THE PSYCHOLOGY OF EXISTENCE
An Integrative, Clinical Perspective

THE PSYCHOLOGY OF EXISTENCE

An Integrative, Clinical Perspective

Kirk J. Schneider

Center for Existential Therapy

Rollo May

McGraw-Hill, Inc.

New York   St. Louis   San Francisco   Auckland   Bogotá   Caracas
Lisbon   London   Madrid   Mexico City   Milan   Montreal   New Delhi
San Juan   Singapore   Sydney   Tokyo   Toronto

This book was set in Times Roman by The Clarinda Company.
The editors were Laura Lynch and David Dunham;
the production supervisor was Diane Ficarra.
The cover was designed by Carla Bauer.
R. R. Donnelley & Sons Company was printer and binder.

Cover photo: *Algimantas Kezys*

THE PSYCHOLOGY OF EXISTENCE

An Integrative, Clinical Perspective

Acknowledgments appear on page 323, and on this page by reference.

 This book is printed on recycled, acid-free paper containing 10% postconsumer waste.

1 2 3 4 5 6 7 8 9 0   DOH   DOH   9 0 9 8 7 6 5 4

ISBN 0-07-041017-8

Library of Congress Cataloging-in-Publication Data

Schneider, Kirk J.
    The psychology of existence: an integrative, clinical perspective
/ Kirk J. Schneider, Rollo May.
        p.   cm.
    Includes bibliographical references and index.
    ISBN 0-07-041017-8
    1. Existential psychology.   2. Existential psychotherapy.
I. May, Rollo.   II. Title.
BF204.5.S35   1995
150.19′2—dc20   94-19497

ABOUT THE AUTHORS

KIRK J. SCHNEIDER, Ph.D., is a licensed psychologist and Director of the Center for Existential Therapy, San Francisco, where he consults and conducts a private practice. He is also an adjunct faculty member at the California School of Professional Psychology and a clinical supervisor for the California Institute of Integral Studies, both in the San Francisco Bay area. Schneider received his Ph.D. degree in psychology from Saybrook Institute, San Francisco, where he worked with Drs. James Bugental, Stanley Krippner, and Rollo May. He is the author of *The Paradoxical Self* (1990), *Horror and the Holy* (1993), and numerous articles in such journals as the *Journal of Humanistic Psychology, Psychotherapy,* and *The Psychotherapy Patient.*

ROLLO MAY, Ph.D., is an internationally acclaimed psychologist, psychoanalyst, and author. Considered the founder of American existential psychology, he is the author of more than a dozen books. Among them are *Existence* (1958), *Love and Will* (1969), *Freedom and Destiny* (1981), and *A Cry for Myth* (1991). May began his psychotherapeutic career in Vienna where he studied with Alfred Adler. He is a founding member of the Association for Humanistic Psychology and a former training analyst of the William Alanson White Institute of Psychiatry, Psychoanalysis, and Psychology in New York City. Recently, Dr. May received the prestigious Gold Medal Award for Life Achievement from the American Psychological Association, and a research center in his name has been launched at Saybrook Institute to carry on his work.

To the Seekers in Psychology—Past, Present, and Future.

CONTENTS

RECENT AND FUTURE TRENDS IN EXISTENTIAL-INTEGRATIVE PSYCHOLOGY

THERAPEUTIC APPLICATIONS OF EXISTENTIAL-INTEGRATIVE PSYCHOLOGY

FOREWORD

What forces shape the architecture of our lives? Arrayed on the right side of the dialectic of the human condition are the constructive designers of Apollo and Company. They are always prepared with their rational plans and sensible blueprints to guide progressions of seemingly orderly experiences in the direction of wise decisions. Their clients come to believe that they will always be able to choose the preferred side of the street on which to live by exercising their free will. But competition is mounted by Dionysus and Sons, well known for their insistence on combining the elements of irrationality, change, and occasional chaos in their plans for how, where, and why people live their lives.

While the Apollonians prefer to sanctify their tenants as exemplars in a divine grand plan, Dionysians treat humankind's tenants as the default value of existence. Apollo folk readily turn to their favorite subcontractors, science and religion, to help build traditional structures. "Sometimes they work and sometimes they give false guarantees of salvation and fundamental truths," counter the supporters of Dionysus.

Nearly forty years ago, a youthful architect of the human imagination offered up an alternate design to these extremes of living in righteous lofts or gloomy basements. Rollo May looked to the very structure of human existence for keys to unlock the resources human beings need to confront the recurring crises in their lives. Those keys were fabricated in the mold of phenomenology. Understanding comes through sharing the perspective of the experiencing person, entering into the life space of the tenant, so to speak, rather than identifying with the authoritative analysis of the landlord. Phenomenology created a subjective, descriptive context for beginning to make sense of the vicissitudes of being and becoming. Its tower of understanding stands alongside the traditional social scientists' tower of objectivity and quantifiability, deemed essential for erecting a science of prediction and control.

As psychological science advances models drawn from physics and biology, the phenomenological rush of existentialism is more toward humanities, philosophy, and the arts.

The former probes human nature vertically, the latter explores its horizontal connections to illuminate the breadth of humanity.

Existential-humanist psychology refuses either to reduce the complexity of human beings to ever more refined variables or to glorify them as masters of their destiny. This approach recognizes that we are all vulnerable to powerful yet subtle situational forces that can bend—and sometimes break—the will of the "best and brightest" of us. Interestingly, this view is echoed by social psychologists who contend that social psychology's major take-home message is that situations exert more powerful influences on our thoughts, feelings, values, and actions than we acknowledge or dare to recognize.

This view does not make us pawns of environmental forces or autumn leaves at the mercy of existential winds. Humans are negotiating continually between realities and illusions, old paths and new destinations, givens and coulds, constraints and freedoms, calibrations and creations.

Rollo May's vision shifted the focus of this new approach to psychology away from rigid determinism and toward understanding how human experiences are challenged and charged by the perils and the prizes of everyday existence. This view would enrich psychology by embracing literary sources, humanistic values, and the power of myth.

I was privileged to meet and break bread with Rollo May some years ago, in sharing the delights of our new existence in the San Francisco Bay Area—so far removed from our former chaotic lives on the East Coast. He was curious about how it was possible to investigate experimentally issues of choice and dissonance, the power clash of situations and dispositions, as I was doing in my research. And I was equally curious about how seemingly elusive existential concepts could be translated into on-line clinical strategies and tactics, as he was doing in his work. From our dialogues and emerging friendship, I began to realize how this existential perspective was more than a philosophy of knowledge or a literary dramatic stance; it could be a powerful foundation for therapeutic practice. Clinicians can utilize existential principles to empower clients in a wealth of ways: to cope more effectively and respond to life's demands, to achieve a deeper understanding of the situational forces operating on them, and to gain a sense of how the individual's interpretation of life creates new possibilities and realities of existence.

Along with Chris Rogers (former psychology editor at McGraw-Hill), I encouraged Rollo May to bring together in one book the many sources of practical wisdom that characterized existential-clinical psychology. Our hope was that he would write a text for the legions of fans of his earlier best-sellers, but also one of value to professional psychologists and students.

Fortunately, Kirk Schneider joined this enterprise at a critical moment when Rollo May's health problems were slowing down his initial progress. Kirk Schneider eagerly shouldered the complex burden of synthesizing diverse sets of source materials, while also integrating general existential perspectives and principles into guidelines of clinical practice. What has emerged from this fortuitous alliance is a unique book presenting the core concepts of Rollo May's existential approach to understanding the psychology of the person, amplified, deepened, and extended by the craftsmanship and theoretical clarity of Kirk Schneider.

I am certain that readers will delight in discovering the interplay and interpretation of existentialism's literary, philosophical, and psychological root concepts in Part One of this work. In addition to excerpts of vital writings by May and Schneider, the opening chapters present the reader with key elements of existential thought from some of the greatest thinkers of our modern era—Kierkegaard, Nietzsche, Husserl, Heidegger, Sartre, Camus, William James, and Maslow, to mention a few.

From these broad roots, the text moves to describing the development of existential-integrative psychology and its future directions. Part Three illustrates clearly the ways and means of applying the core concepts of an existential-integrative psychology in therapeutic settings. These clinical guidelines are embellished with a wonderfully diverse collection of case studies by more than a dozen practitioners of clinical existential-integrative therapy. These cases are so rich with insights into subtle dimensions of human nature that they will delight nonclinical readers as well as professionals and students.

In the end, the reader discovers a goal of this approach that is deeper than merely enabling clients to deal effectively with the issues of their existence. Existential-integrative clinical psychology aspires to guide clients toward personal liberation, an inner sense of freedom, one that absorbs and transforms experiential challenges. Rather than retreat from the onslaught of traumatic experiences or exploit them for personal gain, the client, and all of us, can live most fully, be optimally functional, by developing the mental flexibility to be in the moment, meaningfully rooted in the past, with viable options for the future. This whole person is architect and developer, tenant and landlord, Apollo and Dionysus in the House of Human Nature.

Philip G. Zimbardo
Rome, Italy
February 28, 1994

PREFACE

When Rollo May and I began this textbook, we had four goals in mind: to introduce existential psychology to a new generation; to bring life, passion, and the riches of the humanities back into the psychology curriculum; to render existential psychology accessible—particularly for the training clinician; and to address the integrative implications of existential psychology—in light of our diversifying profession.

We spent many hours planning, envisioning, and detailing this undertaking—and many hours reflecting upon our respective contributions. Suddenly, however—in the winter of 1992—Rollo became ill and had to withdraw from a portion of his involvement. He then—generously—requested that I oversee our project and carry it through to completion.*

The result, I believe, has been salutary—for all concerned. Through a vibrant "chorus of voices," and a rich tapestry of subjects, Rollo's vision has been affirmed on these pages and extended to a new generation.

We have attempted a delicate balance in this book—between organizing the human experience and acknowledging its inherent disorder; clarifying issues while conceding their ultimate obscurity. Yet the task we have set is imperative, we believe, on several counts: meeting the hunger for existential psychology among baffled students and researchers; meeting the challenges of the growing integrationist movements in psychology; and optimally dealing with the health care reality in our society, which is radically curtailing our options.

The timeliness of existential psychology cannot be overstated today; for today so many are perplexed. The blows to traditional worldviews (first religion, then science) in our century have been mind-boggling and have exceeded the human capacity to adapt. After World War II, it is no longer possible in many quarters to expect salvation, purity,

---

*Note: When a perspective is essentially my own in this text, I employ the pronoun "I." When it is essentially shared between Rollo and me, I employ the pronoun "we."

or truth from any of our traditional worldviews, and many of us are debilitated as a result. Our maladies divide into two basic camps: those which are characterized by *retreat* from these bewildering realities (as in depressive and obsessive syndromes), and those which are typified by *exploitation* of them (as in sociopathic and narcissistic profiles).

Existential psychology, on the other hand, may be in a unique position to address these disquieting syndromes—because it evolved during the crises that precipitated them. This is our sincere hope, anyway, and our thesis in this book.

Finally, despite being aimed at graduate students, this book can be accessed by many readers. Professionals interested in enhancing their skills, philosophy and humanities students, and psychologically minded lay readers may all find passages of relevance here—or food for future thought.

A note on our approach: Although this text synthesizes a number of existential standpoints in psychology, it is not a comprehensive or exhaustive formulation. It is *one* existential-integrative viewpoint, based on our own editorial conceptions.

For those readers interested in pursuing other lines of inquiry concerning existential psychology, we spiritedly direct you to the appropriate reference citations, noted throughout the text.

We highly encourage such cross-fertilizing inquiry, moreover, and are grateful if we can inspire it.

Finally, to ensure the confidentiality of the clients discussed in this volume, multiple alterations have been made with regard to their identities. Those readers who think they can identify particular clients are mistaken. Although honesty and accuracy are the cornerstones of scientific research, in this book the preservation of confidentiality takes precedence over the disclosure of unnecessary detail. In many cases, however, readers will recognize people who exhibit the personality dynamics discussed in this book. That will be because despite alterations in case details, these dynamics are common. And it is this very commonality that is a basis for our study.

*   *   *

This text has been the co-creation of so many giving people—both living and dead—that it is impossible to list them all in this limited space. Their spirits, however, will be evident on these pages, and each reader will recognize some or most of them, I am sure.

For their detailed reviews while this text was in preparation, I am indebted to Frank Barron, University of California, Santa Cruz; Maurice S. Friedman, Emeritus, San Diego State University; Thomas Greening, Saybrook Institute; Julius E. Heuscher, Stanford University; George S. Howard, University of Notre Dame; Donadrian L. Rice, West Georgia College; Frederick J. Wertz, Fordham University; and Irvin Yalom, Emeritus, Stanford University; as well as Paul Bowman, Ken Bradford, J. A. Bricker, James Bugental, Robert Flax, John Galvin, Dennis Portnoy, and Ilene Serlin for their informal reviews. I also want to thank my "Existential Theory and Technique" classes at the California School of Professional Psychology for their eager and pivotal feedback.

I can't say enough about the McGraw-Hill editors of this volume, Chris Rogers, Jane Vaicunas, David Dunham, Phil Zimbardo, and especially Laura Lynch—they deeply understood what was at stake.

I am particularly grateful, finally, to my wife Júratė for her cheerful and tireless editing, the bright and sensitive souls who wrote original contributions for the text, and above all, to Rollo and Georgia May, without whose great support and involvement this project would not have been possible.

Kirk J. Schneider

EXISTENTIAL-INTEGRATIVE PSYCHOLOGY: A BEGINNING

In his landmark work, *Existence,* Rollo May outlined one of the boldest psychological agendas in this century. Existential psychology, he wrote,

> does not purport to found a new school as over against other schools or to give a new technique of therapy as over against other techniques. It seeks rather, to analyze the structure of human existence—an enterprise which, if successful, should yield an understanding of the reality underlying all situations of human beings in crisis. (May, 1958, p. 7)

Believe what one will about the ambitiousness of May's proposal, it is both relevant and prophetic. Contemporary existential psychology, for example, is neither a school nor a systematic doctrine; yet it has had a steady and enduring impact on a variety of psychological practices. Indeed, existential psychology is in the ironic position of being one of the most widely influential yet least officially embraced psychological constructs on the professional scene (see Norcross, 1987; Yalom, 1980). This is especially true in the field of psychotherapy, where, as leading researcher John Norcross (1987) put it, "the existential orientation frequently underlies clinical practice without explicit recognition or awareness" (p. 42).

The ambivalent reception of existential psychology among professionals is echoed by an equally mixed reaction among many students. While substantial numbers of psychology majors are intrigued (and sometimes profoundly moved) by isolated existential themes, they are perplexed by the approach as a whole and bedeviled by its implications for practice. Comments such as the following are not infrequent: "The readings in existential psychology are fascinating, but how do you *apply* them?" or "I feel like the material touches something very deep in me and the lives of my clients; I just don't know how or why."

How can we account for these wildly divergent attitudes among scholars? How is it that one of the most potent sources for the comprehension of psychological phenomena is, at the same time, one of the most difficult to coherently discuss or apply? Part of the answer lies surely in the complexity of the project itself. Any psychology that aims to "understand the reality underlying all . . . human beings in crisis" is bound to be a bewildering one. Part of the problem, however, rests with us existentialists ourselves. Although we have made valiant theoretical and therapeutic contributions (see, for example, Bugental, 1976, 1987; May, Angel, & Ellenberger, 1958; and Yalom, 1980), we have yet to cohesively integrate them for practical, clinical use. We have also spent much of our energy in the reactive rather than proactive mode of discourse, as Norcross (1987) noted, especially in the area of psychotherapy.

> In the past . . . existential therapy has often been defined *against* other therapies; that is, in a reactive or negative manner. . . . In the future, existential therapy must move toward a definition *for* something; that is, in a proactive or positive manner. In so doing, its identity must be firmly rooted in a coherent and useful theoretical structure. (p. 63)

But even more important, Norcross declared, *"existential therapists' practices must be examined with particular reference to therapy process and outcome"* (p. 63). [Emphasis added.]

While some in the existential community may resist Norcross' plea, we would do well, I believe, to accord it careful attention. How much longer, for example, can we afford to maintain the position of an elite, underutilized movement? How much longer can we tolerate the incorporation and resultant dilution of our ideas by theoretical traditions foreign to us? Finally, how much longer can we justify informality, obscurity, and disunity simply to oppose rigidity?

These are timely questions today. For today we stand at the threshold of a new consciousness in psychology. It is a consciousness of psychology's rich and complex texture and its many-layered "truths." The quantitative-experimental tradition in psychology, for example, is increasingly acknowledging the validity of qualitative non-experimental designs and approaches (Williams, 1992). It is in the area of psychotherapy integration, however, that psychology's broadened outlook is especially apparent. The impetus for this movement is the proposition, supported by growing evidence (Beutler & Clarkin, 1990; Norcross, 1986), that while all of the major therapeutic orientations are effective, their effectiveness could be enhanced by coordinating which approaches, under what conditions, achieve optimal results.

Recent developments in psychoanalysis also suggest a widened stance. I refer particularly to the shift from biologically derived models of human development to interpersonally based positions. This shift includes a more personal and empathic view of therapeutic relationships and a more generous conception of the self.

The implications of the above trends are revolutionary, indeed, for they signal a revised conception of existence. The question is, What paradigms will lead us in organizing this revision, and upon which data bases will they draw? While many candidates can and should emerge for this task, existential psychology, I believe, is in a particularly suitable position to do so. The basis for this contention is twofold: existential psychology's stated position of comprehensiveness and its direct descent from artistic and literary sources—contexts renowned for their depth.[1]

The premise of this book, accordingly, is that the time for theoretical cohesion in existential psychology is at hand. Not only would such a development benefit existentialists (by rendering their ideas more accessible), it would complement the increasingly interdisciplinary profession as a whole (Norcross, 1986).

To summarize, then, existential psychology (for our purposes) is both complementary to and integrative of other psychological approaches. Not only is it concerned with the psychological influences of biology, environment, cognition, and social relations, but it is also concerned with "the full network of relations," as Merleau-Ponty (1962) put it—including those with cosmic features—that inform and underlie those modalities.

Let us take the case of Diane, for example, to illustrate this integrative view. For years, Diane has felt empty inside, hollow—and for years she has masked over those feelings. She has consumed herself with drugs, for example, gorged herself with food, and inflated herself with falsehoods. But when the shades close at night, or when the partying ceases, the hollowness in Diane returns—and with increasing ferocity.

Diane is exasperated when she steps into my office on this misty evening. She is 40, depressed, and isolated.

She has tried many *treatments,* she tells me bitingly, but they invariably fall short of the mark. To be sure, she is quick to elaborate, they do help to a point. They serve to *maintain* her, or "get her through the night." They help her to change habits, for example, or to chemically alter her mood. They give her thought exercises and practical, rational advice. They reward her when appropriate and discourage her when necessary.

They help her to learn the *reasons* for her despair, and the distortions, consequently, of having misunderstood those reasons.

But the hollowness in Diane remains, she declares to me; and no matter how many ways she thinks about or acts differently toward that experience, she cannot fundamentally alter it.

Existential therapy could help to break this pattern, I think to myself as Diane sits across from me. It could work *in conjunction* with the other therapies, *deepening* her hard-won gains. For example, in addition to helping Diane *think* more logically about her hollowness, I would also work with her to *explore* that hollowness—to see what it is about, to immerse herself in it, and to experience its (immediate, kinesthetic, and affective) dimensions.

The more she can work with these dimensions, I would propose, the less they will threaten her and the more she can range freely within them. She can then be freed from the vicious cycle of compartmentalized therapies to seek richer meanings of a longer term in her life—and she can forgo her compensatory masks.

The problems of Diane and her oversimplified "cures"—indeed the problems of mainstream psychology—are but microcosms of a societywide epidemic. It is an epidemic of part-methods treating part-lives, of quick fixes and easy solutions that console, but fail to genuinely *confront,* human problems.

The signs of this epidemic are legion: The erosion of the environment is traceable to get-rich-quick methods of industrial disposal. Impression management, trickle-down economics, and "just say no" to drugs are the new watchwords of presidential politics. Great procurements of revenue are spent on a bloated and wasteful military (while funds for health care, the homeless, and job training dwindle).

Divisiveness and violence become increasingly acceptable problem-solving strategies.

Given the above, what is our position—the existential-integrative position—in psychology,[2] and how will it be used throughout this text? First, existential-integrative psychology is a revaluation of the oversimplified and one-dimensional thinking that, in our experience, permeates conventional portrayals of the human being. We perceive two basic dangers in the conventional approach—a tendency to unduly both reduce and exaggerate the human condition. On the reductionist side, we see an increasing trend toward conceiving of human beings as machines—precise mathematical tools that can readily accommodate to an automated, routinized lifestyle. With respect to exaggeration, we are concerned about trends in our field that depict the human being as a god (one who can predict and control both internal and external environments) and trends that shun the challenges of human vulnerability.

Finally, we are concerned about more recent trends, such as those of postmodernism, which appear to stridently subvert the (shared) or foundational aspects of human being and leap headlong into relativism.

Beyond these critical analyses, however, existential-integrative psychology also proposes a vision. While we have already hinted at this vision psychotherapeutically, we now present a more comprehensive statement.

Existential-integrative psychology is that confluence of artistic, philosophical, and clinical disciplines that employ what might roughly be called a phenomenological method of arriving at an understanding of human existence. While existential-integrative psychology does not *exclude* other research methodologies from its purview, as we shall see, it views phenomenology as its apotheosis. Formulated by Edmund Husserl (1931) and updated by Maurice Merleau-Ponty (1962), the phenomenological method attempts to grasp the fullness of a given human experience in as rich a language or mode of expression as possible. The phenomenological method combines the artistic approach of "immersing" oneself in and empathizing with a given experience with the scientific approach of systematically organizing and sharing an experience with a professional community. To illustrate the uniqueness of the phenomenological approach to experience, we offer the following comparison. First, we present a phenomenological description of an agoraphobic patient who observes his neighborhood from his house.

> The houses . . . gave the impression of being closed up, as if all the windows were shuttered, although he could see this was not so. He had an impression of closed citadels. And, looking up, he saw the houses leaning over toward the street, so that the strip of sky between the roofs was narrower than the street on which he walked. On the square, he was struck by an expanse that far exceeded the width of the square. He knew for certain that he would not be able to cross it. An attempt to do so would, he felt, end in so extensive a realization of emptiness, width, rareness and abandonment that his legs would fail him. He would collapse. . . . It was the expanse, above all, that frightened him. (van den Berg, 1972, p. 9)

Now let us consider an excerpt from the conventional description of agoraphobia (without panic disorder) given in the *Diagnostic and Statistical Manual of the American Psychiatric Association—Revised* (1987).

> Agoraphobia: Fear of being in places or situations from which escape might be difficult (or embarrassing) or in which help might not be available in the event of suddenly developing a symptom(s) that could be incapacitating or extremely embarrassing. . . . As a result of this fear, the person either restricts travel or needs a companion when away from home, or else endures agoraphobic situations. . . . Common agoraphobic situations include being outside the home alone, being in a crowd or standing in a line. (p. 142)

These excerpts, then, reveal divergent empirical considerations of the same phenomenon. While the latter emphasizes the *exterior* features of agoraphobia—those that can be observed, measured, and specified, the former stresses the *interior* features of the experience—those that can be felt, intuited, and symbolized.

It is out of this personalist-phenomenological tradition, accordingly, that existential-integrative psychology arose. It is out of the desire to base theory on intimate, qualitative data that existential-integrative psychology evolves and exerts its influence.

While existential-integrative psychologists vary to some degree with respect to their interpretations of data such as the above, a consensus has formed around three central themes.

The first core finding is that *human being* (or consciousness) is suspended between two vast and primordial poles: freedom and limitation. The freedom polarity is characterized by will, creativity, and expressiveness; and the limitation polarity is typified by natural and social restraints, vulnerability, and death.* While this thesis may appear commonsensical at first, we will see how complex and subtle it can be and how profoundly it can affect our understanding of psychosocial functioning. The freedom-limitation polarity, for example, forms the template for a revised theory of the psychodynamics of functional and dysfunctional behavior: the productive and unproductive dimensions of choice, self-direction, and desire on the one hand and discipline, order, and accommodation on the other. We will see how traditional psychological views have tended to dichotomize along the freedom-limitation continuum and how the existential-integrative tradition (through art and philosophy) has anticipated and attempted to counter such dichotomizations.

The second core existential-integrative finding is that dread of either freedom or limitation (due generally to past trauma) promotes extreme or dysfunctional counter-reactions to either polarity. A boy who associates limit setting with abuse, for example, is likely to counteract those feelings with a willful, aggressive orientation. Conversely, a woman who associates freedom with unmanageable power and responsibility is likely to become reticent and withdrawn. Many stories from classic myth or literature illustrate this conception. In Goethe's *Faust,* for example, Faust's bargain with the devil for unlimited power is a reaction to the despair and boredom of

---

*This thesis will be elaborated upon in terms of its clinically relevant features—expansion, constriction, and centering—in Part Three, "Therapeutic Applications of Existential-Integrative Psychology."

his ascetic life. Conversely, Ivan Ilych (from the Tolstoy classic) is so petrified by the unpredictability, disarray, and isolation associated with his freedom that he becomes a prisoner of propriety in order to escape.

The final core finding is that confrontation with or integration of freedom and limitation (across numerous spheres of functioning) is enlivening and health-promoting. This finding can be illustrated by the person who has learned to accept his or her contradictory nature and who is thus capable of engaging freedom and limitation more or less as the circumstance demands rather than because of intimidation or panic. Such a person is able to see the beauty of her or his paradoxical situation as well as its tragedy and is thereby inclined to be flexible rather than rigid about life's predicaments. Finally, he or she acknowledges the power of *both* polarities and spurns efforts to defuse or minimize them.

An example of this sort of person is the man or woman who can allow himself or herself to be both bold and tender, creative and disciplined, and exploratory and committed in key life areas. After Faust's deflation, for example, he was able to appreciate the options of his ordinary existence, such as his love for the village girl, Gretchen. Following Ilych's realization of the preciousness of life, he found the courage to expand and transform his social role.

In summary, existential-integrative psychology aims to articulate that which is central and vital to human experience. These shared foundation structures are based on the subjective and intersubjective investigations of phenomenology.

To repeat, the three core dimensions of the human psyche to emerge from such investigations are:

1. Human being is suspended between freedom and limitation. Freedom is characterized by will, creativity, and expressiveness; limitation is signified by natural and social restraints, vulnerability, and death.
2. Dread of freedom or limitation (usually due to past trauma) promotes dysfunctional or extreme counterreactions to either polarity (e.g., oppressiveness or impulsivity).
3. Confrontation with or integration of the polarities promotes a more vibrant, invigorating life-design. This life-design is exemplified by increased sensitivity, flexibility, and choice.

On the pages to follow, we pursue the implications of these operational principles across three broad dimensions: (1) their historical roots, (2) recent and future trends, and (3) clinical applications. The section on historical roots illuminates key literary, philosophical, and psychological lineages within the existential movement. The section is highlighted, not only by excerpts from the leading representatives of these lineages, but also by intimate commentaries by Rollo May, who in some cases knew these luminaries personally. Next, we discuss recent and future trends in existential-integrative psychology. This discussion centers on the role of existential-integrative psychology in the face of the so-called cognitive and biological revolutions, as well as recent counterreactions to those developments (postmodernism and transpersonal psychology). The case of Karen serves to animate this discussion and to demonstrate its clinical relevance. The section concludes, finally, with a perceptive essay by two clinical graduate students—"Existential Psychology from Within the Training Process."

The final part of the text, "Therapeutic Applications of Existential-Integrative Psychology," opens with a preliminary existential-integrative therapeutic guideline. Drawing upon related but less comprehensive existential-integrative purviews (e.g., Bugental, 1987; May, 1958, 1981; Schneider, 1990), this guideline addresses six levels of therapeutic intervention: the physiological (medical), the environmental (behavioral), the cognitive, the psychosexual, the interpersonal, and the experiential. Each level, moreover, is understood as a "liberation strategy," attending to ever-widening spheres of psychophysiological injury.[3] The chief aims of the formulation are twofold: (1) to provide a coherent outline of existential-integrative liberation and (2) to clarify when, how, and with whom given liberation strategies may be appropriate in this (aforementioned) context. Practical, illustrative skill-building exercises are provided at the close of this chapter.

Next we present a variety of case studies—by leading existential practitioners—in order to enliven our formulation. These studies are highlighted by ethnically and diagnostically diverse clinical populations and bold new applications of technique.

In closing, let me take a moment to share my excitement over one of the most distinctive and original features of this book—its stress on *integration.* Never before, to my knowledge, has an existential text attempted to reach out to so many disciplines, settings, and client populations; and rarely has such a work been so focused on the multifaceted concerns of graduate-level practitioners. The section on historical roots, for example, interweaves the poignancy of existential literary narratives with that of parallel developments in philosophy and psychology. The section on recent and future trends combines the perspectives of both graduate students and experienced professionals and also provides an interdisciplinary case study. The section on therapeutic applications, finally, not only integrates a diversity of *procedural* orientations but also embraces a rich (culturally and diagnostically mixed) range of clinical case contributions, reported by an equally diverse set of practitioners.

If there is one group to whom I owe the impetus for this existential ecumenism, it is graduate students themselves; and I am grateful for their appeals.

NOTES

1. It is one of the sad ironies of our field that people like Rollo May had to enroll in nonpsychology graduate programs (like those of theology or literature) in order to study the whole person. While some disaffected students eventually come back to psychology's fold, as did Dr. May, how many do not? How much intellectual talent is discouraged by mainstream psychology?

2. Existential-integrative psychology represents both a broadening of the traditional existential view (e.g., to include mainstream psychological perspectives) and a blending of two other existentially oriented psychologies—humanistic-existentialism and existential-psychoanalysis. Although humanistic-existentialism (represented by such theorists as Carl Rogers and Fritz Perls) and existential-psychoanalysis (represented by thinkers such as

Ludwig Binswanger and Medard Boss) have many features in common, there are several points on which they differ. While humanistic-existentialism emphasizes optimism, potential, and (relatively) rapid transformation, existential-psychoanalysis underscores subconsciousness, uncertainty, and (relatively) gradual transformation. Moreover, whereas humanistic-existentialism emphasizes individual growth, existential-psychoanalysis stresses social, spiritual, and philosophical growth.

Existential-integrative psychology, on the other hand, attempts to make room for all of these dimensions, neither over- nor underestimating their value (see Yalom, 1980, or May, 1958, for an elaboration of this discussion).

Finally, while it is true that *existential psychology* is, by definition, integrative (see Merleau-Ponty, 1962), rarely is this connection made explicit. Here we attempt to redress this significant oversight.

3. Although terms such as *strategy, intervention, psychophysiological,* and the like are frequently considered reductionist and therefore inadequate by existential theorists, there are several reasons why we use them in this text: (1) to reach a diverse and mainstream readership; (2) to limit dry and ungainly jargon; and (3) to ease the reader's transition to more sophisticated coinages that they can readily pursue if they so desire.

From this point on, therefore, terms such as the above are to be viewed as transitional, means to more complicated ends.

More will be said on this subject in Chapter 5.

REFERENCES—INTRODUCTION

American Psychiatric Association (1987). *Diagnostic and statistical manual—revised.* Washington, DC: American Psychiatric Association.

Beutler, L., & Clarkin, J. (1990). *Systematic treatment selection: Toward targeted therapeutic interventions.* New York: Brunner/Mazel.

Bugental, J. (1976). *The search for existential identity: Patient-therapist dialogues in humanistic psychotherapy.* San Francisco: Jossey-Bass.

Bugental, J. (1987). *The art of the psychotherapist.* New York: Norton.

Husserl, Edmund (1931). *Ideas: General introduction to pure phenomenology* (W. Gibson, Trans.). New York: Macmillan.

May, R. (1958). The origins and significance of the existential movement in psychology. In R. May, E. Angel, & H. Ellenberger (Eds.), *Existence: A new dimension in psychiatry and psychology* (pp. 3–36). New York: Basic Books.

May, R. (1981). *Freedom and destiny.* New York: Norton.

May, R., Angel, E., & Ellenberger, H. (Eds.) (1958). *Existence: A new dimension in psychiatry and psychology.* New York: Basic Books.

Merleau-Ponty, M. (1962). *Phenomenology of perception.* London: Routledge.

Norcross, J. (Ed.) (1986). *Handbook of eclectic psychotherapy.* New York: Brunner/Mazel.

Norcross, J. (1987). A rational and empirical analysis of existential psychotherapy. *Journal of Humanistic Psychology, 27*(1), 41–68.

Schneider, K. (1990). *The paradoxical self: Toward an understanding of our contradictory nature.* New York: Plenum.

van den Berg, J. (1972). *A different existence: Principles of phenomenological psychology.* Pittsburgh; Duquesne University Press.

Williams, R. (1992). The human context of agency. *American Psychologist, 47*(6), 752–760.

Yalom, I. (1980). *Existential psychotherapy.* New York: Basic Books.

PART ONE

HISTORICAL ROOTS OF EXISTENTIAL-INTEGRATIVE PSYCHOLOGY

In order to understand the core of any discipline, we must consider its roots, familiarize ourselves with the spirit, vision, and intellectual aims of those who preceded us in the endeavor of psychological practice.

The existential perspective in psychology has a long and distinguished lineage. In this section, we will examine some of the signal developments that make up this lineage, drawing, in particular, from classical literature, philosophy, and Western psychology. Before beginning our discussion, however, several caveats should be kept in mind.

First, our purpose here is to provide you (our readers) with a *feeling* for the various existential influences. We have no pretensions that our survey is exhaustive or definitive; many other works are relevant to the existential overview. For a sampling of these works, we refer you to the references and bibliography at the close of Part One.

Second, we present our survey of historical contributions in a synoptic, highly condensed form. This is done for two reasons: one, to help you grasp the existential significance of the work more readily; and two, to avoid ponderous asides that, while intriguing, would divert us from the task at hand—illuminating existential theory and, more important, its practice.

The historical perspective of existential psychology is distinguished by three thematic elements, each of which was touched upon in the text's introduction.

1. Human experience is characterized by freedom (will, creativity, expressiveness) and by limitation (natural and social restraints, vulnerability, and death).

2. The dread of either freedom or limitation promotes extreme or dysfunctional counterreactions to that dread. These counterreactions often manifest themselves in either fanatical overreaching (if the dread centers on one's limits) or banal timidity (if the dread centers on one's freedom).
3. The confrontation with or integration of the polarities promotes psychophysiological resilience.

CHAPTER ONE

LITERARY ROOTS

The quest for meaning (and moorings) in a seemingly fathomless world can be found in the earliest forms of literature (Otto, 1923/1958). The Assyrian-Babylonian text *Gilgamesh* (3000 B.C.), for example, alludes to a futile search for immortality in an absurd, capricious cosmos. A related Babylonian work, called the *Poem of Creation,* dramatizes a titanic struggle between the forces of chaos (exemplified by the primordial goddess Tiamat) and the forces of order (represented by the upstart deity Marduk).

Written in haunting verse, the Old Testament story of Job tells of an analogous quest for solace in an unconsoling universe. Job's answer to this sorrowful lot is to renew his dialogue with God. But it is not Job's humility alone that makes this drama substantive from an existential view, it is *the way* in which he becomes humble; i.e., through deliberation, struggle, and choice. Job's peers, on the other hand, reveal themselves to be either prideful toward or blindly accepting of God's demands.

Every era stages its own unique dramatization of the struggle to be free. In the pages that follow, we will concentrate on six classic reflections upon this struggle: Sophocles' *Oedipus,* Dante's *Divine Comedy,* Goethe's *Faust,* Fitzgerald's *Gatsby,* Camus' *Sisyphus,* and Hitchcock's 1958 film, *Vertigo.*

THE TRAGEDY OF TRUTH ABOUT ONESELF

Rollo May

What happens when one discovers that one is not all that one wished or hoped to be, when one discovers one's limits, destiny, or mortality? This is precisely the challenge Sophocles's Oedipus sets about to address, according to Rollo May. Departing from the Freudian focus on Oedipus's sexual guilt, May explores a guilt that he suggests even more of us share—that of being fallible and flawed.

Clinical Relevance of the Myth: *If we were to translate* Oedipus *into a clinical paradigm, three themes would become apparent—Oedipus' guilt over his transgressions, his polarization (e.g., rage, self-devaluation), in reaction to this guilt, and his triumphal confrontation with or integration of his transgressions. In the first part of the drama* Oedipus Rex, *Oedipus is like a befuddled alcoholic. All about him his life is breaking down (the "plague"), but he hasn't a clue as to why or how. Then Tiresias (comparable to Oedipus' therapist) induces Oedipus to face his (offensive) impulses, come to terms with them, and reappropriate them into something salutary in his life, something redemptive. That this indeed is what Oedipus is able to do is illustrated by* Oedipus in Colonus, *which can be considered the last stage of his therapy. Oedipus makes three important discoveries at Colonus—that his sense of guilt is overblown, that he has the ability to* respond *to rather than merely* react *against this sense of guilt, and that the guilt and his reactions to it open up new possibilities for him—to understand passion, for example, or the meaning of love.*

When we read the actual drama of Oedipus, as it came to Freud and comes to us from the pen of Sophocles, we are surprised to see that the myth has nothing to do with conflicts about sexual desire or killing one's father as such. These are all done long in the past before the drama begins. Oedipus is a good king ("the mightiest head among us all," he is called) who has reigned wisely and strongly in Thebes and has been for a number of years happily married to Queen Jocasta. The only issue in the drama is whether he will recognize and admit what he has done. The tragic issue is that of seeking the truth about oneself; it is the tragic drama of a person's passionate relation to truth. *Oedipus' tragic flaw is his wrath against his own reality.**

Thebes is suffering under another plague as the curtain rises on the actual drama.

Source: From *The Cry for Myth* by Rollo May (New York: Norton, 1991), pp. 78–87. All other excerpts by Rollo May in this chapter are also from *The Cry for Myth.*

*When Oedipus is born it is predicted that he will kill his father, King Laius of Thebes. To forestall this prophecy, Laius gives the baby to a shepherd with instructions to expose it on the mountainside so it will die. But the kindhearted shepherd takes the baby home. As a boy he goes to Corinth, where he is brought up in the household of the King of Corinth. When he is a young man, he hears the prophecy that he will kill his father so he leaves Corinth to avoid this prediction. On the road he meets a coach. He has an argument with the driver, and the passenger, who is King Laius, gets out of the coach to help the driver, is struck by Oedipus, and falls dead. Oedipus then continues to Thebes, where he solves the riddle of the Sphinx and as a reward is given the kingship and weds Queen Jocasta.

Word has been brought from the oracle that the plague will be lifted only when the murderer of the previous King Laius is discovered. Oedipus calls the old blind prophet, Tiresias, and thereupon proceeds a gripping and powerful unfolding step by step of Oedipus' self-knowledge, an unfolding replete with rage at the truth and those who are its bearers, and all other aspects of our human struggle against recognition of our own reality. It is interesting that Freud, after watching the drama on the stage, cried out, "Ach, it is a psychoanalysis!"

Tiresias' blindness symbolizes the fact that one can more insightfully grasp *inner* reality about human beings—gain *in*sight if one is not distracted by the impingement of external details.

Tiresias at first refuses to answer Oedipus' questioning as to who is guilty with the words:

> How terrible it is to know . . .
> Where no good comes from knowing! Of these matters
> I was full well aware, but let them slip. . . .*

In response to Oedipus' new demands and threats, he continues,

> . . . Let me go home;
> . . . So shalt thou bear thy load most easily.
>   . . . Ye
> Are all unknowing; my say, in any sort,
> I will not say, lest I display my sorrow.

The drama then unfolds as the progressive revelation of Oedipus to himself, the source from which the truth proceeds being not Oedipus himself but Tiresias. *Thus Tiresias is the psychoanalyst.* The whole gamut of reactions like "resistance" and "projection" is exhibited by Oedipus as he fights the more violently against the truth the closer he gets to it. He accuses Tiresias of planning to betray the city; is this why he will not speak? The old seer replies,

> I will not bring remorse upon myself
> And upon you. Why do you search these matters?

This Oedipus myth is particularly cogent in our day because it is central both in psychoanalysis and in literature. We find it, for one example, in the much admired drama by Shakespeare, *Hamlet.* The hero is charged by his father's ghost to avenge his death at the hands of the uncle, who has then married Hamlet's mother. Hamlet, however, is a hero at the beginning of the modern period, and hence in his self-consciousness he always postpones action. When by accident he is killed in the conclusion, he cries out to his friend Horatio,

> If thou didst ever hold me in thy heart,
> Absent thee from felicity awhile,
> And in this harsh world draw thy breath in pain
> To tell my story. . . .

*Quotations from Sophocles, *Oedipus Tyrannus,* in *Dramas,* trans. Sir George Young (New York: Everyman's Library, 1947).

Then in a burst of angry projection Oedipus accuses Tiresias of having killed Laius himself. And when the king is finally told the truth by the goaded prophet that he, Oedipus himself, is the murderer of his father, Oedipus turns upon Tiresias and his wife's brother, Creon, with the charge that these words are part of their strategy to take over the state.

Jocasta, Oedipus' wife, tries to persuade him not to place any weight on the seer's accusation and bursts out in a very human tirade.

> Listen and learn, nothing in human life
> Turns on the soothsayer's art.

Jocasta, the mother whom he has married, now herself becomes aware of the terrible knowledge that awaits Oedipus. She tries desperately to dissuade him:

> . . . But why should men be fearful,
> O'er whom Fortune is mistress, and foreknowledge
> Of nothing sure? Best take life easily,
> As a man may. For that maternal wedding,
> Have no fear; for many men ere now
> Have dreamed as much; but he who by such dreams
> Sets nothing, has the easiest time of it.

When Oedipus still proclaims his resolve to face the truth, wherever it may lead, whatever it may be, she cries,

> Don't seek it! I am sick, and that's enough. . . .
> Wretch, what thou art O mightst thou never know!

Oedipus is not dissuaded but insists that he must know who he is and where he came from. *He must know and accept his own reality, his own myth, and his fate.*

> I will not hearken—not to know the whole,
> Break out what will, I shall not hesitate. . . .

The old shepherd who rescued the infant Oedipus from death on the mountainside is finally brought, the one man who can provide the final link in the fateful story.

"O, I am in horror, now, to speak!" the shepherd cries. And Oedipus answers, "And I to hear. But I must hear—no less."

When Oedipus does learn the final, tragic truth, that he has killed his father and married his mother, he pulls out his eyes, the organ of *seeing*. His punishment is first *exile,* imposed by himself but later, as in *Oedipus in Colonus,* the second drama, imposed by Creon and the state. The tragedy has now come full circle. He was originally exiled when he was a few days old on his father's order, and now, an old man, he will be again in exile.

This exile is a fascinating symbolic act from our modern psychoanalytic viewpoint, for we have held in earlier chapters that the greatest threat and greatest cause of anxiety for an American near the end of the twentieth century is not castration but *ostracism,* the terrible fate of being exiled by one's group. Many a contemporary man castrates himself or permits himself to be castrated because of fear of being exiled if he doesn't. He renounces his power and conforms under the great threat and peril of ostracism.

RESPONSIBILITY NOT GUILT

We now turn to the drama which reveals the healing, integrative aspects of the Oedipus myth, namely *Oedipus in Colonus.* The old blind Oedipus is led by the hand of his daughter Ismene to Colonus, which is a grove of trees a few miles from Athens. There the old man pauses to contemplate his problems and to find some meaning in these horrible experiences he has endured.

There is very little "action" in this drama. It is almost entirely a man meditating on his tragic suffering and what he has learned from it. So far as I know, this drama is never mentioned in psychoanalytic literature in America, an amazing fact in itself. One reason for its neglect is that discussion of the integrative functions of myths in general tend to be omitted in psychoanalytic discussions. But, more specifically, a consequence of the literalistic interpretation of the myth as having to do with sex and killing the father requires that we stop when these are worked through, punishment meted out, and the situation accepted, as at the conclusion of *Oedipus Rex.*

But viewing the myth as a presentation of the human struggle, the truth about oneself, we must indeed go on, as Sophocles does, to see how a person comes to terms with the *meaning* of these acts which Oedipus has committed. This subsequent drama is Oedipus' stage of reconciliation with himself and his fellow men in the persons of Theseus and the Athenians, and it is a reconciliation with the ultimate meaning in his life. "For the gods who threw you down sustain you now," as his daughter Ismene phrases it.

Since it was written by Sophocles when he was an old man of eighty-nine, this drama can be supposed to contain the wisdom of his old age as well.

The first theme we find in Oedipus' meditation at Colonus is *guilt*—the difficult problem of the relation of ethical responsibility to self-consciousness. Is a man guilty if the act was unpremeditated, done unknowingly? In the course of his probing old Oedipus comes to terms with this; the answer is responsibility but not guilt.

Creon has come from Thebes, having heard the prophecy that the city which has Oedipus' body will always have peace, to persuade old Oedipus to return. But the old man defends himself indignantly against the brash accusations of guilt with which Creon attacks him:

> If then I came into the world—as I did come—
> In wretchedness, and met my father in a fight,
> And knocked him down, not knowing that I killed him
> Nor whom I killed—again, how could you find
> Guilt in that unmeditated act? . . .
> As for my mother—damn you, you have no shame,
> Though you are her own brother—
>
> .   .   .   .
>
> But neither of us knew the truth; and she
> Bore my children also— . . .

> While I would not have married her willingly
> Nor willingly would I ever speak of it.*

Again, about his father he cries out that he has

> A just extenuation. This:
> I did not know him; and he wished to murder me.
> Before the law—before God—I am innocent!

It is clear that Oedipus accepts and bears his responsibility. But he insists that the delicate and subtle interplay of conscious and unconscious factors (as we could call them) makes any legalistic or pharisaic imputation of guilt inaccurate and wrong. It is a truism since Freud that the *problem of guilt is not within the act but within the heart,* as indeed Jesus said four centuries after Sophocles wrote this drama. The drama holds that the sins of meanness, avarice, and irreverence of Creon and Polynices are "no less grave than those sins of passion for which Oedipus was punished, that in condemning them to the merciless justice soon to descend, Oedipus acts thoroughly in accord with a moral order which his own experience has enabled him to understand."[†]

In angry, vehement words, Oedipus refuses the tricky proposal of Creon, the present dictator of Thebes, who tries to get the exiled king to return by capturing Antigone as a hostage. Fortunately Theseus, ruler of Athens, comes out in time to send his troops to overtake Creon and bring Antigone back again to the grove at Colonus.

The myth does point toward a conclusion emphasized by modern existential psychotherapists, that because of this interplay of conscious and unconscious factors in guilt and the impossibility of legalistic blame, we are forced into an acceptance of the universal human situation. *We then recognize the participation of every one of us in man's inhumanity to man.* The words to Oedipus from the hero, King Theseus, who exhibits no inner conflict at all, are therefore poignant and eternally important:

> . . . for I
> Too was an exile. . . .
> I know I am only a man; I have no more
> To hope for in the end than you have.

Another theme in this integrative drama is the power of Oedipus to impart *grace*—now that he has suffered through his terrible experiences and come to terms with them. As he himself says to the Athenians who have come out to see him and his daughter in the grove at Colonus:

> For I come here as one endowed with grace,
> By those who are over Nature; and I bring
> Advantage to this race. . . .

---

*Quotations from Sophocles, *Oedipus at Colonus,* in *The Oedipus Cycle,* trans. Robert Fitzgerald (Chicago: University of Chicago Press, 1949).
[†]Note by Fitzgerald, ibid., p. 176.

Theseus accepts this: "Your presence, as you say, is a great blessing." This capacity to impart grace is connected with the maturity and other emotional spiritual qualities which result from [Oedipus'] courageous confronting of his experiences. He cries,

> One soul, I think, can often make atonement
> For many others, if it be devoted. . . .

But there is also a clear symbolic element to make the point of his grace unmistakable: the oracle has revealed that his body after death will ensure victory to the land and the ruler which possesses him. The mere *presence* of his body is enough.*

The last emphasis in the outworking of this myth is *love*. At the end of the drama old Oedipus takes his daughters with him back to a great rock to die. A messenger, who then came back to the group to report the marvelous manner of Oedipus' death, states that his last words to his daughters were:

> . . . And yet one word
> Frees us of all the weight and pain of life:
> That word is love.

Oedipus does not at all mean love as the absence of aggression or the strong affects of anger. Old Oedipus will love only those he chooses to love. His son, who has betrayed him, asks for mercy and states, "Compassion limits even the power of God," but Oedipus will have none of it. The love, rather, he bears his daughters, Antigone and Ismene, and the love they have shown him during his exiled, blind wanderings is the kind of love he chooses to bless.

His sharp and violent temper, present at the crossroads where he killed his father years ago and exhibited in his sharp thrusts with Tiresias in *Oedipus Rex,* is still much in evidence in this last drama, unsubdued by suffering or maturity. The fact that Sophocles does not see fit to remove or even soften Oedipus' aggression and anger—the fact, that is, that the "aggression" and the "angry affects" are not the "flaws" he has old Oedipus get over—all this illustrates our thesis that the aggression involved in killing his father is not the central issue of these myths. Oedipus' maturity is not a renouncing of passion to come to terms with society, not a learning to live "in accord with the reality requirements of civilization." It is Oedipus' reconciliation with himself, with the special people he loves, and with the transcendent meaning of his life.

Finally, the messenger comes back and reports, describing Oedipus' miraculous death and burial,

> But some attendant from the train of Heaven
> Came for him; or else the underworld
> Opened in love the unlit door of earth.
> For he was taken without lamentation,

---

*This "presence" comes up in a number of myths, [such as] Solveig's presence for Peer Gynt, Briar Rose's presence for the Prince, and so on.

Illness or suffering; indeed his end
Was wonderful if mortal's ever was.

This touching and beautiful death of a great character is magnificent as Sophocles presents it dramatically. As *Oedipus Rex* is the myth of the "unconscious," the struggle to confront the reality of the dark, destructive forces in man, *Oedipus in Colonus* is the myth of consciousness, the aspect of the myth which is concerned with the search for meaning and reconciliation. Both together comprise the myth of human beings confronting their own reality.

THE HEALING POWER OF MYTH

From our concern with these dramas of Oedipus, we can see the healing power of myths. First, the myth brings into awareness the repressed, unconscious, archaic urges, longings, dreads, and other psychic content. This is the *regressive* function of myths. But also, the myth reveals *new* goals, *new* ethical insights and possibilities. Myths are a breaking through of greater meaning which was not present before. The myth in this respect is the way of working out the problem on a higher level of integration. This is the *progressive* function of myths.

The tendency has been almost universal in classical psychoanalysis to reduce the latter to the former, and to treat myths as regressive phenomena, which are then "projected" into ethical and other forms of meaning in the outside world. The upshot of this is that the integrative side of myths is lost. This is shown in the great emphasis on *Oedipus [Rex]* in psychoanalytic circles while *Oedipus in Colonus* is forgotten.

But *myths are means of discovery.* They are a progressive revealing of structure in our relation to nature and to our own existence. Myths are *educative*—"e-ducatio." By drawing out inner reality they enable the person to experience greater reality in the outside world.

We now emphasize the side that is generally overlooked, *that these myths discover for us a new reality as well.* They are roads to universals beyond one's concrete experience. It is only on the basis of such a faith that the individual can genuinely accept and overcome earlier infantile deprivations without continuing to harbor resentment all through one's life. In this sense myth helps us accept our past, and we then find it opens before us our future.

There are infinite subtleties in this "casting out of remorse." Every individual, certainly every patient, needs to make the journey in his and her own unique way. An accompanying process all along the way will be the transforming of one's neurotic guilt into normal, existential guilt. And both forms of anxiety can be used constructively as a broadening of consciousness and sensitivity. This journey is made through understanding and confronting myths which have not only an archaic, regressive side but an integrative, normative, and progressive aspect as well.

THE THERAPIST AND THE JOURNEY INTO HELL

Rollo May

In this concise allegory, May shows us the parallel between Dante Alighieri's Divine Comedy *and the client-therapist encounter. Specifically, May introduces Dante and Virgil, the two principal figures in the drama, traces their companionship through Dante's "hell," and explores their re-emergence in the "human community of life." Although this re-emergence echoes "paradise," May suggests, it is something more akin to "paradox"—a "freedom . . . within limits—to take . . . chances on one way of life or another."**

Clinical Relevance of the Myth: *Dante is like a client at middle age—beset by dilemmas. On the one hand, he fears the freedom polarity of his nature—his potential for lust, greed, and power mongering; on the other hand, he dreads the limitation polarity—his entrapment by ignorance, despair, and death. With Virgil's help, he is able to re-experience these agitations, see what they are about, and emerge from them anew. What does this newness mean? It means decreased fear, increased appreciation of complexity, and increased appreciation of the choice within complexity.*

> *No one who, like me, conjures up the most evil of those half-tamed demons that inhabit the human breast, and seeks to wrestle with them, can expect to come through the struggle unscathed.*
>
> —SIGMUND FREUD

Therapists belong to a strange profession. It is partly religion. Since the time of Paracelsus in the Renaissance the physician—and afterward the psychiatrist and psychological therapist—has taken on the mantle of the priest. We cannot deny that we who are therapists deal with people's moral and spiritual questions and that we fill the role of father-confessor as part of our armamentarium, as shown in Freud's position *behind* and unseen by the person confessing.

Therapy is also partly science. Freud's contribution was to make therapy to some extent objective, and thus to make it teachable. Third, therapy is partly—an inseparable part—friendship. This friendship, of course, is likely to be more contentious than the familiar camaraderie of social relationships. Therapists best aid their patients by "evoking their resistances." Even those in the general public who have not entered therapy know this beneficial struggle from published case studies and from popular films like *An Unmarried Woman* and *Ordinary People*.

These three ingredients make a strong brew. Four centuries ago Shakespeare has Macbeth take his physician to hide behind the curtain to watch and hear Lady Macbeth, as she moans in her hysterical guilt feelings. Macbeth then begs the physician,

> Canst thou not minister to a mind diseased,
> Pluck from the memory a rooted sorrow,
> Raze out the written troubles of the brain

---

*This last quote is from Rollo May's commentary on *The Divine Comedy* in Association for Humanistic Psychology, *Perspective*, February 1986, p. 6.

> And with some sweet oblivious antidote
> Clean the stuffed bosom of that perilous stuff
> Which weighs upon the heart?*

Macbeth was indicating that human beings need some new mixture of professions. When the physician answers, in what seems to our age a platitude, "Therein the patient / Must minister to himself," Macbeth rightly retorts, "Throw physic to the dogs, I'll none of it." For physic—no matter how many forms of Valium or Librium we invent—will not basically confront the rooted sorrow or raze out the written troubles of the brain.

Science and technology have, of course, proposed new myths as they displaced or exploded old ones, but the history of technology, so exhilarating at first, has increasingly repelled believers. Now, in the post-industrial age, humanity feels itself bereft of faith, like Matthew Arnold when he wrote more than a century ago the classic epitaph for his dying culture:

> Ah love, let us be true to one another. . . .
>   . . . the world, which seems
> To lie before us like a land of dreams
> So various, so beautiful, so new,
> Hath really neither joy, nor love, nor light,
> Nor certitude, nor peace, nor help for pain;
> And we are here as on a darkling plain
> Swept with confused alarms of struggle and flight,
> Where ignorant armies clash by night.†

. . . [A] loss of this magnitude leaves people en masse without any reliable structure; each one of us feels like a passenger in a rowboat, loose upon the ocean, having no compass or sense of direction, with a storm coming up. Is it any wonder, then, that psychology, the discipline which tells us about ourselves, and psychotherapy, which is able to cast some light on how we should live, burgeoned in our century?

DANTE'S *DIVINE COMEDY*

We propose another such myth, Dante's great poem, *The Divine Comedy*. We shall ask what light it throws on the therapeutic process. This dramatic myth is that of Virgil's relation to Dante as therapist-patient in their journey through hell in *The Divine Comedy*.

Many therapists have no knowledge of Dante's great drama. Even such a humanist as Freud, when asked in 1907 to name his favorite books, cited Homer, Sophocles, Shakespeare, Milton, Goethe, and many others, but ignored Dante. It is a radical deficiency that, in the education of post-Freudian psychotherapists, most students are left illiterate about the humanities. Our literature is the richest source of the presentation

---

*Shakespeare, *Macbeth*, act 5, scene 3.
†Matthew Arnold, "Dover Beach," in *A Treasury of Great Poems* (New York: Norton, 1955), p. 922.

of human beings' self-interpretation down through history. For therapists the peril is greater than for naturalists because the imagination is specifically their tool and object of study, and any abridgement in understanding its workings will significantly limit professional progress.

This *Inferno* starts on Good Friday, when Dante was thirty-five,

> Midway in my life, I found myself in a dark
> wood, where I had lost the way.*

This opening line of *The Divine Comedy* has left an indelible impression on many figures in history. James Joyce once said, "I love Dante almost as much as the Bible; he is my spiritual food, the rest is ballast."[†]

Dante is so lovable because he admits his human problems at every step and never pretends to artificial virtues. He became aware that he had reached an impasse, a psychological place akin to Arnold's in "Dover Beach." As Dante writes in the Prologue of his poem,

> I went astray
> from the straight road and woke to find myself
> alone in a dark wood.[‡]

The *selva oscura* is not only the dark world of sin but of ignorance. Dante does not understand himself or the purpose of his life and requires some high ground, some elevation of perspective, by which to perceive the structure of his experience in its totality. He sights high above him the Mount of Joy, but is unable to make his journey there by himself. In this sense he is like our patients. On the mountainside his way is blocked by three beasts: the Lion of violence, the Leopard of malice, and the She-wolf of incontinence. About the last Dante writes:

> And down [the Lion's] track,
> a She-wolf drove upon me, a starved horror
> ravening and wasted beyond all belief.
> She seemed a rack for avarice, gaunt and craving.
> Oh many the souls she has brought to endless grief![§]

Freud's insight that sexual disturbances were the invariable causes of neurotic afflictions receives support from Dante's confession that it is the *concupiscent appetite* that drives him away from the prospect of joy. But we need not read the allegory narrowly. What for Dante were dispositions to sin we would call mechanisms for rationalizing the private hell of the neurotic: repression, pride, distortion, pretense, and so on. These block our way as effectively, if less interestingly, than the Lion, Leopard, and She-wolf.

---

*Quotations from Dante are from *The Divine Comedy: Dante Alighieri,* trans. John Ciardi (New York: Norton, 1970).
[†]Mary T. Reynolds, *Joyce and Dante: The Shaping of the Imagination* (Princeton: Princeton University Press, 1987).
[‡]Dante, *Divine Comedy,* I, 1–3.
[§]Ibid., I, 47–51.

A person's hell may consist of confronting the fact that his mother never loved him; or it may consist of fantasies of destroying those a person loves most, like Medea destroying her children; or undergoing the hideous cruelty released in wartime when it becomes patriotic to hate and kill. The private hell of each one of us is there crying to be confronted, and we find ourselves powerless to make progress unaided against these obstacles.

Dante's condition on that Good Friday, then, will remind us of numerous testimonies, not excluding our own. His situation recalls Hamlet at Elsinore, or Arnold at Dover Beach, or, to move backward toward Dante's own sources, St. Augustine's, who compared his licentious life in Rome, and its resultant despair, to a journey through hell, and St. Paul's, whose unhappy confession in Romans (7:18–19) resounds through the literature of psychoanalysis no less than through Dante's poem: "To will is present with me, but how to perform that which is good I find not. For the good that I would, I do not; but the evil which I would not, that I do."

VIRGIL AND TRANSFERENCE

At this psychological moment in the poem, Dante sees a figure near him and cries out: "Have pity on me, whatever thing you are, / whether shade or living man." The figure is Virgil, who has been sent to guide him through the Inferno. After some explanations about himself, Virgil concludes:

> Therefore, for your own good, I think it well
>
> you follow me,
> and I will be your guide
> and lead you forth through an eternal place
> There you shall see the ancient spirits tried
> in endless pain, and hear their lamentation.

To whom Dante answers:

> Poet, by that God to you unknown,
>
> lead me this way. Beyond the present ill
> and worse to dread, lead me to Peter's gate
> and be my guide through the sad halls of Hell.*

So Virgil, as guide and counselor, accompanies Dante to interpret the various levels of evil in hell (or, as Freudians would say, the depth of the unconscious). Virgil had shown in his own practice, especially in the *Aeneid,* a thorough familiarity with the dangerous moral landscape they will now traverse. Most of all, Virgil is to be a friend, an accompanying presence for the bewildered pilgrim.

This "presence" in the relation of therapist to patient is the heuristic method most

---

*Ibid., I, 105–109, 123–126.

important but the one we understand least. Virgil will not only interpret these levels in hell but will be a *being,* alive and present in Dante's world. Dante may be taken here as both patient *and* therapist. Some therapists, as John Rosen shows us in his active therapy with schizophrenics, need to have some friend present in order to let themselves go into the depths of the patient's disorder. The friend, who walks slightly behind Rosen, may say nothing at all, but his presence changes the magnetic field; and Rosen can then throw himself into the treatment without himself getting lost in the schizophrenia. Sometimes called empathy or simply relationship, this presence is central to the world of all therapists, I believe, and has a powerful effect upon the patient quite in addition to what the therapist says or the school in which he or she was trained.

In Dante's drama the first hurdle occurs immediately after the "contract" with Virgil and has an amazing similarity to what happens in present-day therapy. Dante is overcome with the conviction that he is not worthy of such special treatment. He cries to Virgil:

> Poet, you who must guide,
>> before you trust me to that arduous passage,
>> look to me and look through me—can I be worthy?*

How often, in doing therapy, do we hear that question, at least with the inner ear, if the patient does not verbalize it directly: why is *he* singled out, among all other people in the world, for this special guidance? Dante, like our patients, cannot "accept acceptance," in Paul Tillich's phrase. Dante recalls to Virgil the images of St. Paul and Aeneas, the hero of Virgil's epic poem, and avers that he can see why *they* were chosen:

> But I—how should I dare? By whose permission?
>> I am not Aeneas. I am not Paul.
>> Who could believe me worthy of the vision?
>
> How, then, may I presume to this high quest
> and not fear my own brashness?

In his pleas to Virgil, he then adds what we might call a statement of positive transference: "You are wise / and will grasp what my poor words can but suggest."

Does Virgil respond in a way that many inexperienced therapists would, namely, to reassure the other person, "Of course you are worthy"? Not at all. He attacks Dante:

> I understand from your words and the look in your eyes
>> your soul is sunken in that cowardice
>
> that bears down many men, turning their course
>> and resolution by imagined perils,
>> as his own shadow turns the frightened horse.†

---

*Ibid., II, 10–12.
†Ibid., II, 31–35.

This can be interpreted as a kind of challenge, which we use in therapy with patients addicted to any kind of neurosis (or habit-forming drug). Reassurance should be rarely used. Psychologists must *not* take the crucial initiative out of the patient's hands, especially at the beginning of therapy.

That sentence of Dante's, "You are wise / and will grasp what my poor words can but suggest," would be, in familiar terms, a buttering up of the therapist. Such a compliment is not going to be met by verbal denial (indeed, we may secretly believe we *can* read his mind!) but rather by a gesture or a wide grin—anyone who grins cannot be all-wise.

There is in Virgil's response to Dante an important sentence: "I was a soul / among the souls of Limbo."* We are all in limbo; we are all struggling along in the human condition, whether we be prince or pauper, patient or therapist, at that particular time. But therapists will not get across to the patient the humanness of it all by telling him their own problems. Frieda Fromm-Reichmann sagely remarks, "The patient is burdened enough with his own problems without having to hear the therapist's also." Again, it can best be communicated to the patient by gesture and attitude, rather than moral lectures, that everyone who lives is in limbo, that the sin (if I may put this in Dante's language) is not to have problems but to fail to be aware of them and fail to confront them.

In any case, Virgil does give some explanation of why he is there. Beatrice in heaven has sent him to help Dante. But Virgil is firm throughout, never sentimental. He concludes:

> And now what ails you? Why do you lag? Why
> this heartsick hesitation and pale fright?

This rebuke has a strong effect upon Dante, who responds,

> As flowerlets drooped and puckered in the night
>   turn up to the returning sun and spread
>   their petals wide on his new warmth and light—
>
> just so my wilted spirits rose again
>   and such a heat of zeal surged through my veins
>   that I was born anew. . . .
>   My Guide! My Lord! My Master! Now lead on:
>   one will shall serve the two of us in this.†

And so they set out on what Dante calls "that hard and perilous track into hell."

We need not be too concerned about the "directive" language here. We must search continually for the inner meaning, which is that Dante cannot find his way alone through human misery. He requires not only the stability of a myth, which Virgil provides, but a myth that he can assimilate to his own purposes. The guide and pilgrim cannot be at cross-purposes or share radically dissimilar cultural myths. Like-

---

*Ibid., II, 51–52.
†Ibid., II, 4–35.

wise, to be a metaphorical Lord and Master, the therapist must paradoxically remain a humble friend, a figure of trust.

Virgil does, however, reassure his friend at certain crucial points in the narrative. In one experience later, when Dante is seized by genuine and profound anxiety, and cries to Virgil:

> O my beloved Master, my Guide in peril, . . .
> stand by me now . . . in my heart's fright.

Virgil does respond:

> Take heart
>
> I will not leave you
> to wander in this underworld alone.*

This is a reassurance which leaves the task of the journey still with the patient, and so does not take over his responsibility. In my own work, I have reached stages parallel to this when the patient is afraid to go farther for fear he will not be able to come out again, or afraid that I will drop him. I may say, "I am glad to work with you so long as it is helpful to you." This puts the emphasis on active help rather than passivity (always a temptation) or stagnation. In the *Inferno,* one is impressed by Virgil's attitude, as Dante describes it: his "gentle and encouraging smile."

THE JOURNEY THROUGH HELL

As they begin their journey, they pause in the vestibule of hell, where they hear the cries of anguish from the Opportunists. These are the souls who in life were neither good nor evil but acted only for themselves. They are the outcasts who took no sides in the rebellion of the angels. In modern psychology these opportunists would be called well adjusted; they know how to keep out of trouble! But Dante sees them as guilty of the sin of fence-sitting. Hence they are neither in hell nor out of it. John Ciardi describes them thus: "Eternally unclassified, they race round and round pursuing a wavering banner that runs forever before them through the dirty air; and as they run they are pursued by swarms of wasps and hornets, who sting them and produce a constant flow of blood." Dante's hell enacts the law of symbolic retribution: since these opportunists took no sides they are given no place. Ciardi remarks, "As their sin was a darkness, so they move in darkness. As their own guilty conscience pursued them, so they are pursued by swarms of wasps and hornets."†

It is highly interesting that classical literature, whether the author is Dante or Sophocles or Shakespeare, has no sympathy with the sentimental or *superficial idea of human perfection.* These authors and myth makers saw the reality of man's inhumanity to man, and they viewed the human condition as essentially tragic. Any character who is neither good nor evil—like Peer Gynt in the first part of Ibsen's drama—

---

*Ibid., VIII, 94–105.
†Ibid., Ciardi's introduction to canto III.

is simply not living an authentic life. The great dramatists take care to punish the evil they depict, but they understand profoundly the passion that drives human beings away from the moral life. With Ibsen they believe that "it takes courage to be a real sinner."* The lovers Paolo and Francesca, who gave way to the concupiscence Dante had been warned against in the poem's opening, provide the most complex case of flawed humanity, sympathetic *because* flawed. Dante, the literary character, must learn by his traversal through hell how to evaluate the variety of sinful examples he witnesses. Again the analogy is apt, for the patient in therapy learns to cope with his problems (not to "cure" them) in part by means of the therapist's superior familiarity with disordered human types, what St. Augustine called "the land of unlikeness."

I will not describe the various levels Dante experiences as he journeys deeper into hell, such as the gluttonous, the hoarders and wasters, the wrathful and the sullen. The *content* of these evils, for which the perpetrators are in hell, varies from era to era; the content of modern sins differs from that of the Middle Ages. The important thing is not the specific evils with which one struggles but the journey itself. In any quest-romance the recognition of negative states leads to a purification of the self, a casting off of the dead/diseased self in favor of a new life. Likewise the function of psychoanalysis, from one point of view, is a movement toward health by traversing the morbid landscape of one's own past. Freud's remark that "hysterical patients suffer mainly from reminiscences" might be extended to include all those who are inwardly compelled to autobiographical narrative. The significant difference is that modern patients, like modern authors, tend to prefer personal reminiscences to the historical people and events of Dante's poem.

The "Inferno"—or hell—consists of suffering and endless torment that produces no change in the soul that endures it and is imposed from without. But in the "Purgatorio" suffering is temporary, a means of purification, and is eagerly embraced by the soul's own will. Both must be traversed before arriving at the celestial "Paradiso." I think of these three stages as simultaneous—three coexisting aspects of all human experience. Indeed, modern literature in the epic tradition of Dante's spiritual poem, such as Joyce's *Ulysses,* Pound's *Cantos,* or Eliot's *Four Quartets,* makes no radical separation of moral landscapes.

I wish to turn now to the problem of the limits of therapy. Does *The Divine Comedy* cast light upon the limits of our work as therapists? I propose that it does.

Virgil, whose relation to Dante I have been taking as parallel to that of therapist to patient, symbolizes human reason. This is made clear by Dante time and again. But "reason" in Dante does not at all mean our contemporary intellectualism, or technical reason, or rationalism. It stands for the broad spectrum of life in which a person reflects on or pauses to question the meaning of experience, especially of suffering. In our age reason is taken as logic, as it is mainly channeled through the left hemisphere of the brain. This does not describe Virgil: he is a great imaginative poet, not a logician. Reason can, if we take it in Dante's broad sense, guide us in our private hells.

But reason even in his amplified sense cannot lead us into the celestial paradise. Dante has need of other guides in his journey. These guides are *revelation* and *intu-*

---

*Ibsen, *Peer Gynt* (New York: Doubleday Anchor Book, 1963), p. 139.

ition. I shall not present any brief for these two functions of human experience. But I do wish to state out of my experience with supervising inexperienced therapists that therapists cut themselves off from a great deal of reality if they do not leave themselves open to other ways of communication than human reason. (I recall Freud's statement that his patients so often saw through any "white lie" he might tell them that he had decided never to lie: this he proposes as his "moral" belief in mental telepathy.) It is interesting to me that Dante identifies intuition as the supreme form of guidance. Therapists who have succumbed to the sin of dogmatic rationalism, if I may be permitted to add it to Dante's hell, might consider the legitimacy of this mental power.

The limits of therapy are illuminated by Virgil's leaving Dante when they have passed through hell and almost through purgatory. When the poets come in sight of the earthly paradise, as Ciardi points out, Virgil "speaks his last words, for the poets have now come to the limit of Reason, and Dante is free to follow every impulse, since all notion of sin has been purged away."* Thus they bid goodbye to each other, with mixed emotions of sadness at leave-taking, comradeship, and loneliness but zest for the future. Once (three cantos later) Dante cries out for Virgil:

> I turned left with the same assured belief
>   that makes a child run to its mother's arms
>   when it is frightened or has come to grief. . . .

> [But] he had taken his light from us. He had gone.
>   Virgil had gone, Virgil, the gentle Father
>   to whom I gave my soul for its salvation!†

In place of Virgil, Beatrice appears as a redemptive and beatific presence. The parallel is that *our therapy is the prologue to life rather than life itself.* We, like Virgil, seek to help the other person to the point where he can "gather the fruit of liberty," not without understandable lapses of need for the therapist's presence, and he moves forward to a place in time where "his will is free, unwarped and sound."

THE FREEDOM TO LOVE

Note that this self-directed life to which Dante, and our patients, go forth, is *life as community,* or more specifically, a freedom to love. This seems to be why the guides at the end of "Purgatorio" and in "Paradiso" are women and why Beatrice is portrayed as saving Dante by sending Virgil to him in the first place. It is in the summoning of Beatrice that Dante most reminds us of a modern analysand.

Beatrice is an entirely personal myth, a Florentine girl of Dante's acquaintance whose death inspired his first great poetic work, *La Vita Nuova.* Her reappearance in the "Purgatorio" shows us Dante successfully overcoming a morbid sense of loss—perhaps the trauma that steered him to the dark wood?—by means of a mystical reunion with this beloved figure from his childhood (they first met when he was nine

---

*Dante, *Divine Comedy,* Ciardi's introduction to canto xxvii.
†Ibid., XXX, 43–51.

years old). She is a reality in Dante's own mind and heart. One wonders what she stands for in Dante's mind—we propose the kernel (heart) of Dante's own inspiration, his spiritual longings, his sense of being guided by ethereal means. This imaginative encounter might be compared to the secular resurrection scene in Wilhelm Jensen's novel of Pompeii, *Gradiva,* about which Freud wrote a book-length study. In both works, a female figure from the protagonist's youth reappears in a radically different landscape in order to restore love and joy to the craving soul of her admirer. We recall other classics which put women in this crucial position: Goethe's *Faust,* where so much importance is given to the inspirational force of Helen and "the Mothers," or *Peer Gynt,* where Ibsen has Peer Gynt come back for his salvation to Solveig. In his essays on the *anima* concept, Jung singled out three novels of H. Rider Haggard—*She, The Return of She,* and *Wisdom's Daughter*—as supreme descriptions of the replenishing libido-object. This myth is of special importance, he claimed, to patients who have reached middle age.

I suggest that women here are symbolic of community. We all experienced life first in the womb and then in the journey from the womb out into the daylight. We were not born alone but in partnership with our mothers. Whether girls or boys, we nursed at our mother's breast, actually or metaphorically. It is in the reunion with a loved one in the sexual function that we participate in the ongoingness of the race. Thus after our journey through hell and purgatory, life itself is the therapist. *Our patients leave us to join the human community of life itself.* This is why Alfred Adler made social interest—the commitment to life in community—the test of mental health.

This view of the limits of therapy implies again that our task is not to "cure" people. I wince to think of how much time has been wasted by intelligent men and women arguing about whether psychotherapy cures and trying to fit psychotherapy into the mode of Western nineteenth-century medicine. *Our task is to be guide, friend, and interpreter to persons on their journeys through their private hells and purgatories.* Specifically, our task is to help patients get to the point where they can decide whether they wish to remain victims—for to be a victim has real benefits in terms of power over one's family and friends and other secondary gains—or whether they choose to leave this victim-state and venture through purgatory with the hope of achieving some sense of paradise. Our patients often, toward the end, are understandably frightened by the possibility of freely deciding for themselves whether to take their chances by completing the quest they have bravely begun.

All through history it is true that only by going through hell does one have any chance of reaching heaven. The journey through hell is a part of the journey that cannot be omitted—indeed, what one learns in hell is prerequisite to arriving at any good value thereafter. Homer has Odysseus visit the underworld, and there—and only there—can he get the knowledge that will enable him to get safely back to Ithaca. Virgil has Aeneas go into the netherworld and there talk to his father, in which discussion he gets directions as to what to do and what not to do in the founding of the great city of Rome. How fitting it is that *each of these gets a vital wisdom which is learned in the descent into hell!* Without this knowledge there is no success in finding directions by which to go, or achieving the things of paradise—purity of experience, purity of heart. Dante makes the journey in person, he himself goes through hell and then is enabled to discover paradise at the end of his journey. Dante writes his great poem to enable the rest of us also to go ultimately to paradise.

Human beings can reach heaven only through hell. Without suffering—say, as an author struggles to find the right word with which to communicate his meaning—or without a probing of one's fundamental aims, one cannot get to heaven. Even a purely secular heaven has the same requirements. Poincaré, for example, struggles for weeks and months, faces depression and hopelessness, but then struggles again, and finally through hell arrives at a new discovery in mathematics, the "heaven" of his solution to the problem that he had posed.

At the beginning of this [essay], I stated that Dante started his journey on Good Friday. The significance of this is that the mordant despair of this day is a necessary prelude to the triumphant experience of Easter, the resurrection. The agony, the horror, the sadness, are a necessary prelude to self-realization and self-fulfillment. In Europe multitudes go to church on Good Friday to hear testimony that Jesus is crucified, for they know that the ascent to heaven must be preceded by death on earth. In America we seem, by our practice, to act on the wish that we could pass over the despair of mortification and know only the exaltation of ascent. We seem to believe that we can be reborn without ever dying. Such is the spiritual version of the American Dream!

The Divine Comedy, like so many other great literary classics, gives the lie to such simplistic illusions. Dante's harrowing and exemplary journey remains one of the greatest case studies the profession of psychotherapy possesses, and is a presentation of a radiant myth of the methods and aims of the best of modern therapy.

GOETHE'S FAUST AND THE ENLIGHTENMENT

Rollo May

In Johann von Goethe's Faust, *the interplay among freedom, limits, and integration is provided yet another classic twist. Rollo May teases out this interplay and its dramatic contemporary relevance.*

Clinical Relevance of the Myth: *Like so many overachieving and narcissistic clients, Faust is inwardly hyperconstricted. He perceives his world as boring and his stature as lowly. He longs to break away from this predicament, to soar—but in the quickest, cheapest way. The devil—who can be likened to Faust's therapist—provides Faust with a mirror on this longing and immerses him in its consequences. Some of those consequences are delightful—as they are for most overachievers—but many of them are disastrous. In the end, Faust is able to reassess his expansiveness, appreciate the value of his limitations, and thus become a more enriched and deliberate person.*

> *Faust:*   When you are labeled Lord of
> Flies, corrupters, liars.
> All right—who are you, then?

> *Mephistopheles:*   . . . Part of that force which would
> Do ever evil, and does ever good.
>   —GOETHE, *FAUST*

When we hear the name "Faust" in our day, we immediately assume the speaker is referring to Goethe's great drama. This masterpiece occupied Goethe, who lived during the Enlightenment in Germany, his whole life long, and he finished it only when he was in his early eighties. It was his work of destiny, as Schiller, in the heated correspondence between these two giants of literature, kept insisting to Goethe. This telling of the myth is great because it is done in such wonderful poetry; everyone seems to quote from this aesthetic triumph.

The drama is great also because it deals with the profound and forever-new problems of how we should live. *Faust* is a philosophical poem in that it centers on what life could be—its temptations, its catastrophes, and its joys. Goethe asks the profound questions, What is life and what are damnation and salvation? As a great humanist, he seeks at every point to deal with the question, What does it mean to be a human being?

Goethe's *Faust* is a poignant and powerful expression of the myth of our modern age in which people yearn to believe that the God of progress—our great machines, our vast technology, our supernational corporations, now even our nuclear weapons—all these, we yearn to believe, will have a beneficent effect upon us and will bring vast gains to humanity. Goethe was caught up in this dilemma, as were his confrères in the Enlightenment and the Industrial Revolution. On his desk he kept a model of the new steam engine and its track which stretched from Liverpool to Bath as a constant symbol of this great hope.

This myth grips the minds of people today because it demonstrates that evil, which in the puppet shows expressed Marlowe's[*] fierce damnation in a literal hell, is now changed in Goethe's poem to good. This amazing tour de force is revealed early in Goethe's drama when Faust demands to know who Mephistopheles is. The devil answers that he is the spirit which seeks to do evil but it always turns to good. Yes, Satan is the apostle of strife, intense activity, even cruelty, but he still ends up after the killings in goodness, according to Goethe's position here.

The intelligentsia of Europe respected Goethe as their titular head. Indeed, Matthew Arnold wrote of him at his death,

> When Goethe's death was told, we said:
> Sunk, then, is Europe's sagest head;
> Goethe has done his pilgrimage.
> Physician of the iron age.[†]

---

[*]*Editor's note:* See Christopher Marlowe's *The Tragical History of the Life and Death of Doctor Faustus* for an elaboration.
[†]We note that, according to Matthew Arnold, Europe is in its "iron age." This points again to the industrial age in the early nineteenth century.

He took the suffering human race,

He read each wound, each weakness clear;
And struck his finger on the place,
And said, "Thou ailest here, and here!"
He looked on Europe's dying hour
Of fitful dream and feverish power.*

The drama of Faust begins just before Easter. Goethe describes this as the time when people

. . . exult in raising of the Lord
For they are resurrected themselves,
Freed from the shackles of shops and crafts,
From stuffy dwellings like narrow shelves,
From smothering roofs and gable lofts,
From the city streets with their smothering press,
From out the churches reverend night,
They have all been raised to light.†

This great vision of Goethe's of what industrialism could bring was shared by a multitude of his fellow writers in this period. His life spanned the Enlightenment in Germany, an enviable time to be alive. Mozart was still living, Beethoven was in his prime, there were important philosophers like Kant, Schelling, Schopenhauer. The Declaration of Independence was written in America when Goethe was twenty-seven. It is indeed thrilling to realize that out of the same milieu came our own political proclamation: "that all men are created equal, that they are endowed by their Creator with certain inalienable rights, that among these are life, liberty and the pursuit of happiness." To read the drama of Faust is to participate in the period when vast numbers of people were dedicated to interpreting evil in such a way that it would eventuate in good.

Faust thus ponders the age-old question of the meaning of evil in a world presided over by a beneficent God. Does creative effort involve the kind of strife which inevitably brings destruction? It is the ancient problem of Job: is there a servant of God so devoted that he will remain true to God even in the worst of human suffering? This fundamental question of human existence has been pondered by almost every sensitive person, a modern one being C. G. Jung in his book, *Answer to Job.*

GOD AND MEPHISTOPHELES

The drama opens with a heavenly council in which God is questioning Mephistopheles, to whom He makes this friendly overture, "I never did abominate your kind."‡

The Norton Anthology of English Literature, vol. 2 (New York: Norton, 1976), p. 1343.
†Goethe, *Faust,* trans. Walter Arndt (New York: Norton, 1976), 1.
‡Ibid., l. 337.

What does Mephistopheles think of things on earth? The devil answers that he "feels for mankind in their wretchedness," and humans have become "more bestial than any beast" because they have "reason." The Lord agrees that human beings too easily become lax; they need vigilance, even though "man ever errs the while he strives." God proposes that human beings should be "ever active, ever live creation."

These opening lines introduce the theme that is crucial to Goethe's whole drama: action, striving, effort. Forever the *active deed* takes supremacy over other forms of human existence. Goethe pictures Faust pondering the Biblical sentence, "In the beginning was the Word,"[*] and Faust shakes his head at that; the "word" is too intellectualistic. Perhaps sensibility will do, so he proposes "in the beginning was the Sense." But that is to be refused as well. Finally, he comes up with, "In the beginning was the Deed." That is it! The expression of action and perpetual striving Faust accepts as final.

As the myth—or drama—unfolds we find ourselves immediately in the consulting room of the therapist. This demonstrates again that, when the would-be patient gives his complaints, he is talking about myths that in his way of life have collapsed. Here Faust is groaning over his failure to gain position or splendor or fortune, and he tells how this makes him feel:

> Each morning I awake in desperation
> Sick unto tears to see begun
>   Yet one more day. . . .
>
> I dread to bed me down, wild visions cumber
> My dreams and wake response unblessed.
> Existence seems a burden to detest
> Death to be wished for, life a hateful jest.[†]

He sums up these morbid imprecations which have led him to consider suicide,

> A curse on faith! a curse on hope!
> A curse on patience, above all.[‡]

Mephistopheles then appears and tempts him with a very different way of life:

> Be done with nursing your despair,
>   Which, like a vulture, feeds upon your mind.[§]

---

[*]Ibid., l. 1224.
[†]Ibid., ll. 1554ff.
[‡]Ibid., ll. 1570–1571. In this very psychoanalytic portion, Faust throws aside with contempt our modern ways in which many people deal with such depression, namely, giving oneself over to money, drugs, and sex.

> Accursed be Mammon, when his treasure
> to deeds of daring eggs us on, . . .
> Cursed be the balsam of the grape!
> Cursed, highest prize of lovers thrall!

[§]Ibid., l. 1635.

The pact is made. Faust agrees that he will be forever unsatisfied, forever moving, forever striving.

> Should I ever take ease upon a bed of leisure,
> May that same moment mark my end!
> When first by flattery you lull me
> Let that day be the last for me! . . .
> Then forget the shackles to my feet,
> Then I will gladly perish there!*

Faust signs this pact with a drop of his blood, saying,

> So may then pleasure and distress,
> Failure and success,
> Follow each other as they please
> Man's active only when he's never at ease.†

Goethe here reflects the essence of the behavior of modern man: rarely serene, always striving, always heaping task on task and calling it progress. The myth shows us the way of life for which Faust sells his soul.

Faust's first adventure is to fall in love with Gretchen, an innocent "child in bloom," and in their lovemaking he impregnates her. This affair between Faust, man of the world, with the fairy-like girl is all directed from the wings by Mephistopheles. Goethe reveals his own ambivalence in that his sympathies and his heart are with the unfortunate Gretchen, who, in her pregnancy, becomes driven out of her mind by her sorrow and by the condemnation of her fellow villagers. Faust, piling cruelty upon cruelty, then fights Gretchen's brother, Valentine, a soldier who has come back from the war to protect Gretchen. In the fight Mephistopheles holds back the brother's rapier so Faust kills him in cold blood. As he dies, Valentine adds his imprecations against the poor Gretchen.

One could make a case for the damnation of Faust simply out of this relationship with Gretchen, even though he so far expresses his love for her. This is the first revelation of Goethe's radical problem with women, which will be visible all through this drama; it is indeed a myth of *patriarchal power*. Goethe pictures Faust as experiencing a foretaste of damnation from the suffering of this fairy-child whom he has made pregnant. Faust, however, grieves at the agony of this fairy-child and is enraged by Mephistopheles' cold remark, "She's not the first." Faust cries,

> I am rent to the living core by this single
> one's suffering; you pass with a carefree
> grin over the fate of thousands.‡

It is clear that Faust has some love, however inadequate, for Gretchen, and he is deeply shaken when she must have her baby in jail. But she cries only that Faust doesn't kiss her with the passion he used to have.

---

*Ibid., ll. 1698, 1702.
†Ibid., ll. 1756–1759.
‡Ibid., ll. 4398 ff.

Having the keys to the jail, Faust begs her to come out. Gretchen can leave the jail "at will," but she has no will to leave; she takes responsibility for her pregnancy and lives out her punishment.

The final scene grows in intensity toward its climax. Gretchen cries out from the jail, "You're leaving now? Oh Heinrich,* if I could too!"

Faust: You can. Just want to! See, the door is open.

Gretchen: It must not be; for me there is no hoping. What use in fleeing? Still they lie in wait for you. . . .

Faust: Oh love,—you rave! One step and you can leave at will![†]

But Gretchen, in her mental derangement, sees the day as both her wedding day and her day of execution. "This day is my undoing," she cries. Mephistopheles can only sneer "Womanish mutter! . . . Vain chatter and putter."[‡] When Gretchen catches a glimpse of Mephistopheles, she knows he is a devil who has come to take her to hell, but Faust cries out a phrase which links him again with our contemporary therapy, "You shall be whole!"[§]

How is this dénouement to be solved? Goethe feels profound sympathy for this creature and her troubles which he has created, yet he must, for the sake of his own integrity as writer, lead her to condemnation. He has Mephistopheles call out, "She is condemned."[¶]

But Goethe inserts the exclamation, "Redeemed!" The notes tell us that this word was not in the first version but was inserted only in a later edition. In other words, Goethe must finally yield to the dictates of his own heart. And he must have some voice cry out "Redemption," whether it makes any sense or not. Thus Gretchen is condemned and redeemed in the same moment.

The first book ends with a voice: "[from within dying away] Heinrich!"

The myth of unlimited power leads Goethe into the greatest of human complications. We can imagine his remembering another verse in his *Faust,* and we wonder if it applies to himself and this drama;

> Spirits sing,
>
> Woe! Woe!
> You have destroyed it,
> The beautiful world,
> With mighty fist.**

Is this why Ortega wrote that Goethe had never really found himself, never lived out his own indigenous form, his true destiny in life?

---

*Faust's first name.
[†]Goethe, *Faust,* ll. 4543–4544.
[‡]Ibid., ll. 4564, 4598.
[§]Ibid., l. 4604.
[¶]Ibid., l. 4611.
**Ibid., ll. 1607–1610.

MYTHIC AGONY

Part Two was put together during the forty years following the publication of part one. We marvel at the thoughts Goethe must have had during all the years when he was turning this myth over and over in his mind. How was he to conclude this myth?

In this second part he deals centrally with the problems of sexuality and power. Some of the verses are slapstick, as when Mephistopheles molds magic gold into a gigantic phallus, with which he threatens and shocks the ladies. But on a deeper level power and sexuality are essential aspects of the Faustian myth. Sex has largely become an expression of power. This is partially seen in our own day with our pornography, our sexy commercialism, our advertising built on luscious blondes and shapely brunettes. There is a curious relationship between our society's attitude toward power on one hand and sexuality on the other.

In the Industrial Revolution there began the radical separation between the product of the worker's hands and his relation with the persons who use his product. Indeed, the worker normally saw nothing at all of the product he helped produce except his own little act. The alienation of labor added to the alienation of persons from themselves and from other people. Their personhood is lost. With the growth of industry and the bourgeoisie, sex becomes separated from persons; one's sexual responses are bought and sold, as is the product of one's hands.

Faust demands to see and have for his lover Helen of Troy, the symbol of beauty and ultimate fulfillment in love.* He thinks it will be easy for Mephistopheles to conjure up Helen.

> *Faust:* I know it can be done with but a mutter,
> Two winks and you can have her on the spot."[†]

But Mephistopheles has a very different view. Faust must go through the Mothers, a strange group which has raised an infinite number of questions since Goethe wrote the play. The Mothers seem to be the only ones who have the power to threaten and to frighten Mephistopheles.

> *Mephistopheles:* I loathe to touch on more exalted riddle—
> Goddesses sit enthroned in reverend loneliness,
> Space is as naught about them, time is less;
> The very mention of them is distress.
> They are—the Mothers.
>
> *Faust:* (starting) Mothers!
> *Mephistopheles:* Are you awed?
> *Faust:* The Mothers! Why it strikes a singular chord.

---

*This relationship presents one of the most profound problems of human life. The connection of form with sex is shown in feminine beauty. This serves the evolutionary survival of the race mythologically and is bound up with the arts and with the relation between the sexes, as we shall see below.

[†]Goethe, *Faust,* 1. 6203.

Mephistopheles: And so it ought. Goddesses undivined
By mortals; named with shrinking of our kind.
Go delve the downmost for their habitat;
Blame but yourself that it has come to that.

Faust: Where is the road?

Mephistopheles: No road! Into the unacceded,
The inaccessible; toward the never-pleaded,
The never-pleadable. How is your mood?*

We pause, for the above lines are for all the world like a session in psychotherapy, especially with that aside, "How is your mood?" The mother, from whom one is born, who gives us form to start with, who carries the survival of the race in her womb—no topic could be more important. Every patient, in learning to love, must confront the psychological remains of his or her mother's imprinting. Mephistopheles presses the point home by making Faust take responsibility for his own anxiety and his own distress—"Blame but yourself that it has come to that."[†]

Is Goethe writing in this myth to relieve his own guilt? And what does this passage have to do with assuaging the guilt of his age? The Mothers certainly seem hostile in this description. I am informed that Goethe never went to see his own mother from the time he was twenty-five until her death, even though he went through Frankfurt, where she lived, often enough. We also know that Goethe was enthralled by women and they by him. Going into a relationship like a storm, he would use the woman up and then leave her. He puzzled his whole life long as to why he could write significant poetry only when in the presence of some femininity. He married late in life and then to his mistress, the last person who would seem suitable; he called her his "bed rabbit." Sixteen years his junior, she was a small vivacious girl, not really pretty or particularly intelligent, but full of spontaneity.

And now to Helen.

May we emphasize again that Helen has a mythic quality in each of these three approaches (Marlowe, Goethe, and Mann). Goethe has Helen herself say when she is questioned about her relationship with Achilles,

I as a myth allied myself to him as myth
It was a dream, the words themselves
proclaim it so.
I fade away, becoming to myself a myth.[‡]

This tells us that Helen was a myth all the way back in history, and the Greeks, in the Trojan War, were fighting for a great myth, the myth of ultimate form. Helen stands for the feminine form, not in the sexual sense (although she may be given that role often enough) but rather in the sense of the Hellenic *arête,* with all the ideal

---

*Ibid., ll. 6224–6225.
[†]Ibid., l. 6221.
[‡]Ibid., l. 8878.

quality that her name stands for in Greek culture. Hence the phrase "form of forms" does indeed fit. It refers to feminine beauty raised to an ethical level, a goal for one's development of the virtue, *arête,* so prized by the ancient Greeks. The path to Helen, as Mephistopheles has already told us, leads only through the Mothers, i.e., it can be followed only by those who have confronted their own mother problem.

When he mentions the Mothers, Mephistopheles asks, "Are you awed?" The awe that Faust feels indicates that some deep conflict has been touched.

Mephistopheles then gives Faust a key with the counsel, "Follow it down—it leads you to the Mothers." At this Faust, like any sensitive client in therapy, shudders,

> *Faust:* The Mothers! Still it strikes a shock of fear.
> What is the word that I am loath to hear?
> *Mephistopheles:* Are you in blinkers, rear at a new word?
> *Faust:* Yet not in torpor would I comfort find;
> Awe is the finest portion of mankind:
> However scarce the world may make this sense—
> In awe one feels profoundly the immense.
> *Mephistopheles:* Well then, sink down! Or I might call it,
> soar! It's all one and the same.*

Indeed it is all the same whether one reaches the Mothers by sinking or soaring, so important are they. Now that Faust has the key, he can "make them keep their distance," and he is suddenly enraptured by the challenge: "Yes, clutching it I feel my strength redoubled, My stride braced for the goal, for heart untroubled."[†] Mephistopheles informs him,

> A glowing tripod will at last give sign that
> You have reached the deepest, nethermost shrine;
> And by its light you will behold the Mothers. . . .
> Some may be seated, upright, walking others,
> As it may chance. Formation, transformation.
> The eternal mind's eternal recreation.[‡]

Then he directs Faust, "Sink down by stamping, stamping you will rise."[§] And Faust stamps and sinks out of sight.

The next scene is in a ballroom filled with persons exhibiting jealousy and repartee. Mephistopheles suddenly cries out, "O Mothers! Mothers! Won't you let Faust go?"[¶] Did he sense some abnormal tie to mothers on the part of Faust? And as Faust continues to seek Helen through the Mothers, Mephistopheles cries, "Mother!

---

*Ibid., l. 6265.
[†]Ibid., l. 6282.
[‡]Ibid., l. 6275.
[§]Ibid., l. 6302.
[¶]Ibid., l. 6367.

Mothers! it is yours to give!" So something of importance is occurring beyond the achievement of Helen, something that makes the "Mothers" of ultimate importance. The form of forms particpates in the universe of reproduction of the species . . . The one in whose womb life is created, the one who carries the implantation of new life, also has these powers such as intuition that alternate between knowledge and magic.

Here we must fall back upon the fundamental truth that Goethe, great poet that he was, possessed a degree of prescience, a capacity to speak from the unconscious depths of his society. The poets as well as the other artists of any culture tell us of myths that go quite beyond anything they consciously know. In this sense they are the predictors of the future. Wizards of femininity, they (the Mothers) must be rescued to help form and reform the new culture. The Mothers have, by nature of reproducing the race, whether they are conscious of it and take responsibility for it or not . . . the key to transformation as they had for the forming of the fetus in the womb at pregnancy.

But this Industrial Age is one of patriarchal power. Such power is gained by overcoming its competitors; it works by thrust, by attack, by mechanical activity. The seamy side of the Industrial Age is sweatshops, life-killing assembly lines, child and women labor, smoke-filled skies over Liverpool and Detroit, the whole arsenal of competitive, adversarial systems. The feminine characteristics ideally are receptivity rather than aggression, tenderness and creating rather than destroying.

Is Goethe doing penance for his worship of progress and for his epiphany of industry? Ostensibly he believed in this patriarchal gospel and he had a long drawn-out battle within his soul as to whether it was good or bad. Faust's later building of the great dike to "give life to millions," where he is on the creative side, is one aspect of the acting out of these beliefs.

Power, attack, the thrusting mode—all these are called, somewhat as a cliché to be sure, masculine and patriarchal. Goethe was in a paradox about this chief myth of modern times, which includes our time in the twentieth century as well as his. The paradox comes out of his poetic soul in dealing with the Mothers as the source of love, tenderness, caring, instead of toughness, cruelty, slaughter. Could the "magic" be the hope that the transformation could occur without great loss of life and without cruelty? The episode of the saving of Gretchen at the very end of the drama would seem to rectify Faust's original cruelty; and the ultimate saving of Faust by having his immortal remains carried to heaven by flocks of angels—all this gives a positive answer to the question. Goethe may have meant it as an affirmative cheer for "progress"; this is the overall impact of this great poem. *We take the drama here as a demonstration that sole patriarchal power is bound to come to grief* * . . .

We have said that the divine element of the forgiveness of Faust is in the last two lines of the drama,

---

*See Chapter 16 [in *The Cry for Myth*].

Woman Eternal
Draws us on high.

One of Goethe's purposes in writing this great drama was to explore the myths of the life of humanism, to search out every way to help human beings discover and live by their greatest callings. He is said to have died with this last word on his lips, "Progress." Progress for him did not mean simply mechanical achievements or achieving wealth. It meant human beings learning to be conscious of their richest unique capacities, and thus have "life and have it more abundantly." Hence he begins his myth of Faust with a description of Easter, the time of the rising of Christ.

There is in Goethe's writing an element of eternity, a sense of the true use of myth. He stretches up toward the divine; he seems always related to transcendent being. This becomes explicit in his last sentence, "Woman eternal / Draws us on high." We have said the principle of forgiving love is present in the person of Gretchen. This is embodied in the "eternal feminine," a force which is an expression of the *deus ex machina* [God in the machine]. This brings us back again to Mephistopheles' statement in his first encounter with Faust: his evil acts are changed to good. The devil is duped, betrayed by his own powers. The motif of the "betrayed Satan" or the "duped devil" has been present in Western theology and philosophy for many centuries, all the way back to Origen. Here it turns up specifically in the ending of Goethe's *Faust*. Thus Mephistopheles is at least partly right when he says that he "does evil out of which there comes good."

GATSBY AND THE MYTH OF SISYPHUS

Rollo May

Shifting now to the literature of the twentieth century, we consider F. Scott Fitzgerald's masterwork, The Great Gatsby. Gatsby *is a story about contemporary overreaching, as Rollo May perceptively remarks; it is also a story about the despair that both precedes and follows the tendency to overreach.*

May finds a remedy to this debilitating cycle in the myth of Sisyphus. By availing us of the "pause," he writes, Sisyphus cleaves between indulgence and despair and alerts us to a fruitful alternative.

Clinical Relevance of the Stories: Gatsby *presents a therapeutic problem; the myth of Sisyphus proposes a therapeutic solution. The problem* Gatsby *poses is the sense of emptiness that some clients feel—even when they are convinced that they are full. What they are actually full of are false highs, dreams with no substance, hypomanic reactions, and an array of compulsions. These extravagances lead inexorably to collapse, as* Gatsby *suggests—and the cycle repeats once again.*

By signaling clients to pause over their emptiness, to explore it, the myth of Sisyphus teaches clients how to break their dysfunctional cycle. They may be poor, Sisyphus intimates, or deprived or deflated, but they do not have to collapse or overreach. They can find possibilities within their restrictedness, to wonder, for example, and to consciously transcend their despair.

TRAGIC SUCCESS

The son of shiftless and unsuccessful farm people of North Dakota, Jim Gatz reflected the American myth of Proteus, in one form. He believed he could recreate himself, deny his parentage and his roots and build a new identity. In his imagination he had never really accepted them as his parents at all.

Already as a boy Gatsby had written in the back of a comic book the self-improving rules to make himself a great success, his own Horatio Alger story. "The truth was," Fitzgerald writes, "that Jay Gatsby of West Egg, Long Island, sprang from his . . . Platonic conception of himself. . . . So he invented just the sort of Jay Gatsby that a seventeen-year-old boy would be likely to invent, and to this conception he was faithful to the end."[*] As his biographer, Andrew Le Vot writes, Fitzgerald in this book "reflects better than all his autobiographical writing the heart of the problems he and his generation faced. . . . In *Gatsby,* haunted as it is by a sense of Sin and Fall, Fitzgerald assumed to himself all the weakness and depravity of human nature."[†]

Like Luke Larkin in the Horatio Alger myth, Gatsby is first befriended by the rich owner of a yacht, Mr. Dan Cody, when he swims out to warn Cody of an unseen rock on which the anchored yacht would founder.[‡] Cody hires him and gives him a blue yachtsman's uniform, the first of Gatsby's line of uniforms—the army uniform in which he courts Daisy, the white suit when he later entertains lavishly in his mansion ("You always look so cool," Daisy was later to remark).

Sent to Louisville for his military training, Gatsby falls in love with the heiress, Daisy. They consummate their love beneath the blossoming lilacs of spring. They promise to wait for each other till the war is over. But he does not count on her conformist nature, her lack of character, her devotion to "the dancing feet, the fortunes behind everything." When in Europe hearing that she has married Tom Buchanan, a monied society man from Chicago, Gatsby vows he will regain her. Committing his whole self to this dream, he changes his name, his manner of dress, attends Oxford for five months, where he acquires a new accent, and comes back to America to become rich, to buy the new mansion with the "blue lawn" on Long Island Sound. All is concentrated on one purpose, to win back Daisy, who with Tom now summers across Long Island Sound.

He has complete faith, in typical American fashion, that he can transform his dreams into action. Nick, the interlocutor who has rented the ordinary house next door for the summer, has his own views about life—conformist, moralistic, Puritani-

---

[*]F. Scott Fitzgerald, *The Great Gatsby* (New York: Scribners, 1925), p. 99.
[†]Andre Le Vot, *F. Scott Fitzgerald, A Biography* (New York: Doubleday, 1983), p. 142.
[‡]Cody, we remember, is the true name of Buffalo Bill. In this Fitzgerald also shows his tie to American mythology.

cal, coming as he did from the midwest followed by Yale—which are exactly opposite to Gatsby's views. But Nick is forced to admit about Gatsby, "there was something gorgeous about him, some heightened sensitivity to the promises of life." Gatsby had an "extraordinary gift for hope, a romantic readiness such as I have never found in any other person and which it is not likely I shall ever find again."*

Gatsby believed unconditionally in the powerful American myth of the "Green Light," a symbol which comes up often in this novel. The green light was on the end of Daisy's dock, as though enticing Gatsby. The first glimpse Nick got of his neighbor was one evening when Gatsby stood out on his lawn looking across the sound at this green light, raising his arms in a yearning gesture, "and I swear I saw him tremble," says Nick.

This eternal Green Light is a revealing myth of America, for it means new potentialities, new frontiers, new life around the corner. There is no destiny, or if there is we construct it ourselves. Everything is ahead; we make anything we choose of life. The Green Light beckons us onward and upward with a promise of bigger and better things in higher and higher skyscrapers, interminably rising into infinity. The Green Light turns into our greatest illusion, covering over our difficulties, permitting us to take evil steps with no guilt, hiding our daimonic capacities and our problems by its profligate promises, and destroying our values en route. The Green Light is the Promised Land myth siring Horatio Alger.

Gatsby certainly was a success in the Horatio Alger sense; he had become literally rich, and though probably unconscious of it, he was completely committed to that myth we inherited from the nineteenth century. His half-literate father, who . . . [came] from North Dakota when he read his son's death notice in the Chicago paper, overcomes his grief at seeing his son in the coffin by his elation at the proofs all about the house of Gatsby's great success: "He had a big future before him. . . . If he'd of lived, he'd of been a great man. A man like James J. Hill. He'd of helped build up the country."†

Obviously Gatsby had money galore—even though the money was gotten illicitly, the way many people in the Jazz Age got theirs. There has been in America no clear-cut differentiation between right and wrong ways to get rich. Playing the stock market? Finding oil under your shack in Texas? Deforesting vast areas of Douglas fir in the state of Washington? Amassing piles of money for lectures after getting out of prison as a Watergate crook? The important thing in the American dream has been to *get* rich, and then *those very riches give a sanction to your situation.* The fact of your being successful is proof that God smiles on you and that you are among the saved. It is not hard to see how this, in true Calvinistic tradition, drifted into getting rich as the eleventh commandment.

If money could buy everything, Gatsby would have been the most fortunate of men. But the success and the money all went to flesh out the vast dream which held Gatsby in its thrall and which he took as the reality of his life. Money could buy the vast par-

---

*Fitzgerald, *The Great Gatsby,* p. 2.
†Ibid., p. 169.

ties, the great glitter of the mansion, the freely flowing liquor, the jazz music which floated from the orchestras as the hundreds of people flocked to the lights like moths at night. But all were important only because sooner or later these accoutrements of Babylon would draw in Daisy. True to his myth, Gatsby was successful at this also—Daisy came out and they gradually rehearsed the lines so dear to Gatsby's heart.

Gatsby's tragic flaw was that he took his dream—the American dream—for reality. He had complete faith in it and never doubted that his transformation and his ultimate success were assured. Nick speaks of "the colossal vitality of his illusion." If Kierkegaard is right that "purity of heart is to will one thing," Gatsby was indeed pure of heart. Strangely, he is the one person in the book who possesses complete integrity. When he tells Nick of his goal to have Daisy confess that she loved and loves only him, and to marry him in the great house in Louisville just as they had originally planned, Nick remonstrates, "You can't re-live the past." Gatsby responds, "Can't re-live the past? Of course you can."*

Nick overcomes his abhorrence of Gatsby's way of life—his having made his money through his connections with bootleggers and his serving as the front for gangsters. The corrupt means Gatsby uses to achieve his ends have not altered his fundamental integrity, his spiritual intactness, writes Le Vot. His means reflect the corruption of the times, they are the only ones available to an indigent cavalier seeking his fortune. True corruption, Nick discovered, lies in the hearts of those who despise Gatsby, especially in Tom's. Gatsby's integrity consisted of his daring to dream and to be faithful to his dream; it never even occurred to him to tell that it was Daisy, not he, who was driving his car when it killed Myrtle Wilson. It was not Gatsby who was to go wrong, says Nick, "it was the foul dust that floated in the wake of his dreams that temporarily closed out my interest in the abortive sorrows and short-winded elations of men." In the same sense, it is not the American myth in itself that leads us astray; it is the "foul dust that floats in the wake" of this dream. It is hanging onto the Horatio Alger myth when it no longer applies; it is using the past myths to rationalize the poverty and hunger in the world; it is the increasing of paranoia out of recourse to a past long since dead.

But Gatsby's dream was too insistent. "You demand too much," Daisy was to whimper in the grand showdown in the Plaza Hotel, when Gatsby insists she say to Tom that she never loved him. Fitzgerald goes on, "Only the dead dream fought on as the afternoon slipped away, trying to touch what was no longer tangible, struggling unhappily, undespairingly."† We note that Fitzgerald writes *un*despairingly. *True despair is a constructive emotion capable of eliciting creative solutions to a situation.* This was just what the Jazz Age was incapable of feeling. Nick mused, as Gatsby lay in his coffin and not a word came from Daisy, that perhaps Gatsby "no longer cared. If that was true he must have felt that he had lost the old warm world, paid a high price for living too long with a single dream."‡

---

*Ibid., p. 111.
†Ibid., p. 135.
‡Ibid., p. 162.

THE MYTH OF SISYPHUS*

Out of that moment . . . is born [a] myth which is new but eternally old, the only myth that fits this seemingly hopeless situation. This is the myth of Sisyphus. The one myth which directly counters the American dream, this myth denies progress, goes no place at all, seems to be a repetition, every day and every act being forever the same in perpetual monotonous toil and sweat.

But that is to omit its crucial meaning. One thing Sisyphus can do: he can be aware of each moment in this drama between himself and Zeus, between himself and his fate. This—because it is most human—makes his reaction completely different from that of the dark night of the mountain up which he rolls his rock.

Punished by Zeus for deceiving the gods, Sisyphus is described by Homer:

> With many a weary step, and many a groan,
> Up the high hill he heaves a huge round stone:
> The huge round stone, resulting with a bound,
> Thunders impetus down.[†]

Indeed, Homer tells us then that "Poor Sisyphus" could hear "the charming sounds that ravished his ear," which came from Orpheus' flute in Pluto's realm.[‡] The myth of Sisyphus is sometimes interpreted as the sun climbing to its apex every day and then curving down again. Nothing could be more important for human life than these circular journeys of the sun.

Out of the melancholy brooding about Gatsby comes the monotony which all human creatures must endure—a [monotony] which the Jazz Age with its boozing and dancing and parties and endless agitation went crazy trying to deny. For we face monotony in all we do; we draw in and exhale breath after breath in ceaseless succession through every moment of our lives, which is monotony par excellence. But out of this repetitiveness of breathing the Buddhists and [Yogis] have formed their religious meditation and a way of achieving the heights of ecstasy.

For Sisyphus is a creative person who even tried to erase death. He never gives up but always is devoted to creating a better kind of life; he is a model of a hero who presses on in spite of his or her despair. Without such capacity to confront despair we would not have had Beethoven or Rembrandt or Michelangelo or Dante or Goethe or any others of the great figures in the development of culture.

Sisyphus' consciousness is the hallmark of being human. Sisyphus is the thinking reed with a mind which can construct purposes, know ecstasy and pain, distinguish monotony from despair, and place the monotony—the rolling of the stone—in the scheme of his rebellion, the act for which he is condemned. We do not know Sisyphus' reveries, his ruminations, as he performed his act, but we do know that each act

---

*Sisyphus is an ancient Greek myth. Condemned by Zeus for spurning and insulting the gods, Sisyphus is consigned (for eternity) to rolling a large stone up a hill, only to witness it fall down again after it has reached the top.

[†]Homer (Pope's translation), in H. A. Guerber, *Myths of Greece and Rome* (London: George Harrap, 1907), p. 144.

[‡]Ibid., p. 60.

may have been again a rebellion against the gods of conformity, or each act could have been an act of penance. Such is the imagination, the purposes and human faiths which we construct. Sisyphus takes his place in that line of heroes who declare their rebellion against the inadequate gods for the sake of greater gods—an illustration and inspiring line consisting of Prometheus,* Adam, and hopefully even down to our own myths and gods. Out of this eternal capacity to see our tasks, as Sisyphus did his, comes the courage to move beyond the rock, beyond the monotony of day-to-day experience.

Sisyphus, furthermore, must have noticed in his trips some wisp of pink cloud that heralds the dawn, or felt some pleasure in the wind against his breast as he strode down the hill after his rock, or remembered some line of poetry to muse upon. Indeed, he must have thought of some myth to make sense of an otherwise senseless world. All these things are possible for Sisyphus—even, if he had been Gatsby, to be aware that the past cannot be relived but in every step he can leave the past behind. These capacities of human imagination are the hallmark of our paradoxical condemnation and our epiphany as human beings.

The myth of Sisyphus needs to be held in juxtaposition with the Green Light to lend some balance, some dialectic to us as individuals as well as to America. It is a safeguard against [the unalloyed] arrogance of the chosen people, and it makes clear that Horatio Alger only leads us astray. Sisyphus balances the myth of the Promised Land: it requires us to pause in our exploitation of this promised America-the-beautiful to meditate on our purposes and to clarify our aims.

It is the one myth which Gatsby so clearly lacked. At the very least the myth of Sisyphus can help us understand why the dream collapsed; and at the most it can show us the way to an ecstasy which balances our hopelessness and inspires us to a new age in which we can directly confront our despair and use it constructively.

We know then that the meaning of human existence is infinitely deeper than Gatsby's dream and the American dream. No matter how far we are borne back into the past of fatigue and ultimate death, we have harbored some ecstatic thoughts, we have wondered and experienced some poignancy as well as sadness in our wondering. And for a while the sadnesses are freed from guilt and the joys are relieved of anxiety. When eternity breaks into time, as it does in myths, we suddenly become aware of the meaning of human consciousness.

The myth of Sisyphyus thus makes sense of our otherwise senseless efforts; it throws light on the darkness of our routine labors and lends some zest to our monotony. This is true whether we row our boats against a current that blocks progress, or work like a robot in a factory, or struggle day after day to express some recalcitrant thoughts in words that always seem to elude us.

The myth of Sisphyus is the ultimate challenge to the American dream. We are required—"destined," if you will—to recognize our human state of consciousness in progress or without it, with the Green Light or without it, with Daisy or without her,

---

*Prometheus is an ancient Greek god who, as the legend goes, ridiculed other gods for their timidity, created human beings, and stole fire from heaven to help people themselves to become creators. His penalty for these acts was to be chained to a rock for thousands of years, as a vulture pecked away at his liver.

with the disintegration of our world or without it. It is this which saves us from destruction when our little rules prove unavailing.

   This is what led Albert Camus to conclude his essay on Sisyphus, "We must consider Sisyphus happy."*

HITCHCOCK'S *VERTIGO:*
AN EXISTENTIAL VIEW OF SPIRITUALITY

Kirk Schneider

Recently we have witnessed an explosion of interest in the transcendental dimension of human experience. While emphatic rationalists (such as Albert Ellis) have perceived little value in the transcendental, ardent transpersonalists (such as Ken Wilber) have stressed its most expansive implications. In this narrative, Kirk Schneider explores a third alternative to these positions—what he terms existential spirituality, *or* wonderment. *To illustrate the richness of this perspective, he discusses and considers the implications of Alfred Hitchcock's acclaimed film* Vertigo.

Clinical Relevance of the Film: Vertigo *takes the Horatio Alger myth of* Gatsby *a step further. The recent collapse of traditions has brought an even greater sense of desolation to many clients and an even greater impulse to compensate for and deny that desolation. Some have turned to drugs to provide that compensation, others to materialism, and still others to relationships and religion.*

   Concerning the last in particular, Vertigo *imparts three basic (therapeutic) messages: Permit your limitations, confront your potentialities, and affirm your contradictoriness.*

> *We burn with desire to find a steadfast place and an ultimate fixed basis whereon we may build a tower to reach the infinite. But our whole foundation breaks up, and earth opens to the abysses.*
>
> —BLAISE PASCAL (1654)

In recent years, we have witnessed an avalanche of studies extolling the transcendental (or transpersonal) dimension of human experience. They have provided a necessary counterweight to the smug, antiseptic traditional psychological theorizing on this topic. Albert Ellis, for example, appears to be so concerned about transcendentalism that he even upbraids James Bugental (who is hardly a flagrant transpersonalist!) for dehumanizing, decerebrating, and desocializing human beings (Ellis & Yeager, 1989, p. 32). Further, he decries, "Transpersonal psychologists encourage their clients to

---

*Albert Camus, *Myth of Sisyphus and Other Essays* (New York: Random House, 1959).
Source: This article (which appeared in the *Journal of Humanistic Psychology*, vol. 33, No. 2, Spring 1993, pp. 91–100. © Sage Publications, Inc.) is adapted from the book *Horror and the Holy: Wisdom-Teachings of the Monster Tale* (1993), Open Court Press. Published by permission of the author, Kirk J. Schneider, and Open Court Publishing Company, La Salle, Illinois. My deepest thanks to Don Cooper for his insightful commentaries on this project.

take guidance not from observed reality or rational thinking, but rather from their intuitive minds and . . . other intangible sources" (Ellis & Yeager, 1989, p. 44). Some transpersonal theorists, on the other hand, are equally insistent about the *virtues* of transcendental experience. Following the lead of Ken Wilber (1981), for example, such theorists unqualifyingly embrace the notion of an "ultimate" or god-like human consciousness, totally unrestricted by time and space (see Schneider, 1987, 1989; Wilber, 1989a, 1989b, for a fuller discussion of this problem).

In this article, I consider a third alternative to these positions that has not been accorded enough of a "voice." This is the alternative of *existential* spirituality, or what I call *wonderment.*

The film I review here, Alfred Hitchcock's *Vertigo,* is a superb illustration of the existential perspective on transcendence. It can also be seen as a compelling synthesis of the theological works of Paul Tillich (1952), Martin Buber (1965), Rollo May (1981), and Ernest Becker (1973).

According to biographer Donald Spoto (1983), Hitchcock supervised the production of *Vertigo* like he did no other film. It appeared to be his most important project, and he was obsessed with every detail. *Vertigo* is also considered by some—for example, the British critic Robin Wood (1969)—to be one of the finest, if not *the* finest, motion picture ever made. At the very least, *Vertigo* is a complex psychospiritual odyssey—a riveting excursion into our most prized and distressing possibilities.

Because of *Vertigo*'s complexity, I will begin by summarizing its basic plot structure. Next, I will consider excerpts that illustrate the film's underlying dilemma—that between freedom and limitation. Finally, I will address the implications of this dilemma for existential spirituality.

PLOT SUMMARY

Ostensibly, *Vertigo* is about Scottie Ferguson (played by Jimmy Stewart), a retired San Francisco police detective. During an incident in which he almost falls from a building, Scottie discovers he has acrophobia (fear of heights) and the dizziness or vertigo which accompanies that fear.

Soon after the accident, Scottie visits his girlfriend Midge. She is cheerful and consoling but cannot seem to grasp the dimensions of his ordeal.

An ex college chum, Gavin Elster, asks Scottie to investigate the strange behavior of his wife Madeline. Allegedly, she is obsessed with a deceased woman (who Elster later claims is a long-lost relative of Madeline's), and because she visits graves and speaks about morbid things, Elster is afraid that Madeline will hurt herself or someone else if she is not deterred. Scottie (somewhat reluctantly) agrees to discover all he can about her and to report his findings back to Elster.

Madeline (played by Kim Novak) is an ethereal beauty, and Scottie soon falls in love with her. She is an enigma, however, and leads him into bewildering situations. He follows her, for example, to the Palace of Fine Arts, where she stares at a painting of a deceased Spanish noblewoman. She stays in the hotel where this woman, Carlotta Valdez, allegedly lived. Finally, she visits her gravesite. In time, Scottie finds that Elster's concerns are valid. Madeline is indeed obsessed with Carlotta Valdez, a 19th-century ancestor of her family. Scottie, however, makes an even eerier observation: Carlotta Valdez committed suicide, and Madeline seems bent on emulating her! The first time she tries to take her own life, by jumping into San Francisco Bay, Scottie rescues her. The second time, however, is a different story. Here, he must follow her up the winding staircase in the bell tower of San Juan Bautista Mission (near Monterey). Ascending this staircase, however, triggers Scottie's vertigo, and he is unable to stop her. The next thing we hear is a scream, and what looks like Madeline's body is seen crashing to the roof below.

Scottie is devastated by Madeline's apparent suicide and begins a long descent into depression. A hearing is conducted in which he is roundly condemned for negligence. He ends up in a sanitarium for a while, but he is beyond help, at least beyond what can be offered by psychiatrists or his girlfriend Midge.

Beleaguered and lovelorn, Scottie takes to the streets and discovers Judy, a rather plainly dressed working-class person who has one outstanding trait—an uncanny resemblance to Madeline. The story's big twist occurs when Scottie discovers that Judy is indeed Madeline, or, more accurately, played the role of Madeline, so that Gavin Elster, who paid her for this role, could kill his wife at the bell tower. Elster, in other words, set Scottie up. He knew he had vertigo and that he would not be able to follow Madeline (who was really Judy) to the top of the bell tower. At that point, therefore, he pushed the body of his actual wife, Madeline, whom he had brought there and killed, out [of] the bell tower and sent Judy back into obscurity.

Overtaken with rage at being duped, Scottie now forces Judy back to the scene of the crime—the bell tower. This time he is not curtailed by his vertigo and takes her to the very top. Judy pleads with him not to harm her but also to believe another complication, that she is in fact in love with him. While he contemplates this dilemma a nun suddenly appears and startles Judy into falling to her death. Scottie is dumbstruck.

Now, this story is about many things. It is a detective story, a love story, a tale of innocence and revenge. But at its deepest level, I believe, *Vertigo* is a metaphor for the human encounter with the transcendent (or infinite, if you will). *Vertigo* (which is holographic in its richness) addresses three key psychospiritual issues: (a) the struggle between freedom and limitation, (b) the mishandling of freedom and limitation, and (c) the integration or negotiation of freedom and limitation. Let us consider excerpts from the film that illustrate these concerns and the implications that they might have for psychospiritual well-being. I will then summarize these implications.

EXCERPTS FROM *VERTIGO*

Credits

Right from the start, Hitchcock graphically introduces his concern. By spiraling into and out of the iris of a woman's eye, the outer world of appearances, surfaces, and limitations is deftly contrasted with the inner world of "reality," depth, and freedom which lies just beneath the veneer.

Opening Scene

The opening scene parallels the credits. First, we see hands tightly grasping a bar, which suggests the tenuous grasp on life. Next, we see Scottie and an officer chasing the man (who grasped the bar) on a series of high-rise rooftops. Finally, Scottie slips as he tries to leap between the rooftops. On his way down, he manages to clutch a highly unstable gutter, which leaves him dangling at the side of a building. The other officer comes to Scottie's aid but plunges violently to his death in the process of trying to save him. Scottie remains hanging. He is in terror, but he is at the same time transfixed. He cannot help but peer into his awesome predicament below. Again, Hitchcock confronts us with life's fragility, with the fear (yet fascination) with what lies beyond, and with the overwhelming danger (i.e., deadliness) of tangling with that reality.

Midge's Apartment

Suddenly, we switch to Midge's apartment. Allusions to the tension between limitation and freedom, ground and groundlessness abound. Scottie is seated comfortably in Midge's living room. Somehow (we don't know how), he has survived his ordeal. He is uneasy, however. He tries balancing the cane he has acquired (for a broken leg), but it falls to the ground. He speaks about how his corset "binds,"* and how much he looks forward to being a "free man" tomorrow when it comes off. But just as he contemplates the prospect, he bristles from the pain. "Do you know many men who wear corsets," he asks Midge rhetorically. Scottie had ambitions to become chief of police, we find out, but he had to quit the force due to his vertigo. Midge tries to pacify him and urges him to take a "desk job." "Don't be so *motherly,*" Scottie snaps. "I'm a man of independent means," he asserts. Then a twinge of pain strikes him and he modifies his statement—"fairly independent." He then asks Midge how she would describe her love life—*"normal,"* she replies. At every turn Scottie is confronted by his dilemma. He is alive but "trapped" in the apartment of (and relationship with) his pedestrian girlfriend (even the name *Midge* is suggestive of smallness). He was strong and brave once, but now he is an invalid, an impotent hobbler. He longs for freedom, but he is dragged down by resignation, guilt (his inability to help the officer), and mundaneness. He longs to enlarge himself, but beyond that, to be superhuman if possible, to undo the death of his fellow officer and his own disability. Later in this scene, Scottie develops a theory that he feels will help him overcome his vertigo. By confronting his fear in steps (with the use of an adjustable chair) he hopes to work through his dilemma. Although this is a potentially viable solution, Scottie is so desperate to deny his fragility that he becomes arrogant and over-reaches himself. "There's nothin' to it," he quips, as he brusquely elevates himself above Midge's picture window. With one sweeping gaze at the streets below, however, Scottie becomes wobbly and collapses onto the floor.

---

*All quotations from *Vertigo* are copyright © 1958 by Universal City Studios, Inc., courtesy of MCA Publishing Rights, a division of MCA Inc., and are reprinted here by permission.

Elster's Office

Again we are besieged by contrasts. Elster's business is "dull," routine, he says. His marriage is empty. Life in San Francisco is not the same as it used to be, he continues. The camera focuses on a painting of San Francisco in the 19th century. "I wish I lived in San Francisco then," Elster sighs, with its "color, power . . . freedom." Scottie is also increasingly lured by these musings, as well as by Elster's plea to investigate his odd wife. This scene, in effect, contrasts the banality of modern life, of institutional life (e.g., business, marriage) with that of history, eternity, and the mysteriousness of human existence (e.g., Madeline).

At Ernie's Restaurant (Scottie's First Glimpse of Madeline)

Per his agreement with Elster, Scottie has his first glimpse of the subject of his investigation. As the camera lovingly closes in on Madeline, her beauty and sensuality are breathtaking. Scottie is aware of this spectacle, but just as he shies away from great heights, he averts his eyes from Madeline. Yet he cannot keep them off her for long, and he abruptly refocuses his gaze. This scene parallels the earlier ones. The object of Scottie's vertigo is gradually shifting from a tall building to a tall blonde named Madeline. (Note the suggestion of madness in her name.) The full extent of his dilemma is becoming plain: Height and depth, beauty and sensuality are gateways to the cosmic; they are dimensions that petrify as well as compel. One is reminded here of Rilke (1982): "For beauty is . . . but the beginning of terror, which we . . . are just able to endure" (p. 151). [Madeline visits Carlotta's hotel and grave.]

At the Museum (Scottie Watches Madeline Observe a Painting of Carlotta)

Increasingly intrigued, Scottie begins melding with Madeline, who in this scene is melding with (a portrait of) Carlotta Valdez, "beauty/eternity." We see intriguing matches between Madeline and Carlotta's portrait, including their vertiginous hair-buns.

[Madeline jumps into San Francisco Bay; Scottie rescues her]

At Madeline's Car (Outside Scottie's Apartment)

Madeline is grateful to Scottie for (allegedly) rescuing her. Scottie is entranced by her, agrees to wander and symbolically merge with her.

At the Sequoias

They take a walk among the tall trees. The freedom, immensity, and longevity of the trees is contrasted with Madeline's foreboding about the unmanageability of death.

At the Beach

Madeline tells Scottie a metaphorical dream. The dream counterposes both fusion with the cosmic and harrowing groundlessness. Her vivid descriptions of corridors and abysses are both repulsive and strangely alluring. Scottie attempts to (rationally) explain her morbid preoccupations, but he is unable. He is unable to maintain his last foothold on conventional reality. "If I were mad," Madeline declares, "that would explain it." And indeed it would, Scottie acknowledges, all too easily.

[Madeline lures Scottie to the bell tower, he cannot handle the ascent, the real Madeline is murdered, and Judy escapes into anonymity.]

Scottie's Dream

Following Madeline's alleged suicide, Scottie is devastated. He becomes increasingly preoccupied by her image and all that she represents. He has a dream that penetrates to the heart of his preoccupation. A bouquet of flowers appears, just like the one Madeline held while staring at the portrait of Carlotta (which also contained a bouquet). The petals begin falling apart, and so does Scottie. In the next scene, Scottie stands next to a woman who appears to be Madeline but emerges as Carlotta. He then focuses on Carlotta's necklace (which is the same kind that Madeline wore). Next, he finds himself walking toward Madeline/Carlotta's gravesite. He plunges into the open pit and begins falling. This image resolves into that of a man falling directly onto a roof (just as Madeline had apparently fallen). The roof disintegrates and the man continues to fall, hurtling *endlessly* into space.

The dream appears to represent Scottie's total giving over to the Madeline-Carlotta-infinitude axis. With increasing degrees of identification and mergence, Scottie discovers the chaos that buttresses that link. He discovers that a *thorough* surrender has no linguistic or cultural context within which to orient oneself, no consoling appeals, but is an absurd, harrowing spin.

[Scottie spots Judy and longs to recapture Madeline's spirit.]

Judy and the Scene of the Crime

Although terrified of Madeline and the cosmic, Scottie continues to be compelled by her/it and desperately tries to make Judy over into Madeline. He then discovers (via Carlotta's necklace) that Judy played a role, that she is indeed human, and this drags him back into cynicism and despair. When one overcomes dazzlement (vertigo), the price is despair.

At the Tower

This is the final scene where Judy's earthly and eternal sides become equally evident. She (like each of us) is both limited, flawed *and* beatific, numinous; Scottie, however, can only see these qualities in isolation. Either he is in despair or unmanageable ecstasy over her. At this point, he is mainly in despair and thus unaffected by his vertigo. As they near the top of the tower, however, he swings back into rapture. Partly, this shift is due to Judy's assurances that she *actually* does love him; partly, however, it is due to his persistent resuscitation of Madeline. At the moment of his possible reconciliation of these poles, the nun (who startles Judy into jumping off the tower) emerges. Her presence intimates that the ecstatic relation has gone too far and that the limited world of flaws and foibles must be addressed. The upshot, she implies, is that neither Judy (who loved but deceived him) nor Madeline (who inspired but overwhelmed him) can survive. He must begin his search anew.

SUMMARY

Vertigo is the story of a person (or by implication, every person) who is caught between the banal (limited), which is represented by Midge (and to some extent Judy), and the fanatical (transcendent), which is signified by Scottie's relation to Madeline. The problem, however, is that neither experience is very fulfilling. The banal is oppressive and the fanatical is disorienting. Indeed, both are reactions to one another. The banal is a defense against the intensity of the fanatical, and the fanatical, as we saw in large part in Scottie's case, is a defense against the devitalization of the banal.

The solution, Hitchcock implies (mainly by vivifying *both* positions), is what I term existential spirituality or wonderment. The Czech novelist Milan Kundera (1986) calls it "the spirit of complexity"; Martin Buber (1964) calls it "holy insecurity." Wonderment cleaves *between* the banal and the fanatical. By acknowledging *both* positions—the cautious and the passionate, the skeptical and the mesmerized—wonderment challenges us to *choose* when and to what degree to modulate these modalities. If Scottie were in wonderment, accordingly, he might have (a) seen through and constructively addressed Judy's duplicity, (b) cultivated the radiance (if any) in his relationship to Midge, or (c) pursued a more substantive transcendental relation.

Wonderment presents three challenges to transpersonal theorists who make totalistic or absolutistic knowledge claims: First, is cosmic surrender (*complete* giving of oneself over as Scottie attempted with Madeline) blissful or harrowing? Is infinitude (best expressed, perhaps, by love and tragedy) genuinely assimilable or is it intolerable, overpowering at certain points? (Recall Scottie's dream sequence, our own loves/losses.) Second, what is the role of danger (destabilization, mortality) in transcendental experience, and how moving (or profound) are transcendental experiences bereft of such elements? Is not danger, some danger, a signal of the magnitude of one's experience—for example, the self edging into the not-self? Is not danger integral to the "growing edge" of any relationship, and does not this growing edge cease where danger ceases? ("Where danger is," Hölderlin reflects, "the delivering power grows too" [Hölderlin, 1986].) Finally, is not the growing edge, the outer limit of our freedom and ecstasy, precisely what makes Hitchcock and art-horror (such as *Frankenstein* and *Dracula*) so compelling?

I believe so, and I believe that such stories are also our most instructive *liberation* stories, because they take our crazy condition (within the boundless) seriously. They harken to that "something more," as Bugental (1990, p. 17) notes, that *sustains* even as it alarms.

REFERENCES—LITERARY ROOTS

Becker, E. (1973). *The denial of death.* New York: Free Press.

Buber, M. (1964). *Daniel: Dialogues on realization* (M. Friedman, Trans.). New York: Holt, Rinehart & Winston.

Buber, M. (1965). *Between man and man* (R. Smith, Trans.). New York: Macmillan.

Bugental, J. (1990). *Intimate journeys: Stories from life-changing therapy.* San Francisco: Jossey-Bass.

Ellis, A., & Yeager, R. J. (1989). *Why some therapies don't work: The dangers of transpersonal psychology.* Buffalo, NY: Prometheus.

Hitchcock, A. (Producer). (1958). *Vertigo* (film). Universal City, CA: MCA/Universal.

Hölderlin, F. (1986). *Hölderlin: Selected verse* (M. Hamburger, Trans.). London: Anvil.

Kundera, M. (1986). *The art of the novel.* New York: Harper & Row.

May, R. (1981). *Freedom and destiny.* New York: Norton.

Otto, R. (1923/1958). *The idea of the holy.* London: Oxford.

Rilke, R. (1982). *The selected poetry of Rainer Marie Rilke* (S. Mitchell, Trans.). New York: Vintage.

Schneider, K. (1987). The deified self: A "centaur" response to Wilber and the transpersonal movement. *Journal of Humanistic Psychology, 27*(2), 196–216.

Schneider, K. (1989). Infallibility is so damn appealing: A reply to Ken Wilber. *Journal of Humanistic Psychology, 29*(4), 498–506.

Spoto, D. (1983). *The dark side of genius: The life of Alfred Hitchcock.* New York: Ballantine.

Tillich, P. (1952). *The courage to be.* New Haven, CT: Yale University Press.

Wilber, K. (1981). *Up from Eden: A transpersonal view of human evolution.* Boulder, CO: Shambhala.

Wilber K. (1989a). God is so damn boring: A response to Kirk Schneider. *Journal of Humanistic Psychology, 29*(4), 457–469.

Wilber K. (1989b). Reply to Schneider. *Journal of Humanistic Psychology, 29*(4), 493–500.

Wood, R. (1969). *Hitchcock's films.* New York: Paperback Library.

WORKS OF RELATED INTEREST

Barron, F. (1963). *Creativity and psychological health.* New York: Van Nostrand.

Bettelheim, B. (1976). *The uses of enchantment.* New York: Vintage.

Bugental, J. (Ed.) (1967). *Challenges of humanistic psychology.* New York: McGraw-Hill.

Friedman, M. (Ed.) (1991). *The worlds of existentialism: A critical reader.* Atlantic Highlands, NJ: Humanities Press.

Heuscher, J. (1974). *A psychiatric study of fairy tales.* Springfield, IL: C. Thomas.

Kaufmann, W. (1960). *From Shakespeare to existentialism.* New York: Anchor Books.

May, R. (1985). *My quest for beauty.* Dallas: Saybrook (distributed by Norton, New York).

May, R. (1991). *The cry for myth.* New York: Norton.

Rank, O. (1932/1989). *Art and artist.* New York: Norton.

Schneider, K. (1993). *Horror and the holy: Wisdom-teachings of the monster tale.* Chicago: Open Court.

Woodruff, P., & Wilmer, H. (1988). *Facing evil: Light at the core of darkness.* Chicago: Open Court.

CHAPTER 2

PHILOSOPHICAL ROOTS

"There is but one truly serious philosophical problem," declared the French philosopher Albert Camus (1955), "and that is . . . whether life is or is not worth living" (p. 3). With these words, Camus inaugurated the fundamental question, not merely of existential philosophy, but of our existence.

"When I consider the short duration of my life," Pascal reflected 300 years before Camus, "I am terrified and wonder that I am here rather than there . . . now rather than then" (quoted in Friedman, 1991, p. 39).

Much like its literary counterpart that we have just discussed, although in more explicit, systematic fashion, existential philosophy is an attempt to grasp "being." It is an attempt to understand the fundamental conditions of human existence and to propose "response-able," that is, thoughtful, deeply searching responses to those conditions.

It is not that other philosophical movements have not attempted to address these fundamental questions. Clearly, they have. The difference, however, can be felt, and I do stress *felt*, in the directness and tone of statements such as those of Camus and Pascal. These philosophers do not merely provide a list of existential attributes or mathematically exacting formulas; they shake you up, let you know in your bones, and give you an *experience* concerning that which they envision. "Truth," the author of modern existentialism, Søren Kierkegaard, once asserted, "exists only as the individual produces it in action," and this is precisely Camus' and Pascal's challenge.

The aim of existential philosophy, accordingly, is to comprehend the human being's immediate, unfolding situation in the world or, to use Heidegger's (1962) phrase, "being-in-the-world." In particular, existential philosophy attempts to clarify the life-designs or experiential perimeters within which we live. What are their shapes, existential philosophers ask, and how much freedom, meaning, value, and so on do they permit us? Finally, how can we optimize them in order to lead fuller, more productive lives?

The impetus for existential speculation is almost always a profound *crisis*. Why else would people ask such poignant questions about who or what they are or where they are headed?* Such questions are almost invariably a response to individual or collective breakdown—a point at which the old patterns no longer work or lead toward catastrophe. Does the periodic quality of existential speculation make it any less significant or profound? To the contrary, we would argue that it is precisely its emergence in the context of *crises*—points of disruption and alarm—that give existential philosophy its depth. It is precisely complacency against which existential philosophers take their stand.

Specifically, then, how do existential philosophers conceive of and respond to the human situation? What are their essential teachings?†

EASTERN ROOTS OF EXISTENTIAL PHILOSOPHY

The search for what it means to be alive is obviously not the province of one single tradition or geographical region. Indeed, it is the fount of many great religions and wisdom teachings all through the world. But the teachings and traditions that can, roughly, be termed *existential*—those that do not resort to formulaic or dogmatic "truths" but emphasize *experiential* knowledge and learning—narrow the list considerably. Although traditionally associated with the West, existential philosophy also draws from and reflects Eastern influences such as Taoism and Buddhism, to which we now turn.

Lao Tzu

Founded in the wake of centuries of oppressive rule, Taoism was formulated in the sixth century B.C. by a little-known Chinese librarian—Lao Tzu. His slim volume, called the *Tao Te Ching* (which means, literally, "way of life") illuminates the fathomlessness of existence and the folly of prideful men. Among his tenets are:

"Existence is beyond the power of words to define: terms may be used but none of them is absolute."

"Existence by nothing bred, breeds everything, parent of the universe."

"Existence is infinite, not to be defined; and though it seems but a bit of wood in your hand, to carve as you please, it is not to be lightly played with and laid down."

To counter his era's "conquest mentality," Lao Tzu advocated a kind of feminine

---

*Depending on the victim's ability to respond, of course, a crisis may or may not lead to deeper reflection; indeed, it can, ironically, lead to the very denials and excesses that fostered it in the first place. For one who is prepared, however, a crisis is often the most illuminating event in life.
†The vignettes to follow are brief and suggestive. They are not designed to be comprehensive. Readers who desire elaboration on the vignettes (and on the complexities of existential philosophy) are directed to the reference and bibliographic sections at the close of this chapter.

softness, receptivity, and acceptance of being. "The way to do is to be," he suggested. Although he seemed to stress "feminine" (*yin*) qualities over "masculine" (*yang*) qualities, he nevertheless acknowledged *both* existential realities. "Rather abide at the center of your being," he proposed, "for the more you leave it, the less you learn" (quoted in May et al., 1958, p. 18).

Siddhartha Gautama

About the same time that Lao Tzu contemplated his *Tao Te Ching,* an Indian aristocrat named Siddhartha Gautama (560–477 B.C.) fashioned a similar, equally challenging orientation. Later to become known as Buddhism, this discipline also arose in the context of strife—the tyranny of the Hindu upper classes, for example, and the excessive ritualism and superstition of the time.

Despite his own privileged background, Buddha (as he came to be known) pioneered a compassionate, wide-ranging path. Against elitism, empty ritual, and grandiose speculation, *between* indulgence and asceticism, Buddha proposed a practical program for liberation. "Whether the world is eternal or not eternal," he is reputed to have said, or "whether a Buddha exists after death or does not exist after death. . . .[These things] do not tend toward edification" (Burt, 1955, p. 142).

"What have I explained?" Buddha asks elsewhere. "Suffering have I explained, the cause of suffering, the destruction of suffering, and the path that leads to the destruction of suffering . . . for this is useful" (Thomas, 1935, pp. 64–67).

Buddha's Middle Way, as he called it, is far too vast to elucidate here. Suffice it to say that through its use of meditation and its disidentification with "roles" and material excesses, Buddhism fosters a larger, more inclusive worldview. By minimizing possessiveness, it maximizes trust, awareness, and equanimity.

To sum up, Eastern and Western worldviews are parallel but not symmetrical. Taoism and Buddhism, for example, place greater stress on detachment, acceptance, and unity than do Western—and in particular existentialist—worldviews. The former, moreover, provide more or less systematized sets of codes for living while the existentialist worldview furnishes directions, suggestions, and a continually evolving *attitude.*

Eastern and Western strands of existentialism, therefore, can be characterized by their complementarity. Their tones and moods are different, but they both underscore "response-ability," profound searching and inwardness, and the integration of self-world relationships, be they soothing or contrary.

THE WESTERN EXISTENTIAL TRADITION

Socrates

During the latter half of the fourth century B.C., in Athens, Greece, there was celebration in the air. Greek military might had just overcome one of the most powerful adversaries in the ancient world—the Persian empire. Amid the pomp and self-congratulation, however, numerous signs of deterioration emerged—a vain and petty aristocracy, for example, and a corrupt political elite.

Enter Socrates (470–400 B.C.)—philosopher, provocateur, and therapist. With proclamations like "Know thyself" and "Life without enquiry is not worth living," Socrates cajoled and prodded his fellow Athenians to reassess their priorities. If they set their sights on the "precious" things in life, as he conceived it, they would achieve both knowledge and compassion—or what he referred to as *soul* (Plato, 1984). Nowhere was this challenging method of self-confrontation more evident than at Socrates' trial where, condemned to death for "corrupting" the young, the ponderer pleaded his case. "All I do," he insisted,

> is to go about and try to persuade you, both young and old, not to care for your bodies or your monies first, and to care more exceedingly for the soul, to make it as good as possible.
>
> If you put me to death, you will not easily find such another, really like something stuck on the state by the god, though it is rather laughable to say so; for the state is like a big thoroughbred horse, so big that he is a bit slow and heavy, and wants a gadfly to wake him up. I think the god put me on the state something like that, to wake you up. (Plato, 1984, p. 436)

Blaise Pascal

Standing singularly proud among those agitators and reformers for whom Socrates was the paradigmatic embodiment is the prophetic French philosopher Blaise Pascal (1623–1662). Pascal was a mathematician, inventor, and acute observer of the human condition. Almost two centuries before Kierkegaard, he outlined what many, even today, consider to be one of the most concise existential commentaries ever written. Following are a few highlights:

> Whoso takes this survey of himself will be terrified at the thought that he is upheld . . . between these two abysses of the infinite and nothing, he will tremble at the sight of these marvels. . . .
>
> For after all what is man in nature? A nothing in regard to the infinite, a whole in regard to nothing, a mean between nothing and the whole; infinitely removed from understanding either extreme. . . .
>
> What shall he do then, but discern somewhat of the middle of things in an eternal despair of knowing either their beginning or their end? . . .
>
> Let us then know our limits; we are something, but we are not all. (Quoted in Friedman, 1991, p. 39)

Elsewhere, Pascal opines:

> We sail on a vast expanse, ever uncertain, ever drifting, hurried from one to the other goal. If we think to attach ourselves firmly to any point, it totters and fails us; if we follow, it eludes our grasp . . . vanishing forever. Nothing stays for us. This is our natural condition, yet always the most contrary to our inclination; we burn with desire to find a steadfast place and an ultimate fixed basis whereon we may build a tower to reach the infinite. But our whole foundation breaks up, and earth opens to the abysses.
>
> We may not then look for certainty. . . . Our reason is always deceived by changing shows, nothing can fix the finite between the two infinities, which at once close and fly from it. (Friedman, 1991, p. 39)

That Pascal (at least partially) *lived* his convictions is borne out by the historical record. He was capable of defending both religious heretics and religious doctrine, both rationality and intuition. His most famous maxim, it seems, is a testament to this dexterity: "The heart has its reasons which reason knows not" (Friedman, 1991, p. 41).

Søren Kierkegaard

Some fifty years before Freud, and unbeknownst to many subsequent psychologists, Søren Kierkegaard (1813–1855) outlined what may someday be seen as a foundational theory of personality functioning (Becker, 1973). Before we summarize this framework, however, it will be helpful to highlight Kierkegaard's other paramount contributions.

Considered the creator of modern existential philosophy, Kierkegaard fervently challenged the rationality, objectivism, and reductionism of his day. Science, Kierkegaard believed, was quietly becoming a new god, and Hegel's metaphysical speculations were the cold and calculating path to that goal. Rather than formulaic truths, therefore, or reductionist explanations of how and why we do what we do, Kierkegaard advocated *inwardness* and *passion*.

Kierkegaard's basic thrust can be understood thusly: Neither objectivism, with its emphasis on the publicly measurable and verifiable, nor subjectivism, with its accent on the private and emotional, can, in isolation, provide us with a complete picture of human functioning. Only taken together can they help us to understand our condition. The problem, as Kierkegaard saw it, was that (particularly) objectivism had grown so monstrous in recent years and had become so top-heavy that it threatened to crush subjectivism—leaving us to pull levers and push buttons for many of our needs.

Contrary to popular belief, Kierkegaard was not a subjectivist. He acknowledged the need for rules, regulations, and formulas; he just didn't believe these things helped us to comprehend the richer aspects of living, such as the capacity to love, create, and marvel at the stars. His purpose, therefore, was to redress the imbalance that had emerged and to forge a broader, more inclusive position.

It is with this background in mind that some of Kierkegaard's most famous statements, make sense:

"Truth exists only as the individual himself produces it in action."

"Away from Speculation, away from the System, and back to reality."

"The more consciousness, the more self."

"Personhood is a *synthesis* of possibility and necessity." [Emphasis added.]

It is no accident that irony and paradox permeate Kierkegaard's prose. Kierkegaard believed that human beings exist on many levels, some of which are contradictory and some of which are fathomless. Our task is to affirm these various facets of our existence and not to reduce or deny them.

Kierkegaard characterizes the various levels of the self in terms of their capacity to limit (or *finitize*) and extend (or *infinitize*). He discusses this brilliantly in "Despair as Defined by Finitude and Infinitude," his comprehensive outline of personality functioning (Kierkegaard, 1849/1980). Here are a few excerpts:

> The self is a synthesis of infinitude and finitude, that relates itself to itself, whose task is to become itself. . . . The self is [a] synthesis of which the finite is the limiting and the infinite the extending [factor]. (Kierkegaard, 1849/1980, pp. 29–30)

He goes on to explain that people become dysfunctional when they overemphasize either polarity, when they become too finitized *or* infinitized. The cold, pedantic objectivist, for example, may be understood as excessively finitized; while the fiery, indulgent subjectivist may be viewed as overly infinitized. These types are described below, beginning with the overly infinitized.

> Infinitude's despair is to lack [or avoid] finitude. . . . Infinitude's despair . . . is the fantastic, the unlimited. . . . As a rule, imagination is the medium for the process of infinitizing. The self then leads a fantasized existence . . . [moving] further and further away [from itself]. It flounders in possibility until exhausted. (Kierkegaard, 1849/1980, pp. 30–37)

Now he describes the excessively finitized, or limited.

> Finitude's despair is to lack [or avoid] infinitude. . . . To lack infinitude is despairing reductionism, narrowness. . . . Whereas one kind of despair plunges wildly into the infinite and loses itself, [this kind] permit[s] itself to be tricked out of itself by [other people]. . . . A person [in such a state] forgets himself, forgets his name . . . does not dare to believe in himself . . . [and] finds it far easier and safer to be like others, to become a copy, a number, a mass man. (Kierkegaard, 1849/1980, pp. 33–34)

Finally, Kierkegaard sums up the healthier, or more integrated, personality. He proposes:

> Good health generally means the ability to resolve contradictions. . . . [It is] a synthesis . . . like breathing . . . which is an inhaling and exhaling. (Kierkegaard, 1849/1980, p. 40)

Kierkegaard's passionate-realistic hero, or what he calls his "knight of faith," has precisely these qualities.

Friedrich Nietzsche

Following closely on the heels of Kierkegaard, yet separately from him, Friedrich Nietzsche (1844–1900) arrived at an equally existential destination. Writing in crisp, authoritative tones and more "penetratingly," as Freud was later to observe, "than any other man who ever lived or was likely to live" (Jones, 1957, p. 344), Nietzsche delineated three contemporary dilemmas: (1) the failure of institutional authority, (2) the rising tide of nihilism, and (3) the struggle for psychospiritual balance, or integration.

When Nietzsche declared that "God is dead," he did not mean all gods or every god to come; he meant the gods, both secular and religious, that no longer bred inspiration and hope, but only disillusionment and decay. He meant the corrupt gods that catered to some greedy elite; the repressive gods that stifled sexuality, creative play, and emotional expressiveness; the technocratic gods that sapped the populace of meaningful and stimulating work; and the scientist gods that denied the legitimacy of nonrational phenomena.

In short, Nietzsche forecast the breakdown of institutional authority, but he did not stop there. He also foresaw a gaping chasm left in the wake of this break-down—a chasm he feared would lead to nihilism. What happens, Nietzsche pondered, when people no longer have traditions to steer them or gods to inspire them? Many of them flounder, he asserted; they become reckless, anarchistic beasts, or they form reactionary, xenophobic enclaves. That these extremisms strike a note of familiarity in our own unstable era, an era bereft of traditions, was precisely Nietzsche's concern.

Nietzsche's worldview, accordingly, can be characterized as a primordial clash of contraries—on the one hand, repression, order, or what Nietzsche termed Apollonian consciousness and on the other hand, indulgence, abandon, or what he called Dionysian awareness. Wherever one is sacrificed, he contended, the other suffers, because neither can operate in isolation (Nietzsche, 1872/1956, p. 64).

How can we cope with these warring (individual and collective) tendencies, according to Nietzsche? By confronting them, by acknowledging both our limits *and* our possibilities, our need for order and discipline, as well as spontaneity and abandon. In so doing, he proclaimed, we foster dynamic, realistic lives.

This is what Nietzsche meant when he talked about "passionate people who master their passions" (Kaufmann, 1968, p. 280) or those, like Goethe, who "self-overcome."

> Goethe sought help from history, natural science, antiquity, and also Spinoza, but above all, from practical activity; he surrounded himself with limited horizons; he did not retire from life but put himself into the midst of it; he was not fainthearted but took as much as possible upon himself, over himself, into himself. What he wanted was *totality;* he fought the extraneousness of reason, senses, feeling, and will. . . . He disciplined himself to wholeness, he *created* himself. . . .
>
> Goethe conceived a human being who would be strong, highly educated, skillful in all bodily matters, self-controlled, reverent toward himself, and who might dare to afford the whole range and wealth of being natural, being strong enough for such freedom; the man of tolerance, not from weakness but from strength. . . .
>
> Such a spirit who has *become free* stands amid the cosmos with a joyous and trusting fatalism, in the *faith* that only the particular is loathsome, and that all is redeemed in the whole. (Nietzsche, 1889/1982, p. 554)

Edmund Husserl

In the early part of the twentieth century, with science and technology in the ascendency, the protestations of Kierkegaard and Nietzsche began to find new adherents. Edmund Husserl (1859–1938), for example, was able to formalize much of what the latter believed in the new discipline he called *phenomenology.*

"The crisis in the European sciences," as Husserl (1936/1970) put it, was the growing effort to impose *natural* scientific attitudes on the study of *human* (or psychological) phenomena. The basic problem with this trend, according to Husserl, was that it reduced, or debased, the human experience. It sought to understand human behavior in terms of only its surface (that is, observable, measurable) features; it equated psychological investigation with the investigation of physical or physiological phenomena, seeking to find invariant, universal laws of psychological functioning (although it must be conceded that Husserl himself appears to have lapsed into this trap from a subjectivist position, as we shall see).

In order to show that a phenomenon such as the smile is more than the contraction of the circumoral muscles or that fear or anger or attraction transcend the conditioned reflex, Husserl returned to investigating *the person* to whom these events occurred.

The aim of phenomenology, accordingly, was to "return to the things themselves" as Husserl put it, or to provide a method whereby (1) human experience can be studied in its immediacy (as opposed to under controlled or laboratory conditions); (2) the researcher suspends her preconceptions (for example, preselected questions) about the phenomenon under study; (3) the researcher immerses herself in as many aspects (e.g., cognitive, intuitive, affective) of the given phenomenon as possible; (4) the researcher richly and fully *describes* the given phenomenon; and (5) the researcher collects and integrates these descriptions to provide a "saturated" (subjective or intersubjective) interpretation of the given phenomenon. (See Giorgi, 1970, and Polkinghorne, 1989, for an elaboration on these procedures.)

That this method has its parallels in the artist's mode of perceiving and apprehending phenomena was not lost upon Husserl's successors. For it was precisely art, or the artistic mode, that best illuminated psychology for these thinkers; it was precisely the artistic mode that could counterbalance reductionism. Merleau-Ponty (1962), for example, wrote,

> If phenomenology was a movement before becoming a doctrine . . . this was attributable neither to accident, nor to fraudulent intent. It is as painstaking as the works of Balzac, Proust, Valery or Cezanne—by reason of the same kind of attentiveness and wonder, the same demand for awareness, and the same will to seize the meaning of the world . . . as that meaning comes into being. (p. xxi)

Phenomenology, on the other hand, is not *merely* an artistic procedure; it is a systematic method of understanding and sharing data—an artistic-scientific blend, if you will. (For more on Husserl's profound and enduring impact on existential psychology, see Giorgi, 1970; Kockelmans, 1978; Spiegelberg, 1976a).

Now let us turn to Husserl's successors, who, drawing upon the techniques of phenomenology, developed their own comprehensive visions.

Martin Heidegger

The chief concern of Heidegger, a student of Husserl's, was what it means to be, to exist. All about him, Martin Heidegger (1884–1976) observed narrow lives, petty concerns, and assembly-line mentalities. *Technocracy,* the management of society by technicians, he felt, had reached fever pitch; and he was aghast at its effects.

What might it be like, Heidegger inquired, to transcend those conformist and role-dominated attitudes and really live, or exist, in our fullness, as Nietzschean "overmen" or Kierkegaardian "knights"? To answer the question, Heidegger decided to perform a phenomenological investigation of being, utilizing himself and Western philosophy as his subjects.

Daunting though it may seem, this is the project that Heidegger (1962) undertook, and it resulted in a foundational thesis.

This thesis can be understood in terms of two basic states of being: (1) being-in-the-midst-of-the-world and (2) being-in-the-world (Olson, 1962, p. 135). Being-in-the-midst-of-the-world entails doing and being for others, functioning as an instrument to do others' bidding; in short, living *inauthentically*. Inauthentic living, moreover, is an expression of complacency. It is designed around habit, custom, and the forgetting of life's *temporality*. Being-in-the-world, on the other hand, is characterized by presence or responsiveness to the world (with all its possibilities and limits). The *authentic person,* accordingly, is one who responds, not just to worldly demands, but to Being itself, or, as Heidegger put it, the "call within." What is this call to Being? While Heidegger is not precise in answering this question (who, after all could be?), he does sketch a picture. It is like the calling of the poet, he says—passionate, poignant, and welling from the depths (Olson, 1962). It is also like the "discoveries" of Ivan Ilych upon learning of his fatal illness—awe-ful and prizing of the moment.

Jean Paul Sartre

For Jean Paul Sartre (1905–1980), whose experiences in the French resistance during World War II were formative, being had particular significance. Sartre (1956) was struck by the idea that though things, or objects, have a radically different existence than do conscious human beings, we so often treat the two in the same way. Increasingly, he felt, society identified people's roles with their overall beings: factory managers, for example, as Heidegger had already observed, perceived their workers as mechanical parts; consumers equated producers with things (e.g., "clerk-things," "waiter-things," "doctor-things"); and even governments, such as Nazi Germany, viewed its citizens as moldable tools of the state.

Yet our authentic existence, according to Sartre, is completely contrary to these frozen interpretations of our lives; it is a "no-thing." At every instant, that is, we are completely free to disengage from who we were the instant before, not in the sense of changing our material reality or the circumstances within which we are thrust, but in the sense of adopting attitudes toward these "facticities," as Sartre called them.

To live authentically, then, one must be prepared, at each instant, to negate one's identities of the past, to create new identities (or attitudes), and to affirm the no-thingness that one is. How workable is this demanding vision of being?

According to Sartre, it is highly workable because we live it whether we want to acknowledge the point or not. "We are condemned to be free," he said. Practically speaking, however, it is extremely difficult to achieve such a liberated state. For unlike Heidegger's "fullness of Being," it would be like a constant state of disorientation, or nausea—a void that we would be perpetually responsible for filling. It would also be a disconnected state for Sartre, completely immune to subconscious (i.e., cultural, historical, or personal) influences.

Recap

It may be clear by now that Husserl, Heidegger, and Sartre had a common mission but took their own unique paths to that goal and achieved varying degrees of success. Each, for example, rebelled against the growing objectivism of his day and developed means of both investigating and interpreting human experience that he considered more suitable to that experience. Heidegger and Sartre, in particular, concerned themselves with authenticity—what it means to fully be—and found their answer in the freedom from socially dictated roles (or, to state it affirmatively, in the presence of inner promptings and attitudes). For Heidegger, this resulted in a fullness of being (that is, a rich, sensual, anticipatory experiential mode); for Sartre, it resulted in an emptiness of being (that is, a disorienting, upsetting, negating experiential mode) (Olson, 1962). Finally, they both highlighted our responsibility for shaping and cherishing these modes before the ever-present givens of life.

Despite their "liberations," however, Husserl, Heidegger, and Sartre all appear to have fallen prey to some of the same tendencies they criticized in others. For all his concerns with objectivism, for example, Husserl appears to have lapsed into an absolutizing mode of his own (Spiegelberg, 1976a, 1976b). His persistent quest—especially in earlier years—was to find the ultimate foundation for all knowledge via subjective (or phenomenological) routes of investigation. Yet such *subjectivism* (the idea that the self holds the key to reality), is just as one-sided as *objectivism* (the idea that the material world holds the key to reality), and was all but dispensed with by Husserl's successors.

Heidegger, on the other hand, criticizes the purveyors of conformity and received views but goes on to formulate his own region of preconceptual influences that he calls *Being*. By so doing, according to his critics, he comes dangerously close to exchanging that which is emancipatory in his philosophical outlook—e.g., presence, immediacy—for that which is presumptive and quasi-deterministic (Olson, 1962; Barnes, 1967).

Sartre, too, displayed extremist tendencies. I refer specifically to his conception of human freedom, which is so antideterministic, so utterly unencroachable, that it threatened to invalidate his otherwise compelling position (Spiegelberg, 1976b). Is it probable, for example, that we exist in the encapsulated moment that Sartre implies? Do we really have to acknowledge *total* freedom to adopt attitudes toward a given situation in order to be considered authentic; or are there mitigating circumstances, pre- or unreflected-upon meanings, that color and limit our attitudinal range?

This was certainly the belief of the existential-phenomenologist Maurice Merleau-Ponty, to whom we now turn.

Maurice Merleau-Ponty

Maurice Merleau-Ponty (1908–1961) is underappreciated by the nonexistential-phenomenological world. He lacked the flash of some of his colleagues, died relatively young, and completed only a fragment of his philosophical project; yet in his short life, he was able to modify, refine, and bring desperately needed balance to existential-phenomenology.

He updated Husserl's views, for example, by modifying his attempt "to find the ultimate foundation for all knowledge in pure subjectivity" (Spiegelberg, 1976b, p. 535). For Merleau-Ponty, phenomenology was no longer a method of unveiling essences or universal truths but a method of revealing the indeterminate intersubjectivity of viewpoints—always open to revision.

At the same time that he argued against essences, however, he also argued against Sartre's radical notion of freedom, or *nonessentialism.* Sartre, he felt, had underestimated the multilayered quality of conscious intention and the limiting effect posed by already established meaning-contexts, such as the body, history, and culture (Spiegelberg, 1976b, pp. 554–555). Using phrases like one "never starts from zero," or I "may confirm or repudiate [my situation] but not annul [it]," Merleau-Ponty (1962, p. 447; 1964) firmly allied himself with psychodynamicists such as Freud, who posit subconscious influence. On the other hand, Merleau-Ponty could agree neither to Freud's determinism nor Heidegger's quasi-determinism (Spiegelberg, 1976b). Whenever human experience was portrayed one-sidedly, Merleau-Ponty indicated, he was there to protest—very much like his existentialist forebears, who challenged the "crimes" of complacency.

In short, Merleau-Ponty stood squarely on the shoulders of those existentialists who ardently spurned philosophical dualisms. We are neither free nor determined, self-created nor externally customized, but an "inextricable intermixture," as Merleau-Ponty (1962, p. 518) put it—and that is precisely our challenge to negotiate.

Next, we turn to philosophers who echo Merleau-Ponty in the domain of spirituality—Martin Buber and Paul Tillich.

Martin Buber*

> In the . . . gaze of Buber's searching eyes is the composedness of him who cannot conform to the established law because he wants to be open and obedient to the demand of the hour.
>
> —MAURICE FRIEDMAN

Martin Buber (1878–1965) led an extraordinary life. Like Goethe, he was a man of great interdisciplinary range; and, like Moses, he was called upon for leadership in a time of great international strife. Many significant turning points in Buber's life presaged his dynamic future career: the desertion by his mother (when he was just 3 years old); the scholarly influence of his grandparents (who tutored him until he was 10); his foundation-shaking encounter with the idea of infinitude (at age 14) that pre-

---

*Source: This passage is adapted from Kirk Schneider's review of Maurice Friedman's *Encounter on the Narrow Ridge: A Life of Martin Buber,* in the March/April, 1992 issue of Association for Humanistic Psychology, *Perspective* (p. 14).

figured his mystical outlook; his controversial appeals—in both Germany and Israel—for a humanistic socialism; and his marriage to Paula, a German Catholic, who supported and eventually converted to Buber's Judaism.

The most important outgrowth of these developments was Buber's formulation of what he affectionately termed the "narrow ridge." The *narrow ridge,* as he saw it, is that delicate passageway *between* the polarized mentalities that have typified—and so often laid waste to—substantial portions of humanity. It is a deeply searching, deliberative position that bridges—but does not fuse—the self-other relation. The person who travels the narrow ridge holds his own perspective but in the context of what might be offered by another or by that which surprises. "I have occasionally described my standpoint to my friends as the 'narrow ridge,'" Buber once stated. "I wanted by this to express that I did not rest on the broad upland of a system that includes a series of sure statements about the absolute, but on a narrow rocky ridge between the gulfs where there is no sureness of expressible knowledge but the certainty of meeting what remains undisclosed" (Friedman, 1991, p. x).

Throughout his life, Buber passionately strove to meet "what remains undisclosed." Time after time, for example, he clashed with dogmatic civic and religious leaders—even during the terrifying Nazi period—and declined the "easy word," as he characterized it, or the expedient path. Even when it came to his beloved Israel, he would not sacrifice the (many-dimensional) "demand of the hour."

Buber's formulation of the concept of the narrow ridge culminated in his most famous philosophical statement (*I and Thou,* 1958). This remarkable document outlines two basic levels of human interaction, the "I-it" and the "I-thou." The I-it level is the treatment of people as things, as objects to be manipulated. Wherever we accept roles, rules imposed from without, or machine-like performances, for example, we countenance the I-it mentality. Many, if not most, of our interactions—as Kierkegaard and other existentialists have pointed out—take place at this level. The I-thou level, on the other hand, is the treatment of people (and even things) as unique, multifaceted beings. It is a level that anticipates surprise, spontaneity, and deviation, and *challenges* those who resist such anticipations. Finally, it is a level that promotes coexistence—self-other distinction in a mosaic of self-other exchange.

Buber's emphasis on the *between* (the narrow ridge, the I-Thou) is foundational for existential-integrative practice. Springing as it does from *psychospiritual* lineages, it shortchanges neither subjective depth nor societal richness, freedom nor sobering limits; and it affirms, thereby, an attainable vision of life.

Next, we turn to Rollo May's mentor and close friend, Paul Tillich. One of the great theologians of our century, Tillich brought "doubt to the faithful and faith to the doubters." The combination of the two sparked hope.

Paul Tillich*

Paul Tillich (1886–1965) was a great teacher. The students who crowded into his classes were not only seminarians but graduate students from Columbia, townspeople

---

Source: This selection is from Rollo May's *Paulus* (Dallas, TX.: Saybrook, 1987), pp. 114, 121, 122–123.

from New York, and fellow intellectuals exiled like Paulus from Hitler's Germany. Later, when he was University Professor at Harvard, the same crowded classes prevailed. What did the students come to hear? Not a flamboyant lecturer (the German-born Tillich always struggled with the English language) and not a colorful speaker. He was the opposite of these.

The reason Tillich was a great teacher was that his lectures always carried a life-and-death significance. He held us spellbound because each of his statements *mattered*. He spoke out of his own doubt-ridden soul—a soul which always existed "on the boundary," as he put it. He once stated, "I am called to give doubt to the faithful and faith to the doubters." Each sentence in his lectures seemed like an ultimate statement. For example, he talked about *Being* in the middle of a century when no one else seemed to take that term seriously. Each of us had, in listening to him, an experience of joyous seriousness. . . .

The value of doubt in Paulus was . . . a great asset in his teaching. It was not at all that Paulus did not know the facts; he had an amazing grasp of history and philosophy and literature, not to say, specifically theology. But one can authentically doubt only to the extent one has authentic knowledge; and the more knowledge one has, the more one can fruitfully doubt. At the conclusion of every lecture, Paulus was ready to entertain any question, no matter how far-fetched it seemed to be. He knew that doubting is the symbol of the growing process, and may lead one into the most interesting and even thrilling phenomena. To doubt constructively requires that one be well fortified with knowledge; the person who knows very little cannot take the risk that doubting requires. When Paulus said that his mission was to bring doubt to the faithful, he meant that these faithful are soundly based and can stand—and even *need* to stand—looking into the abyss of doubt. They are the ones who can take the risk which confronts anyone who gazes into the Holy Void.

It takes more than knowledge to doubt; it takes courage. This is why Paulus did not write his *Systematic Theology* (1963) till the very last; its richness is a product of prolonged and multitudinous doubting. Doubting in this sense is a rich and adventurous back-packing among the high mountains; one's knowledge gives one a firm footing on the trail but one's doubting gives the sense of venture. It opens new trails to the unknown; one learns new paths; one sees new things on the trip; there are fresh winds blowing from different directions. And Paulus, who loved mountain climbing, would thrill with these adventures among the high peaks.

Doubt in this sense is expressive of the courage to venture when one never knows where he will come out. "To venture causes anxiety," wrote Kierkegaard, "but not to venture is to lose one's self." Paulus loved such wisdom from his fellow Northern Europeans. . . .

In the above ways we see Paulus as an exemplar of the great teacher: his use of reason as ecstatic, his courage to doubt, his eternal quest for what he called the "Holy Void," and his use of eros as a teacher. It meant his life was far from simple but at the same time it was glorious. It meant that some theologians would and did attack him strenuously as an atheist; but it also meant that thousands of others would see him as their guide to meaning, to mystery and blessedness. Professor Paul Ricoeur, the great French philosopher, once said to me, "Tillich is *my* theologian." It meant that Tillich would live in doubt—and in ecstasy. No wonder he had to live his life continually under the phrase "in spite of."

THE TASK OF EXISTENTIAL PHILOSOPHY AT PRESENT

Western history can be divided roughly into three philosophical epochs: premodern (3000 B.C. to 1500 A.D.), modern (1500 A.D. to 1900 A.D.), and postmodern (1900 A.D. to the present). While the premodern period (with the exception of eras such as Socrates' Athens) was founded on "secure" religious and cultural beliefs, and the modern era was founded on equally reassuring secular (e.g., scientific, political) ideologies, the postmodern era can boast no such foundations. Today's outlook (among industrialized nations, at any rate) is marked by a deep suspicion of tradition and, conversely, a wholehearted embrace of diversity, sovereignty, and indeterminacy. There are, of course, invariable counteractions to this trend (fundamentalism, for example), but its course, by and large, appears to be irreversible.

Existential philosophy, it may be clear by now, has played a signal role in the promotion of postmodernism. With its accent on freedom, choice, and the co-existence of polarities, existential philosophy has, in many ways, achieved its apotheosis in the postmodern movement. At the same time, however, existential philosophy is not interchangeable with postmodernism and harbors some deep reservations about its direction. Specifically, I refer to postmodernism's own dispositions to excess—overcompensations, perhaps, for the rule-ridden world it abhorred. Among these excesses (which we will have subsequent occasion to address) are the inclinations toward anarchy, the relativization of values, and the decentering of the self. If postmodernism's liberation from dogma is its crowning triumph, existentialists caution, then disavowal of human limits may signify its unheralded demise.

Existential philosophy, accordingly, has a continuing and vital role to play in contemporary discussions about worldviews. To the extent that existential philosophers stress openness in their outlooks, they also attend to our responsibility for channeling and deepening that openness, for making it humanly meaningful; and to the extent that they countenance limitedness, they also remind us of our powers to passionately reinterpret these impasses. While existential philosophy cannot (and will not) provide us with another pat doctrine of knowledge and moral precepts, it can alert us to certain ontological perils—the perils of dichotomizing, for example, and of magnifying our respective autonomous or determined realities. At the same time, existential philosophy can suggest time-tested directions to help us navigate our course—the embracing of paradox, the upholding of choice, and the engaging of what writer-philosopher Milan Kundera (1986) calls a "spirit of complexity" (p. 18).

What is needed today, Kundera concludes, is not so much uncertainty, but a *"wisdom* of uncertainty" (p. 7; emphasis added).

We conclude this chapter, finally, with excerpts from Kierkegaard, Nietzsche, and Camus. Although their topics differ, their themes ring familiar—crisis, searching, and encounter with life's paradoxes.

DREAD AS A SAVING EXPERIENCE BY MEANS OF FAITH

Søren Kierkegaard

Being educated by "the curriculum of misfortune," Søren Kierkegaard intimates in this challenging passage, may be the paramount education that one receives. The more one is shaken, Kierkegaard elaborates, the more one is introduced to possibilities that would not otherwise be available to one. While these possibilities may seem repellent at first, they could eventually prove far superior to one's former prospects and instill a far more enduring faith.

Clinical Relevance of the Passage: *Kierkegaard helps us to throw a new light on crises in this passage. He helps us to view them as openings as well as catastrophes. The loss of a parent, for example, can challenge a client to become more independent in his life, more capable. Fear can awaken humility in some clients and a renewed appreciation for limits. Anger can fuel hope, power, and accomplishment. Depression can fuel sensitivity. The question, of course, is how to promote these discoveries and how to sustain them over an extended period. The answer, Kierkegaard suggests, lies in the faith one acquires by assimilating one's anxiety.*

In one of Grimm's Fairy Tales there is the story of a youth who went out in search of adventures for the sake of learning what it is to fear or be in dread. We will let that adventurer go his way without troubling ourselves to learn whether in the course of it he encountered the dreadful. On the other hand I would say that learning to know dread is an adventure which every man has to affront if he would not go to perdition either by not having known dread or by sinking under it. He therefore who has learned rightly to be in dread has learned the most important thing.

If a man were a beast or an angel, he would not be able to be in dread. Since he is a synthesis he can be in dread, and the greater the dread, the greater the man. This, however, is not affirmed in the sense in which men commonly understand dread, as related to something outside a man, but in the sense that man himself produces dread. Only in this sense can we interpret the passage where it is said of Christ that he was in dread [*ængstes*] even unto death, and the place also where he says to Judas, "What thou doest, do quickly." Not even the terrible word upon which even Luther dreaded to preach, "My God, my God, why hast thou forsaken me?"—not even this expresses suffering so strongly. For this word indicates a situation in which Christ actually is; the former sayings indicate a relation to a situation which is not yet actual.

Dread is the possibility of freedom. Only this dread is by the aid of faith absolutely educative, laying bare as it does all finite aims and discovering all their deceptions. And no Grand Inquisitor has in readiness such terrible tortures as has dread, and no spy knows how to attack more artfully the man he suspects, choosing the instant when he is weakest, nor knows how to lay traps where he will be caught and ensnared, as dread knows how, and no sharp-witted judge knows how to interrogate,

Source: Reprinted from *The Concept of Dread,* W. Lowrie, trans. (Princeton, NJ: Princeton University Press, 1944) pp. 252–256. (Originally published in 1844.)

to examine the accused, as dread does, which never lets him escape, neither by diversion nor by noise, neither at work nor at play, neither by day nor by night.

He who is educated by dread is educated by possibility, and only the man who is educated by possibility is educated in accordance with his infinity. Possibility is therefore the heaviest of all categories. One often hears, it is true, the opposite affirmed, that possibility is so light but reality is heavy. But from whom does one hear such talk? From a lot of miserable men who never have known what possibility is, and who, since reality showed them that they were not fit for anything and never would be, mendaciously bedizened a possibility which was so beautiful, so enchanting; and the only foundation of this possibility was a little youthful tomfoolery of which they might rather have been ashamed. Therefore by this possibility which is said to be light one commonly understands the possibility of luck, good fortune, etc. But this is not possibility, it is a mendacious invention which human depravity falsely embellishes in order to have reason to complain of life, of providence, and as a pretext for being self-important. No, in possibility everything is possible, and he who truly was brought up by possibility has comprehended the dreadful as well as the smiling. When such a person, therefore, goes out from the school of possibility, and knows more thoroughly than a child knows the alphabet that he can demand of life absolutely nothing, and that terror, perdition, annihilation, dwell next door to every man, and has learned the profitable lesson that every dread which alarms [*ængste*] may the next instant become a fact, he will then interpret reality differently, he will extol reality, and even when it rests upon him heavily he will remember that after all it is far, far lighter than the possibility was. Only thus can possibility educate; for finiteness and the finite relationships in which the individual is assigned a place, whether it be small and commonplace or world-historical, educate only finitely, and one can always talk them around, always get a little more out of them, always chaffer, always escape a little way from them, always keep a little apart, always prevent oneself from learning absolutely from them; and if one is to learn absolutely, the individual must in turn have the possibility in himself and himself fashion that from which he is to learn, even though the next instant it does not recognize that it was fashioned by him, but absolutely takes the power from him.

But in order that the individual may thus absolutely and infinitely be educated by possibility, he must be honest towards possibility and must have faith. By faith I mean what Hegel in his fashion calls very rightly "the inward certainty which anticipates infinity." When the discoveries of possibility are honestly administered, possibility will then disclose all finitudes and idealize them in the form of infinity in the individual who is overwhelmed by dread, until in turn he is victorious by the anticipation of faith.

What I say here appears perhaps to many an obscure and foolish saying, since they even boast of never having been in dread. To this I would reply that doubtless one should not be in dread of men, of finite things, but that only the man who has gone through the dread of possibility is educated to have no dread—not because he avoids the dreadful things of life, but because they always are weak in comparison with those of possibility. If on the other hand the speaker means that the great thing about

him is that he has never been in dread, then I shall gladly initiate him into my explanation, that this comes from the fact that *he is spirit-less.*

If the individual cheats the possibility by which he is to be educated, he never
reaches faith; his faith remains the shrewdness of finitude, as his school was that of
finitude. But men cheat possibility in every way—if they did not, one has only to
stick one's head out of the window, and one would see enough for possibility to
begin its exercises forthwith. There is an engraving by Chodowiecki which represents the surrender of Calais as viewed by the four temperaments, and the theme of
the artist was to let the various impressions appear mirrored in the faces which
express the various temperaments. The most commonplace life has events enough,
no doubt, but the question is whether the possibility in the individuality is honest
towards itself. It is recounted of an Indian hermit who for two years had lived upon
dew, that he came once to the city, tasted wine, and then become addicted to drink.
This story, like every other of the sort, can be understood in many ways, one can
make it comic, one can make it tragic; but the man who is educated by possibility has
more than enough to occupy him in such a story. Instantly he is absolutely identified
with that unfortunate man, he knows no finite evasion by which he might escape.
Now the dread of possibility holds him as its prey, until it can deliver him saved into
the hands of faith. In no other place does he find repose, for every other point of rest
is mere nonsense, even though in men's eyes it is shrewdness. This is the reason why
possibility is so absolutely educative. No man has ever become so unfortunate in
reality that there was not some little residue left to him, and, as common sense
observes quite truly, if a man is canny, he will find a way. But he who went through
the curriculum of misfortune offered by possibility lost everything, absolutely everything, in a way that no one has lost it in reality. If in this situation he did not behave
falsely towards possibility, if he did not attempt to talk around the dread which would
save him, then he received everything back again, as in reality no one ever did even
if he received everything double, for the pupil of possibility received infinity,
whereas the soul of the other expired in the finite. No one ever sank so deep in reality
that he could not sink deeper, or that there might not be one or another sunk deeper
than he. But he who sank in the possibility has an eye too dizzy to see the measuring
rod which Tom, Dick, and Harry hold out as a straw to the drowning man; his ear is
closed so that he cannot hear what the market price for men is in his day, cannot hear
that he is just as good as most of them. He sank absolutely, but then in turn he floated
up from the depth of the abyss, lighter now than all that is oppressive and dreadful in
life. Only I do not deny that he who is educated by possibility is exposed—not to the
danger of bad company and dissoluteness of various sorts, as are those who are educated by the finite, but—to one danger of downfall, and that is self-slaughter. If at the
beginning of his education he misunderstands the anguish of dread, so that it does not
lead him to faith but away from faith, then he is lost. On the other hand, he who is
educated by possibility remains with dread, does not allow himself to be deceived by
its countless counterfeits, he recalls the past precisely; then at last the attacks of
dread, though they are fearful, are not such that he flees from them. For him dread
becomes a serviceable spirit which against its will leads him whither he would go.
Then when it announces itself, when it craftily insinuates that it has invented a new

instrument of torture far more terrible than anything employed before, he does not recoil, still less does he attempt to hold it off with clamor and noise, but he bids it welcome, he hails it solemnly, as Socrates solemnly flourished the poisoned goblet, he shuts himself up with it, he says, as a patient says to the surgeon when a painful operation is about to begin, "Now I am ready." Then dread enters into his soul and searches it thoroughly, constraining out of him all the finite and the petty, and leading him hence whither he would go.

When one or another extraordinary event occurs in life, when a world-historical hero gathers heroes about him and accomplishes heroic feats, when a crisis occurs and everything becomes significant, then men wish to be in it, for these are things which educate. Quite possibly. But there is a much simpler way of being educated much more fundamentally. Take the pupil of possibility, set him in the midst of the Jutland heath where nothing happens, where the greatest event is that a partridge flies up noisily, and he experiences everything more perfectly, more precisely, more profoundly, than the man who was applauded upon the stage of universal history, in case he was not educated by possibility.

ON THE DESPISERS OF THE BODY

Friedrich Nietzsche

In this forerunner to Freud's concept of the id and Jung's notion of the Self, Friedrich Nietzsche ponders that great repository of wisdom and reason—the body. Equating "little" reason with the ego and "great" reason with the body and self, Nietzsche upholds experiential knowledge, not merely knowledge that is detached or intellectualized. It is through experiential knowledge, Nietzsche maintains, that the lasting works of history are forged.

Clinical Relevance of the Passage: *Detached knowledge brings detached action. A drug addict can be stopped from using drugs, but she remains an addict. An abuser can be removed from society, medicated, or educated; but his attitude will remain the same. A depressive can be "adjusted," but his depths will remain tormented.*

Unless therapy can reach clients experientially, Nietzsche implies, it cannot promote holistic change. It can promote behavioral and intellectual change, to be sure; but it cannot awaken clients to the affect, sensations, and intentions that underlie that change and that will urge it persistently forward.

I want to speak to the despisers of the body. I would not have them learn and teach differently, but merely say farewell to their own bodies—and thus become silent.

Source: Reprinted from *Thus Spoke Zarathustra* in *The Portable Nietzsche,* W. Kaufmann, Trans. (New York: Viking/Penguin , 1982), pp. 146–147. (Original work published in 1883.)

"Body am I, and soul"—thus speaks the child. And why should one not speak like children?

But the awakened and knowing say: body am I entirely, and nothing else; and soul is only a word for something about the body.

The body is a great reason, a plurality with one sense, a war and a peace, a herd and a shepherd. An instrument of your body is also your little reason, my brother, which you call "spirit"—a little instrument and toy of your great reason.

"I," you say, and are proud of the word. But greater is that in which you do not wish to have faith—your body and its great reason: that does not say "I," but does "I."

What the sense feels, what the spirit knows, never has its end in itself. But sense and spirit would persuade you that they are the end of all things: that is how vain they are. Instruments and toys are sense and spirit: behind them still lies the self. The self also seeks with the eyes of the senses; it also listens with the ears of the spirit. Always the self listens and seeks: it compares, overpowers, conquers, destroys. It controls, and it is in control of the ego too.

Behind your thoughts and feelings, my brother, there stands a mighty ruler, an unknown sage—whose name is self. In your body he dwells; he is your body.

There is more reason in your body than in your best wisdom. And who knows why your body needs precisely your best wisdom?

Your self laughs at your ego and at its bold leaps. "What are these leaps and flights of thought to me?" it says to itself. "A detour to my end. I am the leading strings of the ego and the prompter of its concepts."

The self says to the ego, "Feel pain here!" Then the ego suffers and thinks how it might suffer no more—and that is why it is *made* to think.

The self says to the ego, "Feel pleasure here!" Then the ego is pleased and thinks how it might often be pleased again—and that is why it is *made* to think.

I want to speak to the despisers of the body. It is their respect that begets their contempt. What is it that created respect and contempt and worth and will? The creative self created respect and contempt; it created pleasure and pain. The creative body created the spirit as a hand for its will.

Even in your folly and contempt, you despisers of the body, you serve your self. I say unto you: your self itself wants to die and turns away from life. It is no longer capable of what it would do above all else: to create beyond itself. That is what it would do above all else, that is its fervent wish.

But now it is too late for it to do this: so your self wants to go under, O despisers of the body. Your self wants to go under, and that is why you have become despisers of the body! For you are no longer able to create beyond yourselves.

And that is why you are angry with life and the earth. An unconscious envy speaks out of the squint-eyed glance of your contempt.

I shall not go your way, O despisers of the body! You are no bridge to the overman!

Thus spoke Zarathustra.

THE MYTH OF SISYPHUS

Albert Camus

Making sense of senselessness and finding freedom in a capricious, perilous world are Albert Camus' primary philosophical concerns. In this incisive essay, Camus helps us to live with and even benefit from the unfathomable conditions of life.

Clinical Relevance of the Passage: *When meaning or traditions dissolve, the myth of Sisyphus becomes relevant. Mourners understand it; so do unemployed factory workers. Victims of war, crime, and brutality also know it, as do passionless couples.*

Why do they (or we) get up in the morning? How do they/we face the futility of our lives?

We all have limits and destinies to play out, and we are all used for mysterious ends. The questions are, What are we going to make of our limits and destinies? How are we going to respond to them? Are we going to accept them passively—as many who are depressed and dependent do—or are we going to deny them—as do many who boast? Finally, are we going to engage them, try to fashion something of value from them, and surrender to them only when nothing is left? This is what therapy must inquire.

The gods had condemned Sisyphus to ceaselessly rolling a rock to the top of a mountain, whence the stone would fall back of its own weight. They had thought with some reason that there is no more dreadful punishment than futile and hopeless labor.

If one believes Homer, Sisyphus was the wisest and most prudent of mortals. According to another tradition, however, he was disposed to practice the profession of highwayman. I see no contradiction in this. Opinions differ as to the reasons why he became the futile laborer of the underworld. To begin with, he is accused of a certain levity in regard to the gods. He stole their secrets. Ægina, the daughter of Æsopus, was carried off by Jupiter. The father was shocked by that disappearance and complained to Sisyphus. He, who knew of the abduction, offered to tell about it on condition that Æsopus would give water to the citadel of Corinth. To the celestial thunderbolts he preferred the benediction of water. He was punished for this in the underworld. Homer tells us also that Sisyphus had put Death in chains. Pluto could not endure the sight of his deserted, silent empire. He dispatched the god of war, who liberated Death from the hands of her conqueror.

It is said also that Sisyphus, being near to death, rashly wanted to test his wife's love. He ordered her to cast his unburied body into the middle of the public square. Sisyphus woke up in the underworld. And there, annoyed by an obedience so contrary to human love, he obtained from Pluto permission to return to earth in order to chastise his wife. But when he had seen again the face of this world, enjoyed water and sun, warm stones and the sea, he no longer wanted to go back to the infernal darkness. Recalls, signs of anger, warnings were of no avail. Many years more he

Source: Reprinted from *The Myth of Sisyphus and Other Essays* by Albert Camus (J. O'Brien, Trans.) (New York: Knopf, 1955), pp. 88–91.

lived facing the curve of the gulf, the sparkling sea, and the smiles of earth. A decree of the gods was necessary. Mercury came and seized the impudent man by the collar and, snatching him from his joys, led him forcibly back to the underworld, where his rock was ready for him.

You have already grasped that Sisyphus is the absurd hero. He *is,* as much through his passions as through his torture. His scorn of the gods, his hatred of death, and his passion for life won him that unspeakable penalty in which the whole being is exerted toward accomplishing nothing. This is the price that must be paid for the passions of this earth. Nothing is told us about Sisyphus in the underworld. Myths are made for the imagination to breathe life into them. As for this myth, one sees merely the whole effort of a body straining to raise the huge stone, to roll it and push it up a slope a hundred times over; one sees the face screwed up, the cheek tight against the stone, the shoulder bracing the clay-covered mass, the foot wedging it, the fresh start with arms outstretched, the wholly human security of two earth-clotted hands. At the very end of his long effort measured by skyless space and time without depth, the purpose is achieved. Then Sisyphus watches the stone rush down in a few moments toward that lower world whence he will have to push it up again toward the summit. He goes back down to the plain.

It is during that return, that pause, that Sisyphus interests me. A face that toils so close to stones is already stone itself! I see that man going back down with a heavy yet measured step toward the torment of which he will never know the end. That hour like a breathing-space which returns as surely as his suffering, that is the hour of consciousness. At each of those moments when he leaves the heights and gradually sinks toward the lairs of the gods, he is superior to his fate. He is stronger than his rock.

If this myth is tragic, that is because its hero is conscious. Where would his torture be, indeed, if at every step the hope of succeeding upheld him? The workman of today works every day in his life at the same tasks, and his fate is no less absurd. But it is tragic only at the rare moments when it becomes conscious. Sisyphus, proletarian of the gods, powerless and rebellious, knows the whole extent of his wretched condition: it is what he thinks of during his descent. The lucidity that was to constitute his torture at the same time crowns his victory. There is no fate that cannot be surmounted by scorn.

If the descent is thus sometimes performed in sorrow, it can also take place in joy. This word is not too much. Again I fancy Sisyphus returning toward his rock, and the sorrow was in the beginning. When the images of earth cling too tightly to memory, when the call of happiness becomes too insistent, it happens that melancholy rises in man's heart: this is the rock's victory, this is the rock itself. The boundless grief is too heavy to bear. These are our nights of Gethsemane. But crushing truths perish from being acknowledged. Thus, Œdipus at the outset obeys fate without knowing it. But from the moment he knows, his tragedy begins. Yet at the same moment, blind and desperate, he realizes that the only bond linking him to the world is the cool hand of a girl. Then a tremendous remark rings out: "Despite so many ordeals, my advanced age and the nobility of my soul make me conclude that all is well." Sophocles' Œdipus, like Dostoevsky's Kirilov, thus gives the recipe for the absurd victory. Ancient wisdom confirms modern heroism.

One does not discover the absurd without being tempted to write a manual of happiness. "What! by such narrow ways—?" There is but one world, however. Happiness and the absurd are two sons of the same earth. They are inseparable. It would be a mistake to say that happiness necessarily springs from the absurd discovery. It happens as well that the feeling of the absurd springs from happiness. "I conclude that all is well," says Œdipus, and that remark is sacred. It echoes in the wild and limited universe of man. It teaches that all is not, has not been, exhausted. It drives out of this world a god who had come into it with dissatisfaction and a preference for futile sufferings. It makes of fate a human matter, which must be settled among men.

All Sisyphus' silent joy is contained therein. His fate belongs to him. His rock is his thing. Likewise, the absurd man, when he contemplates his torment, silences all the idols. In the universe suddenly restored to its silence, the myriad wondering little voices of the earth rise up. Unconscious, secret calls, invitations from all the faces, they are the necessary reverse and price of victory. There is no sun without shadow, and it is essential to know the night. The absurd man says yes and his effort will henceforth be unceasing. If there is a personal fate, there is no higher destiny, or at least there is but one which he concludes is inevitable and despicable. For the rest, he knows himself to be the master of his days. At that subtle moment when man glances backward over his life, Sisyphus returning toward his rock, in that slight pivoting he contemplates that series of unrelated actions which becomes his fate, created by him, combined under his memory's eye and soon sealed by his death. Thus, convinced of the wholly human origin of all that is human, a blind man eager to see who knows that the night has no end, he is still on the go. The rock is still rolling.

I leave Sisyphus at the foot of the mountain! One always finds one's burden again. But Sisyphus teaches the higher fidelity that negates the gods and raises rocks. He too concludes that all is well. This universe henceforth without a master seems to him neither sterile nor futile. Each atom of that stone, each mineral flake of that night-filled mountain, in itself forms a world. The struggle itself toward the heights is enough to fill a man's heart. One must imagine Sisyphus happy.

REFERENCES—PHILOSOPHICAL ROOTS

Barnes, H. (1967). *An existentialist ethics.* New York: Knopf.

Becker, E. (1973). *The denial of death.* New York: Free Press.

Buber, M. (1958). *I and thou* (R. G. Smith, Trans.). New York: Scribner.

Burt, E. (Ed.) (1955). *The teachings of the compassionate Buddha.* New York: Mentor Books.

Camus, A. (1955). *The myth of Sisyphus and other essays* (J. O'Brien, Trans.). New York: Knopf.

Friedman, M. (1991). *The worlds of existentialism: A critical reader.* Atlantic Highlands, NJ: Humanities Press.

Giorgi, A. (1970). *Psychology as a human science: A phenomenologically based approach.* New York: Harper & Row.

Heidegger, M. (1962). *Being and time* (J. Macquarrie & E. Robinson, Trans.). New York: Harper & Row.

Husserl, E. (1936/1970). *The crisis of European sciences and transcendental phenomenology* (D. Carr, Trans.). Evanston, IL: Northwestern University Press.

Jones, E. (1957). *The life and work of Sigmund Freud* (Vol. 2). New York: Basic Books.

Kaufmann, W. (1968). *Nietzsche: Philosopher, psychologist, antichrist.* New York: Vintage.

Kierkegaard, S. (1849/1980). *The sickness unto death* (V. Hong & E. Hong, Trans.). Princeton, NJ: Princeton University Press.

Kockelmans, J. (1978). *Edmund Husserl's phenomenological psychology: A historico-critical study.* Atlantic Highlands, NJ: Humanities Press.

Kundera, M. (1986). *The art of the novel.* New York: Harper & Row.

May, R., Angel, E., & Ellenberger, H. (1958). *Existence: A new dimension in psychiatry and psychology.* New York: Basic Books.

Merleau-Ponty, M. (1962). *The phenomenology of perception.* London: Routledge.

Merleau-Ponty, M. (1964). *The primacy of perception.* Evanston, IL: Northwestern University Press.

Nietzsche, F. (1872/1956). *The birth of tragedy and the geneology of morals* (F. Golfing, Trans.). New York: Doubleday/Anchor Books.

Nietzsche, F. (1889/1982). *The portable Nietzsche* (W. Kaufmann, Trans.). New York: Viking/Penguin.

Olson, R. (1962). *An introduction to existentialism.* New York: Dover.

Plato (1984). *Great dialogues of Plato* (W. Rouse, Trans.). New York: Mentor.

Polkinghorne, D. (1989). Phenomenological research methods. In R. Valle & S. Halling (Eds.), *Existential-phenomenological perspectives in psychology* (pp. 41–60). New York: Plenum.

Sartre, J. (1956). *Being and nothingness* (H. Barnes, Trans.). New York: Philosophical Library.

Spiegelberg, H. (1976a). *The phenomenological movement: A historical introduction* (Vol. I). The Hague: Martinus Nijhoff.

Spiegelberg, H. (1976b). *The phenomenological movement: A historical introduction* (Vol. II). The Hague: Martinus Nijhoff.

Thomas, E. (Trans.) (1935). *Early Buddhist scriptures.* London: K. Paul, Trench, Trubner & Co. [as slightly paraphrased by H. Smith (1986). *The religions of man* (p. 143). New York: Harper & Row.]

WORKS OF RELATED INTEREST

Foulcault, M. (1961/1965). *Madness and civilization: A history of insanity in the age of reason* (R. Howard, Trans.). New York: Vintage.

Halling, S., & Nill, J. (in press). A brief history of existential-phenomenological psychiatry and psychotherapy. *Journal of Phenomenological Psychology.*

Jaspers, K. (1971). *Philosophy of existence* (R. F. Grabeau Trans.). Philadelphia: University of Pennsylvania Press.

Kaufmann, W. (1975). *Existentialism from Dostoyevsky to Sartre.* New York: New American Library.

Kierkegaard, S. (1944). *The concept of dread* (W. Lowrie, Trans.). Princeton, NJ: Princeton University Press.

Marcel, G. (1956/1967). *The philosophy of existentialism.* (M. Harari, Trans.). New York: Citadel.

Ricouer, P. (1960/1967). *The symbolism of evil* (E. Buchanan, Trans.). New York: Harper & Row.

Ricoeur, P. (1970). *Freud and philosophy: An essay on interpretation* (D. Savage, Trans.). New Haven, CT: Yale University Press.

Rorty, R. (1979). *Philosophy and the mirror of nature.* Princeton, NJ: Princeton University Press.

Tillich, P. (1952). *The courage to be.* New Haven, CT: Yale University Press.

CHAPTER 3

PSYCHOLOGICAL ROOTS

We now turn to the psychological application of literary and philosophical existentialism. Specifically, we consider leading methodologists, theorists, and psychotherapists who integrated what we now recognize as existential psychology. Again, those readers desiring elaboration on this brief survey are directed to the reference and bibliography sections at the end of this chapter.

To begin our discussion, we feature William James, arguably psychology's first existentialist.

WILLIAM JAMES

William James (1842–1910) is widely regarded as America's foremost psychologist and philosopher. His range was breathtaking, and most of the major schools of psychology could (and indeed do!) claim him as their founder. James was one of the earliest professors of psychology and created the first psychological laboratory (before Wilhelm Wundt and G. Stanley Hall) in 1875. He was also a physician and physiologist, which lent significant authority to his research in psychology (then dominated by physiological precepts).

The holistic nature of James' theorizing is evident in his writings on pluralism, pragmatism, and radical empiricism.

Pluralism is the notion that knowledge is multifaceted and cannot justifiably be confined to one or a few forms. James passionately embraced this interdisciplinary outlook, where ethics, aesthetics, experimentation, practical application, and even religion and mysticism each played an important role. Although James was sometimes self-contradictory, he was unabashedly so. He believed that psychology was at a very early stage of development and that theoretical "play" and ambiguity must be a natural outgrowth of this stage.

Pragmatism is the philosophy (based in part on the writings of Charles Pierce) that the criteria for the validity of knowledge are the consequences that are produced by the (given) knowledge. The validity of James' pluralism, therefore, is the extent to which that approach provides useful implications for understanding human beings (e.g., thoughts or behaviors that give people pleasure or help them to meet basic needs). Now the question, of course, is how one defines *consequences* or that which is useful, and here is where James displays his creative genius. Whereas the conventional scientist based his notion of utility on *traditional empiricism* (that which can be apprehended by the five senses), James based his judgment on the grounds of what he termed *radical empiricism.*

Essentially, *radical empiricism* is a metatraditional, metamaterialistic verifiability criterion for psychology. "To be radical," James (1904/1987) wrote, "an empiricism must neither admit into its constructions any element that is not directly experienced, nor exclude from them any element that is directly experienced" (p. 1160). In another place he stated, "Our fields of experience have no more definite boundaries than have our fields of view. Both are fringed forever by a *more* that continuously develops, and that continuously supersedes them as life proceeds" (p. 1175). Radical empiricism, accordingly, validates not only sense perception, but also affectional, intuitive, imaginal, and spiritual states of experience. It purports that usefulness need not be confined to discrete, overt, or measurable behaviors, but may encompass any experience that a person finds subjectively or objectively of help. For example, James (1904/1987) found that so-called mystical experiences were useful, not only to his subjects in his classic book *Varieties of Religious Experience,* but also to himself. He disclosed that a sense of the divine gave him "a . . . powerful ally [for my] own ideals" (p. 1184). He also viewed the spiritual life as more "richly satisfying" than that of the conventional (logical-positivist) perspective (Myers, 1986, p. 459).

While James' openness to psychological data was profound, he was not always convinced by the inferences or conclusions based on that data. The conception of the absolute, for example, repeatedly incurred his suspicions. He indicated that such doctrines—either of scientific or religious standing—are given to unsupportable claims, rash assumptions, and narrow sectarian beliefs. "The theory of the Absolute," elucidated James (1907/1967),

> has had to be an article of faith, affirmed dogmatically and exclusively. . . . The slightest suspicion of pluralism, the minutest wiggle of independence of any of its parts from the control of the totality would ruin it. . . . Pluralism on the other hand has no need of this dogmatic rigoristic temper. Provided you grant *some* separation among things, some tremor of independence, some free play of parts on one another, some novelty or chance, however minute, she is amply satisfied, and will allow you any amount, however great, of real union. (p. 71)

Real (theoretical) *union* for James was that which passed the acid test of the marketplace, where ideas could be debated, consolidated, and revised (see Myers, 1986).

While James apparently preferred the designation of *humanist* to *pragmatist* (Myers, 1986, p. 491), it was his pragmatic stance that influenced early psychological theorizing. Watson and Skinner, for example, emphasized the *consequences* (or functional outcomes) of behavior with their constructs of classical and operant conditioning.

Concrete and measurable behavioral change was important for them, as it was for James (when addressing certain levels of experience). Despite his reservations over the future implications of these fields, James' influence on the psychology of behavior, cognition, and learning is well illustrated by his *Principles of Psychology* (1890) and *Talks to Teachers on Psychology* (1899). These works, for example, consider the educational "significance of instinct, play, habit, motor responses, and suggestion. . . ." Moreover, they examine "methods of arousing interest and developing voluntary attention, the necessity of routine, the need of effort, the transfer of learning, the value of discipline, methods of punishment, the meaning of [grades], the evils of cramming . . . the relation between teachers and pupils" and offer more psychophysiologically based suggestions to educators (Baldwin quoted in Myers, 1986, p. 11). What we see here are a variety of harbingers of later formulations. Operant behaviorists, for example, would go on to investigate the educational effects of (positive, negative, and aversive) reinforcement schedules; learning theorists would develop the concepts of practice, transfer (and generalization) of learning and optimal memorization strategies; neuropsychologists would probe the relationship between synaptic action in the brain and habit formation; social learning theorists would illuminate the impact of modeling and imitation; and cognitive researchers would elaborate on the impact of (constructive and destructive) beliefs on actions.

Despite, or in great part because of, these developments, however, James' investment in biological and behavioral modification strategies had "definite limits." He cautioned against the "mechanical uses of psychology for the classroom," and stressed the "need for creative, flexible techniques" (Myers, 1986, p. 12).

James' emphasis on introspection and careful description of psychological phenomena had significant implications for the phenomenological movement begun by Edmund Husserl (Giorgi, 1970). Although James' method of introspection differed from that which phenomenologists later advanced, it still inspired their work. Studies such as *Principles* and especially *Varieties of Religious Experience* provided pioneering insights into the most elusive realms of consciousness (realms, incidently, that traditional science eschewed). As a result, psychology has been enriched by such notions as experiential flux, regeneration (through mystical surrender), will and responsibility, the "more" of transcendence, parapsychology, meditation, and mind-altering drugs.

Existential psychology, moreover, is indebted to James for his sensitive and thorough personal discourses on living. He squarely confronted the meaning and value, not just of the lives of those he studied, but also of his own life. He acknowledged both the vastness and the precariousness of existing fully and the courage required to persevere in the face of ill health and depression. In the throes of a profound dysphoria, he wrote: "My first act of free will shall be to believe in free will . . ." (Myers, 1986, p. 389).

OTTO RANK

*My thoughts behave like circles on water. A little stone makes a dot, from which
thoughts spread ever outward until they break on the shores of the unthinkable.*
—O. RANK *(quoted in Lieberman, 1985, p. 7)*

Otto Rank (1884–1939), a young machinist from the Viennese suburb of Leopold-
stadt, grew up to become one of Freud's most cherished and gifted disciples. His
rise to prominence was both early and rapid, but not without its ironies. For
example, Rank was the son of a jeweler but craved books and poetry. He was
trained in a technical school but immersed himself in philosophy and journal writing. Finally, he chose the name Rank—which, in German, connotes "crooked-
ness," "winding course," and "intrigue"—to assert his independence from tradition
(Lieberman, 1985).

Inspired by Freud's *Interpretation of Dreams,* young Otto wrote a fascinating
study of mythology and the artist. At the tender age of 21, on the advice of his family
physician (who happened to be Alfred Adler), he sent Freud his manuscript. Freud
was so taken by the work that he commissioned Rank (for the next twenty years) to
be the recording secretary of his famous Wednesday Psychological Society (or "inner
circle"). In time, however, and after many scholarly contributions, Rank grew dissatisfied with the movement. His artistic inclinations pointed to the need for a wider
psychohistorical view. Impressed by the anthropological investigations of his day, as
well as such thinkers as Friedrich Nietzsche (whose works he presented to Freud on
the occasion of his seventieth birthday), Rank developed a comprehensive psychohistorical position. Although Rank's writings on these matters can be obscure, several
contemporary observers (such as Ernest Becker, E. James Lieberman, and Esther
Menaker) have brilliantly revived his legacy.

The core of Rank's theory, which is eminently compatible with existential philosophy, is as follows: Human consciousness is driven by two basic concerns—fear of
life and fear of death. The fear of life, for Rank, is a concern about separating (from
others), venturing forth or standing out on one's own. Put another way, it is a fear of
becoming free. The fear of death, on the other hand, is a concern about attaching (to
others), retreating back to the womb, or returning to a state of matter. It is a fear, in
other words, of becoming limited.

These fears, according to Rank, can be the cause of a variety of psychological dysfunctions. Depression and dependency, for example, can be traced to a dire fear of
life (separation anxiety); narcissism and mania can be linked to a pronounced fear of
death (attachment anxiety). The greater one's life or death fear, moreover, the greater
one's tendency to swing to the opposite extreme.

Similar operations can be perceived at the level of societies. Societies that stress
protectionism and moral strictness, for example, can be correlated with a pervasive
dread of life. The subtler problems of overspecialization, social malaise, and complacency are also relevant here. Conversely, societies that indulge in national and cultural chauvinism or, to a lesser extent, myriad forms of hero worship can be associated with a global revulsion for death.

At the same time that we fear separation and attachment, however, we also desire them to some degree. For example, most of us desire a measure of self-sufficiency, choice, and adventure. By the same token, most of us seek a modicum of dependency, safety, and order in our lives. The question becomes one of negotiating between these desires and fears.

Although Rank avoids pat or dogmatic responses to such questions, the implications of his work are clear: We must find some kind of balance within which to live. In our quest for vital experience, we must honor *both* our capacity for greatness *and* our (cosmic) meagerness.

The thrust of Rank's therapy, accordingly, is to help clients achieve freedom within a suitable structure. The question as to what is "suitable" for a given client strikes at the heart of Rank's approach. It emerges, that is, from an intense "here and now" encounter with the client, where the actual conditions of life are simulated. This means that not only childhood projections, but also present therapist-client relations are legitimated. "The therapist," Rank enumerates, "may do whatever he believes is pertinent to the process and *moment of therapy* with a particular individual, as long as he takes responsibility for and deals helpfully with what he precipitates in the client" (quoted in Lieberman, 1985, p. xxxvii).

Rank's attempt to reduce the time required for a successful psychoanalysis was a logical extension of this relationship-centered approach. (Such limits, it should be stressed, are not set arbitrarily, but emerge—as does everything else in Rank's method—from deep mutual reflection.) By so implementing, clients are challenged to address their (separation/attachment) concerns more focally, and to mobilize their resources for growth.

Rank left a greatly underappreciated legacy of psychohistorical understanding. Virtually the entire object-relations movement, for example, is indebted to his work. First and foremost, however, is the existential obligation to Rank. His stress on fundamental life-structures, immediacy and relation, and the artistry of psychotherapy have become the standard components of contemporary existential practice.

Next, we turn to Rollo May's important history of existential psychology and his personal understanding of its impact.

ORIGINS AND SIGNIFICANCE OF EXISTENTIAL PSYCHOLOGY

Rollo May

In recent years there has been a growing awareness on the part of some psychiatrists and psychologists that serious gaps exist in our way of understanding human beings. These gaps may well seem most compelling to psychotherapists, confronted as they are in clinic and consulting room with the sheer reality of persons in crisis whose anxiety will not be quieted by theoretical formulas. But the lacunae likewise present seemingly unsurmountable difficulties in scientific research. Thus many psychiatrists and psychologists in Europe and others in this country have been asking themselves disquieting questions, and others are aware of gnawing doubts which arise from the same half-suppressed and unasked questions.

Can we be sure, one such question goes, that we are seeing the patient as he really is, knowing him in his own reality; or are we seeing merely a projection of our own theories *about* him? Every psychotherapist, to be sure, has his knowledge of patterns and mechanisms of behavior and has at his fingertips the system of concepts developed by his particular school. Such a conceptual system is entirely necessary if we are to observe scientifically. But the crucial question is always the bridge between the system and the patient—how can we be certain that our system, admirable and beautifully wrought as it may be in principle, has anything whatever to do with this specific Mr. Jones, a living, immediate reality sitting opposite us in the consulting room? May not just this particular person require another system, another quite different frame of reference? And does not this patient, or any person for that matter, evade our investigations, slip through our scientific fingers like sea foam, precisely to the extent that we rely on the logical consistency of our own system?

Another such gnawing question is: How can we know whether we are seeing the patient in his real world, the world in which he "lives and moves and has his being," and which is for him unique, concrete, and different from our general theories of culture? In all probability we have never participated in his world and do not know it directly. Yet we must know it and to some extent must be able to exist in it if we are to have any chance of knowing the patient.

Such questions were the motivations of psychiatrists and psychologists in Europe, who later comprised the *Daseinsanalyse,* or existential-analytic, movement. The "existential research orientation in psychiatry," writes Ludwig Binswanger, its chief spokesman, "arose from dissatisfaction with the prevailing efforts to gain scientific understanding in psychiatry. . . . Psychology and psychotherapy as sciences are admittedly concerned with 'man,' but not at all primarily with mentally *ill* man, but with *man as such.* The new understanding of man, which we owe to Heideg-

Source: This selection and the one on page 89 are from *The Discovery of Being* by Rollo May (New York: Norton, 1983).

ger's analysis of existence, has its basis in the new conception that man is no longer understood in terms of some theory—be it a mechanistic, a biologic or a psychological one."[1]

What Called Forth This Development?

Before turning to what this new conception of man is, let us note that this approach sprang up spontaneously in different parts of Europe and among different schools, and has a diverse body of researchers and creative thinkers. There were Eugene Minkowski in Paris, Erwin Straus in Germany and later in this country, V. E. von Gebsattel in Germany, who represented chiefly the first, or phenomenological, stage of this movement. There were Ludwig Binswanger, A. Storch, M. Boss, G. Bally, Roland Kuhn in Switzerland, J. H. Van Den Berg and F. J. Buytendijk in Holland, and so on, representing more specifically the second, or existential, stage. These facts—namely, that the movement emerged spontaneously, without these men in some cases knowing about the remarkably similar work of their colleagues, and that, rather than being the brainchild of one leader, it owes its creation to diverse psychiatrists and psychologists—testify that it must answer a widespread need in our times in the fields of psychiatry and psychology. Von Gebsattel, Boss, and Bally are Freudian analysts; Binswanger, though in Switzerland, became a member of the Vienna Psychoanalytic Society at Freud's recommendation when the Zurich group split off from the International. Some of the existential therapists had also been under Jungian influence.

These thoroughly experienced men became disquieted over the fact that, although they were effecting cures by the techniques they had learned, they could not, so long as they confined themselves to Freudian and Jungian assumptions, arrive at any clear understanding of why these cures did or did not occur or what actually was happening in the patients' existence. They refused the usual methods among therapists of quieting such inner doubts—namely, of turning one's attention with redoubled efforts to perfecting the intricacies of one's own conceptual system. Another tendency among psychotherapists, when anxious or assailed by doubts as to what they are doing, is to become preoccupied with technique. Perhaps the most handy anxiety-reducing agent is to abstract oneself from the issues by assuming a wholly technical emphasis. These men resisted this temptation. They likewise were unwilling to postulate unverifiable agents, such as "libido," or "censor," as Ludwig Lefebre points out,[2] or the various processes lumped under "transference," to explain what was going on. And they had particularly strong doubts about using the theory of the unconscious as a carte blanche on which almost any explanation could be written. They were aware, as Straus puts it, that the "unconscious ideas of the patient are more often than not the conscious theories of the therapist."

It was not with specific techniques of therapy that these psychiatrists and psychologists took issue. They recognized for example, that psychoanalysis is valid for certain types of cases, and some of them, bona fide members of the Freudian movement, employed it themselves. But they all had grave doubts about its theory of man. And they believed these difficulties and limitations in the concept of man not only seriously blocked research but would in the long run also seriously limit the effectiveness and development of therapeutic techniques. They sought to understand the particular neuroses or psychoses and, for that matter, any human being's crisis situation, not as deviations from the conceptual yardstick of this or that psychiatrist or psychologist who happened to be observing, but as deviations in the structure of that particular patient's existence, the disruption of his *condition humaine.* "A psychotherapy on existential-analytic bases investigates the life-history of the patient to be treated, . . . but it does not explain this life-history and its pathologic idiosyncrasies according to the teachings of any school of psychotherapy, or by means of its preferred categories. Instead, it *understands* this life-history as modifications of the total structure of the patient's being-in-the-world."[3]

Binswanger's own endeavor to understand how existential analysis throws light on a given case, and how it compares with other methods of psychological understanding, is graphically shown in his study of "Ellen West."[4] After he had completed his book on existential analysis, in 1942, Binswanger went back into the archives in the sanatorium of which he was director to select the case history of this young woman who had ultimately committed suicide. This case comes from 1918, before shock therapy, when psychoanalysis was in its relatively youthful stage and when the understanding of mental illness seems crude to us today. Binswanger uses the case in his endeavor to contrast the crude methods of that day with the way Ellen West would have been understood by existential psychotherapy.

Ellen West had been a tomboy in her youth and had early developed a great ambition as shown in the phrase which she used, "Either Caesar or nothing." In her late teens there becomes evident her perpetual and all-encompassing dilemmas which trapped her like vices; she vacillated from despair to joy, from anger to docility, but most of all from gorging food to starving herself. Binswanger points out the one-sidedness of the understanding of the two psychoanalysts whom Ellen West had seen, one for five months and the other for a lesser time. They interpreted her only in the world of instincts, drives, and other aspects of what Binswanger calls the *Umwelt* (the biological world). He especially takes issue with the principle, stated by Freud, in a literal translation, "In our view, perceived (observed) phenomena must yield their place to merely postulated (assumed) strivings (tendencies)."[5]

In Ellen's long illness, which we would term in our day severe anorexia nervosa, she was also seen for consultation by two psychiatrists of that day, Kraepelin, who diagnosed her as in "melancholia," and Bleuler, who offered the diagnosis of "schizophrenia."

Binswanger is not interested here in the technique of treatment but he is concerned with trying to understand Ellen West. She fascinates him by seeming to be "in love with death." In her teens Ellen implores the "Sea-King to kiss her to death." She writes, "Death is the greatest happiness in life, if not the only one" (p. 143). "If he [death] makes me wait much longer, the great friend, death, then I shall set out to seek him" (p. 242). She writes time and again that she would like to die "as the bird dies which bursts its throat in supreme joy."

Her talent as a writer is shown in her extensive poetry, diaries, and prose about her illness. She reminds one of Sylvia Plath. Binswanger poses the difficult question: Are there some persons who can fulfill their existence only by taking their own lives?

"But where the existence can exist only by relinquishing life, there the existence is a tragic existence."

Ellen West seems to Binswanger to be a vivid example of Kierkegaard's description of despair in "Sickness unto Death." Binswanger writes:

> To live in the face of death, however, means "to die unto death," as Kierkegaard says; or to die one's own death, as Rilke and Scheler express it. That every passing away, every dying, whether self-chosen death or not, is still an "autonomous act" of life has already been expressed by Goethe. As he said of Raphael [and] Kepler, "both of them suddenly put an end to their lives," but in saying so he meant their involuntary death, coming to them "from the outside" "as external fate," so we may conversely designate Ellen West's self-caused death as a passing away or dying. Who will say where in this case guilt begins and "fate" ends?[6]

Whether or not Binswanger is successful in explicating existential principles in this case is for the reader to judge. But anyone who reads this long case will feel the amazing depth of Binswanger's earnestness in his search together with his rich cultural background and scholarliness.

It is relevant here to note the long friendship between Binswanger and Freud, a relationship which both greatly valued. In a small book giving his recollections of Freud, which he published at the urging of Anna Freud, Binswanger recounts the many visits he made to Freud's home in Vienna and the visit of several days Freud made to him at his sanatorium on Lake Constance. Their relationship was the more remarkable since it was the sole instance of a lasting friendship of Freud with any colleague who differed radically with him. There is a poignant quality in a message Freud wrote to Binswanger in reply to the latter's New Year's letter: "You, quite different from so many others, have not let it happen that your intellectual development—which has taken you further and further away from my influence—should destroy our personal relations, and you do not know how much good such fineness does to one."[7] Whether the friendship survived because the intellectual conflict between the two was like the proverbial battle between the elephant and the walrus, who never met on the same ground, or because of some diplomatic attitude on Binswanger's part (a tendency for which Freud mildly chided him at one point) or because of the depth of their respect and affection for each other, we cannot judge. What was certainly important, however, was the fact that Binswanger and the others in the existential movement in therapy were concerned not with arguing about specific dynamisms as such but with analyzing the underlying assumptions about human nature and arriving at a *structure* on which all specific therapeutic systems could be based.

It would be a mistake, therefore, simply to identify the existential movement in psychotherapy as another in the line of schools which have broken off from Freudianism, from Jung and Adler on down. Those previous deviating schools, although called forth by blind spots in orthodox therapy and typically emerging when orthodoxy had struck an arid plateau, were nevertheless formed under the impetus of the creative work of one seminal leader. Otto Rank's new emphasis on the *present time* in the patient's experience emerged in the early 1920s, when classical analysis was bogging down in arid intellectualized discussion of the patient's past; Wilhelm Reich's *character analysis* arose in the late 1920s as an answer to the special need to break through the "ego defenses" of the character armor; new *cultural approaches* developed in the 1930s through the work of Horney and, in their distinctive ways, Fromm and Sullivan, when orthodox analysis was missing the real significance of the social and interpersonal aspects of neurotic and psychotic disturbances. Now the emergence of the existential therapy movement does have one feature in common with these other schools—namely, that it was also called forth by blind spots, as we shall make clearer later, in the existing approaches to psychotherapy. But it differs from the other schools in two respects. First, it is not the creation of any one leader, but grew up spontaneously and indigenously in diverse parts of Europe. Second, it does not purport to found a new school as opposed to other schools or to give a new technique of therapy as opposed to other techniques. It seeks, rather, to analyze the structure of human existence—an enterprise which, if successful, should yield an understanding of the reality underlying all situations of human beings in crises.

Thus this movement purports to do more than cast light upon blind spots. When Binswanger writes "existential analysis is able to widen and deepen the basic concepts and understandings of psychoanalysis," he is on sound ground, in my judgment, not only with respect to analysis but other forms of therapy as well.

When existential psychotherapy was first introduced in the United States by the book *Existence,* there was a good deal of resistance to the movement, despite the fact that it had been prominent in Europe for some time. While most of this opposition has subsided, it is still valuable to look at the nature of those resistances.

The *first* source of resistance to this or any new contribution is the assumption that all major discoveries have been made in these fields and we need only fill in the details. This attitude is an old interloper, an uninvited guest who has been notoriously present in the battles between the schools in psychotherapy. Its name is "blind-spots-structuralized-into-dogma." And though it does not merit an answer, nor is it susceptible to any, it is unfortunately an attitude which may be more widespread in this historical period than one would like to think.

The *second* source of resistance, and one to be answered seriously, is the suspicion that existential analysis is an encroachment of philosophy into psychiatry, and does not have much to do with science. This attitude is partly a hangover of the culturally inherited scars from the battle of the last of the nineteenth century, when psychological science won its freedom from metaphysics. The victory then achieved was exceedingly important, but, as in the aftermath of any war, there followed reactions to opposite extremes which are themselves harmful. Concerning this resistance we shall make several comments.

It is well to remember that the existential movement in psychiatry and psychology arose precisely out of a passion to be not *less* but *more* empirical. Binswanger and the others were convinced that the traditional scientific methods not only did not do justice to the data but actually tended to hide rather than reveal what was going on in the patient. The existential analysis movement is a protest against the tendency to see the patient in forms tailored to our own preconceptions or to make him over into the image of our own predilections. In this respect existential psychology stands squarely within the scientific tradition in its widest sense. But it broadens its knowledge of man by historical perspective and scholarly depth, by accepting the facts that human beings reveal themselves in art and literature and philosophy, and by profiting from the insights of the particular cultural movements which express the anxiety and conflicts of contemporary man.

It is also important here to remind ourselves that every scientific method rests upon philosophical presuppositions. These presuppositions determine not only how much reality the observer with this particular method can see—they are indeed the spectacles through which he perceives—but also whether or not what is observed is pertinent to real problems and, therefore, whether the scientific work will endure. It is a gross, albeit common, error to assume naïvely that one can observe facts best if one avoids all preoccupation with philosophical assumptions. All he does, then, is mirror uncritically the particular parochial doctrines of his own limited culture. The result in our day is that science gets identified with methods of *isolating* factors and observing them from an allegedly *detached base*—a particular method which arose out of the split between subject and object made in the seventeenth century in Western culture and then developed into its special compartmentalized form in the late nineteenth and twentieth centuries. We in our day are no less subject to "methodolatry" than are members of any other culture. But it seems especially a misfortune that our understanding in such a crucial area as the psychological study of man, with the understanding of emotional and mental health depending upon it, should be curtailed by uncritical acceptance of limited assumptions. Helen Sargent has sagely and pithily remarked, "Science offers more leeway than graduate students are permitted to realize."[8]

Is not the essence of science the assumption that *reality is lawful* and, therefore, understandable, and is it not an inseparable aspect of scientific integrity that any method continuously criticize its own presuppositions? The only way to widen one's "blinders" is to analyze one's philosophical assumptions. In my judgment it is very much to the credit of the psychiatrists and psychologists in this existential movement that they seek to clarify their own bases. This enables them, as Henri Ellenberger points out,[9] to see their human subjects with a fresh clarity and to shed original light on many facets of psychological experience.

The *third* source of resistance, and to my mind the most crucial of all, is the tendency in this country to be preoccupied with technique and to be impatient with endeavors to search below such considerations to find the foundations upon which all techniques must be based. This tendency can be well explained in terms of our American social background, particularly our frontier history, and it can be well justified as our optimistic, activistic concern for helping and changing people. Our genius in the field of psychology has been until recently in the behavioristic, clinical, and applied areas, and our special contributions in psychiatry have been in drug therapy and other technical applications. Gordon Allport has described the fact that American and British psychology (as well as general intellectual climate) has been Lockean— that is, pragmatic—a tradition fitting behaviorism, stimulus and response systems, and animal psychology. The Lockean tradition, Allport points out, consists of an emphasis on the mind as *tabula rasa* on which experience writes all that is later to exist therein, whereas the Leibnitzian tradition views the mind as having a potentially active core of its own. The continental tradition, in contrast, has been Leibnitzian.[10] Now it is sobering to remind oneself that every new theoretical contribution in the field of psychotherapy until a decade ago, which has had the originality and germinating power to lead to the developing of a new school has come from continental Europe with only two exceptions—and, of these, one was grandsired by a European-born psychiatrist.[11] In this country we tend to be a nation of practitioners; but the disturbing question is: Where shall we get *what* we practice? Until recently, in our preoccupation with technique, laudable enough in itself, we have tended to overlook the fact that *technique emphasized by itself in the long run defeats even technique.*

These resistances we have named, in my judgment, far from undermining the contribution of existential analysis, demonstrate precisely its potential importance to our thinking. Despite its difficulties—due partly to its language, partly to the complexity of its thought—I believe that it is a contribution of significance and originality meriting serious study. . . .

NOTES

1. L. Binswanger, "Existential Analysis and Psychotherapy," in *Progress in Psychotherapy,* ed. Fromm-Reichmann and Moreno (New York: Grune & Stratton, 1956), p. 144.
2. Personal communication from Dr. Lefebre, an existential psychotherapist who was a student of Jaspers and Boss.
3. Binswanger, p. 145.
4. L. Binswanger, "The Case of Ellen West," in *Existence: A New Dimension in Psychology and Psychiatry,* ed. Rollo May, Ernest Angel, and Henri Ellenberger (New York: Basic Books, 1958), pp. 237-364.
5. Sigmund Freud, *Introductory Lectures on Psychoanalysis,* trans. and ed. James Strachey (New York: Liveright, 1979).
6. Binswanger, "The Case of Ellen West," p. 294.
7. L. Binswanger, *Sigmund Freud: Reminiscences of a Friendship,* trans. Norbert Guterman (New York: Grune and Stratton, 1957).
8. Helen Sargent, "Methodological Problems in the Assessment of Intrapsychic Change in Psychotherapy," unpublished paper.
9. *Existence,* pp. 92-127.
10. Gordon Allport, *Becoming, Basic Considerations for a Psychology of Personality* (New Haven: Yale University Press, 1955).
11. To see this one has only to name the originators of new theory: Freud, Adler, Jung, Rank, Stekel, Reich, Horney, Fromm, etc. The two exceptions, so far as I can see, are the schools of Harry Stack Sullivan and Carl Rogers, and the former was indirectly related to the work of the Swiss-born Adolph Meyer. Even Rogers may partly illustrate our point, for although his approach has clear and consistent theoretical implications about human nature, his focus has been on the "applied" rather than the "pure" science side, and his theory about human nature owes much to Otto Rank.

HOW EXISTENTIALISM AND PSYCHOANALYSIS AROSE OUT OF THE SAME CULTURAL SITUATION

Rollo May

We shall now look at the remarkable parallel between the problems of modern man to which the existentialists on one hand and psychoanalysts on the other devote themselves. From different perspectives and on different levels, both analyze anxiety, despair, alienation of man from himself and his society, and both seek a synthesis of integration and meaning in the person's life.

Freud describes the neurotic personality of the late nineteenth century as one suffering from fragmentation—that is, from repression of instinctual drives, blocking off of awareness, loss of autonomy, weakness and passivity of the ego, together with the various neurotic symptoms which result from this fragmentation. Kierkegaard—who wrote the only known book before Freud specifically devoted to the problem of anxiety—analyzes not only anxiety but particularly the depression and despair which result from the individual's self-estrangement, an estrangement he proceeds to classify in its different forms and degrees of severity.[1] Nietzsche proclaims, ten years before Freud's first book, that the disease of contemporary man is that "his soul had gone stale," he is "fed up," and that all about there is "a bad smell . . . the smell of failure. . . . The leveling and diminution of European man is our greatest danger." He then proceeds to describe, in terms which remarkably predict the later psychoanalytic concepts, how blocked instinctual powers turn within the individual into resentment, self-hatred, hostility, and aggression. Freud did not know Kierkegaard's work, but he regarded Nietzsche as one of the authentically great men of all time.

What is the relation between these three giants of the nineteenth century, none of whom directly influenced either of the others? And what is the relation between the two approaches to human nature they originated—existentialism and psychoanalysis—probably the two most important to have shaken, and indeed toppled, the traditional concepts of man? To answer these questions we must inquire into the cultural situation of the middle and late nineteenth century out of which both approaches to man arose and to which both sought to give answers. The real meaning of a way of understanding human beings, such as existentialism or psychoanalysis, can never be seen *in abstracto,* detached from its world, but only in the context of the historical situation which gave it birth. Thus the historical discussions to follow are not at all detours from our central aim. Indeed, it is precisely this historical approach which may throw light on our chief question—namely, how the specific scientific techniques that Freud developed for the investigation of the fragmentation of the individual in the Victorian period are related to the understanding of man and his crises to which Kierkegaard and Nietzsche contributed so much and which later provided a broad and deep base for existential psychotherapy.

Compartmentalization and Inner Breakdown in the Nineteenth Century

The chief characteristic of the last half of the nineteenth century was the breaking up of personality into fragments. These fragmentations, as we shall see, were symptoms of the emotional, psychological, and spiritual disintegration occurring in the culture and in the individual. One can see this splitting up of the individual personality not only in the psychology and the science of the period but in almost every aspect of late nineteenth-century culture. One can observe the fragmentation in family life, vividly portrayed and attacked in Ibsen's *A Doll's House.* The respectable citizen who keeps his wife and family in one compartment and his business and other worlds in others is making his home a doll's house and preparing its collapse. One can likewise see the compartmentalization in the separation of art from the realities of life, the use of art in its prettified, romantic, academic forms as a hypocritical escape from existence and nature, the art as *art*ificiality against which Cézanne, Van Gogh, the impressionists, and other modern art movements so vigorously protested. One can furthermore see the fragmentation in the separating of religion from weekday existence, making it an affair of Sundays and special observances, and the divorce of ethics from business. The segmentation was occurring also in philosophy and psychology—when Kierkegaard fought so passionately against the enthronement of an arid, abstract reason and pleaded for a return to reality, he was by no means tilting at windmills. The Victorian man saw himself as segmented into reason, will, and emotions and found the picture good. His reason was supposed to tell him *what* to do, then voluntaristic will was supposed to give him the means to do it, and emotions— well, emotions could best be channeled into compulsive business drive and rigidly structuralized in Victorian mores; and the emotions which would really have upset the formal segmentation, such as sex and hostility, were to be staunchly repressed or let out only in orgies of patriotism or on well-contained weekend "binges" in Bohemia in order that one might, like a steam engine which has let off surplus pressure, work more effectively on returning to his desk Monday morning. Naturally, this kind of man had to put great stress on "rationality." Indeed, the very term *irrational* means a thing not to be spoken of or thought of; and Victorian man's repressing, or compartmentalizing, what was not to be thought of was a precondition for the apparent stability of the culture. Schachtel has pointed out how the citizen of the Victorian period so needed to persuade himself of his own rationality that he denied the fact that he had ever been a child or had a child's irrationality and lack of control; hence the radical split between the adult and the child, which was portentous for Freud's investigations.[2]

This compartmentalization went hand in hand with the developing industrialism, as both cause and effect. A man who can keep the different segments of his life entirely separated, who can punch the clock every day at exactly the same moment, whose actions are always predictable, who is never troubled by irrational urges or poetic visions, who indeed can manipulate himself the same way he would the machine whose levers he pulls, is the most profitable worker not only on the assembly line but even on many of the higher levels of production. As Marx and Nietzsche pointed out, the corollary is likewise true: the very success of the industrial system, with its accumulation of money as a validation of personal worth entirely separate from the actual product of a man's hands, had a reciprocal depersonalizing and dehumanizing effect upon man in his relation to others and himself. It was against these dehumanizing tendencies to make man into a machine, to make him over in the image of the industrial system for which he labored, that the early existentialists fought so strongly. And they were aware that the most serious threat of all was that reason would join mechanics in sapping the individual's vitality and decisiveness. *Reason,* they predicted, *was becoming reduced to a new kind of technique.*

Scientists in our day are often not aware that this compartmentalization, finally, was also characteristic of the sciences of the century of which we are heirs. This nineteenth century was the era of the "autonomous sciences," as Ernest Cassirer phrases it. Each science developed in its own direction; there was no unifying principle, particularly with relation to man. The views of man in the period were supported by empirical evidence amassed by the advancing sciences, but "each theory became a Procrustean bed on which the empirical facts were stretched to fit a preconceived pattern. . . . Owing to this development our modern theory of man lost its intellectual center. We acquired instead a complete anarchy of thought. . . . Theologians, scientists, politicians, sociologists, biologists, psychologists, ethnologists, economists all approached the problem from their own viewpoints . . . every author seems in the last count to be led by his own conception and evaluation of human life."[3] It is no wonder that Max Scheler declared, "In no other period of human knowledge has man ever become more problematic to himself than in our own days. We have a scientific, a philosophical, and a theological anthropology that know nothing of each other. Therefore we no longer possess any clear and consistent idea of man. The ever-growing multiplicity of the particular sciences that are engaged in the study of men has much more confused and obscured than elucidated our concept of man."[4]

On the surface the Victorian period appeared placid, contented, ordered; but this placidity was purchased at the price of widespread, profound, and increasingly brittle repression. As in the case of an individual neurotic, the compartmentalization became more and more rigid as it approached the point—August 11, 1914—when it was to collapse altogether.

Now it is to be noted that the compartmentalization of the culture had its *psychological parallel in radical repression within the individual personality.* Freud's genius was in developing scientific techniques for understanding, and mayhap curing, this fragmented individual personality; but he did not see—until much later, when he reacted to the fact with pessimism and some detached despair[5]—that the neurotic illness in the individual was only one side of disintegrating forces which affected the whole of society. Kierkegaard, for his part, foresaw the results of this disintegration upon the inner emotional and spiritual life of the individual; endemic anxiety, loneliness, estrangement of one man from another, and finally the condition that would lead to ultimate despair, man's alienation from himself. But it remained for Nietzsche to paint most graphically the approaching situation: "We live in a period of atoms, of atomic chaos," and out of this chaos he foresaw, in a vivid prediction of collectivism in the twentieth century, "the terrible apparition . . . the Nation State . . . and the hunt for happiness will never be greater than when it must be caught between today and tomorrow; because the day after tomorrow all hunting time may have come to an end altogether. . . ."[6] Freud saw this fragmentation of personality in the light of natural science and was concerned with formulating its technical aspects. Kierkegaard and Nietzsche did not underestimate the importance of the specific psychological analysis; but they were much more concerned with understanding *man as the being who represses,* the being who surrenders self-awareness as a protection against reality and then suffers the neurotic consequences. The strange question is: What does it mean that man, the being in the world who can be conscious that he exists and can know his existence, should choose or be forced to choose to block off this consciousness and should suffer anxiety, compulsions for self-destruction, and despair? Kierkegaard and Nietzsche were keenly aware that the "sickness of soul" of Western man was a deeper and more extensive morbidity than could be explained by the specific individual or social problems. Something was radically wrong in man's relation to himself; man had become fundamentally problematic to himself. "This is Europe's true predicament," declared Nietzsche; "together with the fear of man we have lost the love of man, confidence in man, indeed, *the will to man.*"

NOTES

1. Sören Kierkegaard, *The Sickness unto Death,* trans. Walter Lowrie (New York: Doubleday, 1954).
2. Ernest Schachtel, "On Affect, Anxiety and the Pleasure Principle," in *Metamorphosis* (New York: Basic Books, 1959), pp. 1-69.
3. Ernest Cassirer, *An Essay on Man* (New Haven: Yale University Press, 1944), p. 21.
4. Max Scheler, *Die Stellung des Menschen im Kosmos* (Darmstadt: Reichl, 1928), pp. 13 f.
5. Sigmund Freud, *Civilization and Its Discontents,* trans. and ed. James Strachey (New York: Norton, 1962).
6. Walter A. Kaufmann, *Nietzsche: Philosopher, Psychologist, Antichrist* (Princeton: Princeton University Press, 1950), p. 140.

WHAT PSYCHOLOGY CAN LEARN FROM THE EXISTENTIALISTS

Abraham Maslow

Published at the time of his presidency of the American Psychological Association, and just two years before his untimely death, this essay reflects Abraham Maslow's final sentiments on existentialism. Not only does existentialism have revolutionary implications for psychology's "third [humanistic] branch," Maslow concludes, but it also harbors such implications for the field as a whole. "The existentialists teach that both [creatureliness and godlikeness] are . . . defining characteristics of human nature. . . . And any philosophy which leaves out either cannot be considered to be comprehensive."

Source: From Abraham Maslow, *Toward a Psychology of Being* (New York: Van Nostrand, 1968).

If we study existentialism from the point of view of "What's in it for the psychologist?" we find much that is too vague and too difficult to understand from a scientific point of view (not confirmable or disconfirmable). But we also find a great deal that is of profit. From such a point of view, we find it to be not so much a totally new revelation, as a stressing, confirming, sharpening and rediscovering of trends already existing in "Third Force psychology."

To me existential psychology means essentially two main emphases. First, it is a radical stress on the concept of identity and the experience of identity as a *sine qua non* of human nature and of any philosophy or science of human nature. I choose this concept as *the* basic one partly because I understand it better than terms like essence, existence, ontology and so on, and partly because I feel also that it can be worked with empirically, if not now, then soon.

But then a paradox results, for the American psychologists have *also* been impressed with the quest for identity. (Allport, Rogers, Goldstein, Fromm, Wheelis, Erikson, Murray, Murphy, Horney, May, et al). And I must say that these writers are a lot clearer and a lot closer to raw fact; i.e., more empirical than are, e.g., the Germans, Heidegger, Jaspers.

Secondly, it lays great stress on starting from experiential knowledge rather than from systems of concepts or abstract categories or a prioris. Existentialism rests on phenomenology, i.e., it uses personal, subjective experience as the foundation upon which abstract knowledge is built.

But many psychologists also have started with this same stress, not to mention all the various brands of psychoanalysts.

1. Conclusion number 1 is, then, that European philosophers and American psychologists are not so far apart as appears at first. We Americans have been "talking prose all the time and didn't know it." Partly of course this simultaneous development in different countries is itself an indication that the people who have independently been coming to the same conclusions are all responding to something real outside themselves.

2. This something real I believe is the total collapse of all sources of values outside the individual. Many European existentialists are largely reacting to Nietzsche's conclusion that God is dead, and perhaps to the fact that Marx also is dead. The Americans have learned that political democracy and economic prosperity don't in themselves solve any of the basic value problems. There's no place else to turn but inward, to the self, as the locus of values. Paradoxically, even some of the religious existentialists will go along with this conclusion part of the way.

3. It is extremely important for psychologists that the existentialists may supply psychology with the underlying philosophy which it now lacks. Logical positivism has been a failure, especially for clinical and personality psychologists. At any rate, the basic philosophical problems will surely be opened up for discussion again and perhaps psychologists will stop relying on pseudo-solutions or on unconscious, unexamined philosophies they picked up as children.

4. An alternative phrasing of the core (for us Americans) of European existentialism is that it deals radically with that human predicament presented by the gap between human aspirations and human limitations (between what the human being is, and

what he would *like* to be, and what he *could* be). This is not so far off from the identity problem as it might sound at first. A person is both actuality *and* potentiality.

That serious concern with this discrepancy could revolutionize psychology, there is no doubt in my mind. Various literatures already support such a conclusion, e.g., projective testing, self-actualization, the various peak-experiences (in which this gap is bridged), the Jungian psychologies, various theological thinkers, etc.

Not only this, but they raise also the problems and techniques of integration of this twofold nature of man, his lower and his higher, his creatureliness and his godlikeness. On the whole, most philosophies and religions, Eastern as well as Western, have dichotomized them, teaching that the way to become "higher" is to renounce and master "the lower." The existentialists, however, teach that *both* are simultaneously defining characteristics of human nature. Neither can be repudiated; they can only be integrated.

But we already know something of these integration techniques—of insight, of intellect in the broader sense, of love, of creativeness, of humor and tragedy, of play, of art. I suspect we will focus our studies on these integrative techniques more than we have in the past.

Another consequence for my thinking of this stress on the twofold nature of man is the realization that some problems must remain eternally insoluble.

5. From this flows naturally a concern with the ideal, authentic, or perfect or godlike human being, a study of human potentialities as *now* existing in a certain sense, as *current* knowable reality. This, too, may sound merely literary but it's not. I remind you that this is just a fancy way of asking the old, unanswered questions, "What are the goals of therapy, of education, of bringing up children?"

It also implies another truth and another problem which calls urgently for attention. Practically every serious description of the "authentic person" extant implies that such a person, by virtue of what he has become, assumes a new relation to his society and indeed, to society in general. He not only transcends himself in various ways; he also transcends his culture. He resists enculturation. He becomes more detached from his culture and from his society. He becomes a little more a member of his species and a little less a member of his local group. My feeling is that most sociologists and anthropologists will take this hard. I therefore confidently expect controversy in this area. But this is clearly a basis for "universalism."

6. From the European writers, we can and should pick up their greater emphasis on what they call "philosophical anthropology," that is, the attempt to define man, and the differences between man and any other species, between man and objects, and between man and robots. What are his unique and defining characteristics? What is so essential to man that without it he would no longer be defined as a man?

On the whole this is a task from which American psychology has abdicated. The various behaviorisms don't generate any such definition, at least none that can be taken seriously (what *would* an S-R man be like? And who would like to be one?) Freud's picture of man was clearly unsuitable, leaving out as it did his aspirations, his realizable hopes, his godlike qualities. The fact that Freud supplied us with our most comprehensive systems of psychopathology and psychotherapy is beside the point as the contemporary ego-psychologists are finding out.

7. Some existential philosophers are stressing the self-making of the self too exclusively. Sartre and others speak of the "self as a project," which is wholly created by the continued (and arbitrary) choices of the person himself, almost as if he could make himself into anything he decided to be. Of course in so extreme a form, this is almost certainly an overstatement, which is directly contradicted by the facts of genetics and of constitutional psychology. As a matter of fact, it is just plain silly.

   On the other hand, the Freudians, the existential therapists, the Rogerians and the personal growth psychologists all talk more about *discovering* the self and of *uncovering* therapy, and have perhaps understressed the factors of will, of decision, and of the ways in which we do make ourselves by our choices.

   (Of course, we must not forget that both of these groups can be said to be over-psychologizing and under-sociologizing. That is, they do not stress sufficiently in their systematic thinking the great power of autonomous social and environmental determinants, of such forces outside the individual as poverty, exploitation, nationalism, war and social structure. Certainly no psychologist in his right mind would dream of *denying* a degree of personal helplessness before these forces. But after all, his prime professional obligation is the study of the individual person rather than of extra-psychic social determinants. In the same way, sociologists seem to the psychologists to stress social forces too exclusively and to forget about the autonomy of the personality, of will, of responsibility, etc. It would be better to think of both groups as specialists rather than as blind or foolish.)

   In any case it looks as if we *both* discover and uncover ourselves and also decide on what we shall be. This clash of opinion is a problem that can be settled empirically.

8. Not only have we been ducking the problem of responsibility and of will, but also their corollaries of strength and courage. Recently the psychoanalytic ego psychologists have waked up to this great human variable and have been devoting a great deal of attention to "ego strength." For the behaviorists, this is still an untouched problem.

9. American psychologists have listened to Allport's call for an idiographic psychology but haven't done much about it. Not even the clinical psychologists have. We now have an added push from the phenomenologists and existentialists in this direction, one that will be very hard to resist, indeed I think, theoretically *impossible* to resist. If the study of the uniqueness of the individual does not fit into what we know of science, then so much the worse for that conception of science. It, too, will have to endure re-creation.

10. Phenomenology has a history in American psychological thinking, but on the whole I think it has languished. The European phenomenologists with their excruciatingly careful and laborious demonstrations, can reteach us that the best

way of understanding another human being, or at least *a* way necessary for some purposes, is to get into *his* Weltanschauung and to be able to see *his* world through *his* eyes. Of course such a conclusion is rough on any positivistic philosophy of science.

11. The existentialist stress on the ultimate aloneness of the individual is a useful reminder for us, not only to work out further the concepts of decision, or responsibility, of choice, of self-creation, of autonomy, of identity itself. It also makes more problematic and more fascinating the mystery of communication between alone-nesses via, e.g., intuition and empathy, love and altruism, identification with others, and homonomy in general. We take these for granted. It would be better if we regarded them as miracles to be explained.

12. Another preoccupation of existentialist writers can be phrased very simply, I think. It is the dimension of seriousness and profundity of living (or perhaps the "tragic sense of life") contrasted with the shallow and superficial life, which is a kind of diminished living, a defense against the ultimate problems of life. This is not just a literary concept. It has real operational meaning, for instance, in psychotherapy. I (and others) have been increasingly impressed with the fact that tragedy can sometimes be therapeutic, and that therapy often seems to work best when people are *driven* into it by pain. It is when the shallow life doesn't work that it is questioned and that there occurs a call to fundamentals. Shallowness in psychology doesn't work either as the existentialists are demonstrating very clearly.

13. The existentialists along with many other groups are helping to teach us about the limits of verbal, analytic, conceptual rationality. They are part of the current call back to raw experience as prior to any concepts or abstractions. This amounts to what I believe to be a justified critique of the whole way of thinking of the western world in the 20th century, including orthodox positivistic science and philosophy, both of which badly need re-examination.

14. Possibly most important of all the changes to be wrought by the phenomenologists and existentialists is an overdue revolution in the theory of science. I shouldn't say "wrought by" but rather "helped along by," because there are many other forces helping to destroy official philosophy of science or "scientism." It is not only the Cartesian split between subject and object that needs to be overcome. There are other radical changes made necessary by the inclusion of the psyche and of raw experience in reality, and such a change will affect not only the science of psychology but all other sciences as well, e.g., parsimony, simplicity, precision, orderliness, logic, elegance, definition, etc. are all of the realm of abstraction rather than of experience.

15. I close with the stimulus that has most powerfully affected me in the existentialist literature, namely, the problem of future time in psychology. Not that this, like all the other problems or pushes I have mentioned up to this point, was totally unfamiliar to me nor, I imagine, to *any* serious student of the theory of personality. The writings of Charlotte Buhler, Gordon Allport, and Kurt Goldstein should also have sensitized us to the necessity of grappling with and systematizing the dynamic role of the future in the presently existing personality, e.g., growth and becoming and possibility necessarily point toward the future; so do the concepts of potentiality and hoping, and of wishing and imagining; reduction to the con-

crete is a loss of future; threat and apprehension point to the future (no future = no neurosis); self-actualization is meaningless without reference to a currently active future; life can be a gestalt in time, etc., etc.

And yet the *basic* and *central* importance of this problem for the existentialists has something to teach us, e.g., Erwin Strauss' paper in the May volume.* I think it fair to say that no theory of psychology will ever be complete which does not centrally incorporate the concept that man has his future within him, dynamically active at this present moment. In this sense the future can be treated as a-historical in Kurt Lewin's sense. Also we must realize that *only* the future is *in principle* unknown and unknowable, which means that all habits, defenses and coping mechanisms are doubtful and ambiguous since they are based on past experience. Only the flexibly creative person can really manage future, *only* the one who can face novelty with confidence and without fear. I am convinced that much of what we now call psychology is the study of the tricks we use to avoid the anxiety of absolute novelty by making believe the future will be like the past.

CONCLUSION

These considerations support my hope that we are witnessing an expansion of psychology, not a new "ism" that could turn into an antipsychology or into an antiscience.

It is possible that existentialism will not only enrich psychology. It may also be an additional push toward the establishment of another *branch* of psychology, the psychology of the fully evolved and authentic Self and its ways of being. Sutich has suggested calling this ontopsychology.

Certainly it seems more and more clear that what we call "normal" in psychology is really a psychopathology of the average, so undramatic and so widely spread that we don't even notice it ordinarily. The existentialist's study of the authentic person and of authentic living helps to throw this general phoniness, this living by illusions and by fear into a harsh, clear light which reveals it clearly as sickness, even [though] widely shared.

I don't think we need take too seriously the European existentialists' exclusive harping on dread, on anguish, on despair and the like, for which their only remedy seems to be to keep a stiff upper lip. This high I.Q. whimpering on a cosmic scale occurs whenever an external source of values fails to work. They should have learned from the psychotherapists that the loss of illusions and the discovery of identity, though painful at first, can be ultimately exhilarating and strengthening. And then of course the absence of any mention of peak experiences, of experiences of joy and ecstasy, or even of normal happiness, leads to the strong suspicion that these writers are "nonpeakers," people who just don't experience joy. It is as if they could see out of one eye only, and that eye jaundiced. Most people experience *both* tragedy and joy in varying proportions. Any philosophy which leaves out either cannot be considered to be comprehensive.† Colin Wilson

---

*R. May, E. Angel, & H. Ellenberger, *Existence*. (New York: Basic Books, 1958).
†For further writing on this same subject, see my *Eupsychian Management* (Homeword, IL:, Irwin-Dorsey, 1965), pp. 194–201.

distinguishes sharply between Yea-saying existentialists and Nay-saying existentialists. In this distinction, I must agree with him completely.*

THE WOUNDED HEALER

Rollo May

As Kierkegaard (1954) once said, the "gain of infinity is never attained except through despair" (p. 160). In this little-known commentary, Rollo May recalls some of the greatest therapists and artists in history, their calamitous pasts, and their triumphal emergence as healers and creators.

I'm going to talk with you tonight about something that is very close to my own thoughts—this something I have been thinking about for years in my own heart, and in the period when I spent two years in bed with tuberculosis up in the Adirondack mountains before there were any drugs for this disease—all of these things come together in these ideas I want to share with you tonight.

They came, particularly, when I was interviewing, in New York City, student candidates to be trained in analytic institutions. I was on the committee for two groups, and so I interviewed for these two different groups. What I asked myself was, "What makes a good psychotherapist? What is there in a particular person that would tell us that here's somebody that can genuinely help other people in the fairly long training of the psychoanalyst?" It was quite clear to me that it was not adjustment—adjustment that we talked of so fondly when I was a Ph.D. student, and so ignorantly. I knew that the well-adjusted person who came in and sat down to be interviewed would not make a good psychotherapist. Adjustment is exactly what a neurosis is; and that's his trouble. It is an adjustment to nonbeing in order that some little being may be preserved. An adjustment always flounders on the question—adjustment to what? Adjustment to a psychotic world, which we certainly live in? Adjustment to societies that are Faustian and insensitive? And then I looked further, and I began to realize that the two greatest therapists I ever knew were badly adjusted people.

One was Harry Stack Sullivan, who was the only psychiatrist born in America to contribute a new system that was powerful enough to have an influence, not only on psychiatry, but on psychology, sociology, and a number of other professions. Now

*Wilson, C. *Introduction to the New Existentialism.* (New York: Houghton Mifflin, 1967).
Source: Adapted from a Laurence Lecture delivered October 20, 1984, at the First Unitarian Church of Berkeley, Berkeley, CA.

Sullivan, who was one of my teachers—we all revered him greatly—Sullivan was an alcoholic, and he was latently homosexual—he once proposed to Clara Thompson when he was drunk and got up very early the next morning to take it back. He never could get along with any groups with more than two or three people. Professor Klineberg—Otto Klineberg—who was at Columbia University, tells a story about being on the World Health Organization (WHO)—the mental health association that Sullivan had helped found. There was a meeting of this group in Paris, and after the meeting of this group he saw Sullivan sitting very morosely in the corner. He went over and asked what the matter was. Sullivan said, "It's always the same—I always antagonize everybody." Klineberg said, "But you didn't antagonize *me.*" Sullivan said, "Oh, you, I don't care about you—you don't count." It seems that Sullivan was schizophrenic for a couple of years in his late teens, but he had—I shouldn't say "but"—*and* he had a tremendous insight into what goes on in the troubled human being. Mental problems he defined as problems that always had their beginnings, and their cures, in interpersonal relationships.

The other great psychotherapist I knew and worked under was Frieda Fromm-Reichman. She was the psychiatrist in the book and film *I Never Promised You a Rose Garden.* She was played by Mimi Anderson in the film. Now she was a most unprepossessing person. She was four feet ten inches tall; she was ill at ease with people; she was married for a while to Eric Fromm—that's where she got the Fromm in her name—and in New York it was said, as a kind of wry joke in psychiatric and psychological circles, that the title of Fromm's first book was really *Escape From Freida.* She was once the chairman of a committee—a panel—[that delivered a presentation] at the American Psychiatric Association, a society [of which I was a member]. We were all sitting up there on the platform, and Freida Fromm-Reichman comes up the steps and falls her whole length on the platform. Now I don't know the meanings of these things except that what I am trying to say is that this woman, who always had problems in her relationships with other human beings—this woman had amazing insight, as you know if you have seen that movie or read the book. She died actually of loneliness. Buber, when he was in this country, went to see her. They seem to have been old friends, and he described her as filled with desperate loneliness.

Now let us take a third example—Abe Maslow. He was not a therapist, but one of the great psychologists. Maslow had a miserable time of it. He came from an immigrant family in the slums; he was alienated from his mother and afraid of his father. In New York, groups often lived in ghettos, and Abe was beaten up by Italian and Irish boys in the vicinity (he was Jewish); he was underweight, and yet, this man, the man who had so many hellish experiences—was the one who introduced the system of peak experience into psychology.

Now it's very curious that each of these is great in exactly his weakest point. It is very hard to take in that Harry Stack Sullivan, the person who could never relate to others, founded the psychiatric system of psychiatry as an interpersonal biology; and Abe, who had so many hellish experiences, compensating—if I may use a technical word— . . . then founded just the opposite school of peak experience and the human potential movement.

I want to propose a theory to you, and this is the theory of the wounded healer. I want to propose that we heal other people by virtue of our own wounds. Psychologists who become psychotherapists, psychiatrists, too, as far as that goes, are people who had, as babies and children, to be therapists for their own families. This is pretty well established by various studies. And I propose to carry that idea further and to propose that it is the insight that comes to us by virtue of our own struggle with our problems that leads us to develop empathy and creativity with human beings—and compassion. . . .

There was a study made in England, at the University of Cambridge, of geniuses—great writers, great artists, and so on—and of the forty-seven that this woman took as her sample, eighteen had been hospitalized—in a mental hospital—or had been treated with lithium, or had had electric shock.* These were people that you know. Handel—his music came out of great suffering. Byron—you would think he did everything *but* suffer, but he was a manic-depressive. Anne Sexton, who, I believe, later committed suicide, was a manic-depressive. Virginia Woolf, who I *know* committed suicide, was also very troubled by depression. Robert Lowell, the American poet, was manic-depressive. Now, what I want to point out is that there are some very positive aspects to these mood disorders. This woman was studying manic-depressives, but there are other kinds as well. I would enlarge that to say that there are positive aspects to all diseases, to all illness, whether it is mental or physical. We may say that some form of struggle is necessary to carry us to the depth out of which creativity comes.

Jerome Kagan, a professor up at Harvard, made a long and intensive study of creativity, and what he concluded is that the artist's main capacity, what he calls "his creative freedom" is not born within him. Some preparation for it may be there, but the creativity itself is not born with him. "The creativity," says Kagan, "is made in the pain of adolescent loneliness, the isolation of physical handicap."

A woman who had been in a concentration camp also made a study—for a doctoral degree—over at the Saybrook Institute. She was a survivor of Auschwitz. She studied the survivors of the German death camps, and the curious thing is that they reveal the same things. We would expect these inmates, after the experience of this ultimate in horror in their background, to be broken people. I remember one of them was my patient in psychoanalysis in New York. When I heard what he had been through, I thought, how can a human being survive it? But he not only survived, he was an exceedingly creative and productive human being. What the study by Dr. Eger at the Saybrook Institute pointed out is as follows—that individuals who have suffered calamitous events in the past can, and do, function later at average levels and may even function at higher-than-average levels. Relevant coping mechanisms may avert the potentially detrimental effects of calamitous experiences, but they may also transform these experiences into growth-producing experiences. She adds, "Inmates who have had poor, unpampered childhoods adapted best to the concentration camps, whereas most of those who had been reared by permissive, wealthy parents were the first to die."

---

*See Kay Jamison's *Touched by Fire: Manic-Depressive Illness and the Artistic Temperament* (New York: Free Press, 1993) for an elaboration.

I have thought a great deal about these things, and so have my colleagues at the Saybrook Institute. What some of them have pointed out is that many of our most valuable people have come from the most calamitous early-childhood situations. Investigations of the childhoods of eminent people expose the fact that they did not receive anything like the kind of child rearing that a person in our culture is led to believe is healthy for children. Now, whether in spite of or because of these conditions, these children not only survived, but reached great heights of achievement, many after having experienced the most deplorable and traumatic childhoods.

There was a study also done right here in Berkeley of the long-term development of human beings. A group of psychologists followed people through from birth to 30 years of age. They followed 166 men and women through adulthood, and they were shocked by the inaccuracies of their expectations. They were wrong in about two-thirds of the cases, mainly because they had overestimated the damaging effects of early troubles. They had also not foreseen—this sentence is interesting to all of us— they also had not foreseen the negative effects of a smooth and successful childhood, that a degree of stress and challenge seemed to spur psychological strength and competence.

There was also a British doctor, George Pickering, who wrote a book called *Creative Malady,* subtitled "Illness in the Lives and Minds of Charles Darwin, Florence Nightingale, Mary Baker Eddy, Sigmund Freud, Marcel Proust, and Elizabeth Barrett Browning." These are the people covered in his book, but he could have added Mozart, Chopin, Beethoven—these were all writers and musicians who had a malady, and he points out that each one suffered severe illness and met it constructively in creativity and in contribution to our culture. Pickering speaks of his own arthritic hips as "an ally," and he "puts them to bed," he said, "when they become painful." In bed he cannot attend committee meetings; can't see patients or entertain visitors. He adds, "These are the ideal conditions for creative work—freedom from intrusion, freedom from the ordinary chores of life."

Now you have many questions in your mind about what I am saying, and I certainly had, and have, many questions also. Otto Rank, as a matter of fact, wrote a whole book, *Art and Artist,* on [these ideas]. . . . Overcoming neurosis and creating art are identical things in Rank's work.

What I am doing tonight is challenging our whole view of health in our culture. We keep people living day after day because we think that it is simply the number of days you live. We struggle to invent ways to live longer, as though death and illness were the ultimate enemies. T. S. Eliot has a stanza in his *Four Quartets,* which goes as follows:

> Our only health is our disease.
> If we obey the dying nurse,
> Whose constant care is not to please
> But to remind of ours, and Adam's curse
> And that to be restored, our sickness must grow worse.

These are tremendously significant things—if you can take them in. When he says, "ours, and Adam's curse," he is referring to the fact that we are all the ultimate children of the myth of Adam—this is called in words that don't sound very nice anymore—this is called *original sin,* and the whole idea is that life is not a question of how long you live. It is not a question of how many days you can add. Many people would much prefer to go when their work is finished—to die—but what this verse is trying to say . . . is that disease and illness mean something quite different from what most people in our Faustian civilization take them to mean. . . .

As alienating as illness is, it can also be a connecting of ourselves with new others on a new and deeper level. We see this in compassion. Creativity is one of the products of the right relationship between nature and infinity within us. We see also another gift which Fromm Reichmann certainly had, which Abe Maslow had, which Harry Stack Sullivan had—the gift of compassion, the ability to feel with other people, the ability to understand their problems—this is the other quality that makes a good psychiatrist. The experience of degeneration and of chaos is, I hope, temporary, but this can often be used as a way of reforming or reorganizing ourselves on a higher level. As C. G. Jung put it, "The gods return in our diseases."

ROLLO MAY: PERSONAL REFLECTIONS AND APPRECIATION

James F. T. Bugental

In this moving personal tribute, James Bugental looks back at his long and fruitful association with America's premier existential psychologist—Rollo May.

A few months ago I sat in Rollo May's living room with a small group of therapists and counselors who were the Fellows of the Mentorship in Existential Humanistic Psychotherapy which I was conducting for the Humanistic Psychology Institute.* As the lively talk flowed around the room, I pulled back just a bit to watch the eager faces of the students and the matchingly eager face of our distinguished host. I was moved by his delight in discussion, in the flow of ideas, and in the involvement of the varied people in the room. How typical of Rollo was this readiness to engage in good talk with all comers—so long as they were seriously trying to explore and learn. There was no awkward chasm between this world-famed authority and these animated and bright neophytes; rather they were all caught up in the wonder of emerging understanding—Rollo evoking, teaching, and gently admonishing; the fellows seeing further possibilities, discovering fresh insights, and responding to the challenge of rich knowledge and much thought.

As I watched the scene, I found a shifting succession of images and feelings playing on my inner screen: satisfaction on seeing *destiny* in a fresh way through Rollo's

Source: From Saybrook Institute *Perspectives,* special issue; "Rollo May: Man and Philosopher" (L. Conti, ed.), 2(1), Summer 1981.
*Currently Saybrook Institute, San Francisco, CA.

understanding, envy of his erudition, enjoyment in watching my students meaningfully engage with him, stimulation to think further about the meaning of choice in individual lives, and warm recollection of the many times that Rollo May impacted my own thinking, my career, and my grappling to understand the human situation.

In 1953 I resigned from the UCLA psychology faculty to devote full time to private practice, drawn by the challenges and rewards of working with "real people." That same year—although I did not see it until the next—Rollo published *Man's Search for Himself,* a book that spoke to many of my own inner questionings. Meantime Alvin Lasko, who had taught with me at UCLA, and I founded Psychological Service Associates and began a staff development program which included a variety of further learning experiences among which was the reading of Rollo's book.

For a decade, I tried to match my learnings from graduate school, from my own teaching career, and from these staff seminars with the so very real lives of the people who were coming to see me. Sometimes the matches were successful; often times they left me dissatisfied. The richness and complexity of the lived lives seemed always to go beyond what I was learning, and the procedures and theories in which I had been trained felt as though they were designed for another and simpler species (probably college sophomores or white rats).

Then in 1958 the Los Angeles Society of Clinical Psychologists asked me to chair a committee to develop postdoctoral training opportunities. (At that time there were none on the West Coast, although the East had a variety.) So we brought a variety of distinguished contributors to conduct workshops for us: George A. Kelly, Emanual Schwartz, Rudolf Ekstein, and—of course and especially—Rollo May.

This was at about the time of Dr. May's landmark book, *Existence: A New Dimension in Psychiatry and Psychology,* which he edited (with Ernest Angel and Henry Ellenberger) and for which he wrote two principal chapters. His presentations at that weekend workshop and in those two chapters exploded on me as a major emotional and professional experience: I had found someone who really knew about the unfamiliar territory into which my patients (not "clients" in those days) were taking me. Here was someone who could name, describe, and confirm the phenomena that my training had only vaguely known existed. With this perspective, and borrowing frequently from May's wisdom and experience, I began to articulate what I'd been grappling with and to advance more satisfyingly in the endless work of trying to understand our human condition more deeply and more fully. From then on, I wrote out of my experience rather than solely in the cognitive style I had used before.

Over the subsequent years I took pride in keeping contact with Rollo May. When my first book was readying for the publisher, I asked him to read it. Graciously, he did so and offered several helpful suggestions. One which I recall had to do with the subtitle: at his gentle urging I changed "The Existential-Analytic Approach to Psychotherapy" to " *An. . . .*" In the meantime, Rollo himself was becoming one of the best known of American psychologists. His picture and his opinions were to be seen in many of the media.

After several publications which have remained central to the basic library of existential psychotherapy, Rollo began a series of monumental contributions to the understanding and description of human experience. These books establish his preeminence among psychological observers. Beginning with *Love and Will,* continuing with *Power and Innocence, The Courage to Create,* and the revision of his powerful *The Meaning of Anxiety* (originally his doctoral dissertation), and shortly to be joined by *Freedom and Destiny,* on which he is currently working, Rollo May has drawn careful, scholarly, and notably important portraits of some of the main dimensions of our lives. Somehow he manages to do so while remaining eminently readable, a fact attested to by the best-seller status of *Love and Will*—an astonishing phenomenon for a book as scholarly as it is.

Although Rollo May has published significant works on a variety of topics, I believe his lasting contribution will be judged, in the long run, to be this remarkable series of studies of basic human experiences which have emerged from his mature years. These five books—one hopes that the number will be increased—are the product of his broad, scholarly foundation and his extensive clinical experience. In them he has set forth an integrated set of concepts which provide a language, a dynamic schema, and an inspiring vision of those issues which are at the very core of the human venture: love, will, power, creativity, courage, anxiety, destiny, intentionality, violence—to name only a small part of the vocabulary of life which he has undertaken to spell out.

It is an all too familiar observation that humanistic psychology has been clearer about what it opposes than about what it proposes. The corollary is that the contributions of the third force have been rich in originality, enthusiasm, and promise, but for the most part, they have been equally scattered, incomplete, and shallowly grounded in sophisticated scholarship. Thus the work of humanistic psychologists is an easy target for critics, and the additions to knowledge they offer have been more potential than actual. Rollo May's work is in high contrast to that state of affairs. The body of work which is emerging from his mind and pen is coherent, fertile, and firmly rooted in the highest tradition of learning.

We who are close to the man and his times seldom have sufficient perspective to recognize what a sharp difference there is between May's carefully wrought conceptions in the network of their interrelations and so much else that is appearing on superficially similar topics. Only the passage of time will demonstrate how deeply these two streams of thinking diverge. I feel confident that when students and teachers have had more time to digest the body of work and when researchers have begun to develop the edifice of thought that is set forth, then Rollo May's true gift to psychology and to human beings will stand out clearly.

Thinking about the passage of time recalls to me my personal favorite among Rollo May's books: I am especially fond of Rollo's *The Courage to Create* for he gave me a copy when it was just newly off the presses. The occasion was my sixtieth birthday celebration, and he wrote on the flyleaf a familiar and loved quotation from Browning's *Rabbi ben Ezra,* "The best is yet to be, the last of life for which the first was made," to which he added words I cherish, "Best regards for the second half of a *creative* life" (emphasis in the original). Thus I hope for 120 years of productivity. I shall certainly need them if I hope to come to anything like the creative courage and productivity of Rollo himself.

Following are two tributes to maverick existential psychiatrist R. D. Laing. The first is a personal commentary by Kirk Schneider; the second is a poem by *Journal of Humanistic Psychology* editor Tom Greening. Both commemorate Laing's groundbreaking investigations of freedom, politics, and madness.

R. D. LAING REMEMBERED

Kirk J. Schneider

> *Once people believed that the world was flat; however, science has proved that the world is round. . . . Now in spite of that, one still believes that life is flat and goes from birth to death. However, life is probably round and much superior in extension and capacity to the hemisphere known to us at present. Future generations will probably enlighten us on this so interesting subject; and then science itself might arrive—willy-nilly—at conclusions . . . relating to the other half of existence.*
> —VINCENT VAN GOGH *(quoted in Graetz, 1963, p. 71)*

> *We respect the voyager, the explorer, the climber, the spaceman. It makes far more sense to me as a valid project—indeed, as a desperately and urgently required project for our time—to explore the inner space and time of consciousness.*
> —R. D. LAING, *1967, p. 127*

It was June 15th, 1976. I was 19 years old and about to embark on the journey of my life. Starry-eyed, backpack in hand, I wandered about a bookstore at New York's Kennedy Airport.

Suddenly, I spotted a tiny blue book. The title jumped out at me —*The Divided Self* (Laing, 1969a). "What a moving phrase," I thought to myself, "what a disturbing phrase." When I opened the cover I was no less captivated. I read and kept on reading. I read as the time of my flight drew near. I read as I moved through the jetway. I read and took furious notes throughout my entire seven-hour flight. When I finished I wrote the following inscription:

Author's note: This article conveys some of my thoughts, feelings, and experiences with R. D. Laing. Although I met him only briefly and did not know him personally, I sympathize greatly with his concerns.
Source: This selection by Kirk Schneider and the poem on page 108 by Thomas Greening from *Journal of Humanistic Psychology, 30* (2), Spring 1990, pages 38–43.

This book was written as if Dr. Laing led a team of researchers to a deserted island containing psychotics. . . . The following account is mastered with such intimacy and empathy that it makes me wonder if Laing himself had once been psychotic or had courageously allowed himself to embrace the removed world of psychosis, to further humanity's understanding.

Ronald David Laing died at age 61 on August 23, 1989. The world was not particularly shaken. Instead, as Laing himself might have predicted, a suspended baseball player dominated the news.

And yet the passing of Laing means a great deal to those of us who resonated deeply to his work. Laing was a pioneer in our field. He was one of the first to explore the *meaning* of psychotic experience. In this sense he is comparable to Pinel who "liberated" French mental patients from the dungeon. Laing, likewise, freed contemporary psychiatric patients from the shackles of organized psychiatry. In *The Divided Self* (1969a) and *Politics of Experience* (1967) especially, he articulated a broadened view of "madness."

"No one," observed Laing (1967), "who has not experienced how insubstantial the pageant of external reality can be, how it may fade, can fully realize the sublime and grotesque presences that can replace it, or that can exist along side it" (p. 133). With such statements, Laing sharply counteracted the reductionism of his day (and ours), and heralded a more empathic approach toward clients.

Laing, as I see it, made three important points about psychosis, and about schizophrenia in particular: it represents a great deal more than biochemical action; it has significant implications for the entire spectrum of psychosocial life; and it represents a potential breakthrough as well as breakdown of psychological functioning.

Considering point one, Laing (1967, pp. 114–115) showed that schizophrenia is an *experience,* not just a disease:

In over 100 cases where we studied the actual circumstances around the social event when one person comes to be regarded as schizophrenic, it seems to us that *without exception* the experience and behavior that gets labeled schizophrenic is *a special strategy that a person invents in order to live in an unlivable situation.*

Although recent genetic and biological studies moderate this finding (as Laing well recognized), it is still remarkable and compelling (see Arieti, 1981; Zilbach, 1979).

Second, Laing's descriptions of former clients are so vivid, so accessible that they connect with our own experiences. Witness, for example, the gallery of people in *The Divided Self* who perceived themselves as stones, vapors, or fragments. Consider the little girl who felt like an "A-Bomb"; or the man who thought he was a machine (Laing, 1969a). In his autobiography, *Wisdom, Madness, and Folly,* Laing (1985) details his own struggles. Referring to a picture of his childhood rocking horse he writes: "I was very fond of this little wooden horse. Shortly after this photograph was taken . . . my mother decided I was getting too fond of it and burned it."

We now have a better grasp of our own fragility, our own anxieties, for having pursued these observations.

Finally, Laing showed us how schizophrenia *can* be a potential breakthrough as well as breakdown. Although "Jessie Watkins" in *Politics of Experience* dramatically illustrates this point—as does Laing's (1970) epigramatic *Knots*—the implication is widely dispersed throughout the author's work. Some schizophrenics, according to Laing, are exceptionally bright and sensitive. They cannot dismiss the lies and distortions that beset them (indeed, all of us). They are extremely vulnerable, therefore, and experience the full range of degradations. At the same time, they cannot tolerate these degradations. They do not know how to handle or rechannel them. So they build massive defenses against them, withdrawing, dissociating, or exploding.

Yet these excesses, Laing realized, are also potentialities. They can, if properly integrated, signify the "awakenings" of freer minds. They can point beyond stifling patterns and pave the way to more creative, flexible lifestyles. Romantic clap-trap? To the contrary. Consider such luminaries as Blake, Van Gogh, and Nietzsche. Consider the work of Laing (1967, 1969a, 1969b, 1971) and his colleagues (e.g., Laing & Esterson, 1964) at the Tavistock and Philadelphia Association clinics. Consider numerous studies of the creative process (e.g., Arieti, 1976; Prentky, 1979).

As humanists, scholars, and clients, we owe Laing a great deal. Whatever his faults, he was a caring, attuned human being. He used his personal understanding and vulnerability to further the lives of those less fortunate. He courageously plumbed the inner depths. He was an astronaut of the mind. Baseball and pictures from Neptune may be the current fare, but his time will come.

REFERENCES

Arieti, S. (1976). *Creativity: The magic synthesis.* New York: Basic Books.

Arieti, S. (1981). The family of the schizophrenic and its participation in the therapeutic task. In S. Arieti & H. Brodie (Eds.), *American handbook of psychiatry: Advances and new directions* (Vol. 7, pp. 271-284). New York: Basic Books.

Graetz, H. R. (1963). *The symbolic language of Vincent Van Gogh.* New York: McGraw-Hill.

Laing, R. D. (1967). *The politics of experience.* New York: Ballantine.

Laing, R. D. (1969a). *The divided self: An existential study in sanity and madness.* Middlesex, England: Penguin.

Laing, R. D. (1969b). *Self and others.* Middlesex, England: Penguin Books.

Laing, R. D. (1970). *Knots.* New York: Vintage Books.

Laing, R. D. (1971). *The politics of the family and other essays.* New York: Vintage.

Laing, R. D. (1985). *Wisdom, madness, and folly.* New York: McGraw-Hill.

Laing, R. D., & Esterson, A. (1964). *Sanity, madness and the family.* New York: Basic Books.

Prentky, R. (1979). Creativity and psychopathology: A neurocognitive perspective. In B. Maher (Ed.), *Progress in experimental personality research,* pp. 1-39. New York: Academic Press.

Zilbach, J. (1979). Family development and familial factors in etiology. In J. Nopshitz (Ed.), *Basic handbook of child psychiatry* (Vol. 2, pp. 62-87). New York: Basic Books.

FOR RONNIE LAING

Thomas Greening

Who's mad and who's sane,
and who decides?
If you have to ask,
don't ask out loud,
or you could end up
on the wrong side of the keys,
knife, chemicals, or electricity.
What was a nice Scotch doctor
doing in a world like this?
Rattling paradigms, that's what,
and drinking more than he should.
His time is up,
and the psychiatric pub
is quieter now.
Once he asked,
"Where in the world
are lunatics allowed to bathe
naked in the moonlight?"
At last he has found the place,
but he's probably splashing
more than God allows.

MASTER OF DUALITY: SOME PERSONAL REFLECTIONS ABOUT JIM BUGENTAL*

Kirk J. Schneider

In this intimate commentary, Kirk Schneider compares the life with the work of one of existential psychology's most prominent spokespersons—James F. T. Bugental. In so doing, Schneider unveils parallels between Bugental the person and the profession he helped to shape.

> *I believe that the key to significant life change is to be found in recovering one's centering of life in one's subjective vision. Genuine insight is to my mind inner-sight, subjective vision. So-called "insight" that is chiefly derived from the therapist's*

Source: From The *Script,* Newsletter of the International Transactional Analysis Association, *8,* p. 4, June 1983.

perceptions and interpretations is not inward-seeing; it is objective information about the person the patient has been, but is not evocative of his present being.
—Jim F. T. Bugental

There is a curious duality about one who both preaches and practices intensive psychotherapy. He or she engages in two very different ways of viewing the world, ways which are sometimes in conflict. On the one hand, the therapist (as writer/thinker) participates in the objective, distant, practical world of words, facts, and categories. On the other, he or she (as practitioner/person) is involved with the subjective, intimate, emotional world of revery, fantasy, dreams, hopes and desires. To further complicate the situation, the clients and students with whom the therapist works are often also split between objective and subjective worlds, shifting from the distant and practical to the intimate and emotional.

Given these parallel tasks, it seems clear that the best therapist (preacher/practitioner) is one who has mastered his or her own duality, who has faced his or her own conflicting sides. To the extent the therapist has done this, he or she is in a better position to help others who are struggling to do the same.

For much of his 67 years, Jim Bugental has sought to bridge the gap between these ostensibly rivaling worlds. He is intimately aware of how we divide our experience, often "reporting on" rather than "living" an event or "knowing about" rather than "knowing" a feeling. I have seen Jim convey complex therapeutic issues with great flair and precision and, at the same time, . . . lament the "headiness" of these issues and their inability to reflect the actual work. I have seen him eloquently teach the fundamentals of presence and I have witnessed his actual presence—the unwavering arched posture, the kind, respectful verbal tone, the undeniable mannerisms—each converging as if to say, "I'm here, I'm for you, and I have a sense of where you are."

Jim's awareness of duality, however, was hard won. The feelings, especially, came slowly to him. They were checked, closed off, calling to be acknowledged. In a movingly candid passage from his book, *The Search for Existential Identity,* (San Francisco: Jossey-Bass, 1976), Jim confirms the inner struggle of his early years.

I have always wanted to be one of the "right" people, always since my earliest recollections. . . . My mother was a great admirer of "cultured people." Very early I somehow got the idea that such people had a different skin texture than most people— maybe it was because another favorite word of hers described cultured people as finer. . . . Being "right" is so important and so easily lost. Obviously, being right means pleasing the teachers. . . . Clearly, being right means not being like Dad, who is loving but undependable. . . . And so the explorations go. In some ways, I get confirmation of being right—recognitions, offices, approval. But always the secret self must be hidden, that I know is not right. It is shameful because it is sexual, because it is emotional and unpractical, because it really wants to play many times when I force it to work, because it likes to daydream instead of being realistic. Two selves: gradually one becomes more public, the other more hidden. (Bugental, 1976, p. 280)

And, later in the narrative, Jim surveys his duality from a more ripened, mature perspective.

Now is the time of healing, of hope for a new life. The secret self is hidden no more. I swim in shame and I find I do not drown. With new relationships, I gradually risk letting more and more of me be known, and I find I am welcomed. . . . So is it over, is it healed? Am I "right" at last? No: no to each of these. It is not over; the split is still there—although so small in comparison to before. I heal and I tear open and I heal a bit more. And I am giving up being right in favor of trying to be who I am. (Bugental, 1976, p. 282)

These sensitive passages illustrate how Jim's life forms the basis for his work. The dualities he grapples with—right self/wrong self, practical self/emotional self and, to some extent, preacher/practitioner—echo our own inner struggles. We discover with him how crippled and stifled a life can be when it is half-lived, half-listened to, and half-searched.

And yet, Jim holds out a vision of something more. He suggests that attendant to the process of becoming aware, of inner searching, is another healing process. Jim's mentor, George Kelly, called it "the capacity to reinterpret what cannot be denied." It might also be simply called the capacity for creative change. For Jim, such a capacity means turning his dual nature into rewarding personal and professional activity, including enjoying his family, teaching and practicing psychotherapy. For clients and many of us, creative change also means a wealth of personal and career transformations with fresh ways to reunite and reframe our lives.

Again, I quote from *The Search for Existential Identity:*

Something more has emerged from the explorations of my awareness. . . . Something has been created. New meanings, new perceptions, new relationships, new possibilities now exist where they were not to be found before. In short, my inner vision is a creative process that does more than observe what is already at hand; it brings into being fresh possibilities. This is the astonishing and creative possibility latent in our being. (Bugental, 1976, p. 288).

One of Jim's prized possibilities—now a reality—is Inter-Logue, a non-profit counseling agency. For the past two years, I have been among an energetic group of people who have participated in this reality and we, too, have been inspired to work closely with our inner churnings, becoming perceptibly more real and whole in the process.

Ultimately, however, Jim's journeys between objective and subjective worlds, his brilliance as both scholar and therapist, stand as testament to his "fundamental message." It is a message that reflects a life that searched and found choice, that chose and found change, that changed and found power.

In the closing pages of *The Search for Existential Identity,* Jim relates how elusive this fundamental message is, how hard it is to talk about because, in the very saying, one distorts it. "Again and again," he writes, "I find that those to whom I speak or write take other—and to me, lesser—points as more fresh or meaningful." And yet, it is this very "knowing" as distinct from "knowing about," which must be taken seriously; it is the world which so often calls out to be bridged. It is

our lost sense, the inner awareness that has the potential to let each of us live in wholeness and with true realization of his or her unique nature. [And] it is our avenue toward the most profound meaning of life and the universe. (Bugental, 1976, p. 283)

KIERKEGAARD'S CHARACTEROLOGY

Ernest Becker

The late Ernest Becker (1924–1974) was one of the most innovative existentialists of our age; he was also, unfortunately, one of the least appreciated. His most memorable work, The Denial of Death *(1973), is no less than a comprehensive existential reinterpretation of psychoanalysis. Below we present an excerpt from this project and its edifying inquiry into Kierkegaard.*

Kierkegaard's whole understanding of man's character is that it is a structure built up to avoid perception of the "terror, perdition [and] annihilation [that] dwell next door to every man." He understood psychology the way a contemporary psychoanalyst does: that its task is to discover the strategies that a person uses to avoid anxiety. What style does he use to function automatically and uncritically in the world, and how does this style cripple his true growth and freedom of action and choice? Or, in words that are almost Kierkegaard's: how is a person being enslaved by his characterological lie about himself?

Kierkegaard described these styles with a brilliance that today seems uncanny and with a vocabulary that sums up much of the psychoanalytic theory of character defenses. Whereas today we talk about the "mechanisms of defense" such as repression and denial, Kierkegaard talked about the same things with different terms: he referred to the fact that most men live in a "half-obscurity" about their own condition, they are in a state of "shut-upness" wherein they block off their own perceptions of reality. He understood the compulsive character, the rigidity of the person who has had to build extra-thick defenses against anxiety, a heavy character armor, and he described him in the following terms:

> A partisan of the most rigid orthodoxy . . . knows it all, he bows before the holy, truth is for him an ensemble of ceremonies, he talks about presenting himself before the throne of God, of how many times one must bow, he knows everything the same way as does the pupil who is able to demonstrate a mathematical proposition with the letters ABC, but not when they are changed to DEF. He is therefore in dread whenever he hears something not arranged in the same order.

There is no doubt that by "shut-upness" Kierkegaard means what we today refer to by repression; it is the closed personality, the one who has fenced himself around in childhood, not tested his own powers in action, not been free to discover himself and his world in a relaxed way. If the child is not burdened by too much parental blocking of his action, too much infection with the parents' anxieties, he can develop his defenses in a less monopolizing way, can remain somewhat fluid and open in character. He is prepared to test reality more in terms of his own action and experimentation and less on the basis of delegated authority and prejudgment or preperception.

Source: From Ernest Becker, *The Denial of Death* (New York: Free Press, 1973), pp. 70–75.

Kierkegaard understood this difference by making a distinction between "lofty" shut-upness and "mistaken" shut-upness. He went on to give a Rousseau-like enjoinder for raising children with the right kind of character orientation.

> It is of infinite importance that a child be brought up with a conception of the lofty shut-upness [reserve], and be saved from the mistaken kind. In an external respect it is easy to perceive when the moment has arrived that one ought to let the child walk alone; . . . the art is to be constantly present and yet not be present, to let the child be allowed to develop itself, while nevertheless one has constantly a survey clearly before one. The art is to leave the child to itself in the very highest measure and on the greatest possible scale, and to express this apparent abandonment in such a way that, unobserved, one at the same time knows everything. . . . And the father who educates or does everything for the child entrusted to him, but has not prevented him from becoming shut-up, has incurred a great accountability.

Just as Rousseau and Dewey, Kierkegaard is warning the parent to let the child do his own exploration of the world and develop his own sure experimental powers. He knows that the child has to be protected against dangers and that watchfulness by the parent is of vital importance, but he doesn't want the parent to obtrude his own anxieties into the picture, to cut off the child's action before it is absolutely necessary. Today we know that such an upbringing alone gives the child a self-confidence in the face of experience that he would not have if he were overly blocked: it gives him an "inner sustainment." And it is precisely this inner sustainment that allows the child to develop a "lofty" shut-upness, or reserve: that is, an ego-controlled and self-confident appraisal of the world by a personality that can open up more easily to experience. "Mistaken" shut-upness, on the other hand, is the result of too much blockage, too much anxiety, too much effort to face up to experience by an organism that has been overburdened and weakened in its own controls: it means, therefore, more automatic repression by an essentially *closed* personality. And so, for Kierkegaard, the "good" is the opening toward new possibility and choice, the ability to face into anxiety; the closed is the evil, that which turns one away from newness and broader perceptions and experiences; the closed shuts out revelation, obtrudes a veil between the person and his own situation in the world. Ideally these should be transparent, but for the closed person they are opaque.

It is easy to see that shut-upness is precisely what we have called "the lie of character," and Kierkegaard calls it the same thing.

> It is easy to see that shut-upness *eo ipso* signifies a lie, or if you prefer, untruth. But untruth is precisely unfreedom . . . the elasticity of freedom is consumed in the service of close reserve. . . . Close reserve was the effect of the negating retrenchment of the ego in the individuality.

This is a perfectly contemporary psychoanalytic description of the costs of repression on the total personality. I am omitting Kierkegaard's more detailed and penetrating analysis of how the person becomes fragmented within himself by the repression, how the real perception of reality dwells under the surface, close at hand, ready to break through the repression, how the repression leaves the personality seemingly intact, seemingly functioning as a whole, in continuity—but how that continuity is broken, how the personality is really at the mercy of the discontinuity expressed by the repression. To a modern, clinically-trained mind such an analysis must be truly marvelous.

Kierkegaard understood that the lie of character is built up because the child needs to adjust to the world, to the parents, and to his own existential dilemmas. It is built up before the child has a chance to learn about himself in an open or free way, and thus character defenses are automatic and unconscious. The problem is that the child becomes dependent on them and comes to be encased in his own character armor, unable to see freely beyond his own prison or into himself, into the defenses he is using, the things that are determining his unfreedom. The best that the child can hope is that his shut-upness will not be of the "mistaken" or massive kind, in which his character is too fearful of the world to be able to open itself to the possibilities of experience. But that depends largely on the parents, on accidents of the environment, as Kierkegaard knew. Most people have parents who have "incurred a great accountability," and so they are obliged to shut themselves off from possibility.

Kierkegaard gives us some portrait sketches of the styles of denying possibility, or the lies of character—which is the same thing. He is intent on describing what we today call "inauthentic" men, men who avoid developing their own uniqueness; they follow out the styles of automatic and uncritical living in which they were conditioned as children. They are "inauthentic" in that they do not belong to themselves, are not "their own" person, do not act from their own center, do not see reality on its terms; they are the one-dimensional men totally immersed in the fictional games being played in their society, unable to transcend their social conditioning: the corporation men in the West, the bureaucrats in the East, the tribal men locked up in tradition—man everywhere who doesn't understand what it means to think for himself and who, if he did, would shrink back at the idea of such audacity and exposure. Kierkegaard gives us a description of

> the *immediate* man . . . his self or he himself is a something included along with "the other" in the compass of the temporal and the worldly. . . . Thus the self coheres immediately with "the other," wishing, desiring, enjoying, etc., but passively; . . . he manages to imitate the other men, noting how they manage to live, and so he too lives after a sort. In Christendom he too is a Christian, goes to church every Sunday, hears and understands the parson, yea, they understand one another; he dies; the parson introduces him into eternity for the price of $10—but a self he was not, and a self he did not become. . . . For the immediate man does not recognize his self, he recognizes himself only by his dress, . . . he recognizes that he has a self only by externals.

This is a perfect description of the "automatic cultural man"—man as confined by culture, a slave to it, who imagines that he has an identity if he pays his insurance premium, that he has control of his life if he guns his sports car or works his electric toothbrush. Today the inauthentic or immediate men are familiar types, after decades of Marxist and existentialist analysis of man's slavery to his social system. But in Kierkegaard's time it must have been a shock to be a modern European city-dweller and be considered a Philistine at the same time. For Kierkegaard "philistinism" was triviality, man lulled by the daily routines of his society, content with the satisfactions that it offers him: in today's world the car, the shopping center, the two-week summer vacation. Man is protected by the secure and limited alternatives his society offers him, and if he does not look up from his path he can live out his life with a certain dull security.

> Devoid of imagination, as the *Philistine* always is, he lives in a certain trivial province of experience as to how things go, what is possible, what usually occurs. . . . Philistinism tranquilizes itself in the trivial.

Why does man accept to live a trivial life? Because of the danger of a full horizon of experience, of course. This is the deeper motivation of philistinism, that it celebrates the triumph over possibility, over freedom. Philistinism knows its real enemy: freedom is dangerous. If you follow it too willingly it threatens to pull you into the air; if you give it up too wholly, you become a prisoner of necessity. The safest thing is to toe the mark of what is *socially* possible. I think this is the meaning of Kierkegaard's observation:

> For philistinism thinks it is in control of possibility, it thinks that when it has decoyed this prodigious elasticity into the field of probability or into the madhouse it holds it a prisoner; it carries possibility around like a prisoner in the cage of the probable, shows it off.

REFERENCES—PSYCHOLOGICAL ROOTS

Giorgi, A. (1970). *Psychology as a human science: A phenomenologically based approach.* New York: Harper & Row.

James, W. (1904/1987). *William James: Writings 1902–1910.* New York: Literary Classics/Viking.

James, W. (1907/1967). *Pragmatism and other essays.* New York: Washington Square.

Kierkegaard, S. (1954). *Fear and trembling and the sickness unto death* (W. Lowrie, Trans.). Princeton, NJ: Princeton University Press.

Lieberman, E. J. (1985). *Acts of will: The life and work of Otto Rank.* New York: Free Press.

Myers, G. (1986). *Williams James: His life and thought.* New Haven, CT: Yale University Press.

WORKS OF RELATED INTEREST

Aanstoos, C. (Ed.). (1990). Psychology and postmodernity. Special issue of *The Humanistic Psychologist, 18* (1).

Becker, E. (1973). *Denial of death.* New York: Free Press.

Becker, E. (1976). *Escape from evil.* New York: Free Press.

Binswanger, L. (1975). *Being in the world: Selected papers of Ludwig Binswanger* (J. Needleman, Trans.). New York: Basic Books.

Boss, M. (1963). *Psychoanalysis and daseinsanalysis* (L. Lefebre, Trans.). New York: Basic Books.

Boss, M. (1978). *Existential foundations of psychology and medicine* (S. Conway & A. Cleares, Trans.). New York: Jason Aronson.

Bugental, J. (1965/1981). *The search for authenticity: An existential-analytic approach to psychotherapy.* New York: Irvington.

Bugental, J. (1976). *The search for existential identity.* San Francisco: Jossey-Bass.

Bugental, J. (1978). *Psychotherapy and process: The fundamentals of an existential-humanistic approach.* Reading, MA: Addison-Wesley.

Craig, E. (Ed.). (1988). Psychotherapy for freedom: The daseinsanalytic way in psychology and psychoanalysis. Special issue of the *Humanistic Psychologist, 16* (1).

Frankl, V. (1967). *Selected papers on existentialism: Selected papers on logotherapy.* New York: Washington Square.

Fromm, E. (1955). *The sane society.* Greenwich, CT: Fawcett.

Fromm, E. (1964). *The heart of man: Its genius for good and evil.* New York: Harper Colophon.

Fromm, E. (1969). *Escape from freedom.* New York: Avon.

Fromm-Reichman, F. (1950). *Principles of intensive psychotherapy.* University of Chicago Press.

Lifton, R. J. (1983). *The broken connection: On death and the continuity of life.* New York: Basic Books.

Rank, O. (1936). *Will therapy* (J. Taft, Trans.). New York: Knopf.

Schachtel, E. (1959). *Metamorphosis: On the development of affect, perception, and memory.* New York: Basic Books.

Sullivan, H. (1962). *Schizophrenia as a human process.* New York: Norton.

Taylor, E. (1991). William James and the humanistic tradition. *Journal of Humanistic Psychology, 31* (1), 56–74.

Valle, R., & Halling, S. (Eds.) (1989). *Existential-phenomenological perspectives in psychology: Exploring the breadth of human experience.* New York: Plenum.

van den Berg, J. H. (1972). *A different existence: Principles of phenomenological psychopathology.* Pittsburgh: Duquesne.

Van Kaam, A. (1969). *Existential foundations of psychology.* New York: Image.

Yalom, I. (1980). *Existential psychotherapy.* New York: Basic Books.

MONOGRAPHS AND JOURNALS

Duquesne Studies in Phenomenological Psychology (Duquesne University Press)

Review of Existential Psychiatry and Psychology

Journal of Phenomenological Psychology

Journal of Humanistic Psychology

Humanistic Psychologist (division 32, APA)

Journal of Theoretical and Philosophical Psychology (division 24, APA)

Journal of the Society for Existential Analysis (British)

Daseinsanalyse (Swiss)

RECENT AND FUTURE TRENDS IN EXISTENTIAL-INTEGRATIVE PSYCHOLOGY

CHAPTER 4

FROM SEGREGATION TO INTEGRATION

The world of psychology, as noted earlier, is changing; and existential psychology is on the cusp of that change. In the years since *Existence,* there have been at least four dramatic developments in psychology, and each has reshaped the field. Cognitive psychology, for example, brought welcome attention to the autonomy of the human intellect; biopsychology revealed untold physiological and behavioral interconnections (Beck, 1976; Thompson, 1973). In more recent years, transpersonal (or transcendental) psychology and postmodernist philosophy have ushered in even bolder paradigmatic shifts (Wilber, Engler, & Brown, 1986; Bernstein, 1986). For example, transpersonal psychology inspired (and in some cases revived) an interest in alternative healing methods, Eastern and Western meditative traditions, and paranormal phenomena. Postmodernist philosophy, correspondingly, relativized and thereby broadened scientific and cultural notions of truth. *All* perceptual phenomena are legitimated by this framework; and none can be said to be inherently superior to any other.

There has, however, been a price for these reformative developments; and the outlines of that price have just begun to emerge. First, I refer to contemporary psychology's increasing specialization. We will soon be, if we are not already, threatened by a chaos of competing outlooks. Second, we are threatened by the limitations inherent in the respective points of view. While they are salient within their own domains, they tend to be simplistic or devitalizing when applied beyond those domains. (See, for example, the concerns expressed by May, 1967, and Wertz, 1993.)

Put plainly, we need a psychological foundation that will do justice to both our diversity *and* our particularity, our freedom and our limits. Such a foundation would view human being in its fullness while carefully acknowledging its tragedy and incompleteness. It would honor our biological and mechanical propensities, but not at the cost of compromising our capacity to create and to transcend ordinary consciousness. What, specifically, would such a foundation look like? The following vignette* will serve to illustrate our proposal:

Karen is a 37-year-old, middle-class female. She has a husband and a 15-year-old son who plays Little League baseball. Ordinary in most respects, Karen has one outstanding trait: She is 424 pounds.

What is a 424-pound world like? Karen reflects:

> I weighed [myself on] the freight scale at Johnson's Trucking terminal. I couldn't buy clothes even in large-size women's specialty shops because their sizes stopped at 52 and I was a size 60. My wardrobe consisted of three caftans which I had specially made: one—navy, black, and brown—sewn straight up the sides with openings for my head and arms. I wore slip-on sandals in summer and winter because I couldn't bend over to lace sneakers up and dress shoes buckled under my weight. I didn't own a coat, but that didn't matter since I was hardly ever out of the house anyway. In the morning, I'd maneuver myself out of bed, go to the kitchen, get my stash of food, and settle into my chair in the living room, comforted by the assurance that food was all around me. My days were filled with the drone of soap operas in the background. I lived my life vicariously through my husband and children. They became my arms and legs and my windows to the outside world. When I went anywhere, I drove. The car became part of my insulation, my armor, my protection. I used to drive around town eating, stuffing down anger, guilt, hurt—eating until nothing mattered any more. (Roth, 1991, p. 173)

Let us imagine, now, how a team of contemporary psychologists might understand Karen's condition and what this understanding implies for the integrative vision referred to above.

From the behavioral standpoint, for example, Karen's obesity would probably be understood as a function of her environment. Rearrange her surroundings, behaviorists would contend, and you will significantly modify her compulsion. In particular, they would pin her problem on the wealth of junk foods she keeps around her house (which serve as conditioned stimuli), her consumption of food while engaging in other behaviors (such as television viewing), and her perception of foods as positive (or negative) reinforcers. To redress these concerns, behaviorists would try to help Karen reduce or eliminate the problematic stimuli and replace them with stimuli that are more adaptive.

Physiological psychologists, by contrast, would look to Karen's brain, central nervous system, and cell metabolism for their answers. They might conjecture that deficits in her ability to metabolize her food, for example, render her physiologically predisposed to obesity. Depending on the severity of her predisposition, they might recommend a combination of drugs, dietary restrictions, and surgical procedures. To the extent that Karen was able to lose weight without severe measures, physiological psychologists might suggest that she lose weight gradually through a carefully modified diet and a regular form of aerobic exercise (such as walking).

Cognitive psychologists, on the other hand, would concentrate on the relationship

---

*This vignette is modeled on the case of Karen Russell, who is eloquently described by Geneen Roth (1991, pp. 172–184). Where I have speculated about her condition, I have noted that I have done so.

between Karen's thought patterns and her malady. In particular, they would try to help Karen understand the connection between her faulty beliefs, assumptions, and expectations and her maladaptive behavior. They might point out, for example, that when she is lonely she believes she will always be lonely, and this generalization leads to the faulty belief that food is the only alternative to this loneliness. Once Karen can recognize these maladaptive schemas, the cognitive psychologists would contend, she will be able to modify or restructure them and, hence, her behavior.

Let us pause a moment and reflect on Karen's apparent response to such regimens: "I have tried to break free from my state of nonexistence hundreds of times," Karen tells us. "I'd been to scores of doctors" (Roth, 1991, p. 174). Like many compulsive eaters, moreover, it is a good bet that Karen was helped by some of these doctors—at least temporarily. For example, Karen was probably able to reprogram her life through such contacts. In particular, she probably mustered the will needed to keep junk food out of her house, to devise new links between eating and other behaviors, and to develop fresh, more appropriate ways to reward herself. She also probably took appetite suppressants and a variety of nutritional supplements along her recuperative path.

Yet if Karen sounds bitter about these therapies, it is probably because—in spite of their efficacy—in some intimate, vital way, they failed to address her wound. "'Exercise, dear,'" Karen recalled angrily about the advice she had received at one of her weight-control meetings, "'Just *push* yourself away from the table three times a day'" (Roth, 1991, p. 174).

My own experience with compulsive eaters has convinced me that cognitive-behavioral and physiological treatments can be essential first steps on the path to recovery. They help people understand the importance of reassessing their habits, belief systems, and approaches to food. They educate them about their physiology and the physiology of practice. But most important of all, perhaps, they prompt clients to *begin* a process of deep reflection about their lives—who they essentially are and where they are headed—and this, in turn, sometimes leads to fundamental change (Schneider, 1990).

"Whenever something hurt too much," Karen recollects, "I would pack up and leave myself because I was afraid that if I experienced the fear, it would eat me alive. I made the commitment to stay with myself, [however, and to] let the fear or hurt wash over me" (Roth, 1991, p. 175).

Until now, we have examined treatment regimens that help Karen and countless clients like her to get a "foothold" on their compulsions; they teach them *operational* (measurable, specifiable) ways to change their lives. Yet these methodologies tend to address narrow ranges of the problem, failing to touch the "fear" or "hurt," as Karen puts it, that underlie those ranges. Now let us assess methodologies that purport to confront more substantive domains of psychological functioning—those of transpersonalism and postmodernism. How might they foster Karen's emancipation from food?

Transpersonal psychology encompasses those disciplines and practices that address *transcendental* (or nonordinary) states of consciousness. To the extent that transpersonal psychology accepts existential mystery, for our purposes, it provides vital insights into such transcendental phenomena as energy shifts, paranormal and visionary states, religious and spiritual crises, and unitive experiences. To the extent that the discipline *spurns* existential mystery, on the other hand, it can impose exaggerated or premature solutions on treatment [see Dass, 1992; Ellis & Yeager, 1989; May, 1986; Schneider, 1987, 1989; Zweig & Abrams, 1991; and Bowman (this text) for examples].

How would a team of existentially sensitive transpersonalists understand and help Karen? First, they would probably help her evolve to the point where she could begin to ask deeper questions about herself: What does she want in her life? Where is she headed? Who does she ultimately wish to become? "I grew up to believe in an angry God," Karen acknowledges,

> a God who punishes you, a God who is never pleased, for whom only perfection is enough. I went from an angry mother to an angry God to being angry at myself. Diets were an extension of the angry God; I could never be good enough. I would always rebel and feel horrible about myself afterwards. . . .
>
> I realized that I was not that bad and that openheartedness, not punishment, was the way into my problems with food. (Roth, 1991, p. 181)

Next, the transpersonalists might assist Karen (through meditation, for example) to "dwell" in formerly uninhabitable parts of herself, such as her loneliness or vacuousness. This could have the effect of opening Karen to the deeper meanings of that suffering, and of *reconciling* her with those meanings. No longer would she feel as compelled to "fill" her being with food, she would find, but could realize that solace through living.

After three and a half years of sustained meditative therapy, Karen states: "Now I am living. It's the difference between eating my feelings and feeling my feelings" (p. 180). "I'm alive," she goes on,

> and . . . feel everything with great vibrancy. I walk in the woods and feel a hushed sense of awe. Driving around in the warm spring rain a few weeks ago, I was spellbound by a double rainbow. . . . Last week at work, I saw some bare oak trees covered with raindrops. I knew they were just raindrops on a naked tree, but to me they were diamonds. (Roth, 1991, p. 183)

The *danger* of such a transcendental emphasis, on the other hand, is that it unwittingly implies *salvation* to Karen, or that it shortsightedly implies a resolution. Anxiety can (and fruitfully does) exist alongside glimpses of divinity, and it is in the dialogue *between* that people achieve vitality (May, 1981, 1985). The dialectical features of Karen's struggle, for example, bring a poignancy to her life—a savoring of momentary triumphs—and a wisdom that evolves through humility.

> I wish I could tell you that being a size twelve is all wonderful but I'm finding out that being awake and alive is a package deal. I don't get to go through the line and pick only goodies. On one side is wonder, awe, excitement and laughter—and on the other side is tears, disappointment, aching sadness. Wholeness is coming to me by being willing to explore ALL the feelings.

So . . . 275 pounds later, my life is a mixture of pain and bliss. It hurts a lot these days but it's real. It's my life being lived by me and not vicariously through a soap opera the way it used to be. I don't know where it's all heading, but one thing I know for sure: I'm definitely going. (Roth, 1991, pp. 183–184)

The postmodern approach to Karen's difficulty, finally, draws upon the premise of social constructivism and is just now being therapeutically articulated. Broadly speaking, postmodernism holds three basic assumptions: (1) there are no absolute truths; (2) all realities (or *stories*) are socially constructed; and (3) fluidity among realities is desirable (O'Hara & Anderson, 1991). How, then, might postmodern psychology comprehend Karen?

First, it would seek to understand Karen's *story* about her obesity—how she defines it, what issues she believes contributed to it, and which stories she believes might help her to modify her condition. For example, Karen might tell a kind of psychoanalytically oriented story about how she was abandoned as a child, how she rarely received validation, and how food was substituted for companionship (Roth, 1991, p. 178). She might then talk about the diets and weight-loss programs she'd failed and the deep sense of something missing in her life. Despite her fears, however, postmodernists are likely to respond to Karen with a sense of optimism at this point, a sense that many future stories are available to her and that she—with their guidance—can choose the one(s) that work.

The nagging and unanswered problem here, of course, lies in the criteria the postmodernists choose. Are resultant changes in Karen's symptomatology, for example, the factors that determine her "success;" or are the shifts in her subjective world? Are *intuitive narratives* (such as "message" dreams) worthy of the same attention as *intellectual narratives* (such as statistical judgments)? To whom or what can Karen turn in this menagerie?

One answer lies in the growing movement called *technical eclecticism* (Lazarus, Beutler, & Norcross, 1992). Briefly, this movement holds that the diversity of therapies can be unified by empirical means, or by extant studies of technical effectiveness. Review the literature on therapeutic outcome, technical eclecticists suggest, and you will discern the optimal strategies.

The problem with this standpoint, however, is that the therapeutic-outcome literature is dominated by the quantitative-experimental tradition and neglects or ignores the emerging phenomenological analyses of outcome (Gendlin, 1978; Mahrer, 1986). As a result, technical eclecticism tends to have a cognitive-behavioral bias, and existential (or experientially based) approaches receive short shrift (see Chapter 5 for an elaboration on this point).[1]

Let us return now to the foundational model we have been seeking and review our conclusions thus far. It is clear, first of all, that contemporary "schools" are effective in key areas and that their cultivation must be encouraged. It is equally clear that psychology is in disarray at present and that specialization is largely to blame. Physiological and cognitive-behavioral approaches *work,* for example, but to what ends— external adjustment, transient serenity? While such outcomes are important (and indeed crucial!) for some clients, are they the standards upon which to ground our entire field? Transpersonal and postmodernist approaches, likewise, are emancipatory, but are they attentive enough to our vulnerable and contingent sides—our creatureliness as well as saintliness?

As existentialists, we must (obviously) answer in the negative to these queries and press toward a more fruitful alternative. That existential psychology can provide such an alternative, we believe, is attested to by its *phenomenological* (experiential) data base; its freedom-limitation dialectic, and its challenge to people to fully engage that dialectic.

Furthermore, we believe that the other psychologies can thrive within this multidimensional frame. Physiological and cognitive-behavioral models, for example, can be understood as emancipatory transitions (or footholds) on the path to a broader liberation. Transpersonal and postmodernist (or eclectic) visions, conversely, can be seen as outermost facilitators of liberation which feed back to and bolster the cognitive-behavioral and physiological processes.

While we acknowledge that our conception may sound overly ambitious at points, it is urgent, we believe, to propose it; and we highly encourage an ongoing dialogue at these (integrative) levels.

Accordingly, let us attempt to animate our (existential-integrative) alternative and cast it into the marketplace of ideas.

First, we present the views of two clinical graduate students, who explore the role and challenges of existential psychology in academia. Next, in Part Three, we consider an existential-integrative framework of therapy, and we conclude with case applications that serve to elucidate this framework.

EXISTENTIAL PSYCHOLOGY FROM WITHIN THE TRAINING PROCESS

Ann Bassett-Short and Glenn A. Hammel
California School of Professional Psychology-Berkeley/Alameda

While the impact of existential psychology on mainstream graduate education has been minimal, there are signs—as this book makes plain—that a trend reversal may be occurring. Spearheading this trend reversal are the growing numbers of disaffected professionals that we have discussed. On a quieter, or grass-roots, level, however, a student-based rebellion appears to be coalescing. Aroused by psychology's cultural and theoretical diversity, these students seek commensurately interdisciplinary psychologies. Let us turn now to two graduate students who represent this emerging perspective and to the ground-level insights they offer us.

As clinical practicum and internship students will attest, training to be a psychotherapist is an undertaking of great proportions. Consider the following scene:

> Your first client is looking at you, waiting for a reply. You wonder to yourself how the two of you will build this new and untried relationship into one that could bear painful intensity and encourage this individual toward a life more intentional, spirited, and distinctly her or his own. Where do you start? You could go in a hundred different directions. Fragments of books, supervision sessions, classroom discussions, and experiences in your own life rush past you. Then you notice your client's eyes—their pain, hope, and fear—and you make your response. Later, you realize that you'll be starting over to some degree with each new client throughout your career. You hope for a day when you've become used to starting over.

When student clinicians find themselves disoriented in the therapy hour, it often has to do with the shifting nature of their beliefs about personality functioning, psychopathology, and the conduct of therapy. Students' efforts to find their clinical identities can certainly be furthered by exploring a theoretical orientation whose values seem especially consonant with their own. Schools of therapy, however, vary in their accessibility and usefulness to students. As we will describe below, we find that existential psychology speaks clearly to student concerns and offers considerable aid in meeting some of training's most difficult challenges.

We feel intimately familiar with the challenges of formal training in clinical psychology. We came to this writing when both of us were nearing the end of our doctoral programs in a freestanding school of professional psychology and were conducting our fifth year of supervised therapy in community settings. Although our education in psychology has been fairly mainstream (largely psychodynamic), we began supplementing our programs early in graduate school with study and supervision in existential psychology. Much of our impetus toward existentialism had to do with us as individuals, not with our being students per se. In fact, to imply that we could speak accurately about ourselves only as students would counter the basic existential assumption that humans are indivisible wholes. To emphasize the relevance existential psychology can have for those in training, however, we will restrict our focus here to issues with which students, in particular, wrestle.

What are these student challenges? One part of evolving professionally entails coming to terms with the extraordinary wealth of verbal and nonverbal information clients often present. Students must find a way to conceptualize what they witness and help the client stay oriented in what appear to be the most valuable directions. A complicating issue is that armed with the insights of graduate school, students too often apply their techniques and knowledge *to* clients instead of working *with* them in shared endeavors. For instance, theory can obscure one's clients if one applies it around them like scaffolding. Scaffolding does provide builders a secure place to stand when working in difficult places and gives architects the opportunity to view an emerging building from new angles. But a builder's rough scaffolding can easily camouflage and be mistaken for the intricate architecture it surrounds. Similarly, students erect theory around the client quickly—often automatically—when they are uncertain and hoping for a surer vantage point, as in the opening vignette. One of the most formidable challenges for beginning therapists, then, is to draw structure from a particular orientation without letting theory obscure the complex, unique individual in front of them.

Existential psychology can help with student concerns and challenges like these through four specific features: (1) a focus on the client's immediate experience, (2) an emphasis on the human capacity for choice, (3) an acknowledgment of the limits of action, and (4) an emphasis on phenomenological formulations.

A FOCUS ON THE CLIENT'S IMMEDIATE EXPERIENCE

One way in which the student can lose sight of the client as an individual is by giving too little attention to the client's immediate experiences. Students sometimes fail to notice subtle shifts, for example, in the client's emotional intensity, facial expressions, gestures, or the character of the individual's remarks in session. Missing these nuances means losing some of the person's most telling (and fleeting) disclosures. Conversely, attaining some fluency in the client's unique verbal and nonverbal "dialect" can be an important step in hastening the development of a solid therapeutic alliance.

Students can be distracted from this immediacy in many ways. We have already mentioned the danger of becoming preoccupied in session with one's academic knowledge of psychology. Students may also be preoccupied with the future: thinking, for instance, about how they will describe the session now in progress to their supervisor. Some students may also not yet be accustomed to working with a client in great emotional pain; they may find the individual's distress somewhat overwhelming and seek refuge in more emotionally muted explorations. One area that often falls in this category is exploration of the client's history. History gathering certainly has its place and, indeed, is often explicitly required by field placements.

Unfortunately, the temptation remains strong to collect the information from clients in ways that reduce clients' immediacy and increase their distance and detachment in session.

Training in existential psychology can help students with its consistent and overarching emphasis on immediacy. In fact, existential therapists emphasize that one does not need to fill in all the blanks about a client's past. Instead, one needs to *know* the client (May, 1958). Yalom (1980) adds that exploring deeply can mean thinking "not about the way one came to be the way one is, but *that* one is" (p. 11). If, during history gathering, one focuses on the individual who experienced the events—and who is experiencing something right now—one is much less likely to lose the person for the details. Lastly, existential psychology's demand that therapists remain attuned to their own ongoing, immediate experiences also encourages students to maintain a here-now focus in session.

AN EMPHASIS ON THE HUMAN CAPACITY FOR CHOICE

Another student challenge is to retain awareness of the client's capacity for choice. Clients, for instance, sometimes present their lives as intractably melancholic, downplaying their ability to effect change. Having participated in the therapeutic process comparatively few times (and perhaps having little confidence in their clinical abilities), students may believe such presentations too readily. Existential psychology, however, maintains a clear emphasis on the human capacity for a good measure of choice. Although not all levels of choice are conscious, as Yalom (1980) points out, individuals often have a larger range of choice than they perceive.

Ironically, the pressure to devalue a client's ability to choose sometimes comes from the field placement itself. Some settings, for example, attribute client responses primarily to transference and view this construct in a way that reduces client responsibility. The implication is that clients were driven to respond as they did by echoes of the past within their unconscious. The student's already heightened tendency to minimize the client's degree of choice is compounded when working in such settings.

The existential definition of *transference,* on the other hand, places more emphasis on the client's capacity to choose. May (1958) reminds his readers that constructs like transference draw considerable meaning from the client's immediate circumstances in the session. For May to hypothesize that a client is so demanding because s/he is trying to capture his or her father's love "may be a relief and may also be in fact true." But the crux of the matter, May continues, is that the client "is doing this to me in this given moment, and the reasons it occurs at this instant . . . are not exhausted by" how the client and father related (p. 83). In other words, earlier dynamics and displaced feelings cannot completely explain a client's motivations. The client is also motivated by more contemporary reasons. It may be true that this individual has somehow acquired a distorted way of interpreting and interacting with others, but more important is the fact that s/he *is right now using* that particular style. To some degree, May concludes, the client is choosing to act in that manner to a real person in that room at that minute.

AN ACKNOWLEDGMENT OF THE LIMITS OF ACTION

Amid all this accent on choice, however, it should not escape consideration that individuals also live within constraints. We suggested earlier that student therapists at times underestimate their clients' capacity for choice. This may in part reflect the very real, limiting circumstances with which their clients often struggle. Many students work in community mental health settings and see extremely low fee clients, some of whom live in conditions of poverty, homelessness, and intense discrimination. Many other students work in medical milieus where they witness the physical and social constraints placed on clients by disability or illness.

Theories that emphasize human potential without a concomitant focus on limitation may inadvertently lead students to blame clients for not changing their outward circumstances. Existential psychotherapists recognize and articulate the onerous press of one's social world. Seemingly hopeless and futile experiences like concentration-camp imprisonment and the mythical punishment of Sisyphus (Frankl, 1984; Camus, 1942/1955; May, 1991), for instance, occupy a sobering place in existential thought. Existentialists do not flinch from considering those instances where tangible choices of action are nearly absent.

Existential psychology goes further, though, and emphasizes the transformative power one possesses even in these outwardly hopeless predicaments. Individuals are still capable of choosing the meanings they ascribe to their situation, we are reminded. Writing of his own Nazi captivity, Frankl (1984) asserts that a person can be stripped of all "but one thing: the last of the human freedoms—to choose one's attitude in any given set of circumstances, to choose one's own way. . . . [in his case, to avoid being] molded into the form of the typical inmate" (p. 75). Refusing to relinquish this sort of choice in the face of constraint, an existentialist would argue, helps preserve the humanity of the human being.

Students working with clients in severely constrained external circumstances can thus be assured that their awareness of limitation will find expression in existential psychology. Importantly, it also acknowledges individuals' ability (at least inwardly) to transform their social world. This offers the student a realistic base on which to anchor clinical interventions and a way for both therapist and client to coax meaning from despair.

AN EMPHASIS ON PHENOMENOLOGICAL FORMULATIONS

We have said that part of the challenge of training involves tapping a theoretical orientation when conceptualizing one's clinical work without letting theory obscure the client. Advanced students are expected to use clinical theory in a thorough and formal manner that makes preserving a sense of the client's uniqueness all the more important. These students are frequently asked to integrate the available information about their clients and present "case formulations" in supervision and seminars. The presentations may entail explaining the nature of their clients' defenses, core conflicts, symptoms, level of functioning, personality structure, and diagnostic category.

This type of formulation encourages valuable reflection, but the therapist can slip into perceiving the dynamic and unfolding client in a static and self-fulfilling manner. One's client can become first a "case" and then a "category" ("borderline," for example). What follows from this clinical shorthand is the danger of replacing the individual with a construct ("borderlines tend to . . ."). Yet, to be effective guides, therapists obviously need a coherent understanding of their clients' problems and clear therapeutic strategies. They also need to be able to communicate the basis of their strategies to other clinicians.

An existential approach to formulating client problems and strengths does not ignore diagnostic evaluation or consideration of defenses and conflicts. However, existential formulations are based less on existing clinical and diagnostic categories than they are on the client's phenomenology. The approach emphasizes the personal experience of each client. One attempts to bring a fresh and relatively unbiased mind-set to a consideration of the individual's situation.

An existential psychotherapist might begin a formulation by considering questions of the following nature: What is this client's particular pain? How would the client evaluate her or his day-to-day living? What is getting in the client's way? In what ways is this client getting in her or his own way? How is the client right now treating us both? How am I experiencing this client? How well is the client able to notice her or his own reactions as well as those of others? This kind of reflection keeps the focus on the client and therapist in the moment and can thus be especially constructive for students. Creating and presenting formulations during training tends to be quite anxiety-provoking. The thought of evaluation is constant and can draw students away from therapeutic concerns into solely intellectual pursuits. Remaining committed to understanding and describing the client's world as she or he experiences it—even when formulating—helps students be sure they are focusing on the architecture, not the scaffolding.

We have mentioned only a few of the challenges students encounter in training to be psychotherapists. First of all, student clinicians must come to terms with the amount of information clients present and must work *with* the client instead of unilaterally applying interventions. Students often turn to a particular theoretical orientation in their training and receive valuable guidance and vantage points. However, they must resist letting theory impede their view of the client as a complex and unique individual. Students also face more specific challenges, like remaining attuned to the client's shifting verbal and nonverbal nuances, maintaining belief in the client's ability to effect change, recognizing a client's external constraints without despair, and formulating client material in ways that summarize without distorting.

As we discussed, existential psychology offers considerable help in meeting these challenges. It does so because of its emphasis on the client's immediate experiencing and its focus on our significant capacity for choice. Further, it distinguishes freedom of action from freedom of interpretation and takes a more phenomenologically based approach to formulation. Put simply, existential psychology anchors students to the individuality of their clients.

Thus far, we have restricted our comments to students in formal training. Yet to speak of the client as an individual is to recognize that therapy with her or him will be a novel experience and will require learning a new dialect. In this way, then, all clinicians are to some degree students and may find a number of their concerns addressed within existential psychology as well.

NOTE

1. The validity of so-called objective measures of psychological functioning (including those used in pre- and post-therapy studies) has cogently been called into question recently (see Shedler, Mayman, & Manis, 1993, for an elaboration.)

REFERENCES—RECENT AND FUTURE TRENDS

Beck, A. (1976). *Cognitive therapy and the emotional disorders.* New York: Signet.

Bernstein, R. (1986). *Philosophical profiles.* Philadelphia: University of Pennsylvania Press.

Camus, A. (1955). *The myth of Sisyphus and other essays* (J. O'Brien, Trans.). New York: Knopf. (Original work published 1942.)

Dass, R. (1992). *Compassion in action: Setting out on the path of service.* New York: Crown.

Ellis, A., & Yeager, R. (1989). *Why some therapies don't work: The dangers of transpersonal psychology.* Buffalo, NY: Prometheus.

Frankl, V. (1984). *Man's search for meaning: An introduction to logotherapy* (3d ed., I. Lasch, Trans., part 1). New York: Simon & Schuster.

Gendlin, E. (1978). *Focusing.* New York: Bantam.

Lazarus, A., Beutler, L., & Norcross, J. (1992). The future of technical eclecticism. *Psychotherapy, 29*(1), 11–20.

Mahrer, A. (1986). *Therapeutic experiencing: The process of change.* New York: Norton.

May, R. (1958). Contributions of existential psychology. In R. May, E. Angel, & H. Ellenberger (Eds.), *Existence: A new dimension in psychiatry and psychology* (pp. 37–91). New York: Basic Books.

May, R. (1967). *Psychology and the human dilemma.* New York: Van Nostrand.

May, R. (1981). *Freedom and destiny.* New York: Norton.

May, R. (1985). *My quest for beauty.* Dallas: Saybrook (distributed by Norton).

May, R. (1986). Transpersonal or transcendental? *Humanistic Psychologist, 14* (2), 87–90.

May, R. (1991). *The cry for myth.* New York: Norton.

O'Hara, M., & Anderson, W. (1991, September). Welcome to the postmodern world. *Networker,* 19–25.

Roth, G. (1991). *When food is love.* New York: Plume.

Schneider, K. (1987). The deified self: A "centaur" response to Wilber and the transpersonal movement. *Journal of Humanistic Psychology, 27*(2), 196–216.

Schneider, K. (1989). Infallibility is so damn appealing: A reply to Ken Wilber. *Journal of Humanistic Psychology, 29*(4), 470–481.

Schneider, K. (1990). The worship of food: An existential perspective. *Psychotherapy, 27*(1), 95–97.

Shedler, J., Mayman, M., & Manis, M. (1993). The *illusion* of mental health. *American Psychologist, 48*(11), 1117–1131.

Thompson, R. (1973). *Introduction to biopsychology.* San Francisco: Albion.

Wertz, F. (1993). Cognitive psychology: A phenomenological critique. *Journal of Theoretical and Philosophical Psychology, 13*(1), 2–24.

Wilber, K., Engler, J., & Brown, D. (1986). *Transformations of consciousness: Conventional and contemplative perspectives on development.* Boston: New Science Library.

Yalom, I. (1980). *Existential psychotherapy.* New York: Basic Books.

Zweig, C., & Abrams, J. (1991). *Meeting the shadow: The hidden power of human nature.* Los Angeles: Tarcher.

PART THREE

THERAPEUTIC APPLICATIONS OF EXISTENTIAL-INTEGRATIVE PSYCHOLOGY

CHAPTER 5

GUIDELINES FOR AN EXISTENTIAL-INTEGRATIVE (EI) APPROACH

The following is one way to conceptualize mainstream treatment strategies within an overarching existential framework.* The purpose for this endeavor is severalfold: to clarify what existential therapists do and how they do it; to broaden the treatment options of existential and mainstream therapists; and to elucidate the conditions under which certain treatment modalities will have optimal effects.

Far from being exhaustive or definitive, this approach is provisional. It is a preliminary set of guidelines based on my own theoretical and therapeutic synthesis (Schneider, 1990). For the purposes of this text, I have broadened this synthesis, integrated it with other therapies, and formalized its implications for practice.

The attempt to formulate an existential-integrative standpoint—although theoretically justified—has few (if any) precedents in the therapy literature (Beutler & Clarkin, 1990). It remains for future research, therefore—in particular that of the phenomenological variety—to assess and refine it.[1]

How the Chapter is Organized

To help readers navigate this lengthy chapter, we provide the following thumbnail sketch:

First, we set forth the theory of the existential-integrative (EI) approach—therapy as liberation strategies,[†] consciousness as liberation levels, and experiential consciousness as the culmination of those levels.

---

*Those wishing to apply this approach should have basic knowledge of clinical theory and practice and be appropriately trained or supervised.
[†]*Strategies* (which can also be viewed as "conditions" or "praxes") are to be understood, not as therapist-imposed solutions, but as catalysts to eventual client-based discoveries. As we shall see, this axiom holds for each of the liberation modalities, but it is especially salient where clients' responsibility for change is greatest—the experiential modality.

Second, we elaborate on the personality dynamics that characterize the experiential (and every other) level—the capacities to constrict, expand, and center oneself—and the functional and dysfunctional implications of those dynamics.

Third, we lay out the therapeutic guidelines implied by the theory—how to select appropriate liberation strategies, when to shift among liberation strategies, and how to move toward the experiential core of those strategies.

Fourth, we focus on the experiential liberation strategy itself—which has four intervention phases: (1) presence, (2) invoking the actual, (3) vivifying and confronting resistance, and (4) meaning-creation.

We conclude the chapter, finally, with summaries illustrating the experiential liberation strategy; a summary of the decision points leading up to (or away from) the experiential liberation strategy; and a set of skill-building exercises, designed to apply the experiential liberation strategy.

THEORY OF THE EXISTENTIAL-INTEGRATIVE (EI) APPROACH

Therapy as Liberation Strategies/Consciousness as Liberation Levels

The chief aim of existential-integrative therapy, as Rollo May (1981) succinctly put it, is "to set people free"—physically, cognitively, and emotionally (p. 19). For our purposes, *freedom* is the perceived capacity for choice within the natural and self-imposed limitations of living. These limitations include (but are not exhausted by) culture, genes, biology, and cosmic destiny, such as earthquakes (May, 1981). Now the great question, of course, is how to facilitate existential liberation and under what conditions?

Let us begin our inquiry by considering the following hypothetical position. Human experience (or *consciousness*) can be understood in terms of six (intertwining and overlapping) levels of freedom (see Figure 5-1): (1) the physiological, (2) the environmental, (3) the cognitive, (4) the psychosexual, (5) the interpersonal, and (6) the experiential (*being*). These levels (or *spheres*) of consciousness reflect increasing degrees of freedom within an ever-deepening domain. The outermost (physiological) level, for example, is a simpler and more restrictive manifestation of the environmental level; the environmental level is a simpler and more restrictive manifestation of the cognitive level; and so on.[2]

The range of freedom at any given level is a function of the domain that delineates that level. One's experience of physiological (or *organic*) freedom, for example, is delimited by one's ancestry, physical disposition, diet, exercise quota, substance use (e.g., drugs or alcohol), and other genetic and biochemical equivalents.

One's experience of environmental freedom is similarly delineated by classical and operant conditioning phenomena (see Skinner, 1953; Wolpe, 1969). To the degree that one can manipulate conditioned and unconditioned stimuli (as in desensitization and graded-exposure procedures) or positive and negative reinforcement contingencies (as in reward and avoidance stratagems), one can attain measurable, observable environmental mastery. An example might be rewarding oneself with a vacation for keeping up a high grade average.

Cognitive freedom is demarcated by the principles of logic and rational thought (Beck, 1976; Ellis, 1962). One experiences freedom here to the extent that one can

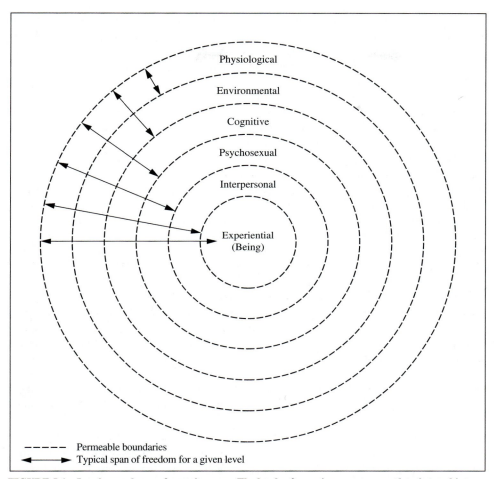

FIGURE 5-1   **Levels or spheres of consciousness. The levels of consciousness are overlapping and inter-twined; the differences among them are a matter of emphasis.**

identify maladaptive schemas (e.g., beliefs, assumptions, and self-statements); change those schemas through practice; and adopt new schemas based on rational and objective evidence. Some of the strategies one might use to bring about this level of liberation are rational restructuring, positive reframing, social modeling, thought stopping, thought rehearsal, and guided visualization. Using one of these strategies might bring about the recognition that one is not a worthless or hopeless person just because of an unsuccessful conversation with a potential romantic partner, for example.

Until now, we have considered relatively conscious, measurable, observable forms of psychophysiological* liberation. We have considered choice at the level of bio-

---

*Unless otherwise indicated, the *holistic* (complex, ambiguous, and intertwining) nature of terms such as *psychophysiological* is always implied (see Merleau-Ponty, 1962, for an elaboration).

chemistry, environmental manipulation, and specifiable thought processes. Now, we will shift our emphasis to comparatively subconscious, nonquantifiable psychophysiological experiences. These experiences are posited to underlie and sometimes subvert the above physiological, environmental, and cognitive levels of freedom (May, 1958; Schneider, 1990).

Freedom at the level of psychosexuality, for example, entails clarification and integration of one's sexual-aggressive past; to the degree that this is not accomplished, one is considered pathogenically vulnerable (Freud, 1963). Liberation at this level means the strengthening of the ego—the capacity to maximize instinct gratification (sexual-aggressive expressiveness) while minimizing a sense of punishment and guilt (super-ego repressiveness). Imbalances either toward overgratification or repression are considered compulsive and therefore unfree. Psychosexual liberation is facilitated by the psychoanalytic techniques of free association, interpretation of the resistances and transference, intellectual insight, and dream interpretation. The emphasis here is on a cognitive understanding of the relationship between present relationships and past psychosexual conflicts. The therapist serves as a surrogate parent here, clarifying and correcting the client's distorted psychosexual reminiscences. For example, the therapist would help the client understand how the childhood dread of castration might manifest itself as an adult fear of assertiveness.

Freedom at the level of interpersonal relations (such as that illustrated by self psychology) both acknowledges and transcends freedom at the level of psychosexual relations (Kohut, 1977). The operative dimensions here are interpersonal attachment and separation, not merely drives and social prohibitions. Freedom at the interpersonal level balances individual striving and uniqueness with interpersonal dependence and connectedness. Although interpersonal liberation also stresses the understanding of early childhood dynamics, the specific components of those dynamics differ from the components of psychosexual liberation. They include (but are not limited to) desires for and frustrations with affection, nurturance, validation, encouragement, and social/moral direction. Interpersonal liberation is facilitated not only by intellectual insight but by re-experiencing the past in the present. The therapist-client relationship is the vehicle for this reexperience, and current separation-attachment issues are focused upon. With time and an appropriately corrective therapeutic experience, the client comes to value her capacity both for separateness and for relatedness, and is markedly less coerced by either position. For example, she might re-experience early nurturance deficits and work through the resultant fears, frustrations, and overcompensations associated with this damage.

Forming the core of our spectrum, finally, is what I term *experiential freedom,* which might also be called *being level* or *ontological freedom.* Experiential liberation embraces not only physiology, environmental conditioning, cognition, psychosexuality, and interpersonal relations, but also cosmic or intersituational relations—the whole human being as far as possible (Merleau-Ponty, 1962). Experiential liberation is intersituational in that it pertains, not merely to this or that content or period of one's life, but to the preverbal/kinesthetic awarenesses that underlie contents or periods of one's life. Experiential liberation is affect-centered and best described by metaphors, works of art, and literary allusions. (Consider, for example, the expressionistic style of Vincent van Gogh, the descriptive richness of F. Scott Fitzgerald, or the symbolic profundity of a Hitchcock film.) Experiential liberation compares favorably to Merleau-Ponty's (1962) "body-subject," Wilhelm Reich's (1949) "bioenergy," and Morris Berman's (1989) "kinesthetic awareness." Each is centered in the body, and each attends to the relatively nonmediated consciousness that radiates through the body.[3] Experiential liberation, finally, is also client-centered—derivative of and pertinent to the client's own particular struggles. This is not to say that the therapist's and society's concerns are dismissed in experiential liberation. Unquestionably, they cannot be dismissed and should be raised responsibly in the course of therapy. However, the ultimate criteria for experiential liberation reside in clients' awarenesses, and it is they who must live with the consequences of those criteria.

To elaborate, experiential liberation is distinguished by four intertwining and overlapping dimensions: (1) the immediate, (2) the kinesthetic, (3) the affective, and (4) the profound, or cosmic. These dimensions form the ground, or horizon, within which each of the aforementioned liberation strategies operate, and they are the context for at least one more clinically significant set of structures. These are, according to phenomenological research, the capacities to constrict, expand, and center one's energies and experiences (Becker, 1973; Binswanger, 1975; Keleman, 1985; Laing, 1969; May, 1969, 1981; Schneider, 1990, 1993). *Expansion* is the perception of bursting forth and extending psychophysiologically; *constriction* is the perception of drawing back and confining psychophysiologically.* Expansion is associated with a sense of gaining, enlarging, dispersing, ascending, filling, accelerating, or, in short, *increasing* psychophysiological options. Constriction, on the other hand, is signified by the perception of retreating, diminishing, isolating, falling, emptying, slowing, or, in short, *reducing* psychophysiological options. *Centering,* finally, is the capacity to be aware of and to direct one's constrictive or expansive possibilities.

Constriction and expansion lie along a potentially infinite continuum, only degrees of which are conscious. Constrictive or expansive dream fantasies (for example, ones in which humiliation or vengeance play a role) may be *sub*conscious. The further one pursues constriction, the closer one gets to a sense of being "wiped away," obliterated. The further one pursues expansion, the closer one gets to an equally excessive perception of "exploding," entering chaotic nonentity (Laing, 1969). (I use the prefix *hyper-* with *constriction* or *expansion* to designate the dysfunctional or unmanageable engagement of either polarity). *Dread* of constriction or expansion (due mainly to past trauma) fosters extreme or dysfunctional counterreactions to those polarities. This sets up a situation where, for example, expansive grandiosity becomes an escape from, or a counterreaction to, the constrictive belittlement one experienced as a child; or constrictive rigidity becomes an avoidance of the expansive disarray and confusion one experienced in a natural disaster. Confrontation with the constrictive

---

*Although *expansion* is often associated with *freedom* and *constriction* with *limits,* they are not always synonymous terms. Restraint, focus, and discipline, for example, can be freeing in some contexts; conversely, activism, assertion, and audacity can be limiting (e.g., when compulsively engaged). In the balance of this text, therefore, freedom and limitation are viewed primarily as *contexts* for constriction and expansion, and not their conceptual equivalents.

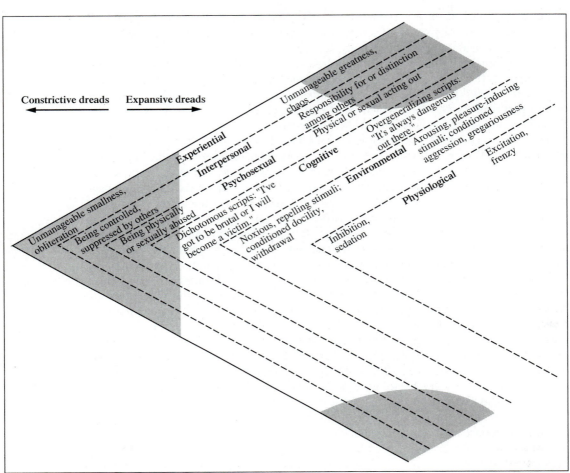

FIGURE 5-2   Levels of consciousness and associated dreads (cross-section of Figure 5-1). These are just a few examples of the dreads (and sometimes fascinations) that can be associated with each of the levels. Shaded sections pertain to regions that many people experience symbolically and subconsciously.

or expansive dreads, on the other hand, can promote renewed capacities to experience the world (e.g., from a standpoint of humility for the grandiose client or from the standpoint of spontaneity for the rigid client).

These two polar eventualities—chaos and obliteration, greatness and smallness—haunt the entire spectrum of freedoms (see Figure 5-2).* They constitute both the dreads and the possibilities underlying physiological elation (arousal) and inhibition (tranquility), conditioned recklessness (conduct disorders) and withdrawal (phobias),

---

*There is an intimate connection, it seems, between our most gripping anxieties (e.g., greatness, smallness) and the primordial forces of the universe (e.g., the "Big Bang")—and the reports of clients confirm it (Schneider, 1990, 1993).

cognitive exaggeration (overgeneralization) and rigidity (dichotomous thinking), gluttony (promiscuity) and psychosexual austerity (abstinence), and separation (estrangement) and interpersonal attachment (dependency).

Experiential liberation is facilitated by careful and sensitive therapeutic invitations to *stay present to* (explore) denied constrictive or expansive parts of oneself. The more these parts manifest anxiety (as opposed to intellectual or detached content), the closer they are purported to be to core constrictive or expansive injuries. The gradual integration of this (preverbal/kinesthetic) material and the sense that one can survive its chaotic or obliterating implications promotes health, vitality, and an enhanced appreciation for spiritual dimensions (e.g., awe, wonder, and connectedness with the cosmos). Although experiential liberation can help to open up extraordinary ranges of possibility, it is not purported to dissolve all conflict or puzzlements. To the contrary, it accepts the dialectical condition *between* self and not-self, freedom and limits, and helps clients to find *optimal* rather than consummate meanings (Bugental, 1987; May, 1981; Schneider, 1987, 1989). The implication here is that although there are always more possibilities for constrictive or expansive encounters, we can't always reach or bear them. It is enough, at this level, to emancipate key blocks and anxieties, to, for example, overcome one's timid, reticent disposition by confronting one's deepest revulsions to brazenness.

Constriction (Smallness) and Expansion (Greatness) as Omnipresent Horizons

Abraham Maslow (1967) once observed that we fear our greatness as well as our lowliness, and this is precisely the core dilemma, from the existential-integrative standpoint. As we have suggested, the fears of both constriction and expansion (or their clinically useful synonyms, *smallness* and *greatness*) haunt the entire spectrum of existential freedoms. They are the keys, moreover, to a full existential restoration. Before considering the clinical consequences of these contentions, however, let us attempt to formalize what we have proposed thus far.

1. The human psyche (*consciousness*) is characterized by a constrictive-expansive continuum, only degrees of which are conscious. For the purposes of our existential-integrative framework, we consider six positions along this continuum: (a) the physiological, (b) the environmental, (c) the cognitive, (d) the psychosexual, (e) the interpersonal, and (f) the experiential (*being*). Whereas physiological, environmental, and cognitive positions along the continuum are dominated by conscious processing, psychosexual, interpersonal, and experiential modalities are accented by pre- and sub-conscious mediation.

2. Dread of constrictive or expansive polarities promotes dysfunction, extremism, or polarization, the degree and frequency of which is generally proportional to the degree and frequency of one's dread. Put another way, one will do everything one can, including becoming extreme and destructive oneself, to avoid the constrictive or expansive polarity that one dreads. The dread of physiological expansion (*arousal*), for example, can promote extreme or dysfunctional measures to constrict (*tranquilize*) oneself. The conditioned fear of enclosures (constriction) can foster excessive efforts to enlarge or expand one's surroundings. The dread of cat-

astrophic (expansive) cognitions can associate with narrow, regimented cognitions. The revulsion for a constricted puritanical upbringing can correlate with an indulgent, expansive adulthood. The horror of a directionless, rootless upbringing, on the other hand, can generate absolutist and fundamentalist tendencies later in life. The terror of being ontologically and cosmically dismissed (*obliterated*), finally, can lead to desperate psychophysiological efforts to manifest ontologically, to be all-important (which too often, tragically, leads back again to the impoverished position because aspirations of the former magnitude cannot be borne for long; consider, for example, the experiential swings of the manic-depressive or borderline personality). (See Table 5-1 for an elaboration on these dreads.)

Developmental View

Although the dread of (and compensation for) constrictive/expansive polarities can be seen at every existential level and is integral to the respective liberation of every level, its genesis is far from uniform. Constrictive or expansive dread can arise in a wide variety of spatial, temporal, and dispositional contexts. Let us consider several of the main ones here—acute, chronic, and implicit traumas (Schneider, 1990).

Acute trauma is the perception of an event as immediately contrary and shocking. It is an existential jolt that produces extreme fear. When a child falls ill, for example, a profound alteration in mobility may be experienced. If this alteration is powerful enough, it can alarm the child, not merely at the level of physiology (pleasure-pain) but at the level of her "groundedness" in the world. It may associate with mortal fears of diminishment, minimization, imperceptibility, and perhaps even dissolution. The intensity of the child's fear is a function of many factors, including (but not limited to) her original psychophysiological disposition (i.e., her hardiness level), the severity of her illness, the cultural and familial contexts in which she contracts the illness, and so on. Discrepancy is the key here. The greater she experiences a discrepancy between her original disposition and subsequent events, the greater is the likelihood that she will deny those subsequent events and hence become experientially debilitated. Such debilitation is likely to manifest itself initially in the form of excessive efforts to expand (e.g., cry out, refuse, defy) her condition of growing immobilization. If these protestations prove comparatively viable, she will be able to maintain her denial of smallness and live out her life in a variety of compensatory fashions. Depending on the severity and subsequent handling of her trauma, accordingly, she is likely to exhibit a range of expansionist traits, from exuberance and feistiness to outright belligerence and imperiousness.

If, on the other hand, the child's attempts to deny her illness are repeatedly and unabatingly rebuffed, then another traumatic cycle may develop—the cycle of *chronic trauma*. Whereas acute trauma focuses on the original dread of constricting (i.e., of becoming immobilized), chronic trauma centers on the counteraction of that dread (fruitless and repeated efforts to become mobilized, expand). The result of this shift is a complete reversal of the original situation. Instead of denying and overcompensating for psychophysiological smallness, the client now does everything she can to render herself small and to avoid psychophysiological greatness.

TABLE 5-1
Some Psychiatric Disorders and Their Associated Dreads*

Hyperconstrictive dysfunctions and the dread of ultimate expansion (greatness, chaos)

Disorder	Dread
Depression	Assertion, stimulation, ambition, standing out, possibility.
Dependency	Autonomy, venturing out on one's own, unmanageable responsibility.
Anxiety	Potency and its associated risks, responsibilities, and strains. Also "foolishness," spontaneity, and unpredictability.
Agoraphobia	Open places, conflict, and confusion.
Obsessive-compulsiveness	Experimentation, surprise, confusion and complexity, disarray, recklessness.
Paranoia	Trusting, reaching out, the confusion, complexity, and brutality of relationships.
Depressant substance abuse (e.g., Valium, alcohol[†])	All of the above

Hyperexpansive dysfunctions and the dread of ultimate constriction (smallness, obliteration)

Mania	Confinement, limitation, delay of impulses, devitalization.
Anti-social personality	Vulnerability, weakness, victimization.
Hysteria	Rejection, insignificance.
Narcissism	Inadequacy, unworthiness, impotence.
Impulsiveness	Regimentation, routine, emptiness.
Claustrophobia	Entrapment, tight or closed places.
Stimulant substance abuse (e.g., speed, cocaine)	All of the above.

Hyperconstrictive/expansive blends

Passive-aggressivity	Belittlement, on the one hand, and, on the other, the rage or fury that results from that dread. (The combination produces such blunted aggression as sarcasm and dawdling.)
Borderline personality	Extreme belittlement, insignificance combined with extreme rage, fury (which leads to both fusion, tyranny and isolation, withdrawal).
Manic depression	Confinement, limitation, and delay on the one hand, and assertion, stimulation, and ambition on the other.
Schizophrenia	Vaporizing (which may lead to disorganized, omnipotence-striving states) and exploding (which may foster obsessive, catatonic-like qualities). Schizophrenia associates with constrictive and expansive dreads in their most radical forms.

*The relationship between the above clinical syndromes and the dreads which may give rise to them is theoretical and provisional. It is based on a small but intriguing body of clinical data, which implicates both temperament and psychological trauma (Schneider, 1990). It remains for future research—especially of a phenomenological nature—to reconsider the soundness of these postulates.
†While alcohol is a depressant, it can also, paradoxically, serve to stimulate (*hyperexpand*) via its disinhibiting properties.

There is yet a third scenario for developing constrictive or expansive trauma. This is the subtler cycle of intergenerational, or implicit, trauma [see the "family systems" literature (e.g., McGoldrick & Gerson, 1985) for a fuller discussion of this cycle]. *Implicit trauma* is the indirect, vicariously transmitted trauma of family and caretakers. Unlike acute and chronic trauma, implicit trauma is never directly experienced by the affected individuals but is learned, accepted, and stored in their memories. While the basis for implicit trauma is relatively obscure, both initial disposition and modeling appear to play instrumental roles. The implicit-traumatic sequence goes something like this: A family member, say our hypothetical client, experiences acute or chronic trauma. Her trauma (i.e., her fear of immobility) leads, in turn, to compensatory behavior (such as overachieving) designed to thwart the precipitating injury. As this cycle solidifies in our client's personal life, it also begins to filter into her relationships with her children. It is at this point, predictably, that her children develop a risk for implicit trauma. For this to occur, however, two basic conditions must be met: (1) the children must idealize, and thereby strive to emulate, their mother's excesses, and (2) they must display inherent dispositions (e.g., ambitiousness) that comfortably conform to these excesses. Given these prime conditions, accordingly, immobility and smallness can prove far-ranging intergenerational enemies, unwittingly internalized and unknowingly transmitted. Only the broken-hearted casualties, such as those who are *not* superachievers, can begin to unravel the contagion (Schneider, 1990). Table 5-2 summarizes the three traumatic cycles.

The operation of the above traumas, it may be evident by now, is confined neither to period nor place, type of polarization (i.e., constrictive/expansive), nor existential

TABLE 5-2
Purported Operation of Three Traumatic Cycles

Type of trauma	Subject's disposition	Perceived environmental demand	Purported psychological effect on subject
Acute	Constrictive	Expansive	$\uparrow^{\dagger}$Constriction
	Expansive	Constrictive	$\uparrow$ Expansion
	Neutral*	Expansive	$\uparrow$ Constriction
	Neutral	Constrictive	$\uparrow$ Expansion
Chronic	Constrictive	Expansive	$\uparrow$ Expansion
	Expansive	Constrictive	$\uparrow$ Constriction
	Neutral	Expansive	$\uparrow$ Expansion
	Neutral	Constrictive	$\uparrow$ Constriction
Implicit	Constrictive	Constrictive	$\uparrow$ /= ‡ Constriction
	Expansive	Expansive	$\uparrow$ /= Expansion

*NEUTRAL means relatively nonpolarized.
$^{\dagger}\uparrow$ means increased constriction or expansion relative to one's disposition.
$^{\ddagger}\uparrow$ /= means about the same or an increased degree of constriction or expansion relative to one's disposition.
Source: Schneider, K. J. (1990). *The paradoxical self: Toward an understanding of our contradictory nature,* p. 85. New York: Plenum, 1990.

level (e.g., physiological). Although childhood, because of its comparative vulnerability, is more susceptible to traumatic impacts, such impacts are not restricted to childhood. Trauma originates, not in relation to parents, peers, or any other stimulus per se, but in relation to being, to the groundlessness that is our condition. Hence it is not so much the specific content of the abuse or pain that unnerves us so, but the implications of that content for our being in the world, for our relationship to the universe. It is in this sense that physical and emotional shocks, parents, family myths, and so on symbolize wider networks of alarm—our smallness or greatness before creation itself.

The third principle that has emerged from our existential-integrative formulation is that the *confrontation with* or integration of constrictive/expansive polarities promotes healing, vitality, and health. This principle also operates at various levels of freedom and can best be understood in terms of these levels. For example, constricting lethargy can be dealt with by nutritional regimens designed to release and expand energy. Expansive criminality can be environmentally modified to constrict via aversive and alternative reinforcements. Constrictive timidity, conversely, can be environmentally conditioned to expand (e.g., by confronting the object of dread). Rigid belief systems can be rationally restructured into expansive, adaptive belief systems. Sexually expansive adult behavior can be explained on the basis of sexually constrictive (or expansive) childhood behavior and thus rechanneled. Compulsive isolation (and constricting) can be explained and transcended through emotionally corrective bonding (and expanding). By facing and experiencing one's frailty, finally, one can learn to understand and transform one's pomposity.

Through these means, then, choice and the capacity for genuine self-encounter broaden while denial and overcompensation shrink. Far from associating with injuries, moreover, smallness and greatness begin associating with growth opportunities. For example, humility can replace docility, discipline can replace obsessiveness, and zest can replace inflation.

Now that we have considered the basic theoretical dynamics of existential-integrative therapy, it is time to put the picture together. It is time to reflect upon the implications of our purview for assessing which treatment, under what conditions, can optimally liberate which existential maladies.

THERAPEUTIC IMPLICATIONS OF THE THEORY

The quest for existential liberation may seem a bit hazy at first—like Dante's quest for Beatrice or Sisyphus' quest for happiness. Yet existential-integration, as I have intimated, provides an organizing principle for this haze (an organizing principle for pluralism, I like to say) and can guide us on our elusive journey.

How to Select Appropriate Liberation Strategies

The *client's desire and capacity for change* are the initial, and foremost, existential-integrative selection criteria.[4] How does the therapist gauge this desire and capacity in the client? First, she needs to explore what it is the client *wants*. What are his short-term objectives and his long-term goals? Is he here to eliminate a particular symptom, such as a simple phobia? Or is he here to deal with complex personality issues, such as depression, anxiety, or hostility?

Next, the therapist needs to reflect on the client's *capacity* to liberate his life. Does he have the intellectual skills to sort through and grasp his dysfunction? Is he emotionally ready for intensive self-exploration? Does he have the ability to deliberate upon and pause over his concerns? To what extent is he delimited by cultural, financial, or geographical concerns?

These lines of inquiry appear straightforward enough, but they are subtler (and more challenging) than they seem. How many clients, for example, present one set of issues upon intake only to alter their story three or four sessions later? Or how many clients state one concern (e.g., anger at a spouse) but imply another issue (e.g., damaged self-esteem)? As noted existential therapist James Bugental observed, one must do more than listen for words; one must hear the "music" behind those words (see also Reik, 1948). The EI therapist, similarly, must attune herself to more than clients' stated reasons—also to their implied and evolving reasons for treatment. To be sure, there are many potential pitfalls in this approach (such as misreading clients' interests). But there are even greater risks in *refraining* from such a course, risks ranging from shortchanging to prematurely aborting the therapeutic project (Bugental & Bracke, 1992).

I take issue with conventional therapeutic integrationists (e.g., Beutler & Clarkin, 1990) who base their treatment decisions on overridingly statistical (and traditionally diagnostic) grounds. While it is true that depth therapists can make "unnecessarily complicated" judgments about clients, as Beutler and Clarkin suggested, it is also true that symptom-oriented therapists can make unwarrantedly facile and restricted therapeutic assessments (see for example, discussions of this problem by May, 1983, and Wolfe, 1992). The EI antidote for these equally undesirable alternatives is to cultivate what Rollo May (1992) calls "therapeutic wonder." *Therapeutic wonder* accepts the need for conventional, experimentally driven assessments, *but only in the context of kinesthetic and intuitive checks* against those assessments. This means that surface impressions about clients are taken seriously and get significant consideration when planning treatment. However—and this is where EI therapy can complement conventional integrationist approaches—supreme consideration is accorded to therapists' *lived* engagement with clients and to the latent possibilities therein.

For example, if a client presents with an ostensibly simple symptom, such as cowering before her boss, an EI therapist would (1) assess the client's singleness of purpose toward this problem; (2) assess her capacity to therapeutically address this purpose; (3) begin opening experientially to the client's own experiential communication (e.g., lability, touchiness around other issues, and so on); and (4) stand *ready* to invite or gently challenge the client to deeper spheres of liberation.*

Most often, in my experience, this sequence of evaluative criteria helps therapists and clients to make substantive, relevant treatment decisions. Usually these decisions

---

*It is extremely important, it seems to me, to be continually open to (and at appropriate times "test the water" for) new levels of depth in our contacts with clients. The fruit that such readinesses can yield—in even the least-likely clinical circumstances—is perpetually astonishing to me.

favor broad rather than narrow-band treatment strategies (e.g., psychodynamic and behavioral as opposed to behavioral techniques only) to achieve their intended effects. (This is not always the case, however, and integrative approaches become relatively superfluous at such times.)

On the pages to follow, accordingly, we will focus on the decision to use broad-band approaches to treatment. Our special emphasis, of course, will be on the existential core of those approaches—the *being,* or experiential, level—and the primary offerings of that domain. Before we turn to this level, however, it is necessary to examine the use of relatively nonexperiential (that is, conscious/programmatic/verbal strategies) as they are understood within the EI framework.

Use of Nonexperiential Liberation Strategies

Part of the therapeutic liberator's task is to recognize when curtailments are called for—nonexperiential footholds along the rigorous journey within. These footholds (which are typified by physiological, behavioral, and cognitive treatment modalities) can serve a variety of purposes. They can contain clients' distress, elevate their motivation, and ready them for deeper self-contact. Let us look more closely at these purposes in a range of clinical situations.

Clients in Acute Crisis   When clients are emotionally overcome, when they are contemplating suicide, or when they are physically acting out, concrete, narrow-band liberation strategies are often the optimal therapeutic choice. Interventions such as supportive reassurance, safety containment, behavioral contracting, meditative exercises, cognitive restructuring, and medication or hospitalization may be the most helpful immediate steps. Although these steps are transitional within the EI framework, they can provide timely and productive reprieves.

During Early Stages of Therapy   Another period during which nonexperiential footholds are advisable is at the outset of treatment. Reframing confusing or fragmentary material, for example, can help beginning clients acquire the patience necessary to address that material. For example, the therapist might say, "Your father just died, you just graduated from college, and your girlfriend has abandoned you for another man. It's no wonder you're feeling rocky." Homework assignments such as simple breathing exercises or positive visualizations can provide a soothing margin of safety in anticipation of intensive self-confrontation. I have found that counting breaths (1 to 10 and back down again) and visualizing temporary "storage bins" for troubling issues can be especially useful at these early stages.

Frequently, cognitive-behavioral techniques can provide a fertile opening for more experientially oriented interventions. Suggesting habit changes for compulsive eaters, for example, can be readily followed up with experiential questions and concerns. These questions might include, "What feelings does it bring up for you to eliminate junk foods from your diet?" "In what way is that reward you give yourself dissatisfying?" "What kinds of feelings come up when you cannot follow the grocery route we designed?" Cognitive restructuring can also stimulate experiential inquiry. For example, the therapist might say, "You asked *one* person on *one* day if he might be interested in getting together with you. What makes it so hard for you to try again?" Or "There you go again, portraying yourself as unredeemably terrible. How do you feel that in your body? What kind of images do those sensations bring up?" The *failure* of cognitive techniques can further stimulate experiential inquiries such as, "What's going on that you can no longer make positive statements toward yourself?" The therapist might also suggest: "Instead of attending to what is *reasonable,* let's look at what you *want* to do right now."

Fragile or Highly Suspicious Clients   It is best to use explicit, low-pressure questions and suggestions when dealing with clients with extremely low self-esteem and tendencies toward paranoia. The most important initial task with such clients is to draw upon the aforementioned modalities to build an alliance. For example, simple, manageable tasks—making a call to a friend, reframing a catastrophic thought, structuring the week's activities—can contribute to the comfort level and effectiveness of the relationship. Although progress is likely to be slow, this safety net can help fragile and suspicious clients to stabilize, and increasingly to tolerate exploration.

Intellectually or Culturally Unprepared Clients   When clients are intellectually or neurologically limited, or when their cultures discourage experiential contact, the most pertinent liberation strategies may be nonexperiential. Such approaches as behavioral shaping, social modeling, and cognitive restructuring may make substantive headway with these clients.

The prospect of *experiential* deepening, on the other hand, should not be discounted. I have found with mentally retarded clients, for example, that relative to the warmth, safety, and genuine disclosures between us, technical achievements, such as instilling good grooming habits, simply do not measure up. Culturally distant clients, similarly, can sometimes achieve intimacy in facilitative settings. It is important that the therapist be *ready* for such engagements—or informative about their availability.

Now let us turn to the use of broader-band semi-experiential interventions within the EI framework. These include, but are not limited to, psychosexual and interpersonal approaches which, while possessing experiential elements, primarily situate those elements within verbal and historical domains.

Use of Semi-experiential Liberation Strategies

An experiential moment, it will be recalled, is characterized by immediate, kinesthetic, affect-laden, and profound or cosmic dimensions. While traditional psychosexual approaches, such as psychoanalysis, recognize these dimensions, they tend to do so peripherally (or, at best, reservedly). Emotion, for example, is subordinated to ego-dominated understanding in psychoanalytically oriented strategies. Although interpersonal approaches (e.g., self psychology) accord a more central role to emotions, therapist-based explanations and historical references tend to truncate this role.[5]

For these reasons, then, psychosexual and interpersonal therapeutic orientations can be called *semi-experiential.* They incorporate but don't quite ground themselves on experiential dimensions. Despite their qualified status, however, semi-experiential treatment strategies can be both illuminating and pivotal for our purposes. Below, we consider the use of such strategies within the EI framework.

When Childhood Sexual Issues Emerge   When clients imply or refer specifically to childhood sexual concerns, traditionally psychoanalytic techniques, such as free association, genetic clarification, and tie-in with the transference, can be of significant initial value (Freud, 1963). Beyond helping clients to understand and re-experience their sexual injuries, however, it is frequently beneficial to invite them into the ontological domains that are purported to underlie those injuries. I use the term *frequently* here because some clients (due either to capacity or desire) intractably resist these ontological domains and are therefore immaterial within the EI context. For those clients who accept the ontological challenge, however, a wide range of experiential strategies is in order. Each of these strategies is designed to enhance the immediate, kinesthetic, affect-laden, and profound or cosmic dimensions of the (aforementioned) material. Discussions of childhood traumas, for example, can be followed up by "here-and-now" explorations of the sensations, images, and feelings unearthed in these discussions. Angry or hurtful reminiscences can be accompanied by role-plays or dialogues aimed at redressing those reminiscences. A hate-filled son, for example, can rehearse or role-play what he would like to say to his father. Drawing upon the same format, a sexually molested daughter can reassess (and perhaps even reverse) her original response to her assailant (Mahrer, 1983).

Transference interpretations can also be supplemented by here-and-now explorations. Attention to the client's *experience* of the interpretation, for example, can help the client verify its accuracy. For example, if the interpretation fails to kinesthetically resonate with the client, it may be fallacious and require further clarification. If the interpretation does resonate, on the other hand, it affords the client a chance to become aware of the affect that underlies and informs his reactions. Such questions as "What are you experiencing right now?" or "How does what I say *feel* to you?" can be effective postinterpretive material.

Free association, finally, can also be complemented by experiential considerations. The awareness of affect and body sensations, for example, can amplify that which is presented verbally. Relevant (or *focused*) free associating, moreover, may be more effective than nondirected, random free associating. In order to be experiential, concludes Bugental (1987), free association (or what he terms "concern-guided searching") must meet these conditions.

> (a) The patient must identify a life issue which he wishes to explore more deeply and fully and describe it to the therapist completely—and often, repeatedly; (b) The patient must be as deeply immersed as possible while carrying out this description . . . . , (c) The patient must maintain an expectancy of discovery, a readiness to be surprised. (Bugental, 1987, p. 167)

When Childhood Interpersonal Issues Emerge   When clients imply or refer specifically to early-childhood relationship deficits (e.g., parental neglect or abuse), the self-psychological use of empathy, explanation, and "optimal frustration" may be in order (Kohut, 1977). Therapeutic empathy, for example, can help restore clients' dignity, encourage their self-explorations, and strengthen their capacities to trust; childhood-based explanations can help clients make sense of (and intellectually contain) their difficulties. Drawing upon both explanation and empathy, finally, optimal frustration embraces the *living* (internal and external) therapeutic relationship. There are four basic components to optimal frustration: (1) repeated and inevitable disruptions of the therapeutic bond (e.g., therapists' decisions to take vacations at certain periods); (2) clients' dysfunctional responses to those disruptions (e.g., rage, anxiety); (3) therapists' empathic and rejuvenating alternative responses to the disruptions (e.g., consistency of support, clarity of explanations); and (4) re-establishment of the therapeutic bond (restoration of the external relationship and reparation of the internal, "self-object" relationship) as a result of the above responses.

While these moderately experiential procedures have been shown to be of significant ameliorative value, several EI accompaniments may markedly enhance that value. For example, empathic bonding—which has overtones of passivity—can be complemented by empathic challenging—which has suggestions of activation, engagement, and mobilization. Such challenges can help clients *experience* their childhood recollections as well as report on them. In addition to sharing with clients that a given memory "may be very difficult for you," for example, therapists can pursue more experiential lines of inquiry, such as, "What are you experiencing in your body right now?" "What other images are associated with that sensation?" "What would you like to say to your mother if she were right here in the room with you?" Timed appropriately, these challenges can accelerate growth processes *in between* periods of optimal frustration and transference.

Once the optimal-frustration period begins, therapists can continue intensifying their experiential challenges. They can deepen the impact of transference explanations, for example, by exploring clients' experiential resonance to those explanations. The therapeutic sequence might go something like this:

> *T (therapist):* You're upset with me because I failed to hear how upsetting my vacation was for you.
> *C (client):* That's right. You don't have the greatest timing, do you?
> *T:* Your father didn't have the greatest timing when he left you alone with your sick mother for all those months either, did he?
> *C: (Winces—tears well up.)*
> *T (warmly, sympathetically):* That struck a chord, didn't it?
> *C:* You could say that.

Let us break off here a moment and consider the critical juncture the therapist has reached. On the one hand, he could pursue his client's developmental history and reminiscences about feeling abandoned. On the other hand, he could go in a more experiential direction. For example, what would happen if the thrust of his inquiry were not so much geared to the "why" and more to the "what" of his client's experience? The possible results are exhibited as follows:

T: See if you can stay with that chord a moment, Joe. Where do you feel it in your body?

C: (*Points to his stomach.*)

T: (*Touches his own stomach.*) What's there, Joe? Slowly now, can you describe it?

C: It's like a big pit, a black hole from which nothing can escape.*

T: What else? Any other images?

C: There I am, this little white face in the midst of that hole. I feel lost, like on a vast, dark sea. I don't know what's happening to me, do you?

T: See if you can stay with it a little longer to find out.

C: I see a cold, black room now. There's a little pudgy kid in that room.

T: Could that kid be you?

C: Yeah, he does feel like me.

T: What are you, or he, doing now?

C: Not doing anything. I'm in a lonely corner of that room just staring, just staring and hurting. . . . (*Tears well up again.*)

T: You're really in that hole now, Joe. See if you can stay with it a bit longer and see what happens.

C: (*Tears flow freely.*)

In time, the client will be able to *occupy* his despair with less panic, and possibly even with a sense of hope.

When Safety and Containment Issues Become Relevant When clients are fragile, or when depth exploration exceeds tolerable limits, semi-experiential treatment strategies can be just the right tonic. Emphasis on genetic (historical) explanations in particular can provide desperately needed structure in given situations. Sometimes the provision of such explanations can mean the difference between suicidal impulsiveness and livable shame, or catastrophic anxiety and manageable fear. Clients with characterological dysfunctions (e.g., borderline personality) can be particularly well served in such contexts (Volkan, 1987).

The use of genetic explanations to quell or bind anxiety, on the other hand, should not be overdone within the EI paradigm. As soon as clients appear anchored enough by the explanatory framework, it is often helpful to follow up with gentle experiential observations or suggestions. In so doing, experiential and explanatory approaches can coexist dialectically with one another, bracing and enhancing each other's power. For example, a recent client of mine (who could be characterized as an ambulatory schizophrenic) has modestly benefited from historical discussions concerning his mother; but he has benefited equally, I believe, by frank here-and-now acknowledgments of affect, sometimes about his mother but just as often about me, society, a philosophy book, or a coworker. We do not *explain* these affects on the basis of his

---

*The *primordial* tone of this response, as suggested previously in another context, is one of the surest signs of its depth.

mother; we do not try to *apprehend* them at these moments; we simply acknowledge them, linger over them a while, and let them be what they are. Remarks or questions like, "You're really turned on by these ideas," "You don't like something that we're doing here," or "What is it you want to say to that fellow who bothered you?" can be deeply self-revelatory and empowering. Too much explaining, on the other hand, can be distancing, deadening, and disempowering—for both client and therapist.

When Clients Are "Stuck" or Seemingly Unreachable   Semi-experiential explanatory frameworks can also be helpful with clients who are "stuck" or appear to be both nonexperientially and experientially unreachable. Such reflections seem to provide foundation-shaking clarity and life-renewing possibilities for these clients. With their motivation for treatment restored and their appetite for exploration sparked, such clients can often be experientially re-engaged.

THE EXPERIENTIAL LIBERATION STRATEGY

Just as physical support is necessary for physiological treatments and interpersonal assistance is central to interpersonal strategies, ontological attention (or the ministration to being) is the sine qua non of experiential approaches.[6]

What do we mean by *ontological attention?* We mean attention that transcends words, contents, and measurable categories. We mean attention, not to physical or interpersonal hurts per se, but to the kinesthetic-affective implications of those hurts—the hurts that are locked up in the body, imagination, fantasy life, and intuition. Finally, we mean attention, not merely to one's physiological or environmental or sexual smallness/greatness, but to one's smallness/greatness before the *universe,* before the general condition of *life.*

Beyond *repairing* ontological wounds, moreover, experiential treatment aims at helping clients *encounter* those wounds—open up to them, see what they are about, discover their future *implications*. It is in this sense that breakdown, from the experiential view, is potentially breakthrough, disability is potentially capability, and anxiety is potentially renewal. The poet Rilke (1991) mused eloquently upon these matters.

> Were it possible for us to see further than our knowledge reaches . . . perhaps we would endure our sadnesses with greater confidence than our joys. For they are the moments when something new has entered us, something unknown. (p. 266)

Our task, then, is to help clients constructively endure, explore, and transform their inmost experiential hurts. Properly carried out, this enterprise leads to deep intra- and interpersonal reconnection, broadened capacities to choose, and a more suitable harness of priorities within which to live.

Let us turn now to the four basic intervention phases of the experiential liberation strategy: (1) presence, (2) invoking the actual, (3) vivifying and confronting resistance, and (4) meaning-creation. Although these phases are often sequential (i.e., presence precedes invoking the actual, invoking the actual precedes vivifying and confronting resistance, and so on), they sometimes cooperate irregularly with one another, so that meaning-creation may directly follow presence or vivifying and confronting resistance may directly precede invoking the actual. The manifestation of these phase alterations is dependent on many factors (such as the rate of the client's progress), and each factor must be responded to accordingly. The phases may also be coordinated, as intimated earlier, with non- and semi-experiential approaches (within our framework), with a resultant deepening and enhancement of those approaches. Therapeutic presence, for example, can complement genetic explanations; invoking the actual can rejuvenate rational restructuring; and meaning-creation can supplement intellectual insight, as we shall see. Taken together, these facilitative strands help clients clarify and apply the EI operating assumptions: *constriction* (making oneself small) and *expansion* (making oneself great) are key existential capacities; dread of either polarity promotes extreme or dysfunctional (constrictive or expansive) counter-reactions to that polarity; the confrontation with or integration of the denied polarities fosters psychospiritual renewal and health. While clients may not grasp these assumptions intellectually (as well they probably should not!), they can often grasp them intuitively, implicitly, and metaphorically—in the successful aftermath of treatment.

PRESENCE: A PRIMARY NUTRIENT

A pivotal moment in Martin Buber's life, according to Maurice Friedman (1991), was a glaring and singular failure to be deeply present. A young man had sought Buber's advice about whether or not to go to the front in World War I, but Buber—due to rhapsodic spiritual preoccupations—could not give him the attention he later realized he should have.

The situation ended tragically, with the young man's death, and, according to Friedman, forever recommitted Buber to being *attuned* in relationships, not merely prepared or available.

"Presence," Bugental (1987) notes with lucidity, "is a . . . quality of being in a situation or relationship in which one intends at a deep level to participate as fully as [one] is able" (p. 27). Such a quality, he goes on to suggest, facilitates attention, concern, aliveness, and exploration.

Rollo May (1981) conceives of presence in terms of the "pause," which "calls forth continuous, unrealized possibilities" (p. 164). "It is in the pause," he elaborates,

> that people learn to *listen to silence*. We can hear the infinite number of sounds we never hear at all—the unending hum and buzz of insects in a quiet summer field, a breeze blowing lightly through the golden hay, a thrush singing in the low bushes beyond the meadow. And we suddenly realize that this is *something*—the world of "silence" is populated by a myriad of creatures and a myriad of sounds. (p. 165)

European existentialists, finally, succinctly characterize presence as *dasein,* which means, literally, to "be there."

Fully "being there" with clients (and oneself) cannot be overestimated as a fundamental experiential task. There are at least three (and probably countless more) therapeutic by-products of this task: (1) it illuminates the construction of clients' (or therapists') experiential worlds—highlighting both the obstacles and promises of those worlds (e.g., the client's desire and capacity for change); (2) it creates a sense of safety—or what Craig (1986) calls "sanctuary"—within which delicate problems can be confronted; and (3) it deepens clients' (or therapists') capacities to constructively act upon their discoveries.

In short, *presence* is an attitude of palpable—immediate, kinesthetic, affective, and profound —*attention,* and it is the ground and eventual goal of experiential work.

Let us turn now to the engagement of presence to illuminate (or assess) clients' worlds—the initial phase of experiential work. One of the first problems therapists encounter at this stage is how to orient themselves in the above worlds. Presence requires such a degree of receptivity to clients' material that not long after one is immersed in it, one is dizzied by its abundance. Fortunately, experiential therapy (within the EI outlook) provides an organizing structure for this dazzlement, a way to harness its receptive power.[7]

Smallness-Greatness "Clustering": Keys to Experiential Work

One of the first areas I reflect upon—even before any words are exchanged—is What is my client expressing in his body? I am particularly alert to the constrictive or expansive *cluster points,* or polarizations, evident in his body.[8] I am also attentive to such resonances in my own body as barometers of his kinesthetic disposition. To the extent that I can register these impressions, I am privy to useful hypotheses about my client's dysfunction—how and why he makes himself small or great and the degree to which he is invested in these stances. Although I initially "bracket" these specula-tions for future consideration, I am often struck by their anticipation of the future concerns of our work. Here is a sample of my meditations:

> What kind of world is this man trying to hold together? What kind of life-design do his muscles, gestures, and breathing betray? Is he stiff and waxy or limber and fluid? Is he caved in and hunched over or stout and thrust forward? Does he curl up in a remote corner of the room or does he "plant himself in my face"? What does he bring up in *my* body? Does he make me feel light and buoyant or heavy and stuck? Do my stomach muscles tighten, or do my legs become jumpy? Do my eyes relax, or do they become "hard," guarded? What can I sense from what he wears? Is he frumpy and inconspicuous or loud and outrageous? What can be gleaned from his face? Is it tense and weather-beaten or soft and innocent?

Each of these observations begins to coalesce with the others, cumulatively dis-closing a world. Each is a sampling of the constrictive or expansive terror my client is experiencing—and the expansive or constrictive armaments he has mobilized in reaction to that terror (see Reich, 1949).

Concurrent with its power to reveal, I am also aware of the power of presence to contain or support experiential material. This support is communicated to my client in the process of my attending. To the degree that I can permit my own embodied responses, my client is also encouraged to respond bodily. To the degree that I can trust *myself* with my client, he is also inspired to trust. My body becomes a sanctuary at such times, intimating a range of silent sentiments, such as, "I am here for you," "I will not waver," and "I take you seriously." "The provision of human sanctuary," Craig (1986) elucidates,

> is manifested in the therapist's attunement as an alert, abiding . . . presence which is both permissive and protecting. Though the particulars of this embodied therapeutic mood fluctuate with the particulars of the therapeutic circumstances, what does endure . . . is a palpable sense of aliveness, respect, and nonintrusiveness. (p. 26)

The engagement of presence, Craig (1986) adds,

> requires constant discipline; discipline in remaining open to all aspects of my experience with the patient; discipline in understanding the salient features of this experience; discipline in determining just what features of this experience hold the greatest promise for opening new possibilities in the patient's existence; discipline in deciding just how these promising possibilities may be framed and offered to the patient in behavior, language, and mood; and, above all, discipline in identifying and transcending all those personal needs, feelings, beliefs, and assumptions of my own which may be interfering with a fresh, virginal perception of and response to the other. (pp. 27–28)

As we can see, the discipline of presence requires a very wide assortment of abilities. Although one can technically develop the art (see the pertinent skill-building exercises), there is no substitute for what one has learned or will learn about it through living one's life. To the degree that one can effectively draw upon this learning, one can dramatically prepare the therapeutic "soil." (See Schneider, 1992, on the link between therapists' personal maturity and their effectiveness.)

To summarize, presence is the *vessel* for experiential work. It holds while illuminating that which is palpably—immediately, kinesthetically, affectively, and profoundly—relevant *between* therapists and clients and *within* clients. Time, intuition, and attention to constrictive and expansive cluster points can help therapists optimize presence. (See "Ways the Intervention Phases Utilize the Constrictive-Expansive Continuum"—close of chapter—for elaboration on this matter.)

Next, we turn to one overarching issue: how to assist clients *into* that which is palpably relevant.

INVOKING THE ACTUAL: CREATIVELY INSPIRING PRESENCE

Recently, a colleague of mine (I'll call him Bob) relayed a most captivating vignette. He was consulting with a group of business leaders about a rift that had broken out in the organization of one of the leaders (I'll call him John). The rift centered on John's decision to fire a disgruntled employee. Before John could explain the reasons for his strategy, however, a highly respected fellow executive (Joanna) began to speak—and her tones were far from measured. She chided John for his presumptuousness, moralized to him about his lack of social conscience, and derided him for his austerity. When Bob urged her to suspend her judgment for a time, she abruptly turned on *him* and began to question *his* partiality and motives. This caused other members of the gathering to remind Joanna of the need for proper decorum. "Be reasonable," they called out, but Joanna refused to yield her ground. Flustered but not daunted, Bob paused, pondered her a moment, and uttered one simple sentiment, "I sense that you are deeply hurting right now, Joanna."

Almost instantaneously, my colleague reported, Joanna doubled over in pain. Thick wet tears began streaming down her face. "You're right," she cried out, "I *am* hurting—and it has nothing to do with this meeting." Bob found out later that what Joanna's pain had *everything* to do with was her abusive, alcoholic father. She had just returned from his funeral, Bob recalled, and she felt betrayed and abandoned by him yet one final time. This was the context for her fierce opposition to John and her exaggerated sympathy for his employee.

There were many ways in which Bob could have intervened with Joanna, and there were many alternative assumptions he could have made about her behavior. He could have assumed, for example, that he could reason with her, the way her associates tried to do. He could have tried to psychodynamically explain or interpret her remarks. Or he could have assumed that she had inside information and that she was justified in her reaction. Yet none of these efforts would have connected with Joanna because none of them would have addressed her *experience*.

When I asked Bob to articulate the basis for his particular intervention, he groped for the right words. "It was something about her intensity," he said, "something about the way she looked when she was speaking and the kinds of words she used when she was speaking. There was a discrepancy there."

What Bob saw, I believe, is what many sensitive therapists see and feel with tormented clients—the extravagances they experience (Binswanger, 1975). In Joanna's case, these extravagances grouped around the need to exhibit greatness, righteousness, and invulnerability. But they also—albeit more subtly—clustered around the fears beneath those displays—fears of smallness, impotence, and helplessness. Bob was able to empathically "home in" on those fears, share them with Joanna, and spur her transformation in consciousness.

By speaking to people's immediate, energetic experience, then, or by encountering their "living" constrictive or expansive panic, therapists can mobilize extraordinary capacities for renewal. Dramatic as it was, Bob's performance is emblematic of one of the most important clinical innovations on the contemporary scene—"invoking the actual." "Words are just brief sounds," Wilson Van Dusen (1965), the man who wrote the landmark article on the topic, elaborates. "Words and symbols are lifeless unless they choke up, frighten, bring tears or alert like the actually numinous. The actualities I speak of are all more or less visible and palpable" (p. 67).

It is hard to overstate the infusion of richness this conception brings to our engagements. From the vantage point of invoking the actual, for example, every therapeutic moment must be seized upon; every transaction amplified. There is no justification for long-term passivity; prolonged inertness is a signal of decay.

The *creative* challenge of invoking the actual, or relevant, is one of its most invigorating features. I am enticed, for example, by the prospect of reaching an intransigent client or of finding myriad routes to her depths. To me, this is what makes our work so awe-filled and so exhilarating in its potential to surprise. Let us look closer now at the use of invoking the actual, drawing from a variety of my own and others' case examples.

The moment a therapist begins to speak to her client, invoking the actual, or relevant, can begin, and it can set the tone for the entire session. Suggestions such as, "Take a moment to settle in," or questions such as, "What's of concern to you?" "What really matters to you right now?" or "Where are you at today?" can help clients begin to center on their concerns. Simple follow-ups to these queries, such as "Tell me more," "Can you give me an example?" or "Is there anything else you'd like to share?" can fruitfully deepen what has been initiated. (See "Enhancing Presence through Focus and Topical Expansion" in the skill-building section.) Finally, suggesting to clients that they speak in the present tense, that they invoke the pronoun "I" when discussing themselves, and that they become more aware of their bodies can consolidate the aforementioned processes. (See Bugental, 1987, for an elaboration on these initial processes.)

At the same time that I try to help clients *center* themselves on their concerns, moreover, I also try to help them actively confront, or encounter, those concerns. For example, I might comment on my experience of them "energetically:" "It feels to me that you are tight right now;" "I hurt when I hear that recollection;" "I feel like I'm spinning—I wonder if you do, too?" Or I might note what I hear and see: "I notice that your fingers are tapping;" "Your voice breaks when you make that statement;" "It seemed hard for you to smile just then." Finally, I might try to underscore the client's experience: "How do you feel as you make that statement? See if you can linger on it a while." (Although such commentaries can be enormously productive at the right moments, it is important to monitor the client's readiness and ability to *handle* them. Fragile or paranoid clients, for example, may not have the tools!)

Clients' investments in smallness or greatness can also help me facilitate their encounters. When I observe a pattern of flamboyance, for example, I am watchful for an undercurrent of shyness, reticence, or self-deprecation that can be explored. When I perceive a clustering of hesitancy and reserve, conversely, I am mindful of the upheaval, rage, and explosiveness that may need to be plumbed. The degree and frequency of these investments, moreover, clue me in on the degree and frequency of future struggles.

Although some clients display consistent polarization patterns, many do not. Some, for example, oscillate *between* smallness and greatness while others fluctuate *within* a given cluster. Some are polarized one way at the beginning of treatment (or at the beginning of each session) and polarized another way at the end of that time period. Still others—and this probably accounts for the therapeutic majority—are polarized in different ways as they uncover deeper levels of their existential pain (see "Ways the Intervention Phases Utilize the Constrictive-Expansive Continuum" at the close of this chapter). Our task as therapists is to help our clients face their polarizations as they arise, and to artfully assist them in deepening those encounters. Eventually, although not invariably, clients will arrive at the experiential core of their constrictive or expansive dreads. To the degree that they can identify (or resonate to) this core, the therapeutic task will become clearer. If they cannot identify it, the therapist's task becomes hazier from the experiential position. This latter outcome is not "bad," however; it merely indicates that (1) more uncovering needs to be done or (2) the client has reached her threshold using the smallness-greatness paradigm.

It is also important to be mindful of any ethnic or cultural predispositions along the smallness-greatness axis that may mislead or confound our assessments. To an American practitioner, for example, an Asian client may appear excessively invested in smallness (e.g., accommodation, deference, and so on). Yet that very same client—relative to his background—may not feel the least bit concerned about that aspect of his experience and may, in fact, view it with some pride. It is of vital importance, therefore, not only to know something about the cultural background of one's clients, but to clarify, to the degree possible, *how the clients themselves* view those backgrounds. Do they experience them as crippling or salutary, forced or natural? If we can attune ourselves to the client's standpoint, we will be in a stronger position to guide.

One last, frequently asked point. What does a therapist do once a client *faces* his or her dread? My answer is threefold: (1) try to stay present to that client, (2) try to trust that the client's pain (as with most things) will eventually transform, and (3) try to assist the *client* to acquire that trust. Almost invariably, in my experience, clients' anxieties do change—especially as they face them. Either they dissipate and give way to liberation (e.g., meaning-creation), shift and become new anxieties or concerns, or overpower the client and engender his or her resistance. Yet each is an instance of change, and each can be dealt with accordingly.

Given these caveats, let us consider some of the most useful strategies for invoking the actual of which I am aware. These derive both from my own and others' existentially oriented practices.

Guided Meditation   Recently I have found guided-meditation to be of value—particularly to clients invested in making themselves small. Ruth, for example, was a repressed, fearful young woman in her mid-30s. She lived alone and spent much of her life worrying about what others thought of her. This concern was especially debilitating to her desire to be more playful, creative, and spiritual in her life. Her life had become a prison. Although we made some headway discussing her personal history in relation to these issues, she continued to describe herself as feeling chronically "heavy," "cramped up," and "blocked." One day I invited her to try something different. "I'd like to try a simple meditation exercise with you," I explained, "that may help you to make fuller contact with yourself. Would you like to give it a try?" Upon her consent, I requested that she sit in a comfortable position (hands to the side, legs uncrossed) and begin to pay attention to her breathing. Next, I suggested that she close her eyes. Although this is not mandatory, I explained to her, it seems to deepen one's participation in the exercise. "Now, as you attend to your breathing," I continued, "you may notice all kinds of extraneous thoughts, feelings, and sensations. Try not to get caught up in those other stimuli. Simply acknowledge them and return to your breathing. To the degree possible," I went on, "try to draw your breaths in slowly, really attending to them, and do the same for your expulsions of air. Let them out slowly, mindfully."

After providing a few minutes for her to center on her breathing, I suggested that as she's ready, she gradually shift her attention to her body. Once she was able to do this, I suggested that she carefully attend to any tension areas in her body, any areas that seemed to "stand out" or "call out" to her, as if in need. She immediately was able to identify such an area—her stomach—and we were off and running.

Me: Can you describe, as fully and *presently* as possible, what it is you sense there, Ruth? What do you feel around your stomach area?

Ruth: I have an image of being bloated, gassy, and disturbed. It's like knives sticking into me.

Me: That's a pretty strong image.

Ruth: Well, part of it is that I'm having my period, but that's not the whole thing. I often feel like this.

Me: What else is there?

Ruth: I feel like it's messy down there, that it's bubbling and teeming with stuff. It's not all bad, though. It feels like it's part of me, part of what I am in my depths. At the same time, I also feel sealed off from these churnings. It's like I'm underneath them, looking up at them. It's like I'm unaffected by them.

Me: Do any images or associations come up around what you're feeling right now?

Ruth: Well, it's like I feel in a great deal of my life. I feel estranged, cut off. It's like I'm cut off from the wild and expressive part of myself, the aspiring part. (*Tears begin to form.*)

Me: See if you can stay with that feeling, Ruth.

Ruth: It's like this very special room I used to have as a child. This was *my* room. It was a place where I could feel safe, where I wouldn't be trampled on or mangled. (*Long pause.*)

Me: What's happening now, Ruth? Do you want to share?

Ruth: Well, I realize how much I miss that room, how much that room meant play and wonder and magic. But as I got older, I just couldn't get away to that room, and I couldn't bring it out or draw on it in my life. I began to feel cut off from it.

Me: It sounds like the way you feel cut off from your gassy, active stomach, like there's something *alive* in there, something of *you*, but you just can't seem to be with it.

Ruth: Yes! It's like so much in my life I've cut off. (*Yells.*) I'm sick of it! I want to dive into it, embrace it, and let myself *be*, just let myself *be a quote mess* for a change! *For a friggin' change!*

Me: (*after a long pause*) What's happening now, Ruth?

Ruth: The seal has broken loose somewhat. I feel like I'm in there with the tumult. I'm with it or near it. It's OK. It's *me*.

Although this single meditation did not transform Ruth overnight, it did—she and I agreed—go a long way toward helping her to identify her fears, find ways to survive them, and see possibilities for rejuvenating her world. That such results are common in connection with guided meditation is illustrated by another client of mine, Bill, who suffered from similar—albeit more complex—strangulations of his life-design.

Bill was a 40-year-old single white male with a well-paying job and a comfortable overall living arrangement. He jogged regularly, met periodically with a small circle of friends, and was fond of mystery novels. Although Bill was outwardly confident, competent, and even commanding at times, in his deepest being he was terrified of these very qualities. He was terrified of strength, power, and greatness in a wide array of forms. For example, he often isolated himself, denigrated his self-worth, and shunned opportunities for intimacy.

At the same time, it was not always clear just *what* Bill feared. His commanding and even condescending manner, for example, contradicted any dread of greatness and implied, instead, anxiety about belittlement, dismissal, and insubstantiality. His indulgence in food and alcohol, similarly, betrayed fears of "emptiness" and a desperation to fill that emptiness.

Bill's greatest suffering, on the other hand, clustered around his inability to reach out to people, to fully expose and express himself, and to trust that he could be looked upon as special. Although we had alluded to these problems in our dialogues, it was not until Bill faced them in the following guided meditation that he genuinely came to understand and redress them:

Me: (*after having prepared Bill as I did Ruth*) See if you can describe, as fully as possible, what it is you *feel* in your stomach area, Bill.

Bill: (*Rubs his stomach, as I respond in kind.*) I feel like there's a huge mass there, a multilayered wall, or fortress. I'm aware of my obesity right now. It's like a tremendous covering of pain. There is some pain in there. It's just not clear what it's about. (*His face exhibits frustration.*)

Me: Slowly now, Bill, just see if you can keep describing what's there. Take your time.

Bill: Yeah, there is something there, beneath the fat. It's like a hunger, or better yet, a hollow feeling. . . .

Me: Something like what you feel when you overeat?

Bill: Yeah, exactly! It's that emptiness, and it hurts real bad. It's *scary.*

Me: Do you feel like you can stay in there with it?

Bill: (*Pauses to reflect.*) Yes, I *want* to stay in there.

Me: Good.

Bill: I suddenly got this image of going with my mother to a gathering of our relatives. I was a little boy—maybe 7 years old.

Me: Bill, see if you can describe it in the present tense, as if you were living it now.

Bill: We arrive at the front door. The house is dark; the relatives are nondescript. The first thing I want to do is dart behind this couch. (*His voice begins to waver, and his face begins to flush red.*) There is this raggedy old couch. I run behind it. I won't even say hello to anyone. I just make a beeline for that couch! I feel tight, real scared. (*He speaks more rapidly, intensively.*)

Me: I'm with you, Bill. Go as far as you feel able.

Bill: I'm this little boy, this little boy who's scared.

Me: Scared of what, Bill. Can you associate?

Bill: Scared of showing himself, scared of hurting himself or of being hurt, scared of "coming out."

Me: What does it mean for you to *come out?*

Bill: I don't know. It's just so frightening. I feel lost, abandoned, exposed—yeah, that's it, *exposed.* It's as if everyone will see me in all my ugliness, all my perverseness. I'm like this big, oozing blob.

Me: So what does that mean for you? What are you afraid will happen if you step out from behind that couch?

Bill: I feel like they're gonna shrink back from me or humiliate me.

Me: Yeah, but what makes that so scary *to you?*

Bill: I just don't feel like I could handle it—being out there in front of them. It's like I would crack up or something, or go out of control. Maybe I'd show them that I was as crazy as they think I am. Oh, it *hurts so much. (Caresses himself.)*

Me: It feels important to keep caressing yourself for a while, Bill. You've gone to a pretty harrowing place. Maybe you can just take some time to soothe that little boy the way you are now. Let him know how you sympathize with him.

This latter comment illustrates the principle of "building up" while you're "stripping the client down." It is essential, during the uncovering process, to help clients "rest" or "gather their resources" from time to time—to bolster their capacities for risk.

Bill began to experience some rather startling shifts within himself after sessions such as the aforementioned. First, he felt increasingly *friendly,* or comfortable, with himself. Although he continued to be alone quite a bit, he was no longer as burdened by or devaluing of that experience. He could even begin to enjoy being by himself, and this helped him to trust and enjoy being with others as well. He felt like a shadow or weight had been lifted from him and that he was freed up to participate more fully in his life. Second, he no longer felt as empty or as wanting as he had before. He still had the urge to overeat or drink on occasion, but the urges were much less frequent than they had been. It was as if the urgency had faded, he said. He couldn't quite articulate it, but he felt like something very significant had happened during our meditation sessions, something that no other aspect of our work had duplicated.

What, specifically, occurred? While neither Bill nor I could answer this question definitively, I would postulate the following: Bill—like many if not most therapy clients—possessed a complex, multitiered experiential profile. At one level he balked at smallness, mustering all his efforts to project dominance, substantiality, and greatness. At another level, he was terrified of these latter qualities. He did everything to *avoid* "coming out," exposing himself, or challenging others. In turn, he made himself small, reticent, and withdrawn.

It was not until I invoked the actual with Bill—through guided meditation—that we could more clearly differentiate his situation. His fears of smallness (of deprivation, of emptiness), for example, were apparent in his references to his weight, his stomach girth, and his need for protective fat. His fears of greatness, on the other hand, were apparent in his memory of hiding behind the couch and appeared to underlie his anxiety about smallness. Although Bill *also* may have felt deprived and empty behind that couch, his *primary* anxiety, it seemed to me, was the effort, risk, and boldness it would take to *step out in front of the couch;* and this was a metaphor for his life. By gradually learning to *survive*—not merely report on—his recollection, Bill was unburdened of its spell.

Experimentation   The idea of using therapy as a *laboratory,* a place to try things out with clients, is neither unique nor original. Cognitive therapies, for example, make abundant use of the concept, and so do such varying approaches as gestalt, psychodrama, and systematic desensitization (see Beck, 1976; Perls, 1969; Moreno, 1959; and Wolpe, 1969). The distinguishing feature of the model we present here is that it combines these respective modalities and creatively synthesizes new ones.

In addition to role-play, rehearsal, and creative visualization, for example, I also find live demonstration to be of benefit. Sometimes I invite artistically inclined—but creatively blocked—clients to draw me, or to draw something in the room. The exercise seems facile at first, but it is often quite profound. One client, for example, rediscovered a long pent-up joy in the artistic process; another simply took pride in expressing herself deeply. One man showed me a twenty-page-long play he had written. It was about an "offensive" therapist he had seen and was full of antitherapist invective. The play, however, was critical for my work with this man because it showed that he could trust me, despite whatever professional identification I might want to preserve.

The old adage that "you don't really know what something is like until you experience it" holds for the subtle as well as the obvious and overt. One of my clients, for example, felt a "lump" in her throat. I asked her to place her hand on that lump and instantly she was able to associate to the abandonment she had once felt as a child. Sometimes I invite clients to pause, stretch in certain ways, or walk around the room. A colleague of mine, John Cogswell (1993), uses what he calls "walking therapy" to invoke the actual. When one of his clients is having trouble articulating who he desires to be, what kind of people hold him back in his life, or, simply, "where he's at" at any given moment, Cogswell invites him to embody that desire, person, or experience in his walk. Hence, for example, one client might walk the walk of her father in order to better understand his influence on her life. Another might imitate the way his boss walks in order to improve his understanding of her personality. Still another might walk the way he is feeling that day in order to *experientially* identify his problem. It is surprising, concludes Cogswell, how much insight clients acquire into themselves and others through walking—as much or more than that typically achieved through role-play, he contends.

The more spontaneous, creative, and absorbing a therapeutic experiment is, the more valuable it is. A client of mine invested in keeping herself small, for example, contemplated a radical change in her career. Although she had begun to *talk* more earnestly about this career change, and although she fantasized about how it could transform her life, she refrained from actually *inquiring* into the prospect. She was on the brink of making such an inquiry, she once confided in me, yet she could not quite go through with it. It was then that I offered her a challenge: "How would you like to make your inquiry *right now,* in the safety of this office? You can use the phone right here—I'll even leave while you make your call. Or, if you wish, I can be right here with you. Then we can look at what came up for you."

At that instant, the entire tenor of our session shifted. What was formerly a rather sober exercise suddenly turned animated. Struggling to respond, my client both laughed (embarrassedly) and grimaced. She also resented *me,* in part, for directly challenging her. Although she ultimately declined my invitation, it was the *experience of being invited*—not its acceptance or rejection—that really seemed to matter. The experience enabled her to look as closely as she ever had at how much she wanted to take a risk in her life and at ways in which she impeded herself from taking that risk. The experience also helped her to reconsider me—the ostensibly warm and gentle listener. How could I "put her on the spot" like that, she pondered, and steer our relationship in such unpredictable directions?

Despite her misgivings, however, her newly acquired ambivalence toward me brought our relationship to an unprecedented level of frankness. She realized that I could no longer be relied upon to magically save her, that only *she* could ultimately save herself. Eventually, she was able to make that terrifying phone call and courageously emerge from her cocoon.

It is not so much the *kind* of experiment that matters, but its capacity to absorb, inspire, and enliven. When I suggest role-plays, for example, I am continually attentive to clients' body positions, breathing patterns, and vocal fluctuations. "How does it *feel* when you say that?" I might inquire. "What's going on in your body as you enact this encounter?"

Role-playing entails more than trying out new interpersonal relationships; it also entails trying out new relationships with one's imagination, energy, and spirit. For example, Rollo May (1969) often speaks about the need for "wishing" within the therapeutic context; and I am in wholehearted concurrence with his position. *Wishing,* May writes, "is the imaginative playing with the possibility of some act or state occurring" (p. 214). To the degree that one is unable to wish, he elaborates, one is unable to will—which "is the full-blown, matured form of wish" (p. 288). To the degree that one is unable to will, I would add, one is unable to fully *be.* In order to foster these capacities, accordingly, I frequently encourage clients to "let their imaginations go" or "throw their judgments aside for a time." "Let's see what happens if you trace that thought or feeling out," I might suggest. "Play with it, embody it, describe it as if it were happening." I often invite clients who are dysfunctionally invested in their greatness, for example, to contemplate stillness, abstinence, or routine. "What might it be like," I'd query, "if you *didn't* get wild tonight or *didn't* 'show up' your peers?" "What fantasies do you have around being ordinary, plain, or slow? Can you tell me in the first person?" It is also helpful for some of these clients to trace out their *manifest* patterns of behavior—their inclinations to dominate others or to take on more than they can handle. Beyond helping them to look at the merely cognitive consequences of such dispositions, however, I am particularly attentive to the toll those dispositions take at the level of their affect and bodies. "See if you can envision yourself beating that fellow," I might inquire. "What kind of feelings, images, or fantasies come up for you?" "Imagine yourself in that prison cell. What are you seeing? What does it feel like in your body?" "See if you can envision *involving yourself* in all those activities we spoke about. What would such a scenario feel like in your stomach, chest, and throat?" I am constantly surprised at how potent such questions can be—even with characteristically "externalizing" clientele.

The more deeply one can describe one's wish or fantasy, the more one can immerse oneself in its possibilities. When I ask clients to visualize a scene, for example, I urge them to "paint," "taste," or fully "re-create" that scene. I asked one man who was envisioning a confrontation with his boss, "What does the setting feel like? How warm is it? What kinds of decorations are around you? How formal is your attire?" I asked a woman reconstructing her dream, "How does the sensation of flying feel in your body? Is it sensual, or is it scary? Do you feel heavy, or do you feel feathery and light?"

If clients are resistant to envisioning an entire scenario, I encourage them to experiment with portions of that scenario—I might ask the man above to imagine being in the same room with his boss rather than confronting her; I might suggest reading up on a job as opposed to calling for an interview; or I might ask an alcoholic to picture one day of abstinence rather than a lifetime. Tiny though they may seem, these increments have proven crucial in my experience because they can shift the momentum of treatment.

Experimenting Outside Therapy   While experimentation within the therapeutic setting is invaluable, experimentation outside therapy, in my opinion, is even more beneficial. This is because (1) outside experimentation reinforces intratherapy work; and (2) it implements that work in the most relevant setting—life.

Accordingly, I encourage clients to *practice* being present and aware, especially in problematic situations. "See if you can stay with the thoughts and feelings that come up," I tell them, "even for the briefest moment." I also encourage clients to sort through what's operating on them in stressful situations—what assumptions they make, how they approach or avoid certain things, and what inner voices they hear. Some clients have found it helpful to observe how readily they give their power away in given circumstances; others have been impressed by their passive-aggressive behavior. Virtually anything clients perceive from this standpoint can be revelatory.

The cultivation of what Zen adepts and others have termed the *observing ego* can also foster extratherapeutic presence (see Bugental, 1978). To nurture this skill, I encourage clients to commit twenty minutes of each week to undistracted self-observation. "As nonjudgmentally as possible," I suggest, "just watch the flow of your inner experiences, and neither try to categorize nor figure out those experiences." Although some clients have difficulty with this exercise, others benefit greatly simply from the time they've taken with themselves and the needs, fears, and desires that they've unveiled.

Challenging clients to experiment with or "act out" extratherapeutic tasks can be of equal benefit. "See what happens if you are honest with your friend," I told one of my image-conscious clients; or "try refraining from one confection tonight," I urged one of my compulsively eating clients, "then look at what that was like for you." Finally, I proposed to a client who was concerned about having children to "try making contact with children, reflecting on your own childhood, and visiting the places and things that children value."

Experimenting with the actual gives clients new opportunities to live. Although they may not always seize these opportunities, they are invariably vibrant and edifying.

Therapist-Client Encounter   One of the most important vehicles for invoking the actual is the therapeutic relationship. This relationship, or *encounter,* as it has come to be known in experiential circles, includes, but also transcends, the psychoanalytic notions of transference, remembering, and explaining (Phillips, 1980).

The therapeutic encounter has three basic features: (1) the real or present relationship between therapist and client; (2) the future and what *can* happen in the relationship (versus strictly the past and what *has* happened in relationships); and (3) the "acting out" or experiencing, to the degree appropriate, of relational material. Let me pose some examples:

I am sitting with a client who communicates to me that "things are going OK right now," that he is really quite "upbeat," and that he had "no problem" with our tension-filled session last week. Yet something about this man's presentation is askew. His mouth is turned down, his gestures are stiff, and his words ring hollow. I could let the man ramble on, I reflect, but the most *relevant* issue, the issue evident *between us,* would not get addressed. Accordingly, I *encounter* him: "I feel like there's something important happening between us right now, Pete, like you have something more to say to me than 'everything's all right.'"

An aircraft engineer succinctly and precisely summarizes his childhood history. He notices that I yawn slightly and that my eyes glaze over as he is talking, but he continues on without pause. I interrupt: "I think we both notice that I'm drifting, Terry; I wonder if you're drifting, too? What is it that really *matters* about what you're telling me?"

An enraged teenage boy has just been sent to a foster home. He stares at me in disdain. Charily, I address him: "I feel like you want to let me or someone 'have it,' John. Is there something you'd like me to know?"

A woman who feels chronically victimized by and unable to confront her ex-husband suddenly bursts out screaming: "That fucking asshole! He makes me so sick. I'd like to kick him where it goddamn counts. *Men* make me sick!" Then she demurs, "present company excepted, of course."

"No!" I reply, "don't qualify yourself. You have more energy than a fireball right now. Now, how can you make that energy *work* for you?"

A client labeled *ambulatory schizophrenic* steps into my office. He is suspicious, disheveled, and "sharp as a tack." "This system is corrupt," he raves. "Look at you all—you professionals, with your smiling faces and your fancy beards. You're just here to pacify me, to make me say 'That's good, doctor. You're right, doctor. You know what's best, doctor.' And behind your masks you're afraid of us, aren't you?

Afraid something's going to rub off on you. Just look right now. You're conniving ways to quiet me, to turn me into your pet-boy."

"You make some valid points, Daniel," I concede. "There *are* people who are afraid of you and who will try to mold you to fit their image. You're also right that I'm one of those people sometimes. I *was,* in fact, a little scared of you back then; even now, I'm both moved and unsettled by your view. But I'm also willing—if you are—to keep taking a look at these problems and to see if we can work them out."

A street-hardened Latino man wonders how I, a Caucasian professional, can relate to him. "I don't know," I respond. "I admit we come from very different worlds. On the other hand, I've also been wounded in my life—in my own ways, within my own cultural context. While these may not be the *same* as your wounds, they may help me connect with yours."

"I'll tell you up front," a court-mandated alcoholic once bragged to me, "I've manipulated every shrink I've had for twenty-five years, and nothing's different here, so far as I can see." "Well, maybe nothing is," I replied, "and maybe you can manipulate me for the next twenty-five years, too. But what will that mean for getting on with your life?"

"I'm horrified by the idea of looking foolish," one client told me as she flushed red with anxiety, "and I can't keep the presence of mind to work with it."

"But you *just were* able to work with it," I responded, "as I surmise that you just now felt foolish!"

She concurred.

The existential psychiatrist R. D. Laing (1985) tells of a perplexing 7-year-old girl he once worked with. For months before he met her, Laing said, she had been both mute and nonresponsive. At their first session together, he tried talking with the girl, but that did not engender any dialogue. Then he tried joking with her, but that, too, garnered negligible results. Finally, Laing gave up on his efforts and simply decided to *be* with her. He sat next to her on the floor and delicately put out his hands. Slowly, she, too, put out her hands and lightly made contact with his fingertips. Then Laing closed his eyes and began to engage in a kind of hand dance with the girl, wordlessly matching her movements.

When the hour was up, Laing reported, the little girl's father asked her how the session went. "None of your business!" she is alleged to have declared, and from that day forward she spoke.

What are the implications of these vignettes? The first implication, I believe, centers on the significance of "realness" in the therapeutic encounter. How else can clients learn to be real with themselves if they cannot be real with their therapists—if they cannot come up against their therapists' love, irritation, recognition of the obvious, and openness to varying approaches? How else can therapists get to know their clients deeply unless some of that depth is shared? It's not that therapists need to "spill their guts" with clients, but they need to be accessible, capable of being known. Bugental has often spoken about feeling deeply *known* by his clients even when he has not exchanged any words with them. Laing, it is clear from the above, would concur with Bugental's observation.

The second implication of the vignettes is that it is the *process*—over and above isolated contents—that fosters intra- and interpersonal growth. My attention to my client's downturned mouth, Laing's suspension of his efforts to speak to his client, and my acknowledgment of ignorance about another client's culture all took our encounters to new levels of possibility. The engagement of content-focused strategies, on the other hand, would probably not have availed us of these opportunities.

Finally, our encounters enabled our clients to experience their smallness or greatness by means of *interpersonal* as well as personal channels. By accepting his client's muteness (or smallness), for example, Laing enabled his client to consider verbalization (greatness). By acknowledging my client's (great) capacity for manipulating, I freed him to explore smaller but more relevant matters, like his life. By directing the aircraft engineer to his mechanistic smallness, finally, I liberated him to consider his spontaneous aliveness, value, and greatness.

Vivifying and Confronting Resistance

When the invitation to meditate, experiment, or encounter is repeatedly declined by clients, then the delicate problem of resistance must be considered. *Resistances* are *blockages* to that which is palpably relevant (i.e., threatening, anxiety-provoking).

Resistances are not to be taken lightly, from the experiential standpoint. To the contrary, they are viewed as vital methods of self-preservation (May, 1983, p. 28). Although such methods may at first seem crude, crippling, or even life-denying, to most clients they are starkly preferable to the alternatives.

Clients invested in smallness, for example, may perceive their sole alternative to be chaos; conversely, clients invested in greatness may perceive their only option to be obliteration. With choices like these, it is no wonder clients sabotage their own growth.

Accordingly, I always try to be respectful of resistances, acknowledging *both* their life-giving *and* their life-taking qualities. I also try to be cognizant of the problems of prematurely challenging clients' resistance, which can often end up exacerbating their conditions rather than alleviating them.

There are two additional points to bear in mind about the experiential approach to resistances. First, it may be overly intense for given clients. To the extent that this is the case, semi- or nonexperiential alternative approaches may be in order. Second, although experiential approaches to resistance are cultivated throughout the treatment process, they are particularly relied upon in the closing stages—when clients face the greatest pressure to change.

Now let us focus on two important experiential tools for handling resistances—therapeutic vivification and confrontation.

Vivifying Resistance   As has been suggested, there are many times when it is better to indirectly, rather than directly, confront resistance. This is so, not only because direct confrontation can therapeutically backfire, but also because it can convey the wrong message to clients—that the power of transformation is possessed by the therapist. But from the experiential standpoint, this is a deception. For it is the *client* who must discover that power, and it is the client who must grapple with its consequences.

Vivifying resistance, accordingly, is one way to empower clients to transform. How does vivification proceed? By gradually and methodically "holding a mirror up" to clients—helping them to see the kinds of worlds they've constructed, the kinds of compromises they've made to maintain those worlds, and the degree of courage necessary to overcome their situations. While these means may seem simplistic at first— for what client would *deny* such knowledge about her world—they are eminently sensible to those who know how deeply one must plumb to *risk the anxieties of growth.* Put another way, vivification helps clients to—supportively and productively—"hit bottom" in their lives and then mobilizes their commitment to change. Now let us look at several ways we can nurture that mobilization and the rewards that attend it.

Verbal and Nonverbal Feedback   These strategies are the most rudimentary forms of vivification. First, let us consider the verbal modality. There are two basic ways to provide verbal feedback—noting and tagging. Noting alerts clients to initial experiences of resistance; tagging acquaints them with those that follow. Some examples of noting are observations such as, "This issue seems really difficult for you," and "You appear to be distracted right now." Some examples of tagging are, "Whenever we discuss this topic, you seem to want to change it," and "There you go again, preferring to argue rather than face your life."

Because I am trying to alert rather than shock, I sometimes find it necessary to temper my appraisals. For example, I might say to a client just beginning treatment: "I wonder if I'm pushing too hard right now. Maybe you can begin again where you feel comfortable." I also try to acknowledge the potential fallibility of my feedback; this helps clients to direct *themselves* to the relevant issues. "My observation may have been off base here," I might remark. "I appreciate your correcting me." Or I might say, "I wonder if we could suspend my observation for a bit, see how it feels to us at a later time."

I find the use of *nonverbal* feedback to be particularly elucidating to clients. Whereas verbal feedback appears to animate predominantly conscious domains of clients' resistance, nonverbal feedback seems to clarify primarily subliminal barriers and domains. By mirroring a client's crossed arms, for example, I was able to help her see how unexpectedly guarded she had been about a particular topic; by echoing a client's sense of being "choked up," I was able to apprise him of his "suffocating" relationship. (See Bugental, 1987, for an elaboration of nonverbal feedback.)

Reviewing Old Territory   Resistances sometimes seem like broken records to clients, endlessly duplicating a theme. While the vivification process can often amplify that sense of repetitiveness, it can also provide fresh opportunities to transcend it. I try to alert clients to these possibilities and to subtle changes in their patterns of defensiveness. For example, I might refer an intellectualized client to his sudden use of the pronoun "I," or direct a client who chronically suppresses her sadness to an abruptly formed teardrop.

Tracing Out and Enabling   Helping clients to trace out the consequences of their resistances and enabling them to be resistant are two other ways to catalyze productive change. I have often found it helpful for clients invested in smallness, for example, to detail the dullness, routine, and oppressiveness that they foresee in their lives. I have found it equally useful for inflated clients to peer into their unsettling futures. While such strategies may acutely frustrate certain clients, they can also alert them to present opportunities, which can head off their nightmarish fantasies.

Ambivalent clients can also benefit from the strategy of tracing out. Experientially detailing the pros and cons of a situation or anticipating the meaning of *remaining* ambivalent have all helped my clients to substantively reassess their predicaments.

One of the most interesting and ironic features of vivification is that when all else fails, *just allowing the client to resist* can be the most salient remedy (see Erickson, 1965, and Frankl, 1965). When I worked with highly resistive (nonviolent) children, for example, I found that divesting of a given treatment plan was more effective, frequently, than pressing for a particular strategy (Schneider, 1990). Highly resistive adult clients also respond favorably to such divestitures. When such clients are allowed to simply *be* their withdrawn, grandiose, or intractable selves, they will frequently begin to *relinquish* those dispositions. For example, I suggested to one intransigent client that she just "be that way," and that she could use her time as she wished. At first she agreed and diverted us to another topic. As time went on, however, it became clear that she felt uncomfortable with this arrangement. When I worked with her to stay *present* to that discomfort, she acknowledged how infuriated she had become with herself and how tired she had become of treating herself like an invalid. It was then that she recommitted to change.[9]

Vivifying or modeling *desired* behavior is another way to catalyze resistant clients. By forming an alliance with the part of a client that *could be,* the therapist can tacitly underscore who that client is; the contrast between the two can invigorate the client to transform. I once told a client who was about to give up on herself, for example, that *I* was *not* about to give up on her, and that I would form an alliance with the part of her that *believed.* Although little changed at first, she gradually realized how absurd her hopelessness had been. Rollo May has also frequently taken these kinds of stands with clients. "As long as I can be of help to you," he is fond of conveying, "I will work with you."

In his classic study of Mercedes, May (1972) used yet another method for vivifying desired behavior to stimulate transformation. Mercedes, May writes, was a repressed African-American female who chronically suppressed her rage. No matter what he tried, May lamented, he could not bring her to stand up for herself and affirm the indignation to which she was entitled. While this state of affairs was a problem in their early relationship, it was not, as yet, a matter of urgency. When Mercedes became pregnant, however, the situation changed. "Every couple weeks," May writes, "she came in reporting that she had begun to bleed vaginally." This was especially true when she dreamed about being attacked by her mother (p. 86). The prospect of miscarrying, May surmised, was one way she could subconsciously avoid these attacks since, in her mind, her mother deeply resented her pregnancy; "Some rage had to be expressed," May declared, or "we were confronted with the likelihood of a spontaneous abortion" (p. 87).

In a determined but "not wholly conscious" move to expedite this expression, accordingly, May "decided to express [*his*] rage in place of hers" (p. 87). "Chiefly," May elaborates, "I attacked her mother with other figures thrown in from time to time. What did these blankety blank people mean by trying to kill her for having a baby," he exclaimed (p. 87).

How did May's diatribes affect Mercedes? She was able to experience them vicariously, May suggested, and rapidly express "her . . . anger at the attackers in the dreams" (p. 88). She was also able to carry her baby to term. By embodying Mercedes' fury, then, May tacitly enabled her to reassess her docility; and by showing her that one could *survive* such a reassessment, he deftly inspired her to reform.

"What she got from me," May concludes, "was not just the *permission* without condemnation to express her struggle to be; she got the prior *experience,* from someone in authority, of her own rights and her own being. . . . My giving vent to my rage was my living out my belief that she was a person with her own rights" (p. 90).

Confronting Resistance   Confrontation, for our purposes, is a direct and amplified form of vivification; instead of *alerting* clients to their self-destructive refuges, however, confrontation *alarms* clients about these refuges and, in lieu of *nurturing* transformation, *presses for and demands* such transformation.

Yet confrontation, within the experiential context, is not synonymous with *dictation* of therapeutic change. Where confrontation challenges, dictation coerces, demeans, and alienates most clients. There are three significant risks associated with dictation: (1) that the client will argue with and further resist the therapist; (2) that the client will give over her power to the therapist; or (3) that the client will be "turned off" and abandon the process altogether.

In order to minimize these risks, experiential confrontation must be done carefully, artfully, and with deep sensitivity to its effects. Use of the first person singular, for example, can minimize unwarranted overtones of accusation or punishment. The statements "I believe you can do more" or "I don't buy what you're saying" serve to illustrate this contention. Posing confrontations in the form of questions or descriptions can also enhance their impact. "You're scared shitless," Bugental (1976, p. 16) reflected to his "hail-fellow-well-met" client Laurence, and this is precisely how his client felt! Following the lead of Rollo May (1969, p. 253), alternatively, I often challenge clients to differentiate between *can't* and *won't* at given junctures. "You mean you *won't* respond to that job offer," I suggested to a client invested in her inadequacy; "You mean you *won't* make time in your day for a lunch break," I remarked to another client invested in his invincibility.

It is sometimes useful, finally, to apprise clients of the difficulty of confronting their resistances, especially when those resistances are threatened with extinction. "A part of you is doing everything it can to keep you where you were," I tell clients in such circumstances. "The most you can do is to realize this and look at what it suggests." (See "Confronting Resistance" in the skill-building exercises.)

Meaning-Creation

As clients begin to realize how imprisoning their usual choices and responses have been and how capable they are of transcending them, they develop new ways of standing in the world and new conceptions of who they will become. They develop a sense of *aha,* or resonance, within themselves that clearly apprises them of their predicaments. They may say things like, "I never realized how deeply these feelings affected me and how strongly I want to experience them again in my life," or "Now I see how so much of my life has been wasted on shame—and it's time I broke the cycle!"

The ingredient that gives these realizations substance, according to Rollo May (1969) is *intentionality,* which precedes that which is traditionally referred to as *insight.* While insight is conceptual and schematic, intentionality is spontaneous and bodily and comprises one's total "orientation to the world at that time" (p. 232). Another precondition for insight is what Bugental (1978) refers to as *inner vision*— which is "a vital sense of one's own powers . . . in directing one's own life" (p. 18). Inner vision, Bugental (1978) elaborates,

> is not to be captured in words. Those who equate a verbal account of inner sight with the inward vision itself make the familiar semantic error of mistaking the map for the territory. What can be said about an inner sight is always less than the sight itself and is always relatively impotent in bringing about true life changes, especially when compared with the power of one's own liberating inward realization." (p. 57)

It is the inward realization, then, the intentionality, that *give experiences meaning* (May, 1969). The chief question, of course, is, How do we, as therapists, help clients to consolidate these meanings—what tools or inspirations can we provide? The answer is, No tools or inspirations are needed other than those they have already gleaned from our being present with them and from their discovering (*internalizing*) the ability to be present with themselves.

Yet it is of vital importance that we reinforce these developments, especially toward the close of treatment. For example, I often invite clients to explore their specific values toward the end of therapy—which values they hold dear and how they plan on implementing those values. I also find it helpful to reflect back to clients, not merely what they say, but what I hear them *intending:* "You seem to be excited about getting out there and doing what you felt you couldn't do all those years;" "I feel exuberance when you speak about marrying your fiancée, a sense that you are deeply ready to be involved;" "I sense that you no longer need to be the flashiest guy on the block, that you can now enjoy quiet moments at home;" "I don't get the sense of you walking on eggshells anymore—you no longer downplay your power;" or "You're not going to let physical handicaps handicap you mentally—this is the message that you have declared to me today."

Embodied Meaning   It is not so much the "why" of a meaning that counts experientially, but the "what": *"What* do you experience when you talk about breaking free of your father?" *"What* would you like to say to that sibling who has neglected you?" *"What* does your dream imply for your life?"

A client of mine recently dreamed that she was in her grandparents' house. It was old, dark, and decayed. "I slipped on something," my client recalled, "but then was able to get a foothold." By the end of the dream, my client found herself looking out into an ocean. "It was green, vast, and just beyond the house," she said.

Rather than inquiring about circumscribed content areas of this dream, such as its potential sexual or archetypal significance, I asked my client what it meant to *her*—here, now, as she was speaking about it. "Can you picture yourself in the house?" I asked. "What do you see there? What is it like to see your grandparents' things, to touch them? Do they remind you of anything you see or possess now? How about your experience of slipping and regaining a foothold—is that what's happening in your life? What is it like, finally, to survey the sea at the end of your dream? What kinds of thoughts, feelings, impressions come to mind when you contemplate the sea? How do they compare with what you experienced in the house?"

After spending some time reflecting on and discussing these issues with my client, I then invited her to ponder a series of suggestions: "I wonder if a part of you feels like the house—old and decaying—while another part feels like the sea—green and vast. This greenness and vastness, however, frightens you a bit—it's a bit disorienting—so you slip back into the old part of yourself—the safe but decaying house. Yet just as quickly, you are able to get a foothold again and face the sea. Might this not be what's going on in your life right now—your struggle to break free?"

That my hypothesis had validity was borne out by my client in a subsequent dream. "I dreamed about a sturdy, self-assured businesswoman," she announced. "This woman was modern, but she could also appreciate the past. I dreamed that she visited the house of her deceased grandmother. Now, however, this businesswoman owned the house—and she had re-arranged it to her own specifications. In so doing, she had brought new life and taste to the house, but she had also preserved many of the things left over from her grandmother. As with me in my life right now, she had found *new ways to arrange old things.*"

To sum up, meaning-creation wells up from the depths. While we, as therapists, can do much to share, reflect, and invite clients into specified meanings, we cannot assign these meanings. Only *clients* can assume that responsibility. On the other hand, we can help clients to articulate their meaning-creations and to consolidate them in actual practice.

Frequently, this means helping clients to clarify the role that smallness has played in their lives—the parts of themselves they refer to as *infantile, bored, trapped,* or *desperately alone.* It also means helping clients to clarify the antidotes to these conditions, the possibilities for assertion, sociability, play, creativity, and spiritual inspiration. Conversely, it also means helping clients to clarify the role that greatness has played in their lives—the aspects of themselves they perceive as *insatiable, reckless, tyrannical,* or *indulgent*—and the opportunities, by contrast, to contain those polarities.

To the degree we succeed in these efforts, clients will no longer experience smallness and greatness as panaceas, necessities—chemical or alcoholic answers—but the rich and complex potentialities to which we have alluded. They are then free to *grapple* with those potentialities, to design the lives they've envisioned.

One final note: To the degree that experientially based meaning has been achieved by clients, nonexperiential and semi-experiential levels of their functioning also tend to be enhanced. Acting as a feedback loop, meaning-creation tends to renew physiological vigor, restore environmental adaptation, optimize cognitive appraisals, revive id-superego integrity, and regenerate attachment-separation elasticity (see Antonovsky, 1979; Bugental, 1976, 1987; Frankl, 1962; Kobasa, Maddi, & Puccetti, 1982; Reed, 1987; and Yalom, 1980, for empirical support for such "loops").

Furthermore, there is almost invariably a spiritual element to the creation of experienced-based meaning (Bugental, 1987; May, 1983). This element enables clients to embrace larger and more comprehensive dimensions of themselves (and others) and may importantly benefit society as a whole (Buber, 1970; Bugental & Bracke, 1992; Merleau-Ponty, 1962).

What is the basis for such holistic reorientations? Perhaps it can be described as follows: The freer that people feel to experience themselves, the less panic they harbor; the less panic, the less urgency they feel to rearrange and hence dysfunctionally distort themselves. To the degree that people can draw upon this strength, the more fully they can subsist.

SUMMARY

In this chapter, we have considered the following main points: The aim of existential-integrative therapy is to set clients free. Freedom can be understood on six increasing and intertwining levels: (1) the physiological, (2) the environmental, (3) the cognitive, (4) the psychosexual, (5) the interpersonal, and (6) the experiential. Each of these levels is characterized by the capacities to constrict, expand, and center (or direct) oneself. Dread of either constriction or expansion promotes extreme and dysfunctional counterreactions to that dread, whereas confrontation with or integration of the polarities fosters vitality.

The basis for determining liberation at each level is the client's desire and capacity for change. Nonexperiential liberation strategies address desires and capacities for change on physiological, environmental, and cognitive levels; semi-experiential strategies address them on psychosexual and interpersonal levels; and experiential strategies address them on the experiential (or *being*) level.

The ability to sense when and how one should move from one liberation strategy to the next and the ability to detect and redress polarizations as they arise constitute the art of this approach.

Next, we provide a series of summaries and skill-building exercises designed to animate the above discussion. These materials emphasize experiential learning and skill building, but they also outline non- and semi-experiential offerings that lead up to the experiential stage.

SUMMARY OF THE FOUR INTERVENTION PHASES OF THE EXPERIENTIAL LIBERATION STRATEGY

Experiential liberation entails four intervention phases ("invitations") (1) presence, (2) invoking the actual, (3), vivifying and confronting resistance, and (4) meaning-creation.*

  I. *Presence* holds and illuminates that which is palpably (immediately, kinesthetically, affectively, and profoundly) relevant *between* therapists and clients and *within* clients. It is the ground and eventual goal of experiential work. Specifically, its goal is:

    A. To illuminate the client's experiential world; to understand that world by deep immersion in the preverbal/kinesthetic experience of the client; and to clarify the salient features of that world (such as the smallness-greatness/constrictive-expansive clusters) that anticipate future problems and directions of treatment. Presence can also alert the therapist to the client's desire and capacity for change, which, in turn, may point in more traditional therapeutic directions within the existential-integrative schema.

    B. To provide the sanctuary, containment, and safety within which deep immersion can take place.

    C. To deepen the client's capacity to constructively act on her discoveries.

 II. *Invoking the actual* is inviting or encouraging the client *into* that which is palpably relevant. The goals of invoking the actual are to help the client clarify, stay present to, and eventually "occupy" her concern; to help her attend to the here and now, make "I" statements, and attend to the preverbal processes behind her words; to use meditation and imagery as vehicles for deep somatic immersion in tensions, fears, and anxieties; to use role-play and rehearsal as vehicles for relevant and immediate exploration; to use interpersonal encounter to experientially consider areas of past and present concern; to use fantasy and dream material; and to encourage extratherapy experimentation to practice and apply experiential skills outside the clinical setting.

III. *Vivifying and confronting resistance* are ways of helping clients overcome *blockages* to that which is palpably relevant.

    Note: It is important that vivifying and confronting be used to empower the *client,* and not the therapist or outside authority, to overcome his resistances. This conforms to our belief that the lasting power for change resides in the client, not in the one who instructs or directs him.

---

*These phases are often sequential, but depending on many factors, such as the client's pace, they sometimes operate irregularly with one another and should be dealt with accordingly.

The goals of vivifying and confronting resistance are:

A. To vivify, feed back, or "hold a mirror up" to moments where the client blocks or defeats himself; to acknowledge erroneous feedback when it is discovered and to suspend judgment about feedback when it is questionable; to mimic or physically mirror the client's resistance where appropriate; to empathically trace out implications of the client's resistance; to model or "act out" the consequences of overcoming the client's resistance (which can, paradoxically, mobilize the client to break out of his victimized stance); and to enable or encourage the client's resistance where appropriate (which can also paradoxically, mobilize him).

B. To empathically confront resistance (when other means fail) by intensifying the vivification, (e.g., by helping to *alarm* the client about, not merely alert him to, the ways in which he blocks or defeats himself); to use challenging questions or suggestions where appropriate to foster that sense of urgency (e.g., "Do you mean you *won't* when you say you can't?")

IV. *Meaning-creation* is the sum total of the understandings and life directions that emerge from "occupying" one's concerns. The goals of meaning-creation are:

A. To clarify an experientially based "story" about what has rendered one dysfunctional and what that implies for the future direction of one's life; to use all the experientially based "invitations" outlined above—presence to one's feelings, meditations, role-plays, interpersonal encounters, associative and dream material, and so on—to develop this story.

B. To *act on* one's realizations.

Note: When engaged maximally, this phase often leads to heightened desires for intimacy, altruism, and spirituality.

WAYS THE INTERVENTION PHASES UTILIZE THE CONSTRICTIVE-EXPANSIVE CONTINUUM

I. *Presence* stresses the question, *what* is palpably relevant *between* T (the therapist) and C (the client) and *within* C. That which is palpably relevant is often (though not necessarily) that which C denies; and that which C denies often clusters around constriction (smallness, fragility, dissolution) or expansion (greatness, audacity, explosiveness). While C may be ostensibly angry (*expanded*), for example, the palpably relevant issue may be sadness (*smallness*). On the other hand, C's anger may indeed be the relevant issue; and discrepancies (such as sadness) may be absent. T needs to give C time, therefore, to explore whether his/her polarity is the palpably relevant one or whether it is essentially defensive in quality—in which case signs of discrepancy and denial should begin to manifest themselves.

II. *Invoking the actual* stresses inviting or encouraging C *into* that which is palpably relevant. This is done by artfully feeding back or providing here/now opportunities for C to "occupy" that which is palpably relevant. T might comment to C, for example, that "a tear has just formed in your eye," "I feel a sudden heaviness in your manner," "I wonder if we could role-play that meeting with your boss—see what feelings come up *now*," or "You're really steaming—how might that help you get on with your life?"

The constrictive-expansive continuum can also alert T to (or make her watchful for) palpable relevancies that are very remote from C's overt presentation. Sometimes, very selectively, it is useful to "test the water" with this kind of foresight. For example, Bugental's (1976, p. 16) comment to his inflated client Laurence that "You're scared shitless!" and Bob's comment to the ostensibly enraged Joanna, "I sense that you are deeply hurting right now, Joanna"* were foundational in their impact and catalyzing of the liberation process.

The worst that can happen in such circumstances is that the client will resist the challenge (in which case the resistance must be worked with). But at least (s)he gets a taste of it (working with him/her more gradually might have postponed this taste, and its momentum, correlatively to encounter it in future).

SUMMARY OF EI DECISION POINTS

Below is a summary of decision points suggested by the EI guidelines. These, too, can be role-played, or simply reflected upon, in the course of study.

1. The first and ongoing question is, What is this client's desire and capacity for constrictive/expansive change? (Use presence, intuition, empirical knowledge, and dialogue with the client to render this judgment.)
2. If the client is in acute crisis, in the early stages of therapy, is fragile, suspicious, or intellectually unprepared—consider nonexperiential liberation strategies (behavioral, cognitive, or medical).
3. If the client emphasizes childhood sexuality or interpersonal issues; or if he is at an impasse with nonexperiential and experiential liberation strategies—consider semi-experiential liberation strategies (psychoanalysis, self psychology).
4. If the client appears physically, cognitively, and emotionally ready, and if he accepts invitations to deepen any of the concerns or conditions above, consider experiential liberation strategies (presence, invoking the actual, vivifying and confronting resistance, and meaning-creation).

SKILL-BUILDING EXERCISES: SUGGESTIONS FOR INSTRUCTORS

The following skill-building exercises—to be facilitated by instructors—can (1) help students *personally* understand experiential liberation and (2) help them translate that understanding into practice. The exercises are divided into two sections: those that are personal and those that are clinical (applied). While the personal exercises may

---

*As suggested in the chapter, such interventions can reflect either invoking-the-actual *or* confronting-resistance phases of treatment.

be engaged variably over a course of study, the clinical exercises should be engaged sequentially, in the order presented.*

I PERSONAL EXERCISES

Exercises that Challenge Students to Be Present, to Face Resistance, and to Create Meaning

The Who Am I Exercise Have students write down ten phrases that best describe who they are (e.g., "I am a worrier," "I am a student"), and order them in terms of priority and centrality to themselves (e.g., tenth is least central, first is most central). Have students do this reflectively, but not labor over it.

Complete the exercise in fifteen minutes.

Immediately following the above, and beginning with the *least* central description, proceed to have students cross out each description, right down to the first and most central, if possible. *Important:* As they are crossing out each description, have them be as mindful as possible of how that particular deletion/relinquishment *feels* to them. What are its implications for their lives?

Complete the exercise in fifteen minutes.

For the next half hour, discuss with students the implications of this exercise. What was it like (for those students willing to engage it)? Did it reveal anything new or surprising to them? What did it imply for prioritizing their lives and for rearranging or losing those priorities? Did they welcome their identity descriptions and loss of identity descriptions, or did they resist them? If they resisted them, how did they deal with the resistance? How *present* were they able to be during the exercise, and what did the exercise imply about the kind of constrictive or expansive life-design(s) they've created? Finally, what did the exercise imply about the clinical work they do, or the kinds of crises their clients experience? (See Bugental, 1987, for an elaboration on this exercise.)

Encountering One's "Double" This exercise is modified from a workshop given by Bugental, (November 1993). An extremely important theme in the psychology of literature (Rank, 1925/1971), the double (or what the Germans call doppelganger) is equally significant for clinicians. Essentially, the double is the suppressed side (or pole) of one's personality; it is the side that is denied. The aim of this exercise is to sensitize students to this phenomenon and its rich EI implications. The exercise proceeds as follows: Have students break up into triads. Request that the members of each triad greet each other—as if they met at a party. Stress that students simply "be themselves" with one another and not try to play a particular role. After four minutes, ask that students reflect on these interactions, and note their verbal and preverbal experiences. Next, request that students try a role-play (to the degree they feel comfortable). Suggest that they role-play a side of themselves that they are intrigued about but generally suppress in everyday life. Recommend that they genuinely

---

*Although these exercises are rudimentary, they can also be emotionally challenging. It is important, therefore, to prepare students for such challenges and to support them as required.

immerse themselves in this role and attune to their manner of engaging it. Give them four minutes for this segment. Next, ask students to write down their experience of role-playing their double: what did it feel like, how much did they resist it, how much did they feel liberated by it, and what are its implications for their lives (e.g., costs, compromises, possibilities)? Stress that these observations do not have to be shared with others. Finally, bring the class back to its normal arrangement and open the floor to discussion. (Tie the discussion to the pertinent EI themes, such as integration of polarities, presence, resistance, and meaning-creation.)

Writing One's Own Obituary   Instruct students to write a one- to two-paragraph description of how they would like to be remembered after they die. Afterward, discuss what this exercise was like for them. What did it bring up as far as how they are currently living their lives? What impact might it have about how they will live their lives in the future. What does it say about time, aging, and death? What fears or concerns does it signal?

This exercise should take approximately a half hour and is best offered on the last day of the term. (See Bugental, 1973/1974, for an elaboration on this exercise.)

II CLINICAL EXERCISES

1. Exercises that Cultivate Presence

Begin this class exercise with the progressive tension and relaxation of group muscles, from the forehead to the toes. Then try a simple meditative exercise, such as attending to breathing or body sensations. Next, have students pair up and sit across from one another in silence for one minute. Ask participants to attune to their partner's body positions, gestures, facial expressions, and other nonverbal signals. Underscore the freshness and uniqueness of these experiential worlds. Then have students attend to their own thoughts, feelings, and sensations in response to their partners' presentations. Afterward, have students record and discuss these respective experiences.

The time for this exercise is twenty to thirty minutes.

2. Exercises Aimed at Invoking the Actual (or Palpably Relevant)[*]

Enhancing Presence through Focus and Topical Expansion   Have students form dyads. One partner plays the therapist (T), and the other partner plays the client (C). T begins by asking C, "What is of concern?" or "What really matters to you right now?" (It is important that C discuss a concern that he or she feels comfortable relating.) T observes C's response and only nods or says, "Tell me more." Afterward, the partners discuss their experiences in terms of presence to body sensations, affect, imagery, and other nonverbal signals. Partners then switch roles.

The time per role-play should be ten minutes. Discussion follows.

---

[*]It is best if instructors themselves role-play the exercises described from this point on, so as to provide students with an example.

Further Enhancing Presence through Focus, Topical Expansion, and Feedback
Have students form trios. One partner observes and records his perceptions of the
students who play C and T. The observer should especially note T's ability to facilitate C's presence and immersion in her concern. T is to do this by gently encouraging
C to stay with and expand on her feelings, by empathically paraphrasing what she
says (repeating key phrases, slowing her down, mimicking or mirroring as appropriate), and having her concretely describe an example of her problem. Afterward, each
party should describe what happened from his or her vantage point and—time permitting—switch roles.
   Time per role-play should be twenty minutes.

Deepening Presence   Have students form trios again. The observer this time is to
note interaction. In addition to the above skills, the therapist is to help the client stay
with "I" statements and personal and relevant content. T is to begin tagging points
where the client diverges from relevant material or intellectualizes. T should also
begin to alert the client to body movements, vocal tones, and points where the dialogue becomes intense or charged, as well as discrepancies between content and
affect. T should use discussion, dream work, role-play, rehearsal, and meditation, and
should even suggest experiments for C to try outside of the session to help him
deepen his self-encounter and begin to understand, in a live way, the basis for his
concern. (This exercise is aimed at deepening C's self-contact and initial *felt* understanding of his concerns. The point should be stressed that insight is to emerge from
deep immersion in the subjective and not from T's interpretation.) Discuss from each
perspective and switch roles.
   Time per role-play should be twenty minutes.

The Therapeutic Encounter   Have students form trios again. This exercise is aimed
at helping students to use the relationship to facilitate self-exploration and integration.
The first focus here is on the impact of T's empathy in facilitating C's self-immersion
and awareness. Second, the focus is not only on T's attention to transference/
countertransference issues but also current interpersonal responses and how they affect
C's self-contact. Observer should watch how T alerts client to and handles disappointments, irritations, pleasures, and so on within the role-play relationship and how these
are worked through. Does T disclose too much, too little? Does she evoke C's affect
productively? The idea is to be able to struggle somewhat but be sensitive to and steadfastly maintain contact with C. Discuss from each perspective and switch partners.
   Time per role-play should be twenty minutes.

3. Exercises Designed to Vivify and Confront Resistance

Vivifying Resistance   Again, set up trios. Here, C agrees to role-play a resistant
client. Discuss importance of being sensitive to resistances—how they are perceived
as familiar and safer than alternative life-designs despite their destructiveness. T
focuses on noting and tagging all resistant behavior—changes in vocal tone, gestures,
facial expression, emotional blocking, intellectualization, projection, divergence from
the present or from the relationship with T, superficial contact, and so on. T should

gently challenge C to weigh (in a felt way) alternative directions or pros and cons of the particular resistance. The idea of this exercise is not to force or eradicate resistances but to vivify them and to help C observe how these resistances cripple his world. Moreover, this vivification helps C move toward taking responsibility for and making a decision about that which holds him back. The therapist cannot really force this, nor should she. Discuss from each perspective and switch roles.

Time per role-play should be twenty minutes.

Confronting Resistance   Form trios again. This time, C will role-play *chronic* resistance. T will attempt to empathically, but firmly, jar C into consciousness of his resistance and his ability to overcome that resistance. She can do this through nonaccusatory, first-person suggestions (e.g., "I believe you can say more") or evocative descriptions (e.g., "You look terrorized right now"). Such confrontation can also be facilitated through challenges to distinguish between *can't* and *won't* and between *might* and *will*. (It is important to alert participants to their option to withdraw from this potentially intensive exercise at any time.) Discuss from each perspective and switch roles. (It is especially helpful to discuss the empathic quality of T's confrontation as well as C's response to that quality.)

Time per role-play should be twenty minutes.

4. Exercise Aimed at Synthesizing Previous Skills and the Embodied Creation of Meaning

This exercise draws upon all previous skills to facilitate meaning-creation and a productive life direction. Form trios. T should help C to (a) focus on and stay present to a relevant concern, (b) meditate on and experiment with that concern; (c) attend to the immediate relationship as appropriate, (d) vivify and work through resistance, and (e) consolidate meaning from the encounter.

Time per role-play should be thirty minutes.

NOTES

1. Although attempts have been made to integrate so-called existential practices into mainstream or transtheoretical frameworks (e.g., see Prochaska & DiClemente, 1986, and Beutler & Clarkin, 1990), few attempts, to my knowledge, have aimed at integrating mainstream approaches into the existential outlook. (See Bugental, 1978, 1987, for fine but brief exceptions; Koestenbaum, 1978, for a philosophical integration; and Barton, 1974, for a synthesis of Freud, Jung, and Rogers.)

    The framework I am about to present, moreover (which I have elsewhere called the "paradox principle," Schneider, 1990), possesses at least one more novel feature—an existential metapsychology. I will elaborate upon this metapsychology (e.g., its dynamic and developmental features), discuss its relevance to therapy integration, and apply it to the clinical context.

    Finally, I cannot overstate the need for students to begin appropriately investigating proposals such as the above. I strongly hope they will take up the cause.

2. This structure of consciousness is both provisional and revisable in the light of new evidence. It is a theoretically useful map, in other words, and is in no way intended to be taken as an actual or ultimate "territory."

3. Body consciousness in this context differs from the physiological or organic consciousness we spoke of earlier. Whereas physiological or organic consciousness is relatively simple (i.e., circumscribed, excitatory), body consciousness is relatively complex (i.e., multitextured, sublime); and whereas physiological or organic consciousness is comparatively overt (i.e., measurable), body consciousness is comparatively intimate (i.e., qualitative). (See Merleau-Ponty, 1962, for an elaboration of these points.)

4. These criteria compare favorably with Prochaska, DiClemente, and Norcross' (1992) five transtheoretical stages of client change. These are the stages of (a) precontemplation, (b) contemplation, (c) preparation, (d) action, and (e) maintenance.

5. There is, of course, a degree of oversimplification in these statements about practitioners from respective orientations: Many are more existential than one might be led to believe. Indeed, recent research suggests that in general, good therapists embody personable, affect-centered qualities and that from the client's point of view, these are the qualities that count (Bugental & Bracke, 1992; Lambert, Shapiro, & Bergin, 1986; Schneider, 1992).

   It is time, it would seem, to make the cultivation of such qualities *central* (rather than peripheral) to the formal education of clinicians.

6. Although my formulation of experiential strategies draws from and parallels those of such luminaries as Bugental (1978, 1987), Gendlin (1978), Mahrer (1986), May (1969, 1981), Perls (1969), and Yalom (1980), it is based on a modestly different set of practical and theoretical assumptions. (See Schneider, 1990, 1993, for the relevant comparisons.)

7. I want to be clear that when I speak of "structure" here, I do not mean some kind of objective, or cookbook, formula. I mean a phenomenologically based metaphor that can (a) help therapists *understand* what is going on in their clients and (b) help therapists *redress* (or heal) what is going on in their clients—based on that understanding. To be sure, some experiential therapists resist even metaphorical criteria for working with their clients because they see in such criteria an element of depersonalization. But to the extent that one views metaphors as subservient to the *person* about whom they are applied, one can counter this objectifying tendency. It is quite probable, moreover, that antimetaphorical therapists themselves use such criteria—albeit implicitly—to organize their own outlooks. Here I simply explicate some of those subliminal criteria.

8. Such underlying qualities are roughly equivalent to May's (1969) concept of "intentionality," which we shall discuss.

9. While this turnaround may be explained on the basis of flooding and desensitization paradigms, I do not believe these are complete explanations. It was the condition whereby my client could fully *experience* rather than merely visualize her defensiveness that led her to substantively change.

REFERENCES

Antonovsky, A. (1979) *Health, stress, & coping.* San Francisco: Jossey-Bass.

Barton, A. (1974). *Three worlds of therapy: Freud, Jung, and Rogers.* Palo Alto, CA: National Press Books.

Beck, A. (1976). *Cognitive therapy and the emotional disorders.* New York: Signet.

Becker, E. (1973). *The denial of death.* New York: Free Press.

Berman, M. (1989). *Coming to our senses: Body and spirit in the hidden history of the West.* New York: Bantam.

Beutler, L., & Clarkin, J. (1990). *Systematic treatment selection: Toward targeted therapeutic interventions.* New York: Brunner/Mazel.

Binswanger, L. (1975). *Being in the world: Selected papers of Ludwig Binswanger.* (J. Needleman, Trans.) New York: Basic Books.

Buber, M. (1970). *I and thou.* (W. Kaufmann, Trans.) New York: Simon & Schuster.

Bugental, J. (1973/1974). Confronting the existential meaning of 'my death' through group exercises. *Interpersonal Development, 4,* 148–163.

Bugental, J. (1976). *The search for existential identity: Patient-therapist dialogues in humanistic psychotherapy.* San Francisco: Jossey-Bass.

Bugental, J. (1978). *Psychotherapy and process: The fundamentals of an existential-humanistic approach.* Reading, MA: Addison-Wesley.

Bugental, J. (1987). *The art of the psychotherapist.* New York: Norton.

Bugental, J., & Bracke, P. (1992). The future of existential-humanistic psychotherapy. *Psychotherapy, 29*(1), 28–33.

Cogswell, J. (1993). Walking in your shoes: Toward integrating sense of self with sense of oneness. *Journal of Humanistic Psychology, 33*(3), 99–111.

Craig, P. E. (1986). Sanctuary and presence: An existential view of the therapist's contribution. *The Humanistic Psychologist, 14*(1), 22–28.

Ellis, A. (1962). *Reason and emotion in psychotherapy.* New York: Lyle Stuart.

Erickson, M. (1965). The use of symptoms as an integral part of hypnotherapy. *American Journal of Clinical Hypnosis, 8,* 57–65.

Frankl, V. (1962). *Man's search for meaning.* Boston: Beacon Press.

Frankl, V. (1965). *The doctor and the soul.* New York: Knopf.

Freud, S. (1963). *A general introduction to psychoanalysis* (J. Riviere, Trans.). New York: Pocket Books.

Friedman, M. (1991). *Encounter on the narrow ridge: A life of Martin Buber.* New York: Paragon House.

Gendlin, E. (1978). *Focusing.* New York: Bantam.

Keleman, S. (1985). *Emotional anatomy.* Berkeley, CA: Center Press.

Kobasa, S., Maddi, S., & Puccetti, M. (1982). Personality and exercise as buffers in the stress-illness relationship. *Journal of Behavioral Medicine, 5*(4), 391–404.

Koestenbaum, P. (1978). *The new image of the person: The theory and practice of clinical philosophy.* Westport, CT: Greenwood.

Kohut, H. (1977). *The restoration of the self.* New York: International Universities Press.

Laing, R. (1969). *The divided self: An existential study in sanity and madness.* Middlesex, England: Penguin.

Laing, R. (speaker). (1985). *Theoretical and practical aspects of psychotherapy* (Cassette Recording No. L330-W1A). Phoenix, AZ: The Evolution of Psychotherapy Conference.

Lambert, M., Shapiro, D., & Bergin, A. (1986). The effectiveness of psychotherapy. In A. Bergin and S. Garfield (Eds.), *Handbook of psychotherapy and research* (pp. 157–212). New York: Wiley.

Mahrer, A. (1983). *Experiential psychotherapy: Basic practices.* New York: Brunner/Mazel.

Mahrer, A. (1986). *Therapeutic experiencing: The process of change.* New York: Norton.

Maslow, A. (1967). Neurosis as a failure of personal growth. *Humanitas 3,* 153–169.

May, R. (1958). Contributions of existential therapy. In R. May, E. Angel, and H. Ellenberger (Eds.), *Existence: A new dimension in psychiatry and psychology* (pp. 37–91). New York: Basic Books.

May, R. (1969). *Love and will.* New York: Norton.

May, R. (1972). *Power and innocence.* New York: Norton.

May, R. (1981). *Freedom and destiny.* New York: Norton.

May, R. (1983). *The discovery of being: Writings in existential psychology.* New York: Norton.

May, R. (1992). The loss of wonder. *Dialogues: Therapeutic applications of existential philosophy, 1*(1), 4–5. (Publication of students from the California School of Professional Psychology, Berkeley/Alameda campus. Glenn Hammel, Ed.)

McGoldrick, M., & Gerson, R. (1985). *Genograms in family assessment.* New York: Norton.

Merleau-Ponty, M. (1962). *Phenomenology of perception.* London: Routledge.

Moreno, J. (1959). Psychodrama. In S. Arieti et al. (Eds.), *American handbook of psychiatry* (Vol. 2). New York: Basic Books.

Perls, F. (1969). *Gestalt therapy verbatim.* Moab, Utah: Real People Press.

Phillips, J. (1980). Transference and encounter: The therapeutic relationship in psychoanalytic and existential therapy. *Review of Existential Psychiatry and Psychology, 17*(2 & 3), 135–152.

Prochaska, J., & DiClemente, C. (1986). The transtheoretical approach. In J. Norcross (Ed.), *Handbook of eclectic psychotherapy* (pp. 163–200). New York: Brunner/Mazel.

Prochaska, J., DiClemente, C., & Norcross, J. (1992). In search of how people change: Applications to addictive behaviors. *American Psychologist, 47*(9), 1102–1114.

Rank, O. (1925/1971). *The double: A psychoanalytic study.* (H. Tucker, Trans.). New York: New American Library.

Reed, P. (1987). Spirituality and well-being in terminally ill hospitalized adults. *Research in Nursing and Health, 10,* 335–344.

Reich, W. (1949). *Character analysis.* New York: Orgone Institute Press.

Reik, T. (1948). *Listening with the third ear.* New York: Farrar, Straus.

Rilke, R. (1991). Letters to a young poet. In M. Friedman (Ed.), *The worlds of existentialism: A critical reader* (pp. 266–270). Atlantic Highlands, NJ: Humanities Press.

Schneider, K. (1987). The deified self: A "centaur" response to Wilber and the transpersonal movement. *Journal of Humanistic Psychology, 27*(2), 196–216.

Schneider, K. (1989). Infallibility is so damn appealing: A reply to Ken Wilber. *Journal of Humanistic Psychology, 29*(4), 470–481.

Schneider, K. (1990). *The paradoxical self: Toward an understanding of our contradictory nature.* New York: Plenum.

Schneider, K. (1992). Therapists' personal maturity and therapeutic success: How strong is the link? *The Psychotherapy Patient, 8*(3/4), 71–91.

Schneider, K. (1993). *Horror and the holy: Wisdom-teachings of the monster tale.* Chicago and La Salle, IL: Open Court.

Skinner, B. F. (1953). *Science and human behavior.* New York: Macmillan.

Van Dusen, W. (1965). Invoking the actual in psychotherapy. *Journal of Individual Psychology, 21,* 66–76.

Volkan, V. (1987). *Six steps in the treatment of borderline personality organization.* New York: Jason Aronson.

Wolfe, B. (1992). The integrative therapy of the anxiety disorders. In J. Norcross & M. Goldfried (Eds.), *Handbook of psychotherapy integration* (pp. 373–401). New York: Basic Books.

Wolpe, J. (1969). *The practice of behavior therapy.* New York: Pergamon.

Yalom, I. (1980). *Existential psychotherapy.* New York: Basic Books.

CHAPTER 6

CASE ILLUSTRATIONS OF EXPERIENTIAL LIBERATION

The following cases elucidate the practical utility of the preceding experiential (and EI) guidelines. Selection of the case material was based on four criteria: (1) its experiential-integrative focus; (2) its clarity and conciseness; (3) its depth and originality; and (4) its ethnic and diagnostic diversity.

A significant cross section of the existential therapeutic community has been chosen to contribute to this section. For example, while some of the authors are world-renowned authorities, others are authorities only in their particular communities; and while most of the authors are senior-level clinicians, a few are creative and enthusiastic mid- and, in one case, junior-level practitioners.

One final note: While the EI guidelines and themes, such as "smallness-greatness," "nonexperiential," "experiential," are notable in each vignette—and will be discussed in my follow-up case formulations—they may not be referred to explicitly in each vignette. This is because of each contributor's unique individual slant on his or her material; but it is also, as previously noted, due to the flexible nature of existentially oriented therapy in general. It is enough, therefore, if the EI guidelines spark a fruitful dialogue about the case material. Ultimately, however, the vignettes must speak for themselves.

BLACK AND IMPOTENT: THE CASE OF MERCEDES

Rollo May

Rollo May, Ph.D., co-author of this book, is an internationally acclaimed psychologist, psychoanalyst, and author. His recent books include The Courage to Create, Freedom and Destiny, *and* The Cry for Myth.

This classic case not only illustrates Rollo May's therapeutic style, it also breaks fresh technical and theoretical ground. For example, by refusing to conceive of his client as "unanalyzable," May takes the first steps toward empowering her; and by showing (*not merely describing*) *what power looks like, he emboldens her to change.*

  This is a pioneering case in another way: It is one of the first to demonstrate the effectiveness of existentially oriented therapy with ethnic minorities. Working creatively with Mercedes's dreams, somatic reactions, and here/now intentions, May lucidly traces her emergence. It is an emergence within the sober parameters of her environment, perhaps, but it is a remarkable unfolding nonetheless.

> *The real tragedy for the [African-American] is that he has not taken himself seriously because no one else has. The hope for the [African-American] is that now he is asserting that he really is a human being, and is demanding the rights due to a human being. If he succeeds in winning these rights he will respect and trust himself, but he cannot win the right to human dignity without the ability to respect and cherish his own humanity in spite of pervasive white rejection.*
> —KENNETH CLARK, *Dark Ghetto*

This . . . is an account of the development in psychotherapy of a young black woman from almost complete impotence to self-esteem and the capacity for aggression. She was born and raised in a state of powerlessness. It is not by accident that she is both a black and a woman, two conditions that decisively increase the usual feeling of powerlessness.

An extreme form of powerlessness can be for a woman the inability to bear a child. Mercedes, as we shall call her, was conscious of only one real desire, a desire her husband shared—to have a baby. But every time she got pregnant, she would have a miscarriage or, for various reasons, have to have an abortion. Whatever else may be said about procreation, it is a special demonstration of one's power, an extension of one's self, a production of a new member of one's kind, a new being. This is especially obvious with women; many a woman blossoms with confidence only when she has a baby. But there is also in men the experience that their manhood is affirmed. The sense of pride of paternity is a cliché, but should not for that reason be derogated.

When I first saw Mercedes, a thirty-two-year-old woman, she looked like a West Indian, striking and exotic in appearance. She explained that she was one-quarter Cherokee Indian, one-quarter Scotch, and the remaining half Negro. She had been married for eight years to a white professional man, whose therapist had referred her

Source: Power and Innocence (New York: Norton, 1972).

to me. The marriage was on the edge of collapse, partly because of Mercedes' so-called frigidity and complete lack of sexual interest in her husband.

She had no active belief that she deserved to be helped, but seemed to accept her problems fatalistically, each hardship being taken as another expression of inevitable doom. The only problem she did recognize and feel with any strength was the already mentioned inability to carry through a pregnancy. Eight experiences of miscarriage or abortion had occurred up to this time.

She had been judged unanalyzable by two other therapists on their belief that she did not have enough motivation, could not generate enough inner conflict about her problems. They felt she was unable to be introspective enough or to feel enough about her problems to engage in the long-term process of working them through. She seemed not to repress her problems, but just to find it inconceivable that she could do anything at all about them.

I accepted her as a patient partly because of my conviction that the label "untreatable" refers not to a state of the patient but to the limitations of an individual psychotherapist's methods. It is important that a psychotherapist try to find the special kind of treatment that will unlock the door to the problems of this particular person.

In the first session Mercedes told me that her stepfather had used her as a prostitute from the time she was eleven until she was twenty-one. The stepfather brought men in to her several times a week after school, before her mother got home from work. Ostensibly the mother knew nothing about this.

Mercedes was not aware of anything she got out of this prostitution; with rare exceptions, she had no sexual excitement, only a feeling that she was being desired. Whatever money was exchanged, none of it ended up in her pocket. But she could not say no to her stepfather and, indeed, could not even fantasy refusing to go along with his expectations. She later went to a community college—an I.Q. test, which she remembers somewhere along the line, gave her a score of 130 to 140. At college she joined a sorority where she went through all the proper motions and emotions. The prostitution continued all the while. It was only when she went to nursing school after college and lived out of her mother's house that she broke away from her stepfather.

Mercedes seemed like a "nice" person, docile, who had adopted the role of harmonizer in the family. Brought up in a Negro section, she had learned almost with her first breath in life that it was her function to please everybody, to be passive, and to accept whatever form of victimization life might bring her. She had taken faithful care of her grandmother, who lived with the family. Not at all a sissy, however, she had learned, like everyone else in her environment, to fight. She had fought not only her own battles at school and on the street—in which she would go into a wild fury—but had also protected her younger brother as he grew up.

My assumption that on some level she must have hated the prostitution was borne out by a childhood memory she was to recount later in the therapy. When visiting relatives in Virginia she had watched a donkey keep trying to get its penis into a mare which stood there apathetically. "I *hated* that donkey!" she expostulated. The vehemence and sincerity with which she uttered this statement indicated that she had always regarded the prostitution as a hated offense against her. But it was totally impossible for some months to get from her any conscious awareness of that conviction.

Beneath the surface I knew Mercedes was profoundly helpless, apathetic, and chronically depressed. Such diagnostic statements don't help us much since anyone in her situation would have been similarly depressed. We have to see more of the inner dynamics of her life.

1. THE MISSING ANGER

When I asked her what she wanted from the therapy and from me, Mercedes could not respond for a while. She finally got out that she found herself often saying as a kind of prayer: "Let me have a child, let me be a good wife, let me enjoy sex, let me *feel* something."

For the second therapy session she brought in the following two dreams. Both were about her dog, Ruby, with whom, as she said, she often identified.

> My dog, Ruby, was hurt. It must be a cut because I have one. I take him home but he runs away again into the subway. A man was there protecting a beagle. I asked, "Which way did Ruby run?" He said a big policeman shot him and they carried him off in an ambulance. I said, "It's my dog," but they didn't let me in to see him.

> Ruby runs away again. I was yelling, running after him. I saved Ruby from a man. Because of this I owed the man some treat. He knew me because he had seen me doing my exercises. I invited him to dinner. He reaches over and touches me sexually. I try to kick him, but I get bumped in the back. I feel a push toward him every time I try to kick him. I turn around and see my mother pushing me toward him.

The dreams give a vivid picture of an extremely helpless woman. When, in the first dream, the dog is shot and carried away, the authorities ignore her cry that he is hers—a graphic picture of the members of the Establishment highhandedly discharging the "white man's burden." They show no respect whatever for Mercedes' feelings or her rights; they assume she simply has none. Such situations which she reflects and creates in the dream would themselves suffice to destroy any nascent individual sense of self-esteem if it were present in her. Anything she does in trying to get to her own wounded dog—or to save herself—is useless; this-is-the-way-the-world-is.

Since these dreams occurred almost at the beginning of therapy, we have to ask whether Mercedes is, in the second dream, also revealing her attitudes toward me, the therapist. All these strains could be read as referring to me—I shoot the dog (or *her,* since she is identified with it); I have no respect for her feelings; I am the man from whom she saves Ruby, the one to whom she "owes something" and who makes sexual passes at her. No wonder she hadn't leaped into therapy! She was completely unaware of these implications toward me (I noted them but judged it was too early in therapy to bring them out). And I am as sure as one can be that nothing happened in the first two sessions to account for this attitude. We must assume that she sees all relationships with men, especially white men, as a power struggle, in which they are the winners and she the powerless victim.

The I-am-only-a-servant attitude is carried further in the second dream: *because she saves Ruby from a man, she owes the man a "treat."* A strange "logic of injustice" is present in such persons who are forced to accept the fact that others have all the rights and they have none. It is the exact opposite of the assumption of one's worth as a person; she is indentured a priori; even saving herself is an act demanding she give some recompense to the man. The one form of giving, the one currency she has which is desired by men, is sex; this is the exploitation men demand as payment. Payment, in this case, is only for what ought to have been hers to start with. If she says no, if she gets what is hers, she is taking away something from the world.

But most important of all in this dream is the role of her mother. She pushes the girl toward the man. The dream says that the mother not only knows what is going on—knows about the prostitution—but actively abets it.

Shortly after Mercedes began therapy, she became pregnant by her husband. I then noted a tremendously interesting phenomenon. Every couple of weeks when she came in reporting that she had begun to bleed vaginally—which was in her judgment as well as medically a symptom predicting a miscarriage—she would also report a dream. This dream would be one in which her mother, and less frequently her father or others, were attacking and trying to kill her. The consistent simultaneity of this kind of dream and the bleeding as a harbinger of a miscarriage was what struck me.

At first I tried to draw out the anger I assumed the young woman must feel toward her assassins. She would sit there mildly agreeing with me but feeling nothing at all. It became clear that she was totally unable to muster any conscious rage toward her mother or stepfather or toward others who were out to kill her. This, again, contradicts all logic: you *ought* to feel rage when someone is out to kill you; that's what anger is for biologically—an emotional reaction to someone's destroying your power to be.

Taking my cue from the second dream, I hypothesized that some struggle with her mother was the reason behind the constant miscarriages, and that if she had a baby, she secretly felt her mother (or stepfather) would kill her. Having a baby was inviting death at their hands.

But we were faced with an immediate practical problem which would not wait: it often takes several months for a theory to become practically convincing and efficacious to the patient, no matter how correct it may be. We were confronted with the likelihood of a spontaneous abortion. Some rage had to be expressed, and I was the only other person in the room. So I decided, not wholly consciously, to express *my* rage in place of hers.

Each time she began vaginal bleeding and brought in such a dream, I would verbally counterattack those who were trying to kill her. Chiefly I attacked her mother with other figures thrown in from time to time. What did these blankety-blank people mean by trying to kill her for having a baby? That bitch, her mother, must have known about the prostitution all along and had been, as in the dream, pushing her into it. She was continually sacrificing Mercedes on the altar of homage to the stepfather, to keep him—or for whatever Godforsaken other exploitative reason. After all, Mercedes (I continued) had done her best, serving everybody, even submitting to sexual exploitation. And here these people still have the power to prohibit her from having the one thing she wants, a baby!

I was giving vent to the rage the girl had never dared express herself. I was allying myself with that faint autonomous element which we must assume is in every human being, although in Mercedes it was practically nonexistent to start with.

At first she continued to sit mute, somewhat surprised at my expressed anger. *But the bleeding would stop.* Each time she would have the warning of a miscarriage and such a dream, I would again leap to the attack, expressing the aggression she could not, or did not dare to, feel. Some of these dreams that occurred during the pregnancy were:

> My father was pounding me to interfere with the baby. He was furious at my having the baby. My husband did not come to help me.

> I was fighting a woman. I was being paralyzed. My voice was leaving me, and I was losing control of my emotions. My father would not leave me in peace. I was screaming to my mother and father. . . . To my mother I screamed, "If you're going to help me, help me. If you are not, leave me alone."

After three or four months she herself began to feel her own aggression and expressed her own anger at the attackers in the dreams. It was as though she took over from me the project of anger; in this sense my anger was her first self-affirmation. She separately called up her parents—her mother, her real father, and her stepfather—and told them in no uncertain terms not to phone her or in any other way get in touch with her until after her baby was born. This act took me by surprise—I hadn't specifically expected it—but I was glad of it. I affirmed it as Mercedes's newfound ability to assert herself and demand her rights.

In the month before the baby was due there appeared some actual affirmation of giving birth. "Lynda Bird [the then president's daughter] is having a baby" was one dream, and "I took a job" was another. When a dream occurred at that point about the stepfather—"He got angry and got a knife"—she apparently had very little fear of him. "So what?" was all she said.

The baby was safely born at its appointed time, to the great joy of Mercedes and her husband. They picked out a name that, like "Prometheus," signifies a new beginning in the history of mankind. She and her husband were totally unconscious, so far as I could determine, of this significance. But I thought it fitting, indeed—a new race of man is born!

Several things about my anger need to be clarified. I was not assuming a role—I genuinely *felt* angry toward her mother and stepfather. The relationship in therapy can be likened to a field of magnetic force. This field has two persons in it, patient and therapist. Into this field is introduced a dream. Some rage was required against the destroyers in the dream. It is more therapeutic if the patient can muster the anger. But if she—as in this case—cannot, the therapist, also feeling the same anger, can express it. I also was not merely "training" Mercedes to establish "habit patterns" by which she herself could become angry. No, we were playing for keeps—to keep a fetus in her womb. Nor is this mere "catharsis" or abreaction in the usual senses of those words. The stakes were life itself—her baby's.

For what is this woman fighting? Why, in her dreams, this great battle with fist and knife? The answer is both simple and profound; she is fighting for her right to exist, to exist as a person with the autonomy and freedom that are inseparably bound up with being a person. She is fighting for her right to *be*—if I may use that verb in its full and powerful meaning—and to be, if necessary, against the whole universe, in Pascal's sense. These phrases—the right to be, the struggle for one's own existence—are poor ones, but they are the only ones we have.

The battle is pictured with knives and fists, which is the language of the streets on which Mercedes was brought up. She knows that she is not permitted to assert her own being except as she establishes herself through brute tooth-and-claw strength. She later stated that she could not have fought her mother without the therapy—"I got my strength from you to stand against my mother"—but obviously it was *her* strength when she got it, and it was *she* who did the standing.

There is yet another point. Mercedes, different from the usual patient in psychoanalysis, could assume her dreams were part of a separate world (and this is what the analysts who had rejected her found lacking in her). This is like the "magic world" of some patients. She could then simply go ahead as if she had no real anger. All the while the rage and the anxiety connected with it were exacting a serious price—her sterility. To *admit* this anger consciously would have been a threat with which she was unable to cope; it would have meant admitting that her mother was her sworn enemy. This mother actually *had* saved her when she was a little girl—i.e., had been the provider for the family when her real father had left. Hence she could not let herself admit any such hostility; she could not lead the double life which is characteristic of middle-class patients, operating under their double binds. Consequently what she got from me was not just the *permission* without condemnation to express her struggle to be; she got the prior *experience,* from someone in authority, of her own rights and her own being which (referring back to the first dream) she had previously lacked. My giving vent to my rage was my living out my belief that she was a person with her own rights. I didn't need to say it because she could see it from my actions.

2. THE RITES OF REBIRTH

But with the birth of her son, Mercedes' life-problem was only half solved. She took a leave from psychotherapy for six months after the birth because she could not (or did not wish to) get someone to take care of her baby while she came to the sessions. I agreed to this since I wanted to keep the therapy geared to her own wishes, directed as autonomously by her as possible. When she did return, I found her in obviously much better shape than when she had originally come. Her hatred of her mother continued—as we filled in the infinite details ("My mother tried to abort me before I was born"; "Her lips are hard, not soft, when she kisses me"; "She was late to every school play I was in, as well as my graduation"; "She goes around looking like a French whore"). But the hatred was not as overwhelming, it no longer caused symptoms, and she could handle it.

Mercedes, however, tended to build her whole life around her son, who was a beautiful, active, blue-eyed, red-haired boy. If he breathed irregularly, she was worried; if he awoke at night, she had to run to him and comfort him. She nursed him a long time at her breast with a perseverance that surprised even her pediatrician. She had trouble sleeping, partly because of her overconcern about her son. As a consequence of all this, she was weary most of the time.

She brought her son to my office one day when her sitter had not arrived. A boy of two at that time, he immediately took charge of the therapy, telling his mother to sit "here; no, there; no, in this other chair" (which she obediently did). He also gave me free directions from time to time. During this period in the therapy I had been hearing continually from her: "He is very intelligent in his nursery school"; "He is special"; "How lucky we are to have such a brilliant child"; and so on and so forth. Regardless of the fact that these comments were generally true, they indicated her subordination to her child, which was actually part of her original problem.

The crucial point is not that she praised the child, which every proud parent rightly does—and Mercedes had plenty of reason for doing so. But she did so as a substitute for her own assertion as a person; she gave him power as an evasion of assuming it herself. In her dreams during this part of the therapy, she and her child were the same person. She regarded herself as the boy's maid (a mistaken identity given to her by some of the other mothers at nursery school where she took her son). She did not like this phrase, but I used it repeatedly, to confront her with it. I pointed out that living through her son was a fine way to evade her own problems and would make him a first-rate candidate for the couch later on.

She heard this in somewhat the same way—though not nearly as pronounced—as she had heard my strictures against her mother. It was as though I were speaking a truth, but it was not yet real to her. Some *experience* seemed to be necessary for Mercedes.

It came when she went to the dentist. She had agreed to take gas, which she had been assured would not be unpleasant. Contrary to expectation, she felt horrible under the gas. She was convinced she was dying. As she felt this doom of death she kept repeating to herself: "Death is for the living, life is for the dying." She cried silently as she lay there. The point is that she did not dare tell the dentist of her terrible experience as she was going through it. She could make no protest, but simply had to endure her fate, do what the authorities expected of her. Finally, as she came out of the gas, she did tell the dentist, who was surprised that she had said nothing before.

For several days after this, the experience clung to her, filling her with sadness and grief. When she got to my office two days later, she was still crying.

Now for the first time with the foretaste of death—which it was to her—she could understand the preciousness of life. Also for the first time she could now experience the fact that she had as much right to live as any other human being.

From then on, a radical change occurred in her life as a whole and in her psychotherapy. The experience seemed to get her over the depression, which, though lightened greatly by the birth of her son, had plagued her continuously during her life. It now *did* make a difference whether she died or not; existence was no mere automatic set of years which one just endures. From now on she felt, as she put it, "simply happy." In the quarrels with her husband that occurred from time to time, she was not overwhelmed as she had been earlier. Some three months after the experience of "death in the dentist's chair," as she called it, she still, to her considerable surprise, found this confident mood still present in her. Even when she was sick with the flu, she would wake up in the morning and ask herself, "Do I feel bad?" and would be amazed to find out that, although she felt *sick,* she didn't feel *bad.*

This elemental experience, simple as it sounds, is one of great importance. What is the meaning of that cryptic sentence she kept repeating under gas: "Death is for the living, life for the dying"? One of the things it says to me is, death is *for* life, and life is for death. That is, you are reborn into life by dying. This would make it an experience in which she joins the race—an experience celebrated in different cultures by the rite of baptism—dying to be born again. It is also the myth and rite of resurrection—dying to be raised again. Therapists see this myth of resurrection enacted, in varying degrees of intensity, every day of the week. It often comes as a prelude to experiencing the right to assert one's self.

This account indicates that, far from toning down aggression, it is of the very nature of psychotherapy to help people *assert* it. Most people who come for therapy are like Mercedes, though less pronounced—they have not too much aggression, but too little. We encourage their aggressiveness provisionally, confident in the hope that, once they have found their own right-to-be and affirm themselves, they will actually live *more* constructively interpersonally as well as intrapersonally. This, of course, means a different kind of aggression from that which is usually implied by the term.

3. VIOLENCE AS LIFE-DESTROYING AND LIFE-GIVING

But what needs to be said of the violence in Mercedes's existence? It was obviously present, and in abundance. Her dreams had so much violence in them that one had the feeling of sitting on a volcano. Most of her violence was in self-defense: she fought with fists and knives in her dreams simply to keep from being killed.

There are, however, several valuable points to be explored. One is the tendency in violence to erupt in all directions, to bypass all rational functions. In her fights at school or on the street she had become wild, not knowing what she was doing. Such letting go of all controls seemed to have worked well in these fights, as it did also in her occasional hysterical fights with her husband. It is helpful to examine Mercedes' experience in this regard since she is a highly intelligent person who, at the same time, was brought up in a primitive background.

Let us go back to the very first session of her therapy, when she told me of two dreams she had had the night before. I take these as both referring, at least in part, to the therapy she planned to commence on the morrow.

> I was asking Percy [her husband] or my brother for help. I didn't get it. My asking him should be enough. I awoke angry, and felt like hitting him.

> Ruby, our dog, was in the house, and had left feces all over the floor. I was cleaning it up. Maybe I was asking Percy for help.

She was aware that "the shit was mine" and of "what happened to me, what I did." But the dreams carry the message that she expected magic help from me: "My asking him should be enough."

This is a common defense of people overwhelmed by feelings of powerlessness. Some other force must have the power to change things since obviously these people don't; *their* actions don't really matter. To fill the vacuum left by their failure to act the powerless frequently rely on the practice of magic rites. Worried about her increasing weight, for example, Mercedes asked me to hypnotize her to cause her to eat less. I refused, saying it would take away her own responsibility; and why did she not learn to be her own hypnotist? The next session she told me that she had been enraged at me by my refusal. She recognized her reliance on magic.

This dependence on magic stretches back through the centuries of oppression of the blacks, colonial peoples, and minorities of whatever sort. It was assumed that the blacks could be made passive, docile, and helpless and could be kept this way by use of built-in threats and an occasional lynching. But in the false calm, we repressed the question we should have been asking: When an individual is rendered unable to stand up for himself socially or psychically, as in slavery, where does his power go? No one can accept complete impotence short of death. If he cannot assert himself overtly, he will do it covertly. Thus magic—a covert, occult force—is an absolute necessity for the powerless. The spread of magic and the reliance on the occult is one symptom of the widespread impotence in our transitional age.

But magic is not the only symptom. Mercedes also fouls her own nest; her violence turns against herself. This is clearly stated in the second dream in which the dog—whom she recognizes as herself—leaves feces all over the floor. True, this can be an indication of hostility toward others (for which feces are often a primitive symbol), an aggressive revenge, an emptying of my refuse on your rug, your floor. But—and this "but" has within it a good deal of the tragedy of suppressed minorities—the feces are on *her* floor. The impulse to aggression, suppressed rage, is turned inward and comes out against herself. The impulse for revenge, the hostile surge, bypasses reason and finds its outlet in the muscles; it *is* irrational in this sense. It erupts against one's self if there is no one close against whom it can erupt; the direction and the aim of violence is secondary, only the eruption is important at that moment. This is the point at which suppressed tendencies for aggression are transformed into violence. Strictly speaking, the object of the violence is irrelevant.

This strange phenomenon, so patently self-destructive, is illustrated specifically in Mercedes. About ten months after her son's birth, she had the following dreams:

> I was being pursued by everyone, I had to kill them, hurt them, stop them in some way. Even my son was one of them in the room. I had to do something to everyone or they'd hurt me. I pinched my son, that was enough for him. But I had to punch everyone else. One at a time, so they wouldn't pounce on me. I awoke with an awful feeling that I was being torn in pieces.

> I was riding in a car with Percy and another man. A man was trying to get in the car. We were then in an office at a place where there was a nurse and a desk. I got under the desk, I chose a knife. The man was looking in, seeing me under the nurse's desk. I went for my knife, but it was gone. Then I got another knife. I now was fighting my son and my grandmother. It didn't bother me; I was parrying their knives. Then it became a woman I was fighting, she was trying to hurt me.

She fights her son as well as her grandmother, the person whom she had taken care of in her childhood and for whom she had a genuine affection. This wild striking in all directions seems a paradigm for irrational violence. Here lies an important part of the explanation of the ghetto riots—the burning, looting, killing, which may turn out, paradoxically, to be against those closest and dearest to the rioters.

Now what do these people whom Mercedes fights have in common? *They are all persons to whom she has subordinated herself.* Whether for good reasons, as in the case of the grandmother and son, or bad, as ostensibly in the case of her mother, they represent people in whom she has submerged herself. In this respect they *should* be fought for the sake of her own autonomy. It is parallel to what Arnold L. Gesell calls the "counter-will," the child's self-assertion in opposition exactly to those upon whom he is most dependent. Thus the life-destroying violence becomes also life-giving violence. They are intertwined as the sources of the individual's self-reliance, responsibility, and freedom.

The "man looking in" may be me, the therapist; and why shouldn't she fight me also as she is asserting her own freedom? This is the unavoidably ambiguous state all persons in therapy are in; they must fight the therapist at some place along the line, although the therapist ostensibly is trying to help, and on deeper examination, precisely *for* the reason that he is trying to help. This occurs partly because in coming for help they have had to surrender temporarily some of the autonomy they do have; partly because of the humiliation of having to ask for help; and partly as a counterbalance to the excessive transference that turns the therapist into a god.

There is thus a self-affirmation precisely in self-destructive violence. Ultimately the affirmation is expressed in the person's demonstration of his right to die by his own hand if he chooses. If, as is our tendency in this country, we condemn all violence out of hand and try to eradicate even the possibility of violence from a human being, we take away from him an element that is essential to his full humanity. For the self-respecting human being, violence is always an ultimate possibility—and it will be resorted to less if admitted than if suppressed. For the free man it remains in imagination an ultimate exit when all other avenues are denied by unbearable tyranny or dictatorship over the spirit as well as the body.

EI CASE FORMULATION (By Kirk Schneider)

The following is an imaginary tour of sorts. In a few concise paragraphs, I will attempt to answer the following question: How might we understand this (as well as each subsequent) case in terms of the previous chapter's existential-integrative guidelines? What would the major diagnostic issues look like, and how would the pivotal interventions be formulated?

Let me be clear that this exercise is meant to supplement—not to replace—the original case formulations, and to further elucidate the utility of our guidelines.

EI CASE FORMULATION—Mercedes

The first theme that strikes me about Mercedes is her degree of hyperconstriction. She is "docile," Dr. May writes, and chronically accommodating and "nice." The roots of this subservience are apparent: She has been devalued as a woman of color and exploited as a sexual object. Yet what is not apparent, and what Dr. May discloses with his presence, is the manner in which these degradations are expressed subconsciously—through Mercedes' body and dreams. Her bearing is stiff, Dr. May intimates; her dreams are life-threatening. She gets along easily enough, but she seems petrified of standing out or being defiant. She shuns expansiveness. To be sure, she does have periods of combativeness, points at which she is no longer able to tolerate the partiality of her existence. But these outbursts are mainly reactive in nature; they do not cultivate genuine power.

Although Mercedes (like many abuse victims) fears physical retaliation, this is not the core, I believe, of her reluctance to stand out. What really seems to have frightened Mercedes was not the overt wrath of her stepfather but the covert threat of her mother's abandonment of her. To defy her stepfather, and to rebel against being a prostitute, then, was to court the possibility, not just of being beaten, but of losing her mother's love—the *ground* that upheld Mercedes' existence. To confront that ground—even with Dr. May—was to confront the nightmare of its absence—too much possibility and responsibility; a surplus of dizzying freedom.

The path of least resistance for Mercedes, therefore, was to push herself into the background, to embed herself in others' agendas and to choke off, as a result, her own ambitions and hopes.

It was not through words, per se, that Dr. May helped her to redress this condition; it was through repeated invitations to be *present* to herself. In his exploration of her dreams, for example, he helped her to acknowledge the anger, power, and energy that had been welling up in her and the transformative potential they had for her life.

Dr. May's attempts to invoke the actual with Mercedes, however, could not afford the luxury of time. Unless he accelerated the process, he conjectured, her dependency on her mother (and extreme avoidance of her own expansive potential) could prompt her to lose her baby. His decision to act out his own indignation toward her circumstances, therefore, proved timely medicine for her, because it catalyzed her resources for change. Put in the language of the EI guidelines, Dr. May's vivification helped Mercedes to discover that she could *survive* explosive tirades against her caretakers, that she could *face* the chaotic and disorienting possibilities that such tirades conjure up, and that she could *transform* these realizations into concrete action.

The meaning created from Mercedes' breakthrough was tangible: a new baby and an enlarged life. No longer did Mercedes accept the passive victim role with her parents. Instead she fought, to the degree possible, to keep appropriate boundaries with them and to define her life as she saw fit. Like the devil in *Faust,* Dr. May helped Mercedes to understand the redemptive sides of her torment—the aliveness in her anger, for example, and the freedom dormant in her rebellion; and, like Dante's Virgil, he provided a way in which she could *experience* these reforms while he steadfastly accompanied her on her journey.

A DEPRESSED ARTIST: THE CASE OF AMANDA

Chris Armstrong and James Bugental

Chris Armstrong, M.F.C.C, has been in private practice for the past seventeen years. She believes that making conscious choices about how one engages existence is the foundation of a meaningful life. Through extensive studies with James Bugental and, more recently, Irvin Yalom, she has found a theoretical and philosophical home in the existential perspective.

James Bugental, Ph.D., is one of the leading existential psychologists in America. The first president of the Association for Humanistic Psychology, Dr. Bugental is currently professor emeritus at Saybrook Institute and emeritus clinical faculty at Stanford Medical School. His recent books include Psychotherapy and Process, The Art of the Psychotherapist, *and* Intimate Journeys.

The case of Amanda is a model illustration of experiential liberation. Amanda is a typical YAVIS (young, attractive, verbal, intelligent, successful) client. The qualities that have sustained her, however, are precisely the qualities that keep her from living fully. In this concise illustration, Armstrong and Bugental show how existential therapy in some cases can redress this contemporary malaise and, in so doing, help to elucidate presence, invoking the actual, vivifying and confronting resistance, and meaning-creation.

I (Chris Armstrong) have selected five segments of a four-year therapy.* In this case, I will illustrate a kind of psychotherapy that is intended to help clients become more alive, more spirited (Bugental, J. F. T., & Bugental, E. K., 1984), more vital, more *present.* I will demonstrate how the theme of awareness of one's presence is essential in each interview and how this awareness helps the client identify the ways in which he/she has been avoiding genuine "aliveness."

November 1988

"How could Mom do this to me? I moved 3,000 miles to get away. How dare she!" Amanda is attractive, well-groomed, 35 years old, and divorced. She is convivial and informative; yet a shroud of reluctance hangs in the room. "I don't want to be here and still be dealing with my mother," she says. With great speed—speed that acts as a buffer between herself and her inner experience—she explains, "My mother, who gets so depressed and helpless, is moving here from Florida, and I'm afraid it will be my job to take care of her."

Amanda tells me how she has always vainly hoped to be close to her mother. She continues, "My mother is so narcissistic. I just can't get close to her! I'm so resentful of the way she neglected me as a child."

Editor's note: The psychotherapy presented here was conducted by Ms. Armstrong, and hers is the bulk of this report. She is regularly part of a consultation group with Dr. Bugental, and he has prepared the commentary on the case report.

"Mom got a housekeeper when I was 4 years old, and then she was gone every day. Mom was very intimidating, cold and aloof; she could cut me to ribbons with her words. Our house was a mausoleum, cool and dark—not a place to bring friends. Mom napped every afternoon; no cookies and milk with a warm welcome for me."

While I listen to what are clearly painful childhood memories for Amanda, I become keenly aware of her intention to keep them tucked neatly in an intellectual box. I want to acknowledge that I recognize she understands her problems intellectually; also, I hope to begin to draw her attention to her delivery, which enables her to keep a safe distance from her inner experience.

"I notice that you speak very quickly, perhaps so fast that you aren't able to experience internally, emotionally, the significance of your words," I say.

"I've never thought of that. Do you think that's important?"

"Right now, Amanda, you have an opportunity to consider this for yourself."

"Well, you're the professional." She is cautious not to expose herself.

"Yes, that's true, but it's also important what *you* think. Do you think that speaking so quickly may make it difficult for you to fully experience your words?"

"That's a new thought to me."

"Take your time; and consider what I've said."

Her speech quickens, and the words start to roll off her tongue. "I've never thought of that. Guess it could make a difference."

"Amanda, here's a chance. You're speaking fast right now. Can you feel the rhythm of your speech?"

"Yes" (*hesitantly, considering*).

"Good. Listen to your voice."

"I'm in a hurry."

"A hurry?"

"It's like I've got to keep moving."

"Sounds important."

"You think it's important?" Here she once again shifts the focus to me.

"Amanda, are you aware that you're asking me rather than yourself?"

"This is very new to me." A long pause, then she states quietly, "I guess I'm not used to considering myself."

Here I repeat what she has said in order to emphasize the importance of her statement. "I'm not used to considering myself."

"It's really new to me." Her tone implies that she is trying the idea on, rolling it around in her mind, seeing if it fits for her.

I am encouraged. Apparently, Amanda is genuinely here to find her inner self, and she appears to have the emotional capacity necessary for the task at hand. She decides that she will come once a week.

In subsequent sessions, I continue to draw Amanda's attention to her words and her delivery. I sense the necessity of the wall of words. Why is it there? What is she protecting? After several sessions, Amanda is ready for me to confront her further with her dependence on her fast talking. With her new awareness, she starts to become more attuned both to how she presents herself and to her avoidance of her inner subjectivity. This allows for a deepening of our work together.

March 1989

"I'm so overwhelmed. Mom expects me to find her a house. She acts as if I have all the time in the world."

"You sound upset."

"Maybe a little. I just have so many things to do." The tone of her voice is thin and tentative.

"Amanda, you're guessing about yourself."

Exasperated, feeling put upon, she states, "This is just too much for me! I can't possibly ever handle all this."

"All this?"

"What's the use? Why should I try to help her?"

With a slight challenging note in my voice, I say, "You sound ready to give up." This catches her attention.

"No. You know that I don't want to do that."

"I do?"

"It's just that I get so overwhelmed and don't know what to do."

"I know that right now all you feel is overwhelmed. See if you can slow yourself down and listen to the tone in your voice. What else is inside of you?" Here I am suggesting that there is more to Amanda than just her anxiety. "You might want to close your eyes and relax in your chair." In previous sessions, closing her eyes has enhanced her ability to search more successfully within herself.

Amanda takes a few deep breaths, exhales, and closes her eyes. After a minute, tears fall down her face. She begins to speak slowly, choosing her words carefully; she is listening to herself. "She expects me to do these things for her, and then when I ask her to take care of the girls, she tells me she couldn't possibly do that."

"I hear irritation and disappointment in your voice."

"I want a different relationship with her. Why can't she appreciate what I do for her?"

"Good, now you're listening to yourself."

"I keep hoping that we'll be close. Then something happens that reminds me that I can't rely on her. She sucks me in for a while, I feel close, and then, when I go to count on her, she pulls back." Amanda has started to deliver familiar information devoid of feeling.

"Slower, Amanda. You're starting to tell me something you already know. Let yourself hear with new ears, new feeling. What's there?"

Earnestly, she attempts to listen. Then she sinks back into herself, more tears fall, and she is silent. After a moment, she says, "It's so painful to feel tricked by her, to trust her and then have her withdraw."

I sit quietly and attentively, not wanting to interrupt her process. Amanda is allowing herself to plumb deeper into familiar territory, but with a different lens.

May 1989

"My daughters are always pulling on me, wanting me to do this and that. Then when I ask them to help me out, they won't. I feel sucked up by them and exhausted. That's when I get angry and bitchy. I hate myself when I get like that." She reports this flatly, like the evening newscast.

"Amanda, do you hear how removed you are?"

"Oh." She reflects on her tone.

"I think . . . I don't like it when I get so angry."

"You *think*? You're not sure?"

"It's so hard for me to know, to feel. . . ."

Interrupting her, I say, "I feel you moving into 'What's the use; I can't.'"

"Maybe that's what I'm doing."

"Maybe?" I continue to press her on her evasive way of talking about herself.

"Maybe I could. . . ." She pauses. "Oh, is that what you mean?"

"Good—you caught yourself."

"Wonder why I do that?"

"Um."

"I think it's familiar."

"There's that *I think* again. It's almost like you're erasing yourself." Here, I am drawing her attention to her *I think* and suggesting a reason for it.

A long silence ensues as she considers my statement. I sense what might be a shift in Amanda's intention: She now seems more willing to look inward. Slowly, clearly attempting not to erase herself, she begins to speak: "When I was a child, being invisible was safer than being seen. It still is today.

"If I don't know what I'm feeling, I can't offend anyone."

"It must be very important not to offend anyone."

Very emphatically, yet removed from the deeper implications, she states, "It's more important for me not to offend anyone than it is to know my own feelings!"

"Do you hear your words?"

"Sort of. Oh, there I go again! It's hard to let all that in."

"Yes, it is. You've taken an important step today by experiencing how you dismiss yourself right here in the room with me."

During the summer months, Amanda experiences the intricacies of erasing herself. "It's as though I cover my feelings with a film so I'll only get a glimmer of my emotions. That way, there's no danger of being able to communicate my feelings to another person or to myself. I'm safe." With this new awareness, Amanda is beginning to question the validity of her "safety." Is she really safe? Or is she crippling herself by dismissing her experience?

October 1989

Amanda comes in and announces that she is terminating her therapy. "My relationship with Mom is better; I'm feeling better about myself as a mother; and I know that I want to be an artist. So it must be time to quit therapy."

"Notice that you're considering an important decision—leaving therapy—and you don't seem certain."

"My relationship with Mom is better, and most of the time I feel like a good mom with the girls."

"You seem clear about that; but I hear some hesitation in your voice."

"Well, it's just . . . when *do* you know it's time to quit therapy?"

"Amanda, you shifted to *you*. When does *Amanda* know?"

"Well, things are better in my life."

"Sounds like deductive reasoning. What does your inner experience tell you?"

Now she becomes quiet. "I'm confused."

"That's a good place to start from."

She struggles with the discomfort of staying present with her confusion. It's clear that she is committed to finding her truth. "I don't want to become dependent on you."

"You sound certain about that. Is leaving the only way to handle your fear?"

Tears start to well in her eyes, "It's so hard for me to let you see who I am."

"So it's better to leave?"

"Well . . ." (*long pause*). She looks a little sleepy but pulls herself back. "I really don't want to leave, but I'm afraid."

"Afraid?"

"I can't keep up this charade that I'm competent."

"So it's better to leave."

"It's hopeless." She pulls herself back with this old familiar dismissal.

"You need to keep your distance."

"I don't want anyone close to me." I feel her shifting her focus back to her subjective experience.

"You don't want *me* close to you?" I draw her focus to the present—and to our relationship.

"It only hurts more."

"If you let yourself connect with me?"

The dam breaks, tears fall. "I don't want to stay so isolated, but it's so frightening to connect with anyone. Because when you see how incompetent I am, you'll leave, and that will be more pain than I can bear."

No wonder she wanted to leave. I am filled with admiration for her as her long-held-secret fear tumbles out.

"You've taken an important step. You've broken your isolation."

"It does feel better. I can feel your caring. I see that this is the same thing that I do with the girls when they want to snuggle. I push them away." Now she is sobbing, reliving all those times that she has pushed the girls away. "I don't want to do this to them; but if something were to happen to them, I wouldn't be able to go on."

"Take it slow, Amanda. If you go too fast, you'll lose the moment." She has made an important discovery. She has experienced how she creates her own isolation. She has allowed herself to struggle with her desire to push me away by terminating therapy. She longs to be seen and accepted for who she is. Furthermore, she experiences directly the emotional costs of her isolation. This awareness is empowering.

"So you have chosen to keep them at a distance."

"I can't do this any more. It's too painful to push them away."

Today is one of those crossroads in therapy, a point at which the client may choose to continue with her self-exploration and delve deeper into the subjective or leave because the original presenting problems have been resolved. Amanda chooses to stay.

February 1990

When Amanda was 22, her father forced her to quit art school because she was not productive enough. Since that time, she has struggled with the demons who whisper in her ear, "You aren't any good; you don't produce fast enough; no one will buy your work."

"I realize that Dad took art school away from me, but I can give it back to myself."

Fear crosses her face as she makes this statement. She holds her breath as she prepares for me to put her down, to say her idea is stupid. I can sense her preparing to let me decide whether she should go to art school. Then something inside of her shifts, and she says, "I'm about to let you decide, just the way I did with Dad."

This is a profound moment. I am deeply touched. She is re-enacting that moment with her father, but this time she is going to make her own decision!

Within two months she has enrolled in art school. "I'm an artist again." Tears of joy well up. "I never thought that I could feel this again."

This is a major victory for Amanda, who was told by her mother, "What's the use? Don't try," and by her father, "You don't have what it takes to succeed." With her decision to return to art school, she is reinvesting in herself, telling herself that she can succeed and that trying is worthwhile. She is stepping out of the shadow into the light, into her life.

COMMENT ON THE CASE OF AMANDA

James Bugental

This case is helpful in demonstrating three important characteristics of our approach to existential-humanistic psychotherapy (Bugental, J. F. T., 1978, 1987; May, 1958): (1) the centering of attention on the immediate subjective experience of the client (i.e., *presence*), (2) the process of working through the layers of the client's resistance to such presence (and thus to taking responsibility for one's life), and (3) the conviction that the locus of the healing/growth process resides in the client (and *not* in the therapist).

Presence is the sine qua non of most depth or life-changing psychotherapy (Bugental, 1983). Presence calls for the client to take aware charge of her/his life, to recognize his/her internal ways of being that are distortive (e.g., Amanda's "safety" through not being definite or explicit), and to confront the responsibility for life choice (as Amanda did when deciding to continue in therapy and again when choosing to return to art school).

The responsibility for life choice is set in contrast to therapeutic modes in which a client is urged and coached to adopt new patterns. Such changes tend to be short-lived and incomplete, and they do not yield the kind of satisfaction Amanda experienced when she made her own decision to go back to art school.

Resistance is a phenomenon familiar to counselors and therapists of all persuasions. As we think of it, resistance has two faces: It arises from the structures that make a person's life possible (e.g., self-definitions and world views) and thus are essential. At the same time, those structure tend to hold off change and thus work against the therapeutic process. For example, Amanda's speaking so rapidly and unheedingly was her attempt to hide her belief that basically, she was not and could not be competent; at the same time, it kept her from changing.

It is important to the power of this mode that the life-distortive patterns be brought into action right in the consulting room rather than being discovered and discussed abstractly. Amanda's handicapping self-image was lived out in her interactions with the therapist before it was identified and named, thus making change possible at a deeper-than-verbal level.

A few words about our characterization of our approach as *existential-humanistic: Existential* means based on the raw fact of existence itself, the fact that we exist. The issue, then, becomes, How will each of us confront and deal with that fact? The first two aspects of the case of Amanda—presence and resistance—particularly manifest the existential perspective. The third—the belief that the healing/growth potential is intrinsic in each individual—expresses the humanistic value system of the orientation. Change, we are persuaded, is the birthright of each human. Therapists can provide a favoring medium or container, a discriminating and encouraging companionship, and a durable faith in the client's potential, but therapists cannot force change to occur. What they can do is vitally important, however, and constitutes a continually challenging yet rewarding calling.

REFERENCES

Bugental, J. F. T. (1978). *Psychotherapy and process.* Reading, MA: Addison-Wesley.

Bugental, J. F. T. (1983). The one absolute necessity in psychotherapy. *The Script, 13*(8), 1–2.

Bugental, J. F. T. (1987). *The art of the psychotherapist.* New York: Norton.

Bugental, J. F. T., & Bugental, E. K. (1984). Dispiritedness: A new perspective on a familiar state. *Journal of Humanistic Psychology, 24,* 49–67.

May, R., Angel, E., & Ellenberger, H. (Eds.). (1958). *Existence: A new dimension in psychiatry and psychology.* New York: Basic Books.

EI CASE FORMULATION—Amanda

This case is a classic illustration of how presence, invoking the actual, vivifying and confronting resistance, and meaning-creation can gradually avail a constricted client of her greatness—her sense of competency and worth. Amanda, we are told, is bogged down by demands. Her daughters are a burden, her mother dominates her, and her father denigrated her potential.

From an early age, Amanda has been convinced of her imperceptibility (or "invisibility," as she put it), always providing a means to others' ends. She feels like a thing, a receptacle, and experiences little "aliveness" of her own. Yet the mechanical nature of Amanda's life is precisely what preserves it, what staves off the vibrancy that is so threatening to her. The message that blares out at her is clear: Pursuit of your desires, your aspiring and playful sides, is synonymous with foolishness and death. "You must remember your place," she has been warned, "and your place is with the meek."

To help Amanda entertain that which is vibrant and strong within herself, Ms. Armstrong provides a series of invitations to her. Sometimes these invitations challenge Amanda to engage her expansive possibilities directly, but mostly they challenge her to face them indirectly, by vivifying her resistance to them. In the end, both strategies help Amanda make conscious decisions about herself and deepen her access to vitality.

The majority of Ms. Armstrong's interventions are aimed at the preverbal, kinesthetic level. She provides Amanda with an *experience,* not merely with a dialogue. Very skillfully, for example, she helps her look at the rhythm of her speech—how she speeds up at certain moments and the distant tone she uses. She notes how difficult it is for Amanda to really hear herself and to pause over her words. She also notes how Amanda abdicates responsibility for her positions, continually appealing to others (such as Ms. Armstrong) to give her answers.

Gradually, and over a sustained period of time, Amanda begins to hear her self-devaluations and to fully see her possibilities for renewal. The practice she gets attending to the blockages within herself mobilizes her to contemplate their reversal—*consideration* for herself and permission for herself to *matter.* The pivotal session, in which Amanda risks and survives appearing incompetent in front of Ms. Armstrong is ample testimony to such developments.

By the end of her therapy, Amanda is able to translate her expansiveness into artistic avenues and to assume the power she previously disavowed.

AN AFRICAN-AMERICAN PERSPECTIVE: THE CASE OF DARRIN

Don Rice

Don Rice, Ph.D., chairs the psychology department at West Georgia College in Carrollton. A graduate of Saybrook Institute in San Francisco, Dr. Rice also received training from R. D. Laing at the Philadelphia Association Clinic in London and is a licensed marriage and family therapist.

With few exceptions, such as Rollo May's case of Mercedes, reports of existential therapy with African-Americans are rare. In this thorough and sensitive study, Don Rice seeks to demonstrate how, as children, African-Americans "become abnormal on the slightest contact with the white world" (Fanon, 1967, p. 143). Bearing this annihilating reality in mind, Rice extends his discussion to the existential-integrative challenge posed by Darrin, a 32-year-old casualty.

The purpose of this contribution is to introduce the reader to an appreciation and an application of existential psychotherapy for the African-American population. More important, I suggest that existentialist concepts such as freedom, being, meaning, identity, choice, and responsibility are relevant to situations faced by African-Americans today. While it is true that these concepts have import for other groups, as well, I find them to be particularly pertinent to African-Americans, considering our unique historical experience.

In treating this topic, the question may be raised whether African-Americans are subject to psychological principles that are fundamentally different from any other group. In response, I submit that there is no evidence in the clinical literature to suggest that African-Americans function differently psychologically. Studies of sociodemographic variables as they relate to mental illness have found little or no support for the notion that racial minority groups in the United States have more mental illness than do whites (Cockerham, 1985). Yet, while the above findings may be true, the real question of therapeutic relevance for African-Americans must be addressed.

What makes the experiences of African-Americans unique from other minority groups and other oppressed groups is the historical fact of slavery. While other groups have suffered discrimination, mistreatment, and isolation from mainstream America, they were never considered to be outside of the human family. Various groups such as the Chinese, Italians, Irish, Germans, European Jews, and others can all tell stories of struggles in the face of opposition in the early days of the formation of this country. Except perhaps for Native Americans, who have endured a different kind of hardship, all of the above-mentioned groups have been able to assimilate into American society and find social as well as personal freedom.

The uniqueness of the African-American experience in a historical context is found in the fact that this is the only minority group to have been systematically stripped of country, culture, language, family, personal identity, and humanness. As Grier and Cobbs (1969) stated:

> The black experience in this country has been of a different kind. It began with slavery and with a rupture of continuity and an annihilation of the past. Even now each generation grows up alone. Many individual blacks feel a desperate aloneness not readily explained . . . non-black groups pass on proud traditions . . . while the black man stands in solitude. (pp. 22–23)

This statement by two prominent African-American psychiatrists makes explicit the uniqueness of the African-American experience and how it is situated in a historical context. When Grier and Cobbs speak of a "rupture of continuity and an annihilation of the past," I would add that this has resulted in a rupture in the continuity of being for African-Americans. One's sense of identity, existence, freedom, and responsibility is inextricably bound up in one's awareness of the past. Not awareness of the past for awareness' sake, but awareness in order to incorporate the past into a meaningful present. Many African-Americans suffer alienation largely because the present is meaningless in light of their past.

Psychological theories and therapeutic techniques that focus solely on internal dynamics and behavioral deficits stemming from early childhood experiences in the family make an assumption that may not be valid for most African-Americans. African-European psychiatrist Fanon (1967) suggested that while many cases of mental disturbance can be traced to the family environment, the opposite of that process seems to emerge in people of African descent. As he states, "A normal Negro child, having grown up within a normal family, will become abnormal on the slightest contact with the white world" (p. 143).

Now, beyond meeting basic needs, the primary function of any family in any society is to ensure the transmission of the operating rules of that society. If we assume that in the "normal" African-American home, the parents are culture bearers of the social system, what, then, can Fanon mean by such a statement? First, Fanon recognizes the significance of the sociohistorical context in which people of African descent find themselves in European and American societies. Second, and perhaps more important, he recognizes the ontological (*being*) obstacles that are necessary for eventual transcendence.

In an attempt to elucidate the psychological impact of European colonization on African nations, Fanon writes,

> In the Weltanschauung of a colonized people there is an impurity, a flaw that outlaws any ontological explanation. Someone may object that this is the case with every individual, but such an objection merely conceals a basic problem. Ontology—once it is finally admitted as leaving existence by the wayside—does not permit us to understand the being of the black man. To be black, he must be black in relation to the white man. (Fanon, 1967, pp. 109–110)

Fanon goes on to explain that while it may seem that being white must also be in relation to being black, he rejects this proposition as false. In Fanon's view, a black person is ontologically inert in the eyes of a white person. One cannot define the being of another when one is essentially powerless. This powerlessness is rooted in the social fabric. Therefore, a person or group repeatedly treated as a fringe member of the human family and stripped of autonomy will react in a certain way, only to be seen by mental health experts as further evidence of their maladjustment.

This unique experience of ontological inertness presents a challenge for the therapist encountering the African-American client. The tendency of therapists to see the problems of African-Americans solely in terms of either genetics, intrapsychic disturbance, or behavioral maladjustment highlights the need for the kind of understanding provided by an existentially based therapy. The existentialist approach helps to explain Fanon's belief that a normal African-American child growing up in a normal home will become abnormal upon the slightest contact with the white world. This "abnormality" is predicated on the rupture in the continuity of being that has been imposed by a sociohistorical context. Hence, questions of being, meaning, freedom, identity, choice, and responsibility emerge as essential themes in the therapeutic process.

Psychotherapists and other mental health professionals treating African-Americans must give consideration to the sociohistorical context that may be contributing to the client's symptoms. I do not intend this statement to mean that one ignores biochemical imbalances, intrapsychic disturbances, and environmental influences. African-Americans are subject to the same psychological and biological factors promoting mental illness or mental health as are other groups. However, it is imperative that the therapist distinguish between a disturbed individual and a disturbed society—a disturbed society being one that wittingly or unwittingly erects barriers to personal freedom for any of its members.

In an article addressing the aftermath of the Rodney King verdict, Johnson (1992) states,

> There remains a system of white privilege in America. There has never been and there is not now a "level playing field." We are twice oppressed. First, by the external forces, stigmas and racial devaluation which is the historical inheritance of America. But more importantly, by our internal oppressors—those images which we in the African-American community hold of ourselves. (p. 6)

Those images we hold of ourselves as ontologically inert, socially restricted, and powerless are the result of the sociohistorical fact of oppression. The images have been internalized and sustained by a residual of negative attitudes directed toward African-Americans and transmitted intergenerationally. For this reason, issues of freedom, power, being, and responsibility must be addressed in a therapeutic context. For the African-American, this is essential. It is essential because, as May (1981) states,

> We choose our way of responding to other people who make up the context in which our freedom develops. The paradox that one can be free only as one is responsible is central at every point in freedom. But the converse is just as true: one can be responsible only as one is free. . . . You have to have some sense that your decisions genuinely matter to take responsibility for them. (p. 64)

The job of the existentially oriented therapist is, as May puts it, "to help the patient discover, establish, and use his or her freedom" (p. 64). In other words, the therapist enables the client to achieve a meaningful life. In the current vernacular, we might say that the therapist *empowers* the client. This empowerment should not be confused with its simplistic use as found in many self-help books but in the existential sense of coming to realize one's freedom and responsibility, regardless of the circumstances.

Noted African-American author Shelby Steele (1990) addresses the existential concerns of African-Americans in a collection of essays depicting the current state of race relations in America. On the issue of responsibility and power, he writes,

> Personal responsibility is the brick and mortar of power. The responsible person knows that the quality of his life is something that he will have to make inside the limits of his fate. . . . With this understanding and the knowledge that he is responsible, a person can see his margin of choice. . . . He can create himself and make himself felt in the world. Such a person has power. (Steele, 1990, pp. 33–34)

Actualizing this awareness of personal responsibility and the freedom to choose in the client is part and parcel of existential psychotherapy. Problems of being, meaning, freedom, responsibility, and their manifest symptomatology (i.e., anxiety, depression, fear, doubt) can only be explored in a context in which the experience of the person is understood as essential to the therapeutic process.

Up to this point, I have tried to develop a general framework for understanding the experiences of the African-American client. In doing so, I have implied a certain prerequisite I believe to be pertinent to existential therapists; that is, an awareness and sensitivity to the effects of social, political, and historical events on the client. This does not mean that the therapist must immerse herself in the intricacies of these areas before treating a client, but being aware of the sociohistorical context helps to establish a framework for understanding the client's present experiences. Certainly a therapist treating a client who experienced the atrocities committed in Bosnia and Serbia or the government-sanctioned starvation of thousands of people in war-torn Somalia would take into account the devastating impact of such experiences. The existential therapist of any ethnic origin should demonstrate social and cultural competence.

THE CASE OF DARRIN

Darrin, a 32-year-old African-American male, was referred to me by a mental health facility, which reported that in their judgment, Darrin could benefit from having a "black therapist." During my initial interview with Darrin, he appeared to be both anxious and depressed. He also showed physical signs of weight loss and sleep deprivation.

Darrin's original contact with the mental health clinic had been made through his company's employee assistance program, which he had consulted because of feelings of depression and an inability to get a "good night's sleep." As part of his treatment at the mental health clinic, he was given a prescription for a sleeping agent and weekly therapy sessions.

His therapist's report to me indicated that Darrin had had no previous emotional problems and there was an improvement in both his state of depression and his ability to sleep after the sessions started. The report attributed his emotional state to overwork and suggested that he take time away from work, and rest. However, after a two-week rest period, his symptoms returned, coupled with a breakdown in rapport between Darrin and his therapist. After three more weeks of sessions with Darrin, the therapist, who was white, decided that a black therapist might have more success with him.

I asked Darrin to tell me about himself and the events that had brought him to this point in his life. He was open and spoke in a very deliberate manner. He described his early childhood as normal for a child growing up in the sixties. He is the oldest of four siblings, and both parents were present in the home when he was growing up. His father worked full time as an electrician for a construction company and often found part-time work wiring homes on weekends. His mother worked as a food services coordinator for a school district. He described his parents as warm and loving but, at the same time, strict in discipline. He elaborated that as children, they were constantly told that they should strive toward a better life than they had then. He said that he had always found this a curious statement because he felt he had a good life already.

While he described his early life as normal and enjoyable, he noted that he began experiencing feelings of despair upon entering junior high school. His entrance into junior high was significant in that he was required by his parents to attend what was then a predominately white school. This particular school district was experimenting with a "voluntary desegregation" plan, which translated into black children volunteering to attend predominately white schools and white children remaining where they were. Darrin's parents decided it would be advantageous for him to attend the "white" school because they perceived it as "better" than the black school. In actuality, there was a measure of truth to this perception because of the disparity in funding.

At any rate, Darrin marked this event as a turning point in his up-to-then uneventful life. Throughout his years in junior high and high school, he was constantly told by his parents how he had to prove himself and be a better student than the white students. Furthermore, he was told that he always had to be on his "best behavior" because his teachers and fellow students would judge his race based on his behavior. This resulted in his feeling that he "could never be himself."

Upon graduating from high school, Darrin received a partial scholarship to attend college. He completed two years and then decided not to continue. After a year of desperate searching, he finally landed a job at a trucking firm. His decision greatly displeased his parents, who, at this point, thought he was "throwing his life away." Within five years, he had risen through the ranks to become a district manager in charge of large portions of the southeast. After three years in this position, his symptoms began to emerge. They began with a general, nonspecific feeling of disinterest in his work and progressed to alternating moments of anxiety and depression.

He also revealed that at this time he was greatly in debt, resulting in frequent letters and phone calls from collection agencies. He described himself as having "expensive taste" which, in his case, included a late-model luxury car, a lavishly appointed condominium, and designer clothes. Furthermore, he expressed the belief that the people whom he managed did not respect him; he was considered incompetent and was only in his position because he was black. He voiced resentment toward his creditors, his fellow employees, his family, and himself. He summed up his situation as not being able to please anyone and, at the same time, trying to do and be what everyone wanted him to do and be.

Existentially, Darrin's feelings of anxiety and depression can be understood as resulting from an interruption in the continuity of his being. His sense of identity, meaning, freedom, and personal power was usurped when his parents redefined his position in life and how he was expected "to be" in the presence of others.

However, keep in mind that the actions of Darrin's parents should be framed in a sociohistorical context. For a black to achieve "success" in the white world, he or she had to be "better" than what would normally be expected for that position. Jackie Robinson had to be a better baseball player; Wilma Randolph had to be a superior runner. Even in the fictional "Guess Who's Coming to Dinner," Sidney Poitier's character had to have the prestigious career of college professor in order to make it palatable for him to be engaged to a white woman. Darrin's parents were conforming to a sociohistorical situation that dictated a prescription for the behavior of any African-American who wanted to gain a minimum of acceptance in the white world.

For Darrin, it is not a simple matter of being black but, rather, his "blackness" in relation to the "whiteness" of others. This is an experience that African-Americans limited to their own social milieu do not have. But at the moment when contact is made with the broader society, the reality of being black takes on a different meaning. Darrin's definition of himself has been replaced by one which allows him no ontological resistance.

My initial work with Darrin began with my efforts to quell the tide of telephone calls and letters from his creditors. I informed them that Darrin was under my care and that arrangements were being made to satisfy his debts. With the cooperation of the creditors, much of Darrin's primary anxiety symptoms, which were associated with threats of repossession, foreclosure, and general financial ruin, dissipated. He reported that he felt less anxious and was sleeping better. Realizing, however, that keeping his creditors at bay was only a temporary measure for alleviating his problems, I knew that additional therapeutic intervention was necessary to effect a more productive change in this aspect of his behavior.

It would be well to pause and take note that existential therapy can involve a variety of specific techniques, not only for different clients, but also for the same client at different times. For Darrin's immediate problem (i.e., his spending habits and creditors), I found behavioral intervention, coupled with rational restructuring, to be most effective (Ellis, 1962; Goldfried & Davison, 1976; Meichenbaum, 1977).

Some of the overt changes in his behavior included establishing a budget that included regular disbursements to his creditors and selling off some of his more financially cumbersome possessions. At the same time, cognitive or rational restructuring was used to help him internalize his behavior at an intellectual and feeling level. Learning to respond differently to a situation in which he had previously felt powerless represented, for him, a new freedom. My role as the therapist is to help the client establish his or her freedom (see May, 1981). For the therapist to understand this role is pre-eminently existential.

Commensurate with freedom is *responsibility,* the ability to respond. While, in one sense, responsibility sets limits on freedom, as May (1981) has pointed out, choices are expanded when responsibility is viewed as the ability to respond (Emery & Campbell, 1986). The cognitive-behavioral techniques served as a tool to help Darrin develop a greater awareness of his existential right of choice. Realizing that he could respond to his situation in a manner that empowered him helped him to eliminate the disabling aspect of his anxiety. It should be made clear here that the cognitive-behavioral techniques were not seen as an all-encompassing theoretical position but, rather, as one method to help Darrin accomplish what he wanted to accomplish for himself.

Psychodynamically speaking, Darrin's free spending patterns could be seen as resulting from a kind of pre-oedipal overgratification. This is an issue that perhaps should not be overlooked and could provide important understandings for the insight-oriented therapist. However, resorting to internal dynamics exclusively can only serve to further comfort and enhance the client's victim status. The essential questions of being, meaning, freedom, and responsibility cannot be addressed in this context. Furthermore, there is no room for understanding the sociohistorical context.

A particular psychodynamic position I found to be relevant in the development of my composite understanding of Darrin was Adler's theory of the inferiority-superiority complex (Ansbacher & Ansbacher, 1956). Stated briefly, it says that every person moves toward a chosen goal and is therefore moving from a feeling of relative inferiority to a feeling of superiority, which includes wanting to be a worthy human being. Darrin's attempt to move from "inferior" feelings of non-self-worth, powerlessness, meaninglessness, and lack of freedom to superiority feelings of self-worth, power, meaningfulness, and freedom could be summed up according to Adler's psychology of the individual. From this perspective, Darrin's feelings and behavior were obviously "neurotic."

However, to stop the analysis here would overlook an essential point. For Adler, these complexes arise within the individual, a point I am not disputing. But for Darrin as an African-American, feelings of inferiority do not stem from the imagined "organ" inferiority or "birth order" inferiority of which Adler speaks but, rather, from an inferiority that is rooted in a sociohistorical context. Since before the establishment of this country as a sovereign nation, the African-American has been considered an inferior being. As Steele (1990) has said,

> The condition of being black in America means that one will likely endure more wounds to one's self-esteem than others and that the capacity for self-doubt born of these wounds will be compounded and expanded by the black race's reputation of inferiority. (p. 43)

The fact that Darrin did not perceive himself as an active force, capable of directing his own life and bringing possibilities into existence, has historical significance that extends beyond the family and environment. While I believe this to be a crucial point, I do not want to suggest that Darrin, or any other African-American, is historically "fixated." I mean only that the therapist should expand the walls of his or her theoretical orientation in order to grasp the fullness of the client's existential situation.

After helping Darrin gain some measure of control over his financial problems, the more important work of helping him to realize his own part in the actualization of his self-worth and sense of power began. Basically, this is a task for each person, to be decided by each person, because the therapist cannot decide for the client how this sense of self-worth and power is to come into being. However, the therapist can facilitate this awareness through a careful prioritizing of the client's concerns.

Darrin's first concern was his dissatisfaction with the direction his life had taken. From his point of view, he had done "everything" to make amends for the disappointment he caused his parents when he dropped out of college. His second concern was that while he was considered extremely competent on his job and commanded the respect of his peers, he *felt* ridiculed and belittled by them. Consequently, all his efforts to meet expectations and to please everyone only resulted in feelings of not being himself.

To offset his negative summation of himself, I asked Darrin to make a list of what he considered to be his strengths. Surprisingly, despite his despondency, he was able to list quite a few. Some of his strengths included good interpersonal skills, intelligence, persistence, and loyalty. He saw himself as being able to handle adversity constructively most of the time and capable of feeling deep empathy toward others. I then asked him to focus on how each one of the strengths he listed had played a role in some of the choices he had made in life.

This exercise brought him to the realization that his decision to drop out of college was based on his desire to assert his freedom and move beyond the environmental, familial, and social restraints that dictated his existence at the time. I pointed out that it was precisely those strengths that had allowed him to succeed in the socio-economic realm on his own terms without the benefit of a college degree. He was able to see how even in his present job, his strengths had been the source of his progress.

What this exercise accomplished was a "reframing" (see Dilts et al., 1980) of the meaning Darrin had attached to his choices. Once he began to view his choices from a different vantage point, I introduced the issue of responsibility—the responsibility that places limits on freedom (May, 1981) and the ability to respond that expands the choices one can make (Emery & Campbell, 1986). I asked Darrin to reflect on what he considered to be the major transformative choices in his life and to state how he had accepted or not accepted responsibility for each of those choices. At the same time, I asked him how he could respond to any of the difficulties in his present situation in a manner that would empower him.

These questions served as a catalyst to help Darrin understand not only his existential freedom but his responsibility in exercising that freedom. Incidentally, the above exercise can be used in any therapeutic orientation, but the very nature of the questions is existential. The exercise gave Darrin a chance to experience himself as an entity separate from his environment, with the capacity to respond upon his own initiative rather than merely reacting.

Finally, I addressed with Darrin the overriding issue of racism and its concomitant effects (i.e., feelings of inferiority, self-doubt, lack of self-worth, and so on). The specific experiences he noted—the beliefs that he had to be better than whites in order to be accepted as an equal or that any progress he made in his career was due to his race rather than his abilities—both have an element of truth when viewed in a sociohistorical context. To invalidate this experience with substitute psychospeak explanations (i.e., inferiority complex, paranoia, and so on) would only serve to "mystify" (Laing, 1967) and do further violence (Laing & Cooper, 1971) to the experience. In other words, it was important for Darrin to understand the sociohistorical precedence for the present attitudes he felt victim to. Whether his experience was valid in an objective sense is irrelevant. It is irrelevant because the sociohistorical context already provides for the possibility of the pervasiveness of these racist attitudes. However, it was equally important for Darrin to realize his own responsibility in exercising his freedom to transcend the negative confines of the sociohistorical context. What Darrin was to confront ultimately was not the inferiority and self-doubt imposed from without but inferiority that emerges from within when the choice is made to abandon, not only responsibility, but also the ability to respond.

For Darrin, the veil of inferiority and self-doubt was lifted when he began experiencing himself as a person apart from his race; that is, as one who is free to choose, to act, and to *be*. While race can be a source of identity, that which is invalid racial-cultural heritage (i.e., nonbeing, inferiority) and that which is valid immediate experience (i.e., freedom, meaning, being) are reconciled in an existential encounter that encompasses the sociohistorical context. To dismiss the influence of either the past *or* present social context would be delusional. However, freedom comes with the awareness that one's personal and collective history does not determine present choice but rather acknowledges the past in order that one may fruitfully move beyond it to facilitate the cycle of freedom (Fanon, 1967).

Darrin's journey toward freedom began with his recognition that the choices he made in the past could be made meaningful in the present when he recognized his responsibility for those choices. Moreover, personal acknowledgment of his ability to respond opened him up to heretofore unrecognized potentialities.

In closing, I want to make the point that the racial/ethnic heritage of the therapist is unimportant. What is important is that the therapist be grounded in a broad education that offers him or her the necessary sensitivity to the sociohistorical influences on the client. An existential framework can lend invaluable perspective to that understanding.

REFERENCES

Ansbacher, H, & Ansbacher, R. (1956). *The individual psychology of Alfred Adler: A systematic presentation in selections from his writings.* New York: Basic Books.

Cockerham, W. C. (1985). Sociology and psychiatry. In Kaplin, H. I., Sadock, B. (Eds.), *Comprehensive textbook of psychiatry IV.* Baltimore: Williams and Wilkins.

Dilts, R., Grinder, J., Bandler, R., & Delozier, J. (1980). *Neurolinguistic programming: The study of the structure of subjective experience.* Cupertino, CA: Meta Publications.

Ellis, A. (1962). *Reason and emotion in psychotherapy.* New York: Lyle Stuart.

Emery, G., & Campbell, J. (1986). *Rapid relief from emotional distress.* New York: Rawson Associates.

Fanon, F. (1967). *Black skin white masks.* New York: Grove Press.

Goldfried, M. R., & Davison, G. C. (1976). *Clinical behavior therapy.* New York: Holt, Rinehart and Winston.

Grier, W., and Cobbs, P. (1969). *Black rage.* New York: Bantam Books.

Johnson, J. (1992). D.C. Counselors speak out on King verdict and its underlying problems. *The Advocate, 16*(1), 6–7.

Laing, R. D. (1967). *The politics of experience.* New York: Pantheon Books.

Laing, R. D., & Cooper, D. G. (1971). *Reason and violence.* New York: Vintage.

May, R. (1981). *Freedom and destiny.* New York: Delta.

Meichenbaum, D. (1977). *Cognitive-behavior modification.* New York: Plenum.

Steele, S. (1990). *The content of our character.* New York: St. Martin's Press.

EI CASE FORMULATION—Darrin

Nowhere is the perception of being hyperconstricted, of being dismissed and wiped away, more acute than in the African-American community; and Darrin is a representative casualty.

From his first days at his mostly white junior high, we are told, Darrin began to disparage himself. Lacking his own cultural yardstick, he squeezed into the yardstick of the majority and distanced himself from that which was dynamic in himself. Becoming increasingly depersonalized, Darrin dropped out of college after two years, abandoning the idea of a degree. Surprisingly, however (or perhaps not so surprisingly, given his driven, overcompensatory needs), he was then able to work his way into a management position. Yet this position resolved little in Darrin's life—especially his desolated core.

Darrin is both attached to and reviled by this core, Dr. Rice informs us. It keeps him safe, buffering him from the risks of success; but it also suffocates him and chokes off his developmental promise. Although Darrin is mostly "depressed," therefore, he is also periodically grandiose—to counter his empty spirit.

The task of Darrin's therapist, accordingly, is to help him break this debilitating cycle. It is to help him pause over his expansive and constrictive fears, clarify them, and learn to become "response-able" toward them, turning them to his advantage.

Yet before Darrin can face this formidable task, he must deal with more immediate matters—such as his debts to his creditors. These, as Dr. Rice shows, can be dealt with at the social-advocacy level by tangibly assisting Darrin with his obligations. This kind of assistance, it should be noted, is extremely significant within the EI framework. Until clients like Darrin are both ready and capable of change, experiential inquiry is fruitless. It is highly important, therefore, to *clear the space* for such experiential inquiry by addressing the crises that prevent it. Once Darrin's debts are alleviated, Dr. Rice helps Darrin to expand his self-esteem. He facilitates this at the cognitive-behavioral levels—reinforcing appropriate spending habits, rationally restructuring his outlook on work, and so on. This reconditioning helps Darrin to feel more accomplished and broadens his capacity for choice. Dr. Rice finds the Adlerian concepts of inferiority-superiority helpful, but limited in their sphere of application.

Soon Darrin becomes amenable to experiential exploration, and this is where Dr. Rice is at his most innovative. Because invoking the actual too directly might prove overpowering to Darrin, the first exercise Dr. Rice proposes is a kind of list-making exercise. This exercise fulfills two purposes: (1) it immerses Darrin in his expansive fears (e.g., the risk of standing out); and (2) it buffers him, at the same time, from being therapeutically immobilized by the encounter, from being overwhelmed.

The second exercise Dr. Rice offers is a kind of vivification of Darrin's resistance. It reveals to Darrin how he *keeps* himself from full presence and thus sets himself up for dysfunction. These two exercises in combination—and Dr. Rice's sensitive demystification of racism—help Darrin to see how he can empower his life and how he can productively respond to adverse conditions. They take him out of the loop of extremism, moreover—where he was either too little or too much—and reveal to him the complexity (both freeing *and* limiting) of his liberation.

In the final analysis, does Darrin become successful? Yes, we are assured—but much in the manner of Sisyphus, who could ultimately respond to, and take responsibility for, his own destiny.

AN OBSESSIVE-COMPULSIVE MALE:
THE CASE OF RON

Ed Mendelowitz

Edward Mendelowitz, Ph.D., is a psychologist in private practice in Lexington, Massachusetts. A graduate of the California School of Professional Psychology, he studied under Rollo May. Dr. Mendelowitz comments: "This business of the obsessive-compulsive has concerned me for a long time, and I have worked hard in this paper to frustrate the left brain of psychology. Also, you will note throughout this paper the evocation of existence as drama, *this, too, for psychologists who may have lost touch with the human story and perhaps feel they have no use for such things."*

There are, of course, a variety of established regimens for the treatment of obsessive-compulsives. Stimulus control and behavioral methods are among them, and so, most recently, is medication. In this vignette, however, Ed Mendelowitz elucidates an experiential approach that squarely challenges his client to struggle with his condition. Through his own empathy and noncompulsive spontaneity, Mendelowitz helps his client to mobilize those qualities within himself and to creatively transcend his rigidity. While Ron's transformation is significant, Mendelowitz suggests that it is neither miraculous nor all-encompassing. He reminds us that the price of liberation is a lifelong commitment to affirm it anew.

> *His disciples questioned him and said to him, "Do you want us to fast? How shall we pray? Shall we give alms? What diet shall we observe?" Jesus said, "Do not tell lies and do not do what you hate."—The Gospel of Thomas*

> *Life is essentially a drama, because it is a desperate struggle—with things and even with our character—to succeed in being in fact that which we are in design.*
> —JOSE ORTEGA Y GASSET, *In Search of Goethe from Within*

There is a Hasidic tale told by Rabbi Hanokh and retold by Martin Buber (1948) of a stupid man, one who could not live without lists and rules. Indeed, so difficult was it for this man to think for himself that he almost hesitated to go to sleep at night for fear of the difficulty he would have in finding his clothes upon waking. One day it occurred to the man to make yet another list and so—with pencil and paper in hand—he duly noted where he lay every article of clothing that he had on. The next morning, the man was very well pleased to consult his list and find hat, pants, shirt, and so on exactly where he had placed them the night before. "That's all very well," thought the man when he was fully dressed, "but now where am I myself? Where in the world am I?" "He looked and looked, but it was a vain search; he could not find himself. 'And that is how it is with us,' said the rabbi" (p. 314).

I relate this little story as a prelude to the present case study because it occurs to me that we psychologists are also often stupid, preoccupied with lists and charts, theories and techniques, and do not know ourselves any better than the fool in the rebbe's tale. Ours is a guild of obsessive-compulsives busily jumping our way through countless academic hoops, overcoming innumerable obstacles on our way toward professional respectability such that we scarcely fare any better than our poor Hasid when thrown back on ourselves and left to our own devices. Otto Rank (1936) referred to this process as one of *partialization,* the all-too-human attempt to encounter the world in manageable doses. The result is a necessarily reduced and leveled-down image of existence and human being. Indeed, Rollo May (1967) makes this same point in *Psychology and the Human Dilemma,* where he unwittingly retells the Hasidic tale with one of his own, this time of the overconfident and ever-industrious psychologist (here we do not laugh so freely!) who is denied eternity because of the crime of *nimis simplicandum,* the crime of oversimplification. "You have spent your life making molehills out of mountains," he is told by an incredulous St. Peter (p. 4). "We sent you to earth for seventy-two years to a Dantean circus, and you spent your days and nights at sideshows!" (p. 4). The psychologist is quick to protest and submit his many publications and countless awards for consideration, but St. Peter interrupts: "Please! Not your well-practiced chatter. Something new is required . . . something new" (p. 6).

Thus humbled, let us proceed to the story at hand.

THE CASE OF RON

I first met Ron in the early summer of 1990. He was 24 years old at that time and had received my name through an employee assistance program counselor following his fiancée's disclosure that she had had an abortion at the age of 16. A good obsessive-compulsive, Ron had a strong moral code and reacted to this disclosure with anger, anxiety, vindictiveness, and feelings of jealousy. Indeed, he once even hit his fiancée. The day after the news, he talked to his EAP counselor and, from there, quickly found his way to my office.

Now, I do not strike a particularly formal pose for a psychologist and believe that the therapist works ideally through his or her own person rather than through some acquired and often disingenuous pose of professionalism. (It was Alfred Adler, I believe, who taught that the therapist's most important asset was her or his own *self.* A simple matter, perhaps, but one which many psychotherapists seem not to get.) I can still remember quite clearly Ron's initial presentation: meticulously dressed in business suit with attaché case in hand. Ron himself seemed to pick up *intuitively* on the incongruity of the situation by elaborating on how organized he was, even opening his perfectly arranged attaché case as if to prove his point. I immediately liked this young man: He had a sense of humor about him and was not so far gone as not to be able to laugh at himself. For the obsessive-compulsive character, this is saying something, indeed!

During this and subsequent hours, I simply tried to listen to Ron, asking questions, not *compulsively* from some textbook evaluation procedure, but rather in order to let the patient's story further unfold. In so doing, I learned the following: Ron was born in rural New England and moved to industrialized southern New Hampshire with his family at the end of his first year of school. He was diagnosed as dyslexic in childhood and spent all his boyhood summers at a special camp for children with learning disabilities. There were other childhood physical maladies as well—problems with his legs requiring a brace, a lazy eye, and so on—bringing to mind Adler's (Ansbacher & Ansbacher, 1956) ideas about *organ inferiority* and *power striving*. Certainly the patient was well aware of his bitter disappointment at not having been able to play varsity sports as an adolescent and, even now, engaged in any number of compensatory endeavors.

Ron described his father as "very successful" but not easy to talk to. His mother, he said, was easier to talk to but had not earned Ron's respect because her world was, as he put it, "too small." Ron's mother had been married once before, as a teenager, and had two older children from that brief marriage. Thus the patient had a half-sister, 29 years of age, whom he described as a recovering alcoholic dependently married to another recovering alcoholic. He also had a half-brother, 27 years old, who was working on his Ph.D. in English somewhere in the Midwest.

Although Ron was not close to his siblings, it was clear that he struggled with turbulent and ambivalent feelings regarding his parents. His father was a self-made man who was both authoritarian and a benefactor. He had not only assisted in Ron's schoolwork but had—more than this—actually *done* much of it. While Ron no doubt had at his disposal a *magic helper* (Fromm, 1941) and possessed consequently, a sense of *specialness* (Yalom, 1980), he never really got the feeling of having accomplished anything of significance in his own right. Consciously, Ron admired his father and emulated his high standards; subconsciously, he harbored enormous resentment. His father had become quite successful as an independent salesperson of paper processing machinery. Ron himself at that time was selling—as we might well have anticipated—stationery products.

Ron's feelings about his mother were equally unsettled. He could, as he noted, relate to her more easily: She was warmer and more accessible. He felt, however, that her life was too severely limited, that she was too dependent on her husband. (Ron's mother had herself become pregnant during her teenage years, a situation forcing a marriage from which Ron's father—always the hero—had eventually "rescued" her.) Ron could easily see women as "weak," and, indeed, his fiancée often frustrated him insofar as he felt that she hadn't "a life of her own."

These, then, are some of the facts of Ron's circumstances up to the point in time when he began working with me. Superficially, it was clear that Ron bore all the earmarks of the obsessive-compulsive personality: perfectionism, preoccupation with details and rules, excessive devotion to work and productivity, inflexibility regarding matters of morality and ethics, restricted expression of affection, and so on. Ordinarily, it seems, the patient's diagnosis and history are meant to provide some sort of key to treatment methodology and goals, and the therapist is only *too anxious* to objectify the data into a neatly defined evaluation and corresponding treatment plan. All of this has its relevance, but first let us pause.

I often think in my life and work about Rollo May's (1981) conception of *freedom* as "the pause between stimulus and response." It is a profound point, really. If, indeed, we rush in to act without giving pause, then we are simply instruments in a great chain of cause and effect and are ourselves hardly free to actualize the patient's own potential in any way. Indeed, we may define *compulsivity* quite simply as "the failure to pause between stimulus and response." I want to underscore this point for we have already noted a professional (to say nothing at all about societal) bias toward compulsivity, and it is clear that nothing of consequence will be accomplished when doctor and patient are equally misguided. Sages from the East have long understood this point in a way that Westerners do not.

> If it could be talked about, everybody would have told his brother.—CHUANG TZU

> Not knowing that one knows is best.—LAO TZU, *Tao Te Ching*

The Polish poet Czeslaw Milosz (1951/1981) explains,

> The man of the East cannot take Americans seriously because they have never undergone experiences that teach men how relative their judgments and thinking habits are. Their resultant lack of imagination is appalling. (p. 29)

It is all too easy for rational, articulate professionals to theorize and discuss end-lessly without truly or deeply understanding, and Dr. May has already warned of the hazards of "well-practiced chatter." "A dog is not reckoned good because it barks well," says Chuang Tzu, "and a man is not reckoned wise because he speaks skill-fully." Let us slow down, then, and pause.

The Czech novelist Milan Kundera (1986/1988) suggests that the means toward apprehension of the self is the grasping of "the essence of [that self's] existential problem": to grasp one's "existential code" (p. 29). Increasingly I find that this is what I am trying to do in my clinical work. It is not merely a matter of determining this or that DSM diagnosis and effecting this or that technique of treatment. It is, rather, an approach to understanding. I say *approach* because I mean to emphasize that the self can never be apprehended with certainty. We may become aware of our themes and those of our patients—indeed we may *act* on these themes—but the themes are never static or fixed, never resolved in any absolute way. Still—and according to Kundera (1991), this is the important point—one cannot escape one's life themes. Rollo May (1981) refers to this, quite simply, as *destiny.*

What, then, can we say about Ron's existential code? First, Ron struggles signifi-cantly with the tension between freedom and destiny. He is ambitious, a go-getter, a young man of action. Superficially, one might say he is his own person. Such is not the case, however. He still lives at home, and even if he did not, his freedom would nonetheless be severely compromised. He idealizes a father who, albeit well-intended and generous, has undermined Ron's self-esteem. He has done this by taking over for Ron while remaining a kind of "ultimate rescuer" (Yalom, 1980), such that Ron has not yet learned to trust in himself. Ron is discontentedly employed in his father's field, and yet he adamantly believes that this very path, if persevered, will bring ful-fillment. It will not. If one travels the wrong path, one does not find fulfillment. External reward and validation, perhaps; fulfillment, no.

> Are you—the real you—a mere corruption? . . . Why do you not examine your own self, and see that you have arisen? (Pagels, 1989, p. 12)

The Baal-Shem said: "Every man should behave according to his "rung." If he does not, if he seizes the "rung" of a fellow man and abandons his own, he will actualize neither the one nor the other. (Martin Buber, *The Way of Man*, in Kaufmann, 1964, p. 430)

"I work hard at living, at getting to the next step," Ron says in his first hour. The question, however, is, Upon whose path are those steps taken?

Without knowing it, Ron is very angry at this state of affairs. There is, consequently, a significant history of acting out of aggression: episodic bouts of overconsumption of alcohol, periodic frays with authority and the law, even—shortly after the onset of therapy—a vandalized automatic teller machine that failed to operate. One might say that such behavior is a bad sign for an obsessive-compulsive personality; I, however, consider it a good omen for it indicates a man who is in touch (indeed, violently so) with his daimon. The task will be to harness the daimonic forces in *willing one's own life*.

This tension between freedom and destiny is played out, too, in the patient's relationship with his fiancée and in his attitude toward women in general. His fiancée is herself the daughter of alcoholic parents and very much a product of anxious family enmeshment. The patient is frustrated with the limitations of a relationship based, in the end, on mutual insecurity, mutual *fear of becoming*, and yet he lacks the courage to move beyond it in pursuit of a more satisfying relationship. Women whom Ron sees as being at his level are devalued as weak and dependent; they are resented and yet desperately needed to divert the patient's attention from his own failure of nerve. Stronger, more confident women whose worlds are not so finite are seen as highly desirable, yet off limits. Ron does not feel deserving of them and rather prefers to deny their existence: They give the lie to Ron's show of autonomy. Anxiety, as Kierkegaard (1944, p. 55) has said, is "the dizziness of freedom." Indeed, this tension is played out in other aspects of Ron's interpersonal life, such that—although the patient is rarely aware of it—extant relationships fail to assuage his chronic existential loneliness. He is ever afraid to move further out into life, where he might find circumstances more rewarding.

Finally, yet related to these themes, is the patient's spiritual void, a thoroughly modern dilemma. From the earliest sessions, Ron speaks of a "need to find meaning in life," a desire that "life should matter." Although brought up in a Protestant home, the patient considers converting to Catholicism in an effort to ease his religious discontent. Certainly, we may view this along the lines of the perennial human struggle between meaning and meaninglessness, but it is by no means unrelated to the basic polarity between freedom and destiny. To the extent that one avoids personal responsibility for one's own life one forfeits a sense of fulfillment at living authentically.

From becoming an individual, no one at all is excluded, except he who excludes himself by becoming a crowd. (Kierkegaard, 1939, p. 121)

What does your conscience say?—"You shall become who you are." (Nietzsche, 1974, p. 219)

Irrespective of the external rewards that may accrue, the patient is unable, in his avoidance of himself, to experience a genuine sense of peace with either himself or the world.

These, then, are some of the more prominent themes that I take to compose Ron's existential code. To be sure, these themes define, to a greater or lesser extent, all human beings insofar as they are ontological themes and, more particularly, the compulsive personality in which life has become constricted and leveled down. We are concerned, however, with seeing Ron, not as a member of this or that diagnostic category, but, rather, as a unique individual. This, to my way of thinking, is the distinguishing feature of the existential emphasis in psychotherapy. Theories, techniques, diagnostic formulations are all important aspects of our work, but they are always ancillary to the living human being who is before us. We seek first "to understand, to uncover, to disclose human existence" (May, 1958a, p. 24). If these conceptions appear to bear little relevance to the therapist's workaday responsibilities, I would suggest that they represent a starting point, indeed, the foundation, without which creative work cannot occur.

The existential approach to therapy proceeds with an emphasis upon the real relationship between therapist and patient. Without a genuine *encounter,* it is doubtful that the therapeutic process will be anything but superficial. As Frieda Fromm-Reichmann used to say, "the patient needs an experience, not an explanation" (May, 1958b, p. 81). This encounter, moreover, can be accomplished only to the extent that the therapist herself or himself has achieved some degree of authenticity. This point is crucial, and yet I am afraid that this quality is a rare bird these days, particularly among professionals who spend years and years in training programs unwittingly learning to define themselves from the *outside in,* by (in Kierkegaard's terminology—"externals."

> In Christendom he too is a Christian, goes to church every Sunday, hears and understands the parson, yea, they understand one another; he dies; the parson introduces him into eternity for the price of $10—but a self he was not, and a self he did not become. . . .
>
> For the immediate man does not recognize his self, he recognizes himself only by his dress. . . . He recognizes that he has a self only by externals. There is no more ludicrous confusion, for a self is just infinitely different from externals. (Kierkegaard, 1954, pp. 186–187)

Indeed, we can easily see the prototype of May's "well-practiced psychologist"—and not just that of our patient—in Kierkegaard's model Christian.

Early on in therapy, I tried to relate genuinely to Ron and listen carefully to his story. Obvious as this may seem, it is a rare enough occurrence for most of us: to be heard without preconceived judgment or theory. In this way, Ron was tacitly encouraged to take the themes which he had brought to therapy more seriously, to bear *responsibility* for these themes. This contrasted antithetically with the others in Ron's life and past, who had discouraged him from confronting his anxiety (a thoroughly modern philosophy, really: *kitsch,* we may say, or the *denial of the ontological dimension).*

Ron was not used to this sort of reception, and he tested it as he would any seemingly authoritarian relationship. Early on in treatment, he missed an appointment. Several days later, I received the following note:

Dr. Mendelowitz:

I'm sorry that I missed my apt. I forgot all about it, I've had a lot on my mind, you can bill me for the apt. b/c it was my fault.

I believe that the treatment is helping but I have along way to go. Thanks for your help, I think we have a nice relationship.

I will call you sometime this week. Until then have a nice week. I won't forget about the apt. again.

Take care,
Ron

When Ron arrived for his next appointment, he apologized once more. I accepted his apology graciously, commenting only that it would be helpful to have advance notice of a missed session. I did not interpret this "forgetfulness" as resistance, which, indeed, it was on a certain level. Resistance, however, has many dimensions and refers at its deepest level to the all-too-human tendency toward *self-betrayal,* the maneuvering by which one avoids oneself.

Perhaps the most tragic thing about the human situation is that a man may try to supplant himself, that is, to falsify his life. (Ortega y Gasset, 1991, p. 119)

Or, as Nietzsche somewhere states, "the most common lie is the lie which we lie to ourselves." Thus I do not interpret resistance in a strictly psychoanalytic or self-referential way but rather *existentially,* as an "avoidance of self." This is a point of fundamental importance for it emphasizes once again the tension between freedom and destiny and one's ultimate responsibility for oneself.

Many patients go to psychiatrists as if to psychic surgeons. When such a patient comes to such a therapist a relationship of considerable length may result, but little else. For the job can be done, if at all, only by the patient. To assign this task to anyone else, however insightful or charismatic, is to disavow the source of change. In the process of personality change the role of the psychiatrist is catalytic. As a cause he is sometimes necessary, never sufficient. (Wheelis, 1973, p. 7)

Once the client realizes this, therapy proceeds quite naturally: The patient *chooses* change, supported—now gently, now more forcibly—by the therapeutic *relationship* within the therapeutic container.

Essentially, then, the therapist needs to let go of her or his own *compulsivity;* that is, of the compulsion to act or solve. This is harder than it sounds, but it serves to underscore the essential tension between the patient's compulsive search for answers and clearly delineated techniques of change and the ultimate realization that one is responsible, in the end, for oneself.

> When the Zen master Po-chang was asked about seeking for the Buddha nature he answered, "It's much like riding an ox in search of the ox." (Capra, 1975, p. 124)

Like Wheelis, the Zen master understands the futility of the search for magic fluid.

With these thoughts in mind, let us review some of the salient aspects of Ron's course of psychotherapy. Ron has been with me for something over two years in weekly psychotherapy and is currently winding down his sessions. Early in his treatment, Ron was able to recognize that his exaggerated reaction to his fiancée's disclosure (that she had had an abortion) unveiled his own significant impulse to antisocial behavior, an impulse—as we have noted—periodically acted upon. With this realization, he quickly settled into the real therapeutic struggle: confronting himself. He gradually acknowledged that beneath a veneer of bravado, he harbored deep-seated feelings of insecurity and a concomitant resentment of authority. Clashes with the law and its enforcers, ambivalence about a rigid moral code that the patient had inherited but not chosen, an oftentimes judgmental and supercilious attitude toward his fiancée—indeed, toward women in general—all related to unresolved themes revolving around an overly constricted world.

It is important to emphasize that because the patient's insecurity, his reactive egotism and relentless need to succeed, had its roots in his past relationships, his authentic confrontation with these themes could come about only through a corrective relationship, one based on presence and genuine empathy. Once the patient had tested the new relationship to his satisfaction (and this was a far more stormy process than I will elaborate upon here), he was able to settle into the real work of therapy. (Although certain similarities exist between existential approaches to change and the so-called Eastern "ways of liberation," there is an important way in which the two approaches differ significantly: for the existentialist, *relationship is paramount.*)

Gradually, using the therapist as support and guide, the patient was able to move forward in embracing existential freedom. Realizing that his work was not satisfying in any fundamental way, and acknowledging further that what truly interested him was teaching and working with adolescents, Ron began to focus more on dissatisfaction with self and situation and rehearsed in therapy for the *possibility* of change. Within months, Ron gave up his position as a sales representative, finding odd and temporary employment while pursuing his teaching credentials. Moreover, he did all this without the initial support of his parents, risking considerable uncertainty about his future in an economic climate that did not augur well for prospective teachers. Eventually (and here the therapist was as much surprised as anyone), the patient's efforts paid off: He acquired a teaching position in his hometown. The work has been frustrating, challenging, but ultimately rewarding. It is no longer a fixed end point, however, nor does the patient any longer tread a carefully planned professional itinerary. He is more willing to live in the moment, accepting the inevitable pangs of the life and death anxiety that will lead, yet again, to further change. Already, he foresees a time when teaching will not interest him as much, and he is looking into graduate work in administration. Anxiety, no longer circumvented, is now accepted as the way of life—indeed, as *normal.*

Working with adolescents has elicited a periodic return of a moral rigidity that has, at times, limited Ron's ability to relate to and ultimately help his students. With each new "return of the repressed," however, Ron is quickly able to look within and recognize that the struggle is significantly internal. To the extent that he does this, he becomes more self-accepting (of doubt, of passion, of the daimonic) and better able to accept others. Interestingly, Ron has received numerous accolades in his two years of teaching, but these awards seem not to carry the weight they possessed when the patient worked so "hard at life, at getting to the next step." The emphasis is now on self and genuine relationship, not on external validation.

On the interpersonal front, my sense is that Ron has not fared quite so well. About a year after the initiation of therapy, the patient married his fiancée. Ron and I agree that there have been compromises here insofar as his feelings about his wife have never matched those he had for a former girlfriend. These perceived compromises were gently brought up by the therapist prior to the marriage, without any presumption whatsoever of knowing what was best for the patient. Respect for autonomy is absolutely essential to effective psychotherapy. Patients will change, if at all, in their own direction, at their own pace.

This marriage has been supportive for Ron, and yet also limiting, as his wife, too, struggles with relentless insecurity. Ron realizes the compromises herein—compromises that bother him more at certain times than at others—but has been less than successful at getting his wife to seriously pursue her own course of therapy. "She is a good person," he often sighs, fully aware that for him this is no longer always enough. Here, as elsewhere, I have maintained a nonjudgmental stance. I understand well the difficulties involved in seeking one's "soul image" (Jung, 1921/1961) and find few individuals who choose relationships for pure reasons. (Woody Allen investigates this ubiquity of compromise in his film *Husbands and Wives,* just as Ingmar Bergman did so convincingly before him.) Also, compromise—if it is *conscious* compromise—is still being addressed and need not be taken as failure: it may be modified at a future point.

At the very least, Ron seems to have significantly worked through his sexist attitudes toward women. He now freely accepts that his wife's insecurity mirrors his own and that his father is entirely as dependent on his hero identity as is his mother on her subsidiary role. In this respect, his relationships with both mother and wife have improved, and he is more discerning of his father's shortcomings. Thus the patient's former world of absolutism has slowly yielded to one of relativity and the ambiguity of the human enterprise.

As Ron winds down his present course of therapy, I ponder the relationship and the process of change. Ron is undoubtedly more fulfilled in his work and life than before. He has "seized his own rung." Whatever frustrations now ensue, they are, at least, a consequence of choosing his own life rather than of what Freud called "soul murder." This is genuine freedom, one that encompasses destiny. In relationships, Ron still struggles with feelings of uneasiness and inconsistency. Here, too, however, there are signs of real growth as the patient is far less defensive and more open to others than was once the case. The psychotherapeutic process has separated the patient further from anonymous and everyday relationships while heightening an existential loneliness as he searches for others to whom he can deeply relate. This is, perhaps, the price one pays for "authentication of one's existence." The patient now seeks *authentic* relationships, hardly something that can be ordered up at will. Also, Ron is only 26; I foresee a future for him that is open and full of possibility.

Although Ron's progress has been impressive in many respects, it is necessary to point out that I do not make of it a trophy unto myself. Just as the patient is ultimately responsible for himself, so, too, in the end is he due the lion's share of credit for growth achieved. The therapist's role, as Rollo May has often observed, is like that of Virgil in Dante's *Divine Comedy:* The therapist is a *guide.* (I am well aware of the many individuals whom I have *not* helped, and so I do not choose to shoulder accountability for all that is and isn't accomplished in therapy.) The patient's youth and turbulence, and perhaps my own genuineness, all augured well in the present instance, but it was Ron himself who, in the end, took up the gauntlet. In a similar vein, I no longer try to be overly objective about the precise means by which change occurs in therapy. The brilliant Otto Rank once treated a patient who, curious about a sudden and uncharacteristic burst of self-assertion moments before his psychoanalytic hour, later recalled,

> And so Rank said, "Well, I will tell you something that you may find rather comforting. I don't understand what happens." He said, "You don't understand, and neither do I." He just simply knew that from experience he could expect that certain things could happen if they were handled rightly and if the person's psyche and personality could be influenced for the better along certain lines. But he wouldn't pretend at all to try to give me a lecture on why it was happening because he said, "I don't know." (Lieberman, 1985, p. 272)

The sages of old had nothing on Rank.

Finally, in many respects Ron's compulsive traits remain, but they have certainly abated. Many of his current laments and longings are strikingly reminiscent of early sessions, reminding us of the wisdom of Jung's comment that the fundamental problems in life are never resolved in any final way. Still, there is a real pleasure that Ron and I have experienced in this relationship, one that has enabled the patient to open himself further to life in a way hitherto unthinkable. If Rank is right about the human tendency toward "partialization" of the world, Ron's purview is now at least broader: He sees further into life as he embraces the joys and burdens of freedom. He is no longer a wheelhorse. The result, I am convinced, will be a more fulfilled existence, one in which he does not flinch from life or death, nor from his *particular way.*

> And that's life: it does not resemble a picaresque novel in which from one chapter to the next the hero is continually being surprised by new events that have no common denominator. It resembles a composition that musicians call a *theme with variations.* (Kundera, 1991, p. 275)

Who can say more?

REFERENCES

Ansbacher, H. L., & Ansbacher, R. R. (Eds.) (1956). *The individual psychology of Alfred Adler.* New York: Basic Books.

Buber, M. (1948). *Tales of the Hasidim: Later masters* (O. Marx, trans.). New York: Schocken Books.

Buber, M. (1965). The way of man according to the teachings of Hasidism. In W. Kaufmann (Ed.), *Religion from Tolstoy to Camus.* New York: Harper Torchbooks.

Capra, F. (1975). *The Tao of physics.* Boulder, CO: Shambala Publications.

Fromm, E. (1941). *Escape from freedom.* New York: Holt.

Jung, C. G. (1921/1961). *Psychological types* (R. F. C. Hull, trans.). New York: Bollingen Foundation.

Kaufmann, W. (Ed.). (1964). *Religion from Tolstoy to Camus.* New York: Harper Torchbooks.

Kierkegaard, S. (1939). *The point of view* (W. Lowrie, trans.). London: Oxford.

Kierkegaard, S. (1944). *The concept of dread* (W. Lowrie, trans.). Princeton University Press.

Kierkegaard, S. (1954). *Fear and trembling* and *The sickness unto death* (W. Lowrie, trans.). New York: Anchor Books.

Kundera, M. (1986/1988). *The art of the novel* (L. Asher, trans.). New York: Harper & Row.

Kundera, M. (1991). *Immortality* (P. Kussi, trans.). New York: Grove Wiedenfeld.

Lieberman, J. (1985). *Acts of will: The life and work of Otto Rank.* New York: Free Press.

May, R. (1958a). The origins and significance of the existential movement in psychology. In R. May, E. Angel, & H. Ellenberger (Eds.), *Existence: A new dimension in psychology and psychiatry.* New York: Basic Books.

May, R. (1958b). Contributions of existential psychotherapy. In R. May, E. Angel, & H. Ellenberger (Eds.), *Existence: A new dimension in psychology and psychiatry.* New York: Basic Books.

May, R. (1967). *Psychology and the human dilemma.* New York: Norton.

May, R. (1981). *Freedom and destiny.* New York: Norton.

Milosz, C. (1981). *The captive mind.* (J. Zielonko, trans.). New York: Vintage Books.

Nietzsche, F. (1974). *The gay science* (W. Kaufmann, trans.). New York: Vintage Books.

Ortega y Gasset, J. (1991). In search of Goethe from within (W. R. Trask, trans.). In M. Friedman (Ed.), *The worlds of existentialism.* Atlantic Highlands, NJ: Humanities Press.

Pagels, E. (1989). *The gnostic gospels.* New York: Vintage Books.

Rank, O. (1936). *Will therapy* and *truth and reality* (J. Taft, trans.). New York: Knopf.

Wheelis, A. (1973). *How people change.* New York: Harper & Row.

Yalom, I. (1980). *Existential psychotherapy.* New York: Basic Books.

EI CASE FORMULATION—Ron

The conditions of sickliness, of fragility and dependence, are the bedrocks of Ron's dysfunction. Although he contradicts these dispositions periodically, he basically operates within them.

With a dominant father and weak mother, and with maladies aplenty, Ron seems to have been given the message that he is too frail for this dangerous world and that his life must be maximized for *protection.* This protection, Dr. Mendelowitz tells us, has many manifestations—perfectionism, moral rigidity, and compromising love and career interests.

Occasionally, as Dr. Mendelowitz alerts us, Ron unbinds these tortuous constraints. He becomes aggressive, as Dr. Mendelowitz puts it, and as expansive as his former state had been constrictive. Yet Dr. Mendelowitz is not pessimistic about these transitory shifts for they are signals, to him, of Ron's "aliveness."

To cultivate this aliveness, Dr. Mendelowitz offers Ron a genuine relationship. He attempts to be present to Ron, with as little pretense as possible. There is even a sprinkling of humor in this relationship, and some candid sharing of emotions. The relationship is tested early on when Ron misses one of his appointments. Far from admonishing Ron about this breach (as his father might have done), Dr. Mendelowitz mirrors it back to Ron thus letting *him* dwell upon its implications.

In time, Dr. Mendelowitz helps Ron to see how his world is constructed and to experiment with possible rearrangements. By vivifying Ron's avoidance of therapeutic spontaneity, for example, Dr. Mendelowitz helps him to recognize similar avoidances in his extratherapy relationships and to contemplate alternative responses. Beyond merely intellectualizing about these responses, however, Dr. Mendelowitz encourages Ron to *rehearse* them and to *experience* them within the therapeutic container.

By the end of therapy, Ron seems genuinely expanded. He no longer lives under the shadow of his father and is more fully immersed in the moment. Alternatively, Ron has less need to inflate himself—less impetus to be condescending toward women, less of an urge to aggrandize himself, and less drive—we can presume—to imbibe and intoxicate himself.

While Ron is still blocked in significant ways—such as in his love relationship—he is more actively aware of these blocks and more capable, therefore, of redressing them.

Since Ron will not compromise himself as he had earlier, the price of his liberation is loneliness. But this price is anticipated, Dr. Mendelowitz asserts, for it is the price of paradoxical living. Yet there *is* a community for "survivors" like Ron, and Rollo May refers to it in his commentaries on myth. It is the community of those who can love.

A GAY AND LESBIAN PERSPECTIVE: THE CASE OF MARCIA

Joan Monheit

Joan Monheit, L.C.S.W., board-certified Diplomate in Clinical Social Work, is a psychotherapist and consultant in private practice in Berkeley, California. She is an adjunct faculty member at John F. Kennedy University and has trained extensively with James Bugental.

The freedom to be who one deeply is strikes an especially resonant chord in the gay and lesbian communities. Ironically, however, existential therapy has had relatively little to say on the matter—until now. In her lucid and concrete discussion, Joan Monheit highlights freedom, limits, and sexual identity and outlines their impact on treatment.

A primary concern of existential psychotherapy is the relationship among freedom, limitation, and choice. For lesbians and gay men, the choice is not in being lesbian or gay; that is a given. Rather, the choice is either to embody one's affectional and erotic desires and allow for all the possibilities of who one is or to limit oneself by imitating the perceived norms of the culture, thereby constricting expression of not only one's sexuality but many other aspects of the self as well.

Inherent in this concern is the issue of self-acceptance: the freedom to express oneself fully in relation to self, others, and the world. This very human struggle is intensified for lesbians and gay men because of both *homophobia* (the fear or dislike of lesbians and gays by others) and *internalized homophobia* (self-hatred). Lesbians and gay men must daily answer the question: "With whom can I be myself?" The dangers are real. Physical safety, economic security, and acceptance by others are all threatened. And hiding *one* aspect of the self affects other dimensions of the self, such as self-esteem, creativity, and the ability to love.

Even for those who appear to be comfortable with being gay, the issue goes deeper. One of my clients, whom I will call Gary, was "out" as a gay man. He wore gay buttons, did not hesitate to tell others that he was gay, held strong political beliefs, and displayed a good intellectual understanding of being gay. Gary's parents and siblings knew he was gay, although no one would talk about it with him. It especially saddened and angered him that he could not talk with his mother about his life, which included his relationships with his friends and his activities. As he said to me at one session, "I can't just change the subject; this *is* my life."

While Gary appeared to be comfortable with himself as a gay man, he was not. After the breakup with his first lover, Gary stopped being sexual for over six years, adopting one strategy used by lesbians and gay men: "It's OK to be gay as long as I'm not sexual." But since he could not be sexual, he was unable to fully embody who he was as a gay man, nor, for that matter, could he express his full humanness.

Therapeutic work concerning the freedom to express oneself and therapeutic work touching on lesbian and gay identity issues is mutually reinforcing. As clients gain a greater sense of self and possibilities, they also learn to accept themselves as lesbian or gay; as they learn to accept themselves as lesbian or gay, they become increasingly more able to express all of who they are and to experience a widening sense of possibilities.

THE CASE OF MARCIA

The interweaving of the concerns of freedom, limitation, choice, and sexual identity is illustrated in greater depth in my work with a client I will call Marcia. While there are differences between lesbians and gay men, not the least of which is gender, the basic issues are the same.

Marcia was a 28-year-old Jewish woman referred to me by another lesbian client. "I'm very unhappy and need help from you," she said to me with tears in her eyes the first time we met. We worked together for four years.

Marcia was in a secret sexual relationship with a married but separated woman, a relationship she ended shortly after we began therapy. Marcia was fighting constantly with her mother, who lived in the area and with whom she had almost daily phone contact. She experienced herself as highly critical and judgmental, which she said created much conflict in all her relationships. She also described herself as "very needy."

Since early childhood, Marcia has had psoriasis that flares up under stress. Ten years previously, while away for her first year of college and during her first serious relationship with a young man, Marcia had a psychotic break and was hospitalized. She was diagnosed as manic-depressive at that time and has been on lithium ever since.

Marcia was the eldest of three children and the only girl. Her family was religiously observant and identified strongly with Jewish culture. She was expected to date and marry within the Jewish religion. No one in her family knew of her sexual relationships with women. In fact, Marcia hid the existence of all of her intimate relationships from her family, including an on-again, off-again, five-year relationship she had with a non-Jewish man. Marcia's fear was so great that she worried about her mother calling her early one morning, finding her not at home, and surmising that she had spent the night with a lover. Marcia's symptoms (e.g., psoriasis) appeared to be unconscious expressions of this oppressive fantasy.

The two areas of her life on which Marcia wanted to focus in her therapy were her sexuality and her relationships. Though she acknowledged her emotional and sexual attraction to women, she could barely use the "L" word, lesbian. Although she wanted to explore being a lesbian and her attraction to women, for almost two years we could barely touch the topic. When we did, she would change the subject.

Marcia's experience had taught her that she had very few options in life: She had to be a good, attentive daughter or her behavior might, literally, kill her parents. Because of her belief that she had no choice, she rebelled the only way she could, by keeping her life secret and having loud, angry fights with her mother, fights which would end with both of them in tears.

A significant aspect of our work was Marcia's learning how to make contact with her subjective self. I would encourage Marcia to sit or lie on the couch quietly and make contact with her body and then with any thoughts or emotions relating to her inner life. She was so used to focusing "out there," onto others, imagining stories about people's lives, that she did not know how to pay attention to herself. She focused on me, as well, wondering what kind of car I drove, what I thought, what my life might be like. The combination of her learning to "stop and check in with yourself," as I would say to her, along with my listening to her and letting her know that she was acceptable, was instrumental in her coming to accept herself and her sexuality.

I wondered how I could help Marcia to have a clearer sense of herself, to distinguish her needs from other people's needs of her, particularly her parents' needs. Could I help her act from a sense of herself instead of either trying to appease her parents or reacting against them? Could I enable her to find out who she was as a sexual being?

First, we looked at two symbols of her freedom and her developing sense of identity: being responsible for her own money and her own health. To this end, we talked about Marcia opening her own checking account. Up to this point she had only a joint account with her mother, an account into which her parents would sometimes deposit money. Ostensibly, her parents' rationale, she thought, was to make sure they could keep track of her spending, in case she had another manic episode. We talked about her fears of being financially independent, what it would mean for her to be in charge of her own finances. Soon she opened a new checking account for herself and stopped receiving money from her parents, relying, instead, on the income she made from her own small business.

Next, we looked at the second symbol of her freedom: being responsible for her own health. Marcia had told me that she wanted to begin to decrease her lithium and see if she could eventually get off it entirely. Not only was Marcia's physician father monitoring her lithium levels and supplying her with the lithium, she was also going to the same doctor, a friend of the family's, that she had been seeing since childhood.

First, I made a referral for her to see a psychiatrist, who made an evaluation and began a very gradual process of decreasing her lithium. Marcia began buying her own lithium and had the psychiatrist, rather than her father, monitor her periodic blood tests. Second, Marcia chose a woman physician to oversee her general health needs, one whose medical philosophy included a holistic approach more in keeping with Marcia's own beliefs about health care.

Marcia felt some anxiety when she began exploring the areas of managing her money and her health, but eventually she was able to make these two significant transitions fairly easily. Her actions enabled her to have primary experiences in being responsible for herself, which reinforced her sense of freedom to express who she truly was.

Weaving in and out of our sessions was the theme of her sexuality. For over two years, Marcia was celibate, choosing to focus on building nonsexual, though increasingly intimate, relationships with other women. Being celibate also enabled her to establish a deeper relationship with and reliance on herself and gave her time to gently dance with the "L" issue. It was important that she take all the time she needed to explore her sexuality and the meaning of being a lesbian.

As Marcia began to embody a sense of herself, she began to become more involved in social activities with women in general and lesbians in particular. She tentatively started to date women. As our work progressed, she became aware of her need to integrate an identity of herself as a lesbian and also as a Jew. She began to attend religious services at a lesbian and gay synagogue and joined a Jewish women's spiritual group. Earlier in our work, Marcia could not have involved herself in these activities; but now it was important to her to decrease her isolation and receive support and acceptance from people similar to her.

A year and a half into our psychotherapy, Marcia and I had our first pivotal conflict. Just as, without awareness, she had reacted against her parents instead of choosing her own way, Marcia stopped being the "good" client and began to reject my facilitation of her work in our sessions. Whereas she had long been trying to do what I suggested in order to explore her concerns, she would now sit straight up on the couch and, as she had done at the beginning, talk about other people. When I pointed that out, she would say, "What good is therapy anyway? I'm spending too much money. Maybe I should just stop." Marcia was trying, in the only way she knew how, to assert herself. And so, staying with her subjective experience, we began to talk about that.

"Marcia," I said, "what do *you* want to do right now?"

"Nothing," she said stubbornly.

"You sound so young. How old do you feel?"

"Seven," she replied. "I'm not going to do what you want me to do!"

"You don't have to. You get to do whatever you want. You can be here, you can leave, you can talk or not. It's all up to you."

Sometimes I would ask her about feeling 7 years old and protecting herself. "How do you feel, insisting that you won't do what I suggest?" As we explored this, I was able to point out that by saying only "no" to me, like she had with her family, she was acting, once again, from a set of limited possibilities on how to assert herself. I suggested that she might *want* to be quiet, check in with herself, and see what she was aware of—even if that *was* what I was suggesting that she do. She could make the choice for herself. Perhaps there were more meaningful ways in which she could now assert herself?

"I'm not your mother, and you're not really seven anymore, even if you feel that way," I said to her. By Marcia's being able to see and experience her process of reacting by saying "no" instead of acting from within herself, she became aware of how she limited herself and, therefore, began to feel a true sense of choice in how she responded.

During our third year of work, Marcia became sexually involved with a close woman friend. While this relationship was mutually supportive, the other woman was basically heterosexual. This seemed to reflect Marcia's own ambivalence regarding her lesbian sexuality. Although the relationship was brief, Marcia was able to use her new self-awareness to explore many crucial issues. She could identify her own fears, or internalized homophobia. What would her parents think if they knew? (*Total panic!*) How would the rest of the world treat her? What would it be like to give up being in an "acceptable" relationship? How was it to make love with another woman? How did she feel touching and being touched?

During this relationship Marcia did "come out" to one of her brothers; and despite her fears, his reaction was quite supportive. Then came a family crisis: Marcia's brother reported to her that their mother had deduced the fact that Marcia had been lovers with another woman. Marcia became frightened and wasn't able to talk directly to either parent about her lesbianism, nor did they initiate a dialogue with her. It was crucial that Marcia choose for herself when and how to tell her parents. In therapy, she decided that she wasn't yet ready to have that conversation.

At the end of our third year of work came our next major conflict, which, though extremely difficult for both of us, was crucial in helping Marcia understand that she could have a serious disagreement with someone, be angry, stay instead of leave, and actually work out the conflict. One session, Marcia told me that the local health club, the YMCA, was offering a membership special and that she was going to join. I had been encouraging her to exercise more, so that she could also support herself through being more fully in her body. She knew that I had been a long-standing member of the health club myself. I felt myself grow concerned, realizing that being at the same gym might create difficulty in our working together. How would it be for us to run into each other while working out or in the locker room? How would she be able to focus on herself if I was there? We took a couple of weeks exploring these questions, and she finally decided she would not join this particular gym. Then she went on a month-long vacation. During the first session upon her return, after telling me about her travels, Marcia said, "Joan, I decided I still really want to join the Y, and if you don't want me to, then maybe I should just stop therapy!"

"Marcia," I said, "I know this is really scary for you to talk about, and I really appreciate you telling me. I don't think you'll have to quit therapy over this. Let's hang in here together and see how we can deal with this situation. Are you willing?"

Session after session she'd come in, angry and scared, and we'd discuss the problem. I was certain that I was right that we shouldn't be at the same gym, yet neither of us knew how to solve the problem. "Marcia, we're in the soup. I don't know how we'll solve this, but I know that what we're doing is really significant," I said. "That we can both stay here and talk, and even be angry together, is important. You don't have to leave. You can stay and tell me what you think. I trust our relationship."

Finally, we did work out a compromise, which entailed setting up certain hours when each of us could go to the gym so that we wouldn't run into each other. I know there were other possible solutions to the problem—I could have changed gyms, for example—but what was important was that we were able to stay together in a place of disagreement and uncertainty and work it out together. Our grappling with this conflict further reinforced Marcia's experience that she could express herself and her needs and still stay in relationship with someone, a freedom she hadn't trusted before.

We were gradually coming to the final phase of our therapy, termination. Marcia took a job for five weeks at a resort in Idaho, where she spent much of her nonworking time alone, reading, writing letters, bike riding, and generally enjoying her solitude, a new experience for her. At the end of the five weeks, she went to a week-long women's festival in Yosemite. Here, Marcia was with many other lesbians and experienced herself as attractive and well-liked. She became sexually involved with a woman who lived on the opposite coast. This time, the woman was a lesbian. Over several months, the two women became more and more intimate, through visits, letters, and many hours of phone calls. When they decided to live together, Marcia chose to move to where her new partner lived.

Marcia and I set the date of our last session for three months in the future. Given a supportive relationship that satisfied her both sexually and emotionally, one in which she could feel positive about her lesbian identity, Marcia was now ready to "come out" to her parents.

Marcia and her mother were able to spend time together, disagreeing, but not having the destructive fights that had been such an old pattern. They went to family therapy, and her parents continued ongoing couples therapy. Marcia even brought her new partner to her parents' home for dinner during one of her visits.

We ended therapy acknowledging all the difficult work Marcia had done to bring her to this point in her life at 32. She was establishing an adult relationship with her family and forming a positive and mutually supportive relationship with a woman.

She now had greater ability to control her psoriasis. As Marcia developed the freedom to express herself, she began to feel more secure with her lesbian identity; and, as she experienced more fully what it meant to be a lesbian, she became more content and accepting of herself. In Marcia's therapeutic work, the dynamic interaction of freedom, limitation, and choice provided a context within which Marcia could discover and experience her ability to respond to her own nature and to make decisions that expressed her sense of self.

EI CASE FORMULATION—Marcia

The freedom of consenting adults to be sexual with one another is one of the elemental freedoms we enjoy. Indeed, few of us think twice about it; and many view it as a God-given right. For the gay and lesbian population, however, the picture is quite different. Daily they are threatened with curtailments to their sexual freedom, and daily they are challenged to protect it.

Marcia is a casualty of this fervent struggle. For years, Ms. Monheit informs us, Marcia has suppressed her sexual identity, and paid dearly for it—physically, emotionally, and intellectually. Yet if she steps out of her closeted existence, she risks paying an equally heavy cost: parental and social ostracism.

These are the torments, then, that Marcia brings to her therapy and that Ms. Monheit is called upon to address. Before anything is clarified, however, Ms. Monheit first simply listens to Marcia and patiently attends to her experience. This listening and attending is pivotal, Ms. Monheit tells us, because it grounds the balance of their work. Next, Ms. Monheit helps Marcia to "check in" with herself—not merely to think about particular issues but to *resonate* to them, to experience them kinesthetically.

Gradually, Ms. Monheit helps Marcia to become more aware of her dilemma and to face its consequences nonjudgmentally. While Marcia is constricted during this period, she becomes increasingly aware of how she can counter that constriction and productively regenerate her life. For example, she quits seeing her parents' physician and refuses her parents' financial assistance. She decreases her lithium intake, moreover, and begins to sense her own potency.

This increase in freedom generally emboldens Marcia to turn her attention to sexual matters, like the question of "coming out." By being celibate for a period, and by getting to know her needs deeply, Marcia begins to reconnect with herself sexually. She also joins several groups that give her support and acceptance, while Ms. Monheit continues to invoke the actual with her in session.

Suddenly—as so often happens with clients on the verge of a breakthrough—Marcia becomes resistive with Ms. Monheit. She refuses Ms. Monheit's therapeutic invitations and flaunts her authority. Through vivifying these resistances, Ms. Monheit and Marcia observe that they serve two disparate functions. On the one hand, they derail Marcia and prevent her from attending within. On the other hand, ironically, they *manifest* what she feels within by validating her newfound power.

In the final challenge to their relationship, Marcia decides to join Ms. Monheit's local YMCA. This leads to many rounds of tension—and even anger—between Ms. Monheit and Marcia. But it also deepens their relationship. By inviting Marcia to be real with her, Ms. Monheit offers two challenges to Marcia: (1) to trust Ms. Monheit as a person and (2) to trust *herself* in response to Ms. Monheit. She meets these challenges.

By the end of therapy, Marcia is liberated enough to seek new meanings in her life. These affirm her sexuality, to be sure, but they also expand her sensitivities more generally. They inspire her to become "response-able"—personally, socially, and spiritually.

PSYCHOTIC CLIENTS, LAING'S TREATMENT PHILOSOPHY, AND THE FIDELITY TO EXPERIENCE IN EXISTENTIAL PSYCHOANALYSIS

Michael Guy Thompson

Michael Thompson received his analytic training from R. D. Laing and his associates at the Philadelphia Association in London and his Ph.D. in psychology from the Wright Institute in Berkeley, California. He is the founder and director of Free Association in San Francisco, a training program in psychoanalysis, and the author of The Death of Desire, *and* The Truth about Freud's Technique.

Counting to a million and back again isn't the typical avocation for most people; but for some, it may be the only way to feel free. In this seminal and moving report, Michael Thompson recounts his experience with Jerome, one of the most difficult patients at R. D. Laing's renowned Philadelphia Association Clinic. Dr. Thompson suggests that while Jerome is incorrigible, he is not unlike others of his ilk—both logical in his own way and profoundly desirous of validation. The challenge is deciphering Jerome's logic and helping him work out his "truth." That Dr. Thompson draws from experiential *sources to answer this challenge is both the subject and lesson of this study.*

What is "existential analysis"? This question is asked more urgently today than ever before, probably because its allure is fading while the competing forms of psychotherapy are taking the field. Even in the 1960s, when terms like "existential analysis," "existential psychoanalysis," and "existential therapy" were on the lips of every psychology student in America, no one knew what it meant. Everyone talked about it all the same. Why? There's no denying that the word itself sounds good. The term "existential" has a wonderful flavor to it; it's full of depth, resonance, meaning. It sounds at once European and personal; humanistic yet vaguely wise; intellectual but not academically so. It was the perfect word for anybody who professed to be "in the know," both streetwise and learned. To be "existential" was synonymous with being hip, modern, on the cutting edge. Existential therapy seemed to define itself, epitomized by spontaneous, in-the-café encounters. Surely specialized "training" was irrelevant, if not obscene. Existentialism itself, a philosophical school of thought, was somehow related to the technique of existential therapy, but one shouldn't make too much of the relationship between them. If you did, you might be accused of confusing therapy with philosophy. Yet, existential analysis—whatever "it" is—is based on the work of a group of philosophers who are bound by *existentialism*. It's no wonder it was hard to fathom the meaning of a school of clinical intervention whose roots were frequently suppressed.

Today the question, What is existential analysis? is still being asked, but not for the same reasons. Today, the question is asked because it's *out* of fashion. Most of the people who made existential analysis and existential therapy famous are either dead or aging. Ludwig Binswanger, Medard Boss, Victor Frankl, R. D. Laing, David Cooper, Rollo May, Ludwig Lefebre, and Eugene Minkowski are only some of the names of clinicians who promoted the cause of the existential approach to psychotherapy and—in the case of some—psychoanalysis. Their transitions have struck a near-death blow to the movement and the rationale that supports it. This is why the question, What is existential analysis? *should* be asked today—and why it is more imperative than ever before to answer it.

EXISTENCE AND EXPERIENCE

I would like to answer the question by addressing an important aspect of how I conceive the existential approach to clinical practice. It concerns the perhaps unanticipated significance of an everyday term—*experience*—and how that word is conceived "existentially." I hope you will forgive me, because I plan to say something slightly philosophical in my exploration of this term, even if this paper is specifically clinical in nature. I will avoid the risk of obtuseness, however, by couching my remarks in the very practical context of my association with R. D. Laing, whose clinical work, since his death in 1989, has aroused a certain curiosity because he wrote almost nothing about it.[1] More than most existential psychotherapists, Laing linked experience with existential thought in such a way that the one became synonymous with the other. I would like to show how the two are interrelated by sharing with you the treatment of a young psychotic male who stayed at one of Laing's post-Kingsley Hall therapy centers. I will try to explain how Laing's unorthodox treatment of psychotic patients worked and the philosophical basis of his unorthodox treatment of a large number of people going through psychotic episodes. I believe this is the first published attempt to situate Laing's treatment philosophy at Kingsley Hall in the inherently transformative nature of experience as he understood it. Though this connection is frequently alluded to in his writings, it has never been explored in the context of his treatment of schizophrenia.

It should be noted, however, that Laing's work wasn't based simply on a reading of existential philosophy. He owed a great deal to psychoanalysis, particularly Freud's earlier work and his papers on technique. Freud's conception of "free association" was the centerpiece of his technique. Laing, as a consequence of his analytic training in London, was thoroughly schooled in this method. The rule of free association is to utter out loud whatever comes to mind during a therapy session, refraining from keeping specific thoughts to oneself *no matter how personal or private or embarrassing* it feels. This rule was gradually introduced because Freud, in the early years of his clinical investigations, concluded that neurosis is the consequence of extremely personal secrets that we somehow *hide from ourselves.* These secrets are repressed from consciousness because they concern terrible disappointments we experienced early in our development. Suppressing our knowledge of these experiences by "forgetting" them temporarily relieves the anguish and frustration they originally elicited. Freud believed that the suppression of painful experiences produced psychical conflicts which, in turn, gave rise to psychopathology, symptomatic expressions of the pain that was being denied. This led to Freud's conception of a treatment for psychical symptoms: psychoanalysis. Its cornerstone was the "fundamental rule," the *pledge* to be completely candid with one's therapist during the analytic hour. If carried out sincerely, the exercise of candor should reverse the conflicts that had been caused by repression. In other words, the fundamental rule of psychoanalysis was, in effect, the promise to *be honest with one's analyst* by agreeing to "free associate" with him (Freud, 1913/1958, pp. 134–136). Unnoticed by many, Freud's conception of "psychical" therapy was rooted, on a deeper level, in a form of *moral* therapy because the curative power lay in one's *pledge* to be honest, something that, given the cause of psychopathology—self-deception—we are reluctant to do.

Laing accepted Freud's basic premise and took it a step further. He believed that our tendency to conceal painful experiences from ourselves could be compounded by families who keep secrets *from each other:* I know what you are thinking, but you deny it and pretend to think the opposite; or I know how I feel, but you insist that I really believe the opposite. This kind of mystification can become so extreme that a child doesn't know *what* he thinks (Laing, 1965). His sense of reality becomes so compromised that he seeks refuge in a psychotic—rather than merely neurotic— withdrawal from an intolerable situation (Thompson, 1985, pp. 88–117).

Following Freud's lead, Laing concluded that the therapeutic treatment of psychosis should serve to reverse the pathogenic process that had been initiated in the first place to escape an unlivable experience. Laing decided that this could best be realized in a familial setting, where the "fundamental rule" could be adapted to a more disturbed population. Each person's relationship with the others would be characterized by candor, in deed as well as in word. Why confine a relationship rooted in free association to only one hour a day, and with only one person? Why not apply it to a setting in which one *lived,* where mutual candor was the *only* rule? This approach would inevitably be more existential, since each person's efforts at self-disclosure would be *lived out* in the course of the community's day-to-day existence.

In order to make this transition possible—the transition from the treatment of neurotic to the treatment of psychotic loss of experience and the transition from individual (actually one-to-one) to group dynamics—Laing needed a more radical conception of experience than even Freud had formulated. He turned to the philosophers who had made experience the cornerstone of their thinking. He turned to Hegel and Heidegger, whom he had studied as a medical student at the University of Glasgow. In the briefest possible terms, I will try to summarize Hegel's and Heidegger's respective conceptions of experience, particularly those aspects of it that influenced Laing's clinical theories.

Hegel believed that experience can't be reduced simply to one's subjective aware-ness of or involvement in an event, in the sense that I have an experience of writing this sentence. According to Hegel, when I truly experience something, I'm *affected* by it. It comes as a shock. *It changes everything.* My experience of something con-fronts me with the unexpected. It violates my familiar view of things by forcing something new into consciousness. Due to its intrinsically unsettling nature, Hegel concluded that experience elicits despair because it disturbs my cozy accommodation to reality. On the other hand, despair leads to something new because experience always occasions a transformation of some kind. In other words, since experience displaces what is familiar to me, it doesn't simply *cause* change: It *is* change. Hegel was the first to realize that experience isn't simply subjective. It's also transcendental because it takes me outside myself and places me inside a situation that alters my perspective. The effect that my experience has over me changes, to some degree, *who* I am. Hegel's term for my relationship with the things that affect me through my experience of them is *dialectical.*

> This dialectical process which consciousness executes on itself—on its knowledge as well as on its object—in the sense that out of it the new and true object arises, is precisely what is termed Experience. (Hegel, 1949, p. 142)[2]*

Hegel arrived at this unusual conception of experience while exploring the nature of consciousness and its relationship to change and history. It had an enormous impact on the way philosophers saw the relationship between thought and action. Heidegger was influenced by Hegel's work, but took it further. He emphasized the *revelatory* aspects of experience as well as the transformative ones. In other words, experience doesn't merely change the world I inhabit, it also reveals things to me that I hadn't known. Consequently, *experience elicits truth.* Heidegger, however, was even more interested in the "handy," practical aspects of experience than was Hegel. He realized that one's experience could be nudged in a certain direction for a specific purpose so long as one prepared oneself for it. In other words, by anticipating my experiences purposefully, deliberately, and thoughtfully, I can make use of experi-ence to gain knowledge about myself. There are *degrees* to which I experience things; it isn't all or nothing. Experiences don't just fall on me whether I want them to or not. I am capable of *resisting* experience. In turn, the degree to which I am able to experience something is determined by how willing I am to submit to whatever it is that I want to experience. According to Heidegger,

> To undergo an experience with something—be it a thing, a person, or a god—means that this something befalls us, strikes us, comes over us, overwhelms and transforms us. When we talk of "undergoing" an experience, we mean specifically that the experience is not of our own making; to undergo here means that we endure it, suffer it, receive it as it strikes us and submit to it. It is this something itself that comes about, comes to pass, happens. (Heidegger, 1971, p. 57)

---

*Editor's note: On this specific point, Kierkegaard and Hegel agreed, but Kierkegaard apparently did not feel that Hegel's general philosophy or way of employing experience was very deeply lived, or experi-enced.

This view of experience is remarkably close to Freud's conception of the "fundamental rule" of psychoanalysis, the conscious willingness to comply with the injunction to be candid with one's analyst. The extent to which I am able or willing to listen to what my experience tells me will determine how fully I experience what I'm doing, whether I'm eating a meal, solving a problem, or undergoing psychoanalysis. Heidegger recognized that because experience is transformative, I am afraid of it and resist it by holding back. I'm perfectly capable of suppressing my experiences (if they happen to be painful) and even repressing the significance or memory of experiences I've had in order to "forget" them. In other words, I can resist change by suppressing experience, just as I can elicit change by being open to it.

Laing was formally schooled in Hegel's and Heidegger's views about experience as a student in Glasgow. He conceived of Kingsley Hall as a place where one would be free to *undergo* experience in the way that Hegel and Heidegger described it. It was a place where one had permission—in effect, license—to endure the types of experience that we are typically alarmed by—such as psychotic experience. In other words, he conceived of psychosis as a sort of process that some feel *compelled* to undergo, given their circumstances.

His views about this process were complex, but briefly, he conceived of psychosis as a desperate effort to stay in touch with one's experience of reality when the environment that one is in is violently opposed to that experience. This is paradoxical because psychosis, as Laing understood it, is an attempt both to escape the experience of an unlivable situation *and* hold onto that which one is escaping—via a "psychotic breakdown." In other words, the psychotic individual is simply trying to *be true* to his experience. Because of the opposition that he encounters in his environment, he is compelled to withdraw from the reality that he is in in order to protect what experience tells him. This "compromise" comprises his psychosis. Laing's theory about the nature of psychosis, as unorthodox as it sounds, actually conforms with Freud's view that a psychotic symptom is a desperate attempt to heal the rift with reality that the pre-psychotic person created (Freud, 1924/1961, pp. 185–186). The problem with this strategy is that it usually ends in failure. The psychotic gets stuck in his psychosis and can't find his way out of it.

LAING AND EXPERIENCE

Laing believed that anything we are capable of experiencing can't, in and of itself, be pathogenic. Rather, it's the *suppression* of experience that gives rise to distortions in consciousness that we associate with psychopathology. Hence anything that we're called upon to experience must have a purpose. Following Heidegger, Laing decided that fidelity to experience was a vehicle for change, given time.

The emphasis Laing gave to the transformative nature of experience as a therapeutic tool epitomizes the specifically existential component of his clinical work. Existential therapy should be structured in such a fashion that it gives rise to experience by giving voice to it, regardless of how frightening or anxiety-provoking it may be. It's important, however, not to make the mistake that some existential therapists make in equating existential therapy with simply eliciting "experiences" in the pre-

Hegelian sense of simply bringing something to conscious awareness, such as being "in touch" with one's feelings, for example. In order to be therapeutic, in order to facilitate change, one's conception of experience should be intrinsically "revelatory." It should exploit the way consciousness aspires to keep pace with events by yielding to the effect they have on us. This is why Freud's innovation of free association embodies an existential conception of experience—because its efficacy rests on a willingness to submit to our experience *of the analytic hour,* by verbalizing what those experiences are.

Before turning to my clinical material, I should say one last word about Laing's conception of groups and their transformative power. While engaging in family research at the Tavistock Clinic, Laing was exposed to Wilfried Bion's famous experiments with group dynamics, particularly the employment of "leaderless" groups (Bion, 1961). Laing conceived of a place where psychotics could *live,* rooted on the same principles of the group whose leader abstains from assuming the *function* of a leader. In order to create a similar feeling, Laing decided that no staff or attendants should be paid to "run" things. Therapists would be involved with the people who lived there, but, like the analyst in psychoanalytic treatment, they would refuse to assume responsibility for anyone else's experience. Nor would they attempt to "normalize" anyone's behavior, no matter how crazy that behavior was. Laing wanted an environment that resembled a home more than an institution, a place where—stripped of coercive rules—the relationships that people formed with one another would be more personal and less stereotyped. The gulf in power that one typically encounters in institutions—even analytic ones—would be diminished, if not entirely erased, in such a place. Finally, "group therapy" per se—in the sense of formal sessions—would be eschewed in favor of spontaneous conversations that arose naturally, like those around the dinner table or in the heat of the moment. In other words, Freud's conception of the analytic session (as with Bion's of the group) would be transplanted to a lived situation, where it would become a piece of "real life." Freud's model of candor would serve as the principal therapeutic agent, but instead of emphasizing the interpretation of experience in psychoanalysis, the emphasis would be on *eliciting* experience and living through it.

Kingsley Hall was the first of the household communities set up by Laing to serve as both places where patients could live through their madness in order to achieve a more viable existence and asylums from the treatment—psychiatric or otherwise—that some believed was the instrument of (not the answer to) their insanity. Laing and his colleagues at that time—including David Cooper and Aaron Esterson (Cooper, 1967; Laing & Esterson, 1971)—leased a building from a London charity and occupied it from 1965 to 1970. The house was of historic importance, having been the residence of Mahatma Gandhi while he was negotiating India's freedom from British rule. Apparently the trustees of Kingsley Hall were impressed with Laing and his plans for the building's use. It was leased to his organization—the Philadelphia Association—for the sum of one pound per annum.

In 1970, when the lease ran out, Laing moved his operations elsewhere. By this time, Esterson and Cooper had departed and been replaced with other colleagues who shared Laing's unorthodox—and by now, increasingly famous—views on the treatment of schizophrenia. They included Leon Redler, an American; Hugh Crawford, a fellow Scotsman and psychoanalyst; John Heaton, a phenomenologist and member of the British aristocracy; and Francis Huxley, an anthropologist and nephew of Aldous Huxley. In addition, there were several second-generation psychotherapists who had trained with Laing and his associates. A number of post-Kingsley Hall houses began to emerge, each adhering to the basic philosophy of the first—"live and let live"—as the paradigm of its clinical philosophy. Each place reflected the personalities of the people who happened to be living there as well as the therapist (or therapists) who took it upon themselves to be available to the residents.

By the time I arrived in London in 1973 to study with the Philadelphia Association, there were four or five such places, primarily under the stewardship of Leon Redler and Hugh Crawford. I opted to join Crawford's house on Portland Road. Though it was essentially like the others, I was particularly drawn to Crawford himself and the extraordinary involvement he enjoyed with the people who lived in his house. While some of the houses took elaborate pains to perfect a hands-off approach to the crazier members of their community, Crawford used a profoundly intensive, even "familial" intimacy that felt inviting, warm, reassuring. Joining wasn't easy. No one was "in charge," so there was no one to whom to apply to gain admittance. Since I wasn't psychotic myself, I lacked the most obvious rationale for asking to join. Other students I had met told me how they had visited Portland Road and, while sipping tea, offered to "help out." "What's in it for you?" they were asked. When they replied that because they were students, they wanted to learn firsthand about psychosis, that they were confident the experience would prove beneficial, they were promptly rejected and never invited back.

It occurred to me that it would take time to get in, as with any other relationship. They would have to know me, and I, in turn, should get to know them. I attended Crawford's seminars on Heidegger and Merleau-Ponty and went to the occasional "open house" that tolerated curiosity seekers. Eventually, I was invited to participate in a *vigil,* an around-the-clock group effort to stay up—and with—somebody who was going through a psychotic episode. Generally, these affairs lasted a couple of weeks. I volunteered to participate on two different evenings from midnight to eight in the morning. At one of these vigils, a man in his twenties was in the throes of what resembled an extraordinary LSD trip from which he never came down. Having managed to keep my cool and mind my manners throughout this vigil, I guess I proved to their satisfaction that I was someone who could be counted on, someone who would be less of a burden than an asset. In time, I was accepted into the house.

It took six months to be invited to live at Portland Road. Crazier people fared better. Typically, a person would call, say he or she was going through something terrible, and be invited to drop around. Upon arrival, everyone who lived in the house—about a dozen people—and Hugh Crawford would be present. The visitor would have the evening to make his case heard. What were they looking for? What criteria were used for allowing someone to move in? It's hard to say. What criteria do psychoanalysts use to admit someone to analysis? That is also somewhat difficult to articulate. At Portland Road, it was more difficult because none of the applicants were *analyzable* in the conventional sense of that term. However, there were similarities.

At bottom, Freud was looking for patients who, irrespective of how neurotic they were, could be honest with him. The "fundamental rule" of analysis required a capacity for candor. Similarly at Portland Road, no matter how crazy a person was, he was expected to be candid with the people to whom he made his case. They were looking for signs of sincerity, genuineness, and goodwill underneath all the symptoms they would inevitably be burdened with. As Wilfried Bion himself might have said, they were looking to make contact with the *sane* part of the personality, irrespective of how insane the rest of it might be.

Since people were admitted only by unanimous vote—even one dissenter was enough to reject an applicant—once in you could count on everyone's commitment to the person you happened to be. The sense of community was extraordinary. So was the brutal frankness with which everybody typically expressed their opinions about everyone else. The effect was startling, like being stripped of the ego one has so carefully created for society's approval. I came to realize that candor is actually something most of us would prefer to avoid, however much we complain about its absence. Again, the similarity to the analytic experience was apparent. Only now, instead of having to contend for one hour a day with one analyst who serves as a mirror to the unconscious, at Portland Road one was confronted with an entire *cadre* of mirrors, all of whom engendered transference relationships with which one had to contend twenty-four hours a day, seven days a week.

THE CASE OF JEROME

With these particulars in mind, I would like to introduce Jerome, a 20-year-old man who, ironically, had been referred to Laing by a psychiatrist at the local hospital. At the time, Portland Road tended to take the more difficult cases, and Laing, for some reason, was especially concerned about the prospects for this particular fellow. Jerome was a rather slight, dark-haired, and extremely shy young man. In a quiet voice and tentative manner, he told his tale.

He didn't know why, but Jerome had developed an irresistible habit of withdrawing from his family—mother, father, and a younger sister—by going to his bedroom and closing himself inside. When he refused to come out, his parents tried first to cajole him, then became angry and threatening. Eventually, after several days, they called in a psychiatrist. He was forcibly taken from his room and removed to the hospital via ambulance and in restraints. In the hospital, he persisted in his behavior. He refused to speak or cooperate in any way. All the while, he said, he didn't know *why* he was behaving this way. He just felt that he had to.

The psychiatrist diagnosed him as suffering from catatonic schizophrenia with depressive features. Electroconvulsive therapy was ordered, and soon Jerome was fine again, his ordinary, friendly, cooperative self. Six months after he returned home, it happened again. Withdrawal. Removal to the hospital. Shocks. Recovery. Jerome still had no idea why he was acting this way, but each time a lengthier course of "therapy" was required to bring him out. He and his family had been through this routine three times in the two years before Jerome came to Portland Road.

The psychiatrist had called Laing because his colleagues at the hospital were fed up with Jerome and had vowed that if he came back a fourth time, "he wouldn't leave." This, now, was the fourth such episode, in its earliest stages. This time, as his parents beseeched Jerome to come from his room, he replied that he would agree to do so but only on the condition that Laing would see him. He'd read *The Divided Self* and decided he was the only psychiatrist he would be willing to trust. Hence the hospital psychiatrist—one of the few who sympathized with Laing's treatment philosophy—decided to intervene on Jerome's behalf. Now we realized why Laing had been so concerned about the outcome of Jerome's journey. He had managed to orchestrate a competition of sorts between Jerome's family and conventional psychiatry on the one side, and Laing and his unconventional ways on the other. Everyone was watching. It seemed assured that should we back down, Jerome's future was decidedly bleak. But if we failed, Laing's—and, by extension, our—reputation, marginal as it was, would suffer, too.

Jerome, to make matters worse, insisted on dictating precisely what *he* believed was the therapeutic course to follow. He sought *asylum,* in the truest sense of that word. He proposed to go to his room and stay there till he felt able to come out. We, in turn, were asked to agree with this plan. We decided, rather reluctantly, to accept his terms.

I single Jerome out, of all the people I came to know and lived with over the four years I spent at Portland Road because, in many ways, he confronted us with probably our biggest challenge. Due to the nature of his terms, he effectively robbed us of our most effective therapeutic tool: the communion that was shared by the people who lived there. His plan challenged the treatment philosophy that Laing and Crawford had so painstakingly formulated and crafted: the call for *fidelity to experience,* no matter how crazy or ridiculous it seemed. Jerome asked that Laing and his associates be true to their word. We couldn't bring ourselves to say no.

True to *his* word, no sooner did Jerome move in to Portland Road than he took to his room and stayed there. He had a room of his own, so no one saw him. It wasn't uncommon for residents to forgo meals and other opportunities to fraternize, but the way Jerome cut himself off was radical. No one even saw him sneak downstairs for food in the middle of the night. Or use the bathroom. We became alarmed. It was obvious he wasn't eating anything and that he was using his bed—from which he refused to move—for a bathroom.

We tried talking to him. "This wasn't part of the deal," we said. "Oh yes it was!" he shot back. Jerome didn't seem to be in any particular pain. He didn't seem depressed, or anxious, or remotely "schizophrenic." He was just *stubborn*! He insisted on having his way. He needed to do what he needed to do, even if he couldn't or wouldn't tell us why. He resented our appeals for cooperation. We, on the other hand, felt that we had put ourselves out on a limb for him. And where was the gratitude, the goodwill, in return?

Jerome wouldn't talk about underlying motives for his behavior; nor would he acknowledge his withdrawal as a symptom that demanded to be understood. He simply submitted to his *experience*—and we were being forced to submit to ours, of *him.* He agreed to eat cereal, to prevent starvation, so long as we brought it to him. The stench from his incontinence didn't bother him. If it bothered *us,* that was our problem. He became the topic of conversation every night around the dinner table. "What are we going to do about him?" Ironically, he had turned us into a hospital. We were concerned about his health, his diet, possible bedsores. He was losing weight precipitously. We either had to tell him to get out—in effect, have him removed—or abide by his extraordinary demands. Laing was concerned. If he developed bedsores, he would have to be taken to the hospital anyway. And it was imperative that he take some nourishment. Compounding everything, he couldn't keep even his cereal down and vomited, on the average, every other meal. This added to the stench of his urine and feces.

We weren't a hospital staff. By now, two months after he moved in, most of us hated him and didn't care if he starved. Who was going to clean him, bathe him, and do all the other things that were essential if he was to survive? Some of us—only two or three, really—were willing to play nurse and keep it going, probably out of some sort of misguided neurotic guilt. But at least he was still there, more or less alive, surviving. How long would it take for him to come out of it?

Two more months went by. Now Jerome's family was insisting on visiting and threatened legal action if we didn't allow them to. We weren't about to. Crawford insisted we could hold the course. Laing was uneasy but protective and was ready to back us up, whatever that entailed. Jerome continued to lose weight. He was on the verge of becoming ill. Now six months into it, we were on the brink of a crisis. Through it all, Jerome refused to talk to anybody in a meaningful way. He bitterly protested our efforts to keep him clean and fed.

We decided a change of some kind was vital. Jerome needed to be in closer proximity to the people he lived with, somehow or other. In addition to the physical threat to his health, the lack of *human* contact was alarming. If he couldn't join us, perhaps we could join him. We moved him into my bedroom. In exchange, everyone else agreed to bathe him regularly, feed him, change his bed every day, spend more time with him, talk to him even if he wasn't inclined to talk back. We gave him regular massages to prevent loss of muscle tone and for an excuse to get close. We felt confident that things would get better. Before you know it, Jerome will be back on his feet. He'll even tell us what this was all about.

His condition stabilized, but that's about all. I grew accustomed to the stench, the silence, the close quarters; but Jerome was hardly a congenial roommate. I grew depressed, living with a ghost who haunted our space but couldn't *occupy* it. I needed something to change the sense of deadness that surrounded us. I invited the most floridly schizophrenic person in the house—a sweet guy who thought he was Mick Jagger—to move in with us. He serenaded Jerome morning and night and more or less adopted him as a kid brother. At least it was a livelier, if "crazier," arrangement. I came out of my depression.

A year went by without a change. In the meantime, many crises transpired between Jerome's family and Laing, between Laing and us, between us and Jerome, and between ourselves and Crawford for not supporting the occasional mutinous attempts to kick Jerome out. I needn't go into the details. You can imagine how trying and disillusioning the situation became. We were ready to admit defeat and resign ourselves to having failed. Jerome wasn't going to come out of his self-imposed exile from life. For him, this had *become* life. This was apparently all that he wanted from it.

I don't know how or why, but as time went by, the urgency of Jerome's situation and its resolution became somehow less urgent. Naturally, other things were happening all the while. Probably because Jerome was living in my room, I was more concerned than most about when this would end. I was eager to have my room back. But as one month slipped into another, even I lost track of time. Nobody even noticed when the year-and-a-half (*eighteen-month*) anniversary came by. We were so used to his odd definition of *cohabitation,* so accustomed to the routine of the baths, the linen changes, the bowls of cereal, the serenades, that we hardly noticed that evening by the fire, the evening of the anniversary, when Jerome walked downstairs to use the bathroom. He nonchalantly flushed the toilet, peeked his head in to say "hi," and went back upstairs. We hardly noticed it at first, but then I nearly gagged when I realized what had happened.

An hour later, Jerome came back downstairs, announced he was famished, and proceeded to terminate the bizarre fast that had reduced him to ninety pounds. This was a Jerome we'd never seen. Talkative, natural, shy but social. We pinched ourselves, wondering how long it would last. But the next day Jerome got dressed and cleaned up his (our) room. He had clearly taken a new turn. He was through with whatever it was he had needed to do, up there in his bed, cut off from the world, engaged in God knows what manner of meditation. Naturally, we wanted to know. "What on earth were you *doing,* Jerome, all that time by yourself? What was it that you finally got out of your system?"

We didn't really expect an answer. We didn't believe that Jerome himself knew. You can imagine the shock when he gave us the answer, when he told us the reason he had to be alone all that time in his bed in order to feel sane. You won't believe this, but it's true. Jerome said he had to count to a million, and then back to one, in order to be "free." This is what he had been trying to do for four years, every time he withdrew. No one had let him do it.

But why, we asked, did it take so long once he had moved into Portland Road? After all, we had *let* him withdraw, hadn't we? According to Jerome, "yes and no." We kept intruding and interfering, talking to him, distracting him from his task. Every time he got to a few thousand, even a few hundred thousand, someone would break his concentration, and he would have to start all over again. The worst, he said, was when he was moved into my room with that *guitar player!* But why didn't you *tell us,* we said, what you were doing? We would have helped. "That wouldn't have counted," he said. "It was important that you trust me, that you just let me do it my way."

Apparently it was only when our collective anxiety over Jerome's behavior subsided, toward the end, when we, in effect, "backed off," that he was able to finish his task. We finally submitted to *our* experience of him and his presence, and thus he was able to submit to *his* experience, too, of whatever it was that called him to count to a million and back again, uninterrupted. He had come so close, he said, *many* times. Finally he did it, and he was free.

I know you have many questions. It's hard to compare the unorthodox therapy that Jerome got at Portland Road with more conventional treatment modalities. The most obvious question is, Did it work? Jerome never experienced a psychotic episode again. He resumed his life as a basically normal, average, everyday person. Naturally we wondered why Jerome had felt the need to withdraw from his family in the first place. What were the dynamics and the unconscious motives that prompted such a radical symptomatic solution to his concerns? These were questions that Jerome himself couldn't answer. After he got back on his feet and regained his weight, he decided to undertake individual therapy to see what he could find. In time, he found his answers.

It wasn't hard to guess, just the same, what some of Jerome's grievances against his family might have been, based on his behavior at Portland Road. For example, he must have felt that his integrity as a person was somehow injured or belittled by his family. When he closed himself off in his bedroom at home, he was protesting something about his experience there. He was staking a claim for a kind of independence. This isn't an unusual form of protest for adolescents to make, but Jerome must have felt he had to go to extremes to be heard. He was demanding recognition, on *his* terms. Apparently he was prepared to die for it. A battle of wills ensued between Jerome, on the one hand, and his mother and father on the other: the proverbial immovable force against the intractable object.

This drama, which we can conjecture from its resurgence—its *transference*—at Portland Road, isn't untypical of the sort of impasses that so-called schizophrenic individuals get caught in. The way that we struggled with this impasse when it arose would no doubt be regarded as reckless, indulgent, needlessly dangerous, even bizarre by the staff of nearly all the mental hospitals around the world. His kind of behavior—intransigence, stubbornness, resistance—is usually met with an even greater force of will, determination, power. Naturally, the use of medicating drugs would be an asset to that approach. And electric shock. Or, if that fails, even surgery. On the other hand, many psychoanalysts have felt it is possible to work *with* these impasses through analysis. Our treatment of Jerome, you might say, was a modified form of analysis. Since Jerome refused to talk, we were compelled to let his experience do the "talking." D. W. Winnicott, Harry Stack Sullivan, Frieda Fromm-Reichmann, Otto Will, and others have described the many hours they spent with silent patients, allowing them the time they needed for something, anything, to break through the impasse that appeared to impair progress. Some, if not all, analysts would depict Jerome's behavior as blatant resistance to treatment. His behavior would be characterized as a form of "acting out." They would consider him unanalyzable.

In my opinion, "acting out" is not necessarily, strictly speaking, nor always a pathological defense. It may be, on a certain level and on some occasions, a plea for patience. We can't always be sure that we understand what another person's behavior means or what he may be experiencing. With psychotics, we seldom do. Perhaps the critical difference between a typical *psycho*analysis and an existential analysis is that the former relies to an extraordinary degree on the client's facility for speech. The latter, also, values speech highly, but we all sometimes speak in mysterious ways. Sometimes, the only vehicle that we have for listening, when our ears fail us, is our hearts. We're obliged to let our conscience be our guide. As we did with Jerome, we may have no other recourse than to "live and let live" and see where it leads us.

Existential analysis isn't contrary to psychoanalysis. It is the heart of what psycho-analysis was originally about. It speaks to an emphasis that psychoanalysis, properly understood, may assume. It is, perhaps, a more personal vision of analysis. It may break some rules of convention. Nonetheless, it is dedicated to the same premise that the most conventional forms of analysis are: that *listening is transformative.* When all was said and done, odd as it seemed, Jerome finally got to express what anyone who was able to listen could hear—something, perhaps, that words alone couldn't say.

The question that I would like to close with concerns the application of this method to other, nonpsychotic, scenarios. As you have probably already guessed, I believe that *fidelity to experience* is the agent of change in every successful therapeutic endeavor, whatever school of therapy is used, whatever technique is credited with the success. The roots of Laing's therapeutic program are in Freud. Somehow, trends in psychoanalytic theory and practice since Freud have drifted away from its connection with his voice. Every time two human beings look at each other for the purpose of baring their souls, experience is waiting its say. Whether we call that experience *existential* or something else, its voice has to be heard by someone, however frustrated he may become, who is willing to give it its say.

NOTES

1. See Laing (1972) for a singular exception.
2. See also Heidegger's commentary on Hegel's critique of experience in Heidegger (1970).

REFERENCES

Bion, W. R. (1961). *Experiences in groups and other papers.* New York: Basic Books.

Cooper, D. (1967). *Psychiatry and anti-psychiatry.* New York: Ballantine Books.

Freud, S. (1913/1958). *On beginning the treatment (further recommendations on the technique of psycho-analysis I).* Vol. 12, pp. 121–144. London: Hogarth.

Freud, S. (1924/1961). *The loss of reality in neurosis and psychosis.* Vol. 19, pp. 182–187. London: Hogarth.

Hegel, G. W. F. (1949). *The phenomenology of mind,* 2d ed. (J. B. Baillie, trans.). London: Allen & Unwin.

Heidegger, M. (1950/1970). *Hegel's concept of experience* (orig. *Hegels Begriff der Erfahrung*). New York: Harper & Row.

Heidegger, M. (1959/1971). *On the way to language* (P. Hertz, trans.). New York: Harper & Row.

Laing, R. D. (1965). Mystification, confusion and conflict. In I. Boszormengi-Nagy and J. Framo (Eds.), *Intensive family therapy* (pp. 343–363). New York: Harper & Row.

Laing, R. D. (1972). Metanoia: Some experiences at Kingsley Hall, London. In H. M. Ruitenbeek (Ed.), *Going crazy: The radical therapy of R. D. Laing and others* (pp. 11–21). New York: Bantam.

Laing, R. D., & Esterson, A. (1971). *Sanity, madness and the family,* 2d ed. New York: Basic Books.

Thompson, M. (1985). *The death of desire: A study in psychopathology.* New York: New York University Press.

EI CASE FORMULATION—Jerome

Regardless of the genetic or environmental forces that produce schizophrenia, we should not forget the *person* on whom these forces act; the one who *experiences* them. While existential therapy may not be the only or even the best means for addressing this person, there are several reasons why it should be taken seriously. First, conventional treatments tend to have damaging side effects, such as tardive dyskinesia, memory loss, and lethargy. Second, while conventional treatments manage (or *maintain*) patients, they tend not to nurture and support them. Third, while conventional treatments foster behavioral changes, they neglect the underlying perceptual changes—which could significantly reinvigorate patients' lives.

Since the 1970s, there has been a steady decline in milieus like that of Kingsley Hall. This decline is due primarily to the appeal of antipsychotic drugs (and other expedient modalities) which sap the resources for funding such alternative environments. However, it is also due partly to the alternative communities themselves, which failed to methodically document their experiences. While there are many favorable anecdotes concerning these communities, few have been organized or published.

The case of Jerome is a welcome exception to this situation. Stubborn, silent, and withdrawn, Jerome is a challenging subject for existential inquiry.

From the EI standpoint, Jerome is a bit of an anomaly. He not only *flirts* with constrictive and expansive groundlessness, but he *becomes* that groundlessness and is reachable in few other positions. Withdrawn to the point of paralysis, isolated to the point of encapsulation, something harrowing must have happened to Jerome. But as Dr. Thompson recognizes, what occurred to Jerome is not as important as how Jerome experiences it, and this is where therapy begins.

By sensitively being *present* to Jerome, and by ensuring him an atmosphere of safety, Dr. Thompson starts to learn about Jerome and to wordlessly sense how to approach him. One of the first things that Dr. Thompson discovers about Jerome is how defiant he is and how thoroughly he is locked in his position. Jerome's resistances, it appears, serve two important functions: (1) they keep him from venturing out in the world, from risking himself, and from establishing challenging relationships, and (2) they prevent him from suffocating in this paralyzed condition and from dissolving into insignificance. At the same time that Jerome is withdrawn, therefore, he is also extravagantly rebellious; and at the same time that he is still, he can be mentally awhirl.

While efforts to modify these polarizing mentalities backfire (because they deprive Jerome of his refuges), one approach does instill hope, Dr. Thompson realizes: *enabling Jerome to resist.* This approach presses *Jerome* to assess his resistances and challenges *him* to set the pace for addressing them. Let me be clear here that Dr. Thompson (and the staff) did not simply *abandon* Jerome in this process. Quite the contrary, they steadfastly remained supportive and available to him. What they did do, however, was to acknowledge Jerome's *need* to resist, and the room, correspondingly, to work himself out of it.

Slowly, painfully, Jerome begins to recognize how unnecessary his resistances are in this nurturing atmosphere and how brutally his resistances have divided his life. He sees that he no longer needs to hide, for example, nor inflate himself, in order to survive. Alternatively, he begins to entertain more conscious constrictive and expansive possibilities, which soothe and rejuvenate his spirit.

By the time Jerome steps out of his room on that fateful evening, and withdraws from his counting, he confirms that he can be a "self" in the Kierkegaardian sense. He can retract (e.g., from extravagant behavior) and extend (e.g., to housemates) more or less because he *chooses* to; and he can relax, finally, because he has been so generously permitted to *live*.

EXISTENTIALISM OF PERSONALISM:
A NATIVE AMERICAN PERSPECTIVE

Royal Alsup

Royal Alsup, Ph.D. is a therapist and adjunct faculty member of Saybrook Institute in San Francisco. A codirector of the Transpersonal and Existential Psychotherapy Center in Arcada, California, he has over twenty-five years of experience living with, advocating for, and counseling culturally diverse clients in northern California. His special area of interest: the social consciousness of mental health professionals.

Existential therapy with Native Americans, suggests Royal Alsup, is a wide-ranging, holistic enterprise. Freedom is defined by a mosaic of realities—individual, social, and archetypal. Drawing upon his work with a teenage Native American girl, Alsup depicts the rich and evocative tools used in her liberation. These include deep empathy for and experience with her sociocultural background, legal-communal advocacy, and experiential engagement with her ancestral mythology.

Existentialism of Personalism sees the human personality as sacred and punctuates both inner and outer life as sacred. An "I-and-Thou" encounter with the Supreme Personality of the Creator takes place through dialogical meeting in the three aspects of human life: (1) interpersonal relationships; (2) the physical, natural world; and (3) inner psychic phenomenology. Existentialism of Personalism embraces interconnected attitudes of aesthetic, sacred consciousness with social, political awareness. Transpersonal and existential realities are captured in the sacred and profane events of life. The ecstasy and numinous awesomeness of an I-and-Thou encounter with the Supreme Personality can be experienced in any time and in any place and through any object, person, or event. It is not limited to an inner, individualistic mysticality, nor is it particular to community worship and ceremony. The personal relationship with the Supreme Personality creates a "sense of being" and "becoming" that is spontaneous and goes on ceaselessly in a constant dialogue with self, other, and nature. It is contained in form and is experienced in existential, concrete, everyday lived life.

Flora Jones, Wintu medicine woman, speaks about the spirits like they are living personalities in a partnership of existence with human beings. Witness the following statement, quoted by Knudtson (1975):

> This is what the spirit tells me—get my people together. . . . Whoever has sacred places must wake them up, the same as I am doing here—to keep my old world within my heart and with the spiritual. For them to help me and for me to help my people. (p. 14)

The personalism expressed by Flora Jones is the basis of most African-American and American-Indian traditions. Both of these traditions have a dual theme of Being-in-the-World and Being-beyond-the-World. The Supreme Personality is experienced as an integrated intelligence and love that is expressed through the archetypes of mythologies, rituals, worship, dreams, and visions.

The archetypal spirituality of the meeting in the Between confirms that the Supreme Personality lies within the human personality and in the meeting as the Ground of Being. The Supreme Personality, as a living personality, offers love, knowledge, mystery, gift giving, and sharing in relationship with the human person. The I-and-Thou encounter brings to "awareness" constellations of fascination and fear, destiny and freedom, death and life, anxiety and joy, interest and surprise, love and shame, and guilt and excitement.

Existentialism of Personalism came out of my practice and theory in a circle of understanding and interpretation through dialogue with American Indians and African-Americans. Alex Haley in his book *Roots* (1976) describes how the father of Kunta Kinte presented his infant son to the universe. He writes, "Carrying little Kunta in his strong arms, he walked to the edge of the village, lifted his baby up with his face to the heavens, and said softly, . . . Behold—the only thing greater than yourself" (p. 13). Haley is showing that the living universe is the father/mother of Kunta Kinte and that the child's personality is sacred. In the Navajo tradition, the man who holds his infant up to Father Sun and says, "Father Sun, this is your child" (J. Rivers & J. Norton, personal communication, June 1, 1992), is expressing that the universe is personal and loving. The Navajo infant is a direct descendant of the living universe, and, therefore, its personality is sacred. African-American and American-Indian traditions demonstrate a continual dialogue between the human personality and the Supreme Personality that reveals the sacred and the profane as not separated but forming an interconnected metaphysical reality that is remythologized in every I-and-Thou meeting.

American-Indian ceremonies emphasize the sacredness of the human personality. The Hupa Boat Dance ritual creates sacred space for a community mysticism that revitalizes the community and makes the tribal members feel special in the perceptions of the Creator. This is a spirituality in which the tribal members "know" they are recognized by the Creator. The Boat Dance honors the dead and helps their spirits to make the crossing into the Great Mystery. It is also a ritual for reminding the living that they are sacred and that every individual is important in this communitarian worldview. The archetypal sounds from the dance and the archetypal experiences of the observer/participants allow this serious ontological enactment of death to become an experience of beauty.

The following case is presented to demonstrate effective psychotherapy based on Existentialism of Personalism and its use with American-Indian clients. Mental health professionals working with American-Indian clients need to practice indwelling, which brings about the joining of the therapist and client in a cultural context and makes diagnosis and treatment culturally appropriate. Indwelling requires the professional to go to gatherings and ceremonies, such as the Boat Dance, attend funerals of tribal members, do home-visit psychotherapy with immediate and extended families, and work with the Indian shamans. Therapists need also to practice communicative social action, which is the use of cultural knowledge to educate and inform county, state, and federal agency workers about cultural values and attitudes concerning aspects of life such as death, silence, limitedness, and freedom in their professional treatment of American-Indian clients.

The case example is typical of ones involving American Indians, especially if there has been a death in the family. Although the death is not to be talked about, the cultural tradition provides that the death experience for the person and the survivors be settled in ritual and ceremony. In cases pertaining to American-Indian youth, there is often involvement in the juvenile justice system. A non-Indian therapist who is not familiar with the American-Indian cultural stricture against talking about the deceased may make assumptions in court reports that the adolescent Indian client is not cooperating with treatment. For example, the youth may not disclose that his or her recent substance abuse problems arose as a result of the emotional trauma surrounding a death; and the therapist unfamiliar with the culture will label the nondisclosing, nonverbal Indian youth *untreatable*. Often in such a case, the district attorney will recommend that the youth be placed in a residential treatment facility or in the state's youth prison. These placements are usually far from the youth's home, separating him or her from the healing, cultural matrix of family, tribe, landscape, and shaman. This separation further aggravates the grief process and, for most American-Indian youth, superimposes post-traumatic stress symptoms upon the death and grief trauma.

The psychology and worldview of the American Indian holds that it is in the silent solitude of the mind and heart, along with the ceremonial way, that one understands one's "limitations and freedom." When an American-Indian youth is pressured by the dominant culture's mental health professionals to speak about a death in the family, he or she becomes painfully caught in a clash of cultural values. The cultural conflict over how to process the experience of death brings about feelings of dread, despair, anxiety, isolation, and limitedness. American-Indian cultural norms prescribe that one can only speak with respect for the dead; and it is better not to speak at all than to risk drawing the spirit of the deceased back into the world. The therapist's ignorance of the importance of silence, words, rituals, and ancestors disrupts the dialogical healing process in the meeting of client and therapist. The tribal tradition is a stronger determinant of what the youth will share with the psychotherapist than is the court's intimidation.

THE CASE OF AN AMERICAN-INDIAN GIRL

This case study concerns a 15-year-old American-Indian girl who resisted treatment of substance abuse that was a symptom of unresolved grief from the loss of a family member. She had been to approximately five culturally insensitive therapists to whom the juvenile justice system had referred her. The reports from the therapists consistently labeled her as silent and resistant and concluded that she could not benefit from treatment and therefore that incarceration in a youth prison was the only solution.

Session One

The American-Indian girl entered the therapy session saying that she had seen me at a tribal ceremony and funeral and that she trusted me. Then she fell into silence for about ten minutes. I then told her a Coyote-Buffalo story that deals with tradition and one's role and function in tradition. In traditional Indian stories, Coyote-Buffalo are seen as both transpersonal and existential; and the stories teach moral development that balances the sacred and the profane. The Coyote-Buffalo story became a touchstone of reality for her to relate to instead of to the therapist. The story took her out of her silence, made her feel cared for, and brought about excitement and inspiration that helped her relate her own personal story to the mythic tale. At my suggestion, she used art materials with enthusiasm to make a collage to express herself symbolically.

By projecting her intimate feelings and the caring of her tribal traditions onto the symbols of the collage, she was able to integrate cognitively and affectively her tribal moral tradition as it was expressed in the story. The storytelling made her aware that the choices she was making had been taking her away from her "path of life," causing her to be psychologically and spiritually out of balance. She used alcohol and drugs to mask the pain of her feelings of disharmony, discomfort, and suffering.

Through the storytelling and art making, she had an experience of her personal mythology and how it was unfolding in the greater tribal mythology. She saw her personal life story reflected in the character who is both ordinary and divine (Coyote) in struggle with the wholly transpersonal, the Great Spirit (Buffalo). The cognitive and affective domains of learning and moral development were both evoked and brought to "self-awareness" through the Coyote-Buffalo story.

Session Seven

In this session, I gave the Indian girl an assignment to do a collage of how she saw her tribe and what the tribe represented in her life. As she worked, her tribal story unfolded, and she expressed the feelings of safety, security, belonging, and love that she received from the experience of being known by the Creator. Being known by the Creator allowed a unity of consciousness and a peak experience for her in the concrete making of the collage. Her collage showed a landscape symbolizing her tribal land within certain boundaries. The symbols of rituals, the landscape, and the Creator expressed that these touchstones of reality talked to her personally to reassure her of her Indianness within the sacred cathedral of her tribal land. The symbols in her collage brought about a psychological transformation of her attitude from one of depression, constriction, and limitedness to one of joyfulness, expansiveness, and freedom.

By the end of this session, the girl was more "self-affirmed" and seemed to have more of a sense of how she fit within the boundaries of her daily life because she felt more "centered." She started talking about how she had been losing her sense of being and her sense of identity. Now she could see her limitedness within this mythological world, but she was also inspired and excited about claiming her freedom by not feeling driven to conform to the non-Indian youth at her high school. Now she saw that to follow her tribal ways and the morals of living nonindulgently would help free her from her addiction to methamphetamines. It gave her an experience of how the limitations of her Indian traditions also gave her meaning, purpose, and freedom.

Session Twelve

At this session, I suggested she do a collage about her family and the role or function her family members played in the tribal community. I also told her another Coyote story. In this one, Coyote reverses all the destruction caused by the loggers' greed. All the trees are returned to the forest by blue-shirted logger-shamans, who put the trees back in the ground, re-attach the boughs and limbs, and thus re-establish all the natural habitats of the animals. American-Indian stories unite consciousness with the unconscious, thereby giving the Indian a deep sense of direction and purpose. The structure that gives meaning in this psychological process is what existentialists call *intentionality* (May, 1969).

The girl enthusiastically started a new collage that showed her family members, who were loggers as well as dance people. Members of her family traditionally brought their dance regalia and dancers to help with the tribal renewal ceremony that puts the earth back in balance. This artistic moment was literally a renewal of her personality in that it gave her a real sense of her identity as an Indian person. The affective awareness of her family as loggers who were also dance people working for the earth's balance made her feel a deep I-and-Thou meeting with me. This dialogical presence was the true healing event because it made her feel her connectedness to a therapist who was truly interested in her family mythology and her tribal community. She felt proud of belonging to her family and tribe, and her sense of freedom sparkled through her joy and excitement.

There were several more sessions in which the girl further strengthened her sense of Indian identity. She started living according to her traditions; and the pride she took in her family's role in the tribal community as dancers and regalia makers helped her to abstain from using drugs. In a year, she was released from probation and became an honor student. Her new, stronger sense of identity as a tribal member helped her to confront the isolation that resulted when she lost her substance-abusing friends, and this gave her a context of greater freedom and potential.

The death-and-grief issues were addressed in psychotherapy through the indirect, symbolic processes of storytelling, art making, and dreamwork that honored her need for silence and her sense of being. During therapy, she had a dream that reassured her that her family member had survived the journey from ordinary life to the spirit land. The dream relieved her depression and her grief and put her back on her tribal path of life.

CONCLUSION

The mental health professional needs to be alert to the following for the healing dialogue to be created in the Between with American-Indian clients:

1. A mythological worldview that is based in the concrete, existential events of daily life and reflects a personalism of the transpersonal and immanent Creator.
2. The sacredness of all human personality.
3. The social existence of the Supreme Personality, who addresses the American Indian through various touchstones of reality—ritual, story, song, myth, dreams, visions, regalia, and the landscape that is more global than regional.
4. The independence, uniqueness, and wholeness of the American-Indian client in response to the address from the Supreme Personality.
5. The individuation process of the American Indian that helps maintain and develop a "we" psychology and brings about individuation through participation in community.
6. The importance of confirming American Indians' identity or sense of being, their tribal family, and their personal mythology as these unfold in the I-and-Thou moment within the therapeutic setting.
7. The need to practice indwelling by attending ceremonies, visiting families, working with tribal healers, and engaging in communicative social action.

The existential psychotherapist who uses storytelling, art making, and dreamwork facilitates the creative pause as it is described by Rollo May (1981).

> The pause is the essence of creativity, let alone of originality and spontaneity. One cannot avail oneself of the richness of preconsciousness or unconsciousness unless one can let oneself periodically relax, be relieved of tension. It is then that the person lets the silences speak. (p. 176)

Finally, it is ontologically necessary in psychotherapy with American-Indian clients to draw upon silence, or the creative pause, and to use tribal symbol systems through storytelling and art making. Silence in the therapeutic mileau creates an environment where the internal conflict of opposites—death and life, meaninglessness and meaning, limitedness and freedom—can be creatively resolved. Silence allows the symbols to emerge and to integrate the troubled psyche. Through the use of tribal symbols in the therapy session, the therapist witnesses and confirms the integrity of the Indian person. In this manner, an I-and-Thou meeting is created that brings about the client's confrontation with his or her freedom. This shift in attitude brings about the existential healing.

REFERENCES

Haley, A. (1976). *Roots.* New York: Doubleday.
Knudtson, P. N. (1975). Flora, Shaman of the Wintu. *Natural History,* May, 6–18.
May, R. (1969). *Love and will.* New York: Doubleday.
May, R. (1981). *Freedom and destiny.* New York: Doubleday.

EI CASE FORMULATION—A Native American Girl

The girl in this case carries a double burden. Not only is she bereft of a loved one; she is deprived of a culture, an inheritance from the past.

This deprivation is enormous, Dr. Alsup realizes, because it strips her of dignity and pride and abandons her to those she mistrusts.

Through his sympathetic worldview and understanding of her heritage, Dr. Alsup attempts to redress this situation. He respects her need for silence, for example, and her estrangement from conventional treatment. He engages her, but delicately, metaphorically—without compulsive agendas.

Dr. Alsup is soon able to invoke the actual with his client—through storytelling and other experiential media. The story of the Coyote, for example, helps the girl to feel cared for by Dr. Alsup and directs her attention within. It also inspires her to use collage to further her inquiries.

The collage helps her to realize how lackluster her life has become and how far she has drifted from her roots. She realizes how small she feels, for example, and how dysfunctionally she has attempted to counter that smallness. Yet, increasingly, she feels the echoes, the pulsations of her forebears. She feels the throbbing of the ceremonial dances and the vibrant colors of the regalia. She reconnects with community life and the radiant splendor of creation.

In time, she feels substantial enough to reduce her drug intake and to stem her compulsion to be popular. She becomes secure enough to *constrain* herself in certain ways—by committing to her tribal traditions, for example, and by disciplining herself in school. She permits herself to be cared for by others and to subordinate herself before creation. Whereas before she felt *driven* to contract or enlarge, inhibit or stand out, she now feels more flexible about these capacities—more deliberate.

While she begins to partake of her tribal ceremonies, however, she also acknowledges life's contemporary realities and demands. Dr. Alsup's story about the shaman-loggers is a reflection of this integration. By inviting her to see loggers (such as her family members) as *tribal* role models, he helps her to bridge experiences, backgrounds, and future possibilities.

To summarize, Dr. Alsup has used culturally relevant liberation strategies with his client. He approached her culturally prepared; he attended to her in her personal and cultural context; and he challenged her with culturally sensitive exercises. The combination of these modalities helped his client to *experience*—not merely report on or analyze—her predicament. She was then able to pause over this predicament (e.g., constriction, fear of distinction), acknowledge it for what it was worth, and find ways to respond to it, to enhance her life's meaning.

BRIEF ENCOUNTERS WITH CHINESE CLIENTS: THE CASE OF PETER

John Galvin

John Galvin, Ph.D., is a licensed psychologist, management consultant, and fellow of the University of Hong Kong Business School. A graduate of Saybrook Institute in San Francisco, he has over twenty years of therapeutic experience in the Asian community.

Although brief treatment is often disparaged in existential circles, there are times when it may be appropriate. John Galvin shows how brief or what he terms "sudden" existential encounters can be especially salient with Chinese (and other ethnic or demographically appropriate) clientele. When combined with empathy, presence, and sensitivity to the client's pace, such encounters foster pivotal reassessments of priorities.

Following Dr. Galvin's case, and serving to complement it, we present "sketches" for a short-term existential-humanistic therapy by Dr. James Bugental.

Throughout the ages, writers have found the journey a powerful metaphor for reflecting on and describing life's experiences. Homer's Ulysses journeyed back from Troy; Chaucer's pilgrims traveled from inn to inn; Mark Twain's Huck Finn rafted down the Mississippi; and Melville's Ishmael set sail with Captain Ahab and the crew of the Pequod.

An event common to all these travel books is the encounter of the hero and some stranger or some strange event. As the encounter unfolds, we find the traveler risking a genuine confrontation with some aspect of the human condition or in some way revealing his or her deepest thoughts and feelings.

Existential therapists develop an affinity for these moments of encounter. They are the points in the therapeutic "journey" where healing takes place, if healing is possible. They are the moments when choices are made and when choices are required.

They are the moments when life is affirmed, despite all the forces that negate it. These encounters are the moments when consciousness affirms or denies what the will desires and when the client begins to take a hand in creating him or herself.

As an existential therapist, I see myself as a traveler journeying through life prepared for these encounters. The existential literature highlights the importance of the existential encounter, and my experience as a therapist frequently confirms that it is extremely important.

Much of the therapist's training is directed at developing the knowledge and skills required to make the most of these encounters. The therapist learns to recognize the client's often vague, indirect invitation to encounter; to understand and overcome the barriers the client raises to avoid encounter; to listen and understand and *not* to interfere in the unfolding of the client's experience. But most fundamental is the therapist's commitment to be genuinely available to share in these moments of encounter.

Even when dealing with psychotic patients, I have learned not to rule out the possibility of encounter. The presence, the authenticity, the respect, and the humility that invite encounter may even pierce the veil of psychosis. When working with psychotic patients, I maintain the same attitude I maintain with other clients. I knock politely at their hospital doors and ask if I can come in. I listen attentively to their psychotic conversations, and, as best I can, allow myself to be moved emotionally.

On several occasions, I have been astonished to discover that an encounter did take place. One Chinese youth whom I had evaluated when he was admitted to the hospital in the midst of a severe psychotic episode remembered me most vividly when, months later, we met by chance in a busy vegetable market. He told me how he had felt frightened and alone at the time we met and that I had given him a sense of hope.

Existential encounters, as they are called in the literature of psychotherapy, can happen at almost any time. Some come in the context of therapy, and others come on the occasion of some brief, chance meeting.

Over the years, my work with the Chinese has led me to particularly value the power and importance of brief, sudden existential encounters. Unlike Americans, who have come to appreciate the professional role of the therapist and commonly engage in extended periods of psychotherapy, the Chinese are not likely to seek help from a therapist. What I have come to appreciate are the short, often one-time, encounters with these people. They are usually people with whom I have already established a relationship through some other activity. Despite the brevity of the encounter, much of what I recognize as therapeutic takes place.

THE CASE OF PETER

One such encounter took place after a presentation I gave on loneliness and the new immigrant. As the audience dispersed, Peter, a young Chinese man who had recently immigrated to the United States from Southeast Asia, approached me and started a conversation. Initially, he asked some theoretical question. We sat down together in one corner of the room. As the room emptied, I asked Peter if he had ever experienced loneliness when he first immigrated to the United States. His response was immediate, without thought: "No, I didn't!" His denial was intense. An experienced therapist develops a sixth sense for self-deception, those lies directed at oneself and designed to protect. Peter's denial, artificial in its intensity, actually suggested to me that he wanted to talk about an experience of loneliness. I prepared myself for a quick reversal. I gave him my full attention, kept silent, and waited.

A brief silence followed Peter's denial. When he sat back in his chair, his body stiffened, his breathing stopped, and his expression went blank. Then, just as suddenly, life came back into him. He sat forward and said,

"Yes, I did experience loneliness."

I replied, "Please, tell me about it."

Peter wanted to speak, to open up. This was a critical moment. My attitude, my words could slam the door shut as quickly as it had opened. The process of socialization makes judges of us all. The therapist must learn to remove the judicial robes and stop being the gatekeeper who only allows the appropriate and logical to enter consciousness. Presence and empathy are the keys that open the door to encounter.

The choice to continue was his. I communicated, more by my attitude then verbally, that I was ready to listen and understand. He was free to talk or not to talk.

An individual's life is a rich tapestry of experiences. Some of the threads that make up this tapestry we weave with our own hands, and some the hands of fate weave for us.

Peter's narrative began.

He was born Chinese in a Vietnamese city, Saigon. He belonged to a community of migrant Chinese who had left their own lands seeking opportunities in a foreign culture. In Vietnam, they chose to maintain their Chinese identity, and the Vietnamese chose to view them as foreigners.

At the end of the Vietnam war, North Vietnamese troops occupied Saigon. These "liberators" forced many Chinese, mostly traders and business executives, to leave Vietnam. The contingencies of life had ended their comfortable middle-class lifestyle and scattered Peter's family among three countries. Several brothers went to Canada, his oldest brother and his parents went to Great Britain, and Peter and his sister went to the United States.

Peter explained that he was the youngest in a large family. As he grew up, he enjoyed the companionship of his father, who, older and retired, had time to appreciate the joys of nurturing a young son.

Peter's father made a powerful impression upon him. He gave Peter a sense of security in a turbulent world, and, though he was the youngest and the least experienced of the children, Peter's sense of self-esteem was enhanced by his father's attentions.

As I listened, I understood that Peter's father was a central figure in his world, Peter's primary source of meaning, of self-esteem, of security—what existential therapists call the *existential ground* that supports one's psychological existence.

As a refugee, Peter was separated from his father, but the bond remained strong. Peter's father wrote letters, and there were occasional telephone conversations. Frequent talk of a future reunion of the entire family gave Peter hope and a goal.

In life, our strengths can easily become our weaknesses. The bond between Peter and his father fostered psychological vitality, but if broken, it might leave him shattered, thrown into a crisis. This happened one cold English day.

While walking the streets of London, his father slipped on a piece of ice and fell. His head injury was fatal. He never regained consciousness, and doctors pronounced him dead upon arrival at a London hospital.

An ill-placed step and a life ends. There was no time for last good-byes, no slow unraveling of the bonds that gave Peter security, and no time to develop a more mature sense of independence. His father was dead, and Peter faced the world alone, an unwilling master of his fate.

"I felt a deep sense of loneliness. Memories of my father and our experiences together filled my waking hours and haunted my dreams. I wanted to see my father but knew I would never see him again."

During our encounter, Peter relived the loneliness and depression that had followed his father's death. I encouraged and supported him by reflecting back to him his feelings and the meanings he expressed in sentences such as the following:

"You knew he was gone forever but couldn't accept it."

"He departed so suddenly."

"You felt so isolated when you were unable to attend his funeral in London."

"He made you feel important."

Peter's longing for his father and the undeniable fact of his absence reminded me of a line of poetry: "We long for what has been and desire what is not." (For a moment, I, too, felt a longing for what had been and for what was not, a longing for my younger brother, who had died.) I directed my awareness back to Peter, who explained:

"I worked during the day and went to school at night, but it all seemed meaningless. I got up in the morning, dressed, went to work, attended school. I didn't speak with people unless they spoke to me. I couldn't start a conversation. I didn't want to talk to anyone. After school, I went home to sit alone in my room. I turned off all the lights and sat curled in a chair. I sat there for hours until I fell asleep exhausted."

Alone in his room, shrouded in darkness, he brooded. He clung to the memories of his father. While these memories caused him pain, they offered comfort, as well. Human experience is paradoxical. We can entertain both joy and sorrow simultaneously, and one can evoke the other.

The darkness of Peter's room represented how he experienced his present life. All the people and the things around him had fallen away. Only he was left, alone with the memories of his father and, gradually, alone with less and less will to live.

Peter felt himself like a man clinging to the jagged edge of a rock, legs and body dangling precariously, while below him loomed a vast and empty pit. He was tired, alone, and in pain. The only thing that kept him from letting go were those brief moments when a memory of his father gave him a sense of value.

I commented: "Death would be an escape from the pain."

Peter looked at me. I suddenly felt as if I were in that dark room with him. He said:

"I knew this couldn't go on. I had to do something, end it all."

"To be or not to be"—like Hamlet, Peter struggled with indecision, unable to choose either life or death. How long this struggle lasted, he found it difficult to say. Three weeks, four weeks . . .

"I lost all sense of time. Each day was the same. I can only remember sitting in the darkness, paralyzed, unable to do anything."

Then, one evening, a memory of something his father once said tipped the balance.

"I remembered my father saying, 'Life is full of opportunities, but you must grasp them and work hard for success.'"

These were simple words of advice from a retired Chinese business executive to his youngest son. However, in Peter's dark cave of depression, these words echoed in his memory. The insight was simple: He had to make a choice, and it was *his* choice. To live or to die? It was up to him.

Peter's paralysis of will ended.

It is difficult to describe in words the depth of feeling that accompanied this narrative. Peter's face reflected, in its quick changes, the moods that filled him as he struggled with his choice. At one moment he argued for the meaninglessness of it all and, in a voice full of rancor, described the burden of pain that life offers the weary in place of a helping hand. Then, the next moment, he countered this mood with happy memories of family and friends. It was not an objective debate, but a deeply personal struggle. I felt as if Peter had grabbed me by my arm and hustled me onto a roller-coaster. A slow, reflective ride up toward hope, then a horrific rush of air as we careened downward into anxiety, then banked sharply right, then left, and up once again.

The intensity of this encounter left a lasting impression on me. Not all meetings are so vigorous. Some are calm, gentle, as pleasant as a summer breeze under a clear, star-filled sky. Others are full of anguish and struggle, with a sense of helplessness threatening—like finding oneself caught in an undertow, with the fingers of death pulling one down.

As therapists, our own fears and anxieties limit our work. Our own inner paradoxes, our undigested memories, our compromises with life, pull us back from encounter. For me, it was the death of a younger brother, the sorrow that still remained, the courage I needed to continue living my own life with a heightened sense of mortality. During moments of encounter, I have often wondered at the dexterity of conscious awareness, how it jumps between my experiences and the experiences of others.

At some point Peter made a choice for life; his conscious intellect served to provide the rationale. His father would want him to go forward, to make something of himself. It was his duty to live and to remember his father. He recalled many things his father had said and wove into the tapestry of his life, a philosophy of hope and purpose. He would finish his studies; he would do something for other people; he would make his father proud.

I asked: "What did this experience mean to you?"

He sat thoughtfully for several moments, then responded, "People need to make choices in life. We need other people, but sometimes we need to stand alone. I learned I needed to grow up. I was too dependent upon my family." He made it sound so simple and so obvious.

I was curious and perhaps somewhat selfish. I asked what, if anything, did it mean to him to have shared these experiences with me.

He responded: "I never talked to anyone about what happened. I feel I understand it all a bit better now. I never thought it through like this. I felt I relived it all, but with more self-awareness. In some way I feel happy, proud, and I am more aware of my strength."

The encounter ended there. He said good-bye. I think I saw him twice briefly after that, and it has been years since this encounter took place. This and similar experiences have left me with vivid memories, and I find my own life strangely enriched by them.

A conventional perspective perceives existential psychotherapy as an intensive, long-term process. As such, few would judge the interaction between Peter and myself as a form of existential therapy.

I have never been inclined to limit psychotherapy to the formal setting of a psychologist's office. Throughout the years, I have worked primarily with disadvantaged and troubled teens, the mentally ill, ethnic minorities in the United States, as well as the less-affluent Chinese population of Hong Kong. Intensive, long-term psychotherapy requires a great outlay of money, not to mention a cultural milieu that encourages and supports this form of therapy. For the most part, these were lacking among the people I have served.

Even though the conditions that might support a psychological practice of intensive existential psychotherapy were lacking, I regularly encountered people who were struggling with issues that commonly surface during existential psychotherapy; accepting responsibility for one's life, integrating a growing sense of one's individuality with the powerful demands of a communalist culture, facing the anxieties of choice, accepting limitations, having the courage to create, searching for meaning, confronting life's paradoxes.

Professionals whose formal practice of psychotherapy overlaps with other mental-health and social-work activities may find many people engaging them in brief, intensive interactions that have the potential for significant existential liberation.

Over the years, I have developed four guidelines that I attempt to follow when I sense a person is inviting me to engage in an existential encounter. Perhaps others may find these guidelines helpful:

1. Never underestimate the willingness of people to open their hearts and minds during these brief encounters. Many people have an intuitive understanding of existential themes. They may not have read the literature or attended courses, and they may not belong to an ethnic and social group known to be psychology minded, but they have in some way departed the safe havens of conventional society and undertaken the path of existential liberation.

2. Focus on a particular life situation, a concrete, specific event in a person's life. Avoid an intellectual discussion. The genius of the existential perspective lies in its appreciation for the *existential moment,* an intense conscious engagement with

a salient, specific, concrete life event. As the story goes, a person asked a chess master, What is the best move in chess? Of course this question cannot be answered in any absolute sense, so the master replied that the best move at any given time depends on the ability of the person and the specific context of the game. A person who is confronted with a choice, with the paradoxical pull of two equally valid concerns—community and individuality, limitations and possibility, or any other significant existential issue—begins to find liberation by being more immersed in the experience itself. There is no absolute answer. How a person thinks, feels, and acts depends upon her abilities and the context as she understands it.

3. An ability to hear, understand, and reflect back the explicit and implicit feelings and meanings that a person is expressing is crucial to evoking an existential moment. I continue to be amazed at how rapidly a conversation moves to a deeper level when one listens for feelings and meanings.

4. Accept and understand a person's defenses, his or her reluctance to express certain feelings and to confront certain issues. It is easy to feel pressured by the lack of time and to try to push the person forward. An existential therapist engaged in long-term, intensive psychotherapy greatly appreciates the importance of working through the client's defenses. This principle applies even when one is seeing a person only once. Often it is by helping a person face certain defenses that one makes a contribution. Various forms of brief psychotherapy are increasingly popular, and the therapist is inclined to play a very active and directive role in order to achieve results within the limited time available. In my view, during these existential encounters the therapist can accomplish more by doing less.

Let me end with the image of two road-weary travelers meeting by the fire in the corner of a dimly lit inn that gives temporary shelter to life's wandering pilgrims. In the morning these travelers will part, but each will feel better-prepared for the journey that still remains. For me, this simple image says much about what it means to be an existential therapist.

EI CASE FORMULATION—Peter

In light of therapy's funding problems—and its increasingly diverse clientele—many depth therapists are becoming brief therapists, or curtailing their ambitious goals.

While existential therapy has been a latecomer to this movement, it, too, is rethinking its assumptions and provisionally offering alternatives.

Dr. Galvin's case study is a creative example of short-term existential therapy. He begins by being *present* to Peter and by inviting Peter to be present with him. He refrains from rushing Peter, moreover, and supportively holds a space for him (the image of the inn at the end of Dr. Galvin's commentary is illustrative of this). Although Peter resists this space at first, Dr. Galvin does not press the matter with him. Instead, he *mirrors* (or vivifies) Peter's resistance and simply makes himself available. This helps Peter to trust Dr. Galvin and to relinquish the anguish he has striven to hide.

The case can be summarized as follows:

1. Dr. Galvin creates a fertile context for Peter.
2. He focuses him on one concrete and specific experience (i.e., his loneliness).
3. He invites him to contact this experience bodily and to sort out its salient features.
4. He asks him to summarize his discoveries and to consider their present and future implications.

Although Peter had expanded beyond his isolation before he met Dr. Galvin, their encounter served to consolidate this expansiveness and to illuminate critical developments in his life.

PRELIMINARY SKETCHES FOR A SHORT-TERM EXISTENTIAL-HUMANISTIC THERAPY

James Bugental

James Bugental, Ph.D., is professor emeritus, Saybrook Institute, and author of The Art of the Psychotherapist, Intimate Journeys, *and numerous other publications.*

While Dr. Galvin's approach stresses informality, other existentially oriented therapists have begun to consider more structured short-term positions. Recently, James Bugental identified six phases important to a highly structured short-term existential-humanistic model.* Since these phases may be of interest to many readers—and because they nicely dovetail with our discussion—we report them below. Before we do, however, there is one essential point to bear in mind: Dr. Bugental's comments are preliminary, with further development forthcoming. Those intending to use his suggestions with clients, therefore, should await publication of a more fully developed statement. Even more desirable would be participating in training for the approach.

INTENTION PARAMETERS

In sketching a shorter-term regime for psychotherapy, I have been guided by three principles.

1. Emphasize the autonomy of the person who is the client; i.e., insist that the change agency is the client's own self-discovery rather than the insight, power, or manipulations of the therapist.
2. Demonstrate to the client the power of the natural *searching process*† and help the client learn to continue to use this power in her/his post-therapy living.

---

*These phases were presented at a workshop conducted by Dr. Bugental in the summer of 1993.
†For an elaboration on the *searching process,* see J. Bugental *Psychotherapy and Process.* (Reading, MA: Addison-Wesley, 1978).

3. Avoid building habits or expectancies that would be countertherapeutic if and when the client undertook further and deeper therapeutic work.

PHASE-STRUCTURED PROCEDURE

Short-term work requires a clearly (and usually explicitly) defined and limited focus of effort (*goal of treatment*) and thus a more overt structure to maintain maximum gain from limited opportunity.

This structure is best grasped when it is organized into the phases detailed below. It is not intended that each of these phases occupy an interview. The pace of moving through them will vary with each client-therapist pairing. Generally, however, these phases need to follow the sequence described here.

First Phase: Assessment

Is the presenting problem such that it can be isolated to some extent and made explicit or objective?

Is the client's urgency (pain, anxiety, other distress) such that the client can still detach sufficient ego function to sustain the apparently indirect approach?

Is the ego function such as to support intensive searching; i.e., can the client's observing ego make a truly therapeutic alliance?

If the answer to one or more of these questions is negative, that condition must be addressed before undertaking to move to the next phase. If each answer is favorable, the next phase may be begun.

Second Phase: Identifying the Concern

Encourage the client to present his/her concern in the most succinct form.

Seek to shape the issue into as explicit or objective a form as is valid. This is a delicate operation in which the therapist's intent to shape the issue must not be allowed to introduce an artifactual distortion of the client's actual concern.

Contract to work with the client toward greater understanding and some resolution of the issue. The contract needs to be as explicit as is realistic and may well be reduced to written form as an aid to maintaining its focusing effect.

Third Phase: Teaching the Searching Process

The client is instructed in how to engage in the searching process by:

Getting centered (present).

Mobilizing concern (the identified issue plus the emotional energy attached to it).*

---

*This is similar to what was previously described in this text as *invoking the actual;* see also Bugental's discussion of the concept in *The Art of the Psychotherapist* (New York: Norton, 1987), pp. 207–212.

Learning the significance of resistances and of not working them through (i.e., shorter-term, less deep or lasting changes are explained).

Beginning the search.

Fourth Phase: Identifying Resistances

As the searching goes forward and resistances are encountered, the therapist teaches their significance as cues to what is conflicted.

The client is encouraged to take note of these occasions and then to return to the search. *Again, this is a key point of difference from long-term therapy: There is no working through of resistances. As a consequence, changes are apt to be more shallow and possibly less lasting.*

It is essential that the client recognize the difference, for otherwise he/she may not appreciate the limits of short-term work and mistake them for limits of all therapy.

Fifth Phase: The Therapeutic Work

From the beginning and regularly the therapist needs to bring to the client's attention in a meaningful way the two crucial parameters of the work:

This is a time-limited effort; that limit needs to be recognized and not ignored.

This is work directed toward the identified concern. Other issues will repeatedly appear, but they must not displace the central and contracted concern.

It is important and difficult often to keep this focus on the contracted concern. By the very nature of the searching process, that concern will be redefined and reidentified more than once.

The sensitivity and skill of the therapist are tested here, for the work can easily degenerate in a seeming randomness (which might be valuable in longer-term work) with a resulting inadequate therapeutic impact when the allotted time is exhausted.

Another hazard is that an overly literal and zealous rigidity about the focus on the explicit concern can similarly lead to so superficial an inquiry as to be impotent therapeutically.

Sixth Phase: Termination

Handling the time parameter is an important part of the therapeutic process itself. If a fixed number of sessions has initially been agreed upon—as is usually desirable—then that limit must be observed. Of course, a new contract can be negotiated if both parties agree to it, but the original plan should not be casually dismissed. Clients need to recognize the aborting of the work as arbitrary and something they may want to address. Similarly, clients may gain from the confrontation with their finitude that this ending demonstrates and the way it reflects the limit to life itself.

As the last session of the contracted time occurs, it is desirable to call on the client to assess what has been accomplished and what remains to be done.* Concurrently, some attention may be given to the client's having begun to incorporate the searching process into his/her extra-therapy living.

While clients and therapists may negotiate a follow-up contract to continue the work, there is a potential countertherapeutic pitfall to be avoided: A series of short-term therapeutic efforts is *not* the equivalent of long-term psychotherapy. The effort to insist on one limited engagement after another is a major resistance to commitment to one's life, disguising a deeper sense of genuine need.

A PERSPECTIVE ON ALCOHOLISM:
THE CASE OF MR. P

Barbara Ballinger, Robert Matano, and Adrianne Amantea

Barbara Ballinger, M.D., is a staff psychiatrist in the department of psychiatry and behavioral sciences, Stanford University School of Medicine, Stanford, California.

Robert Matano, Ph.D., is director of the Stanford Alcohol and Drug Treatment Center, part of the department of psychiatry and behavioral sciences, Stanford University School of Medicine, Stanford, California.

Adrianne Amantea, M.S., is an intern at the Stanford Alcohol and Drug Treatment Center.

Despite the many treatment regimens for alcoholism, few appear to concern themselves with the meaning, experience, or, in short, existential facets of the syndrome. In this pioneering analysis, Barbara Ballinger, Robert Matano, and Adrianne Amantea attend precisely to the existential issues and deftly apply them to their case.

Alcohol abuse and dependence are burgeoning problems in American society, often with devastating and wide-ranging social consequences. One source states that over 59 million Americans abuse alcohol and tobacco (Witters, Venturelli, & Hanson, 1992). Another estimates that 18 million Americans 18 years of age and older experience problems associated with their alcohol abuse (Moos, Finney, & Cronkite, 1990).

Alcohol is involved in 10 percent of all deaths in the United States. It is the leading cause of accidental death for people 15 to 24 years of age (Cahalan, 1987; NIAAA, 1987; Saxe et al, 1983). It can damage virtually every organ in the body and has the potential for causing chronic deficits or even death. It is also associated with

---

*Similar to what was previously described in this text as the "meaning-creation" phase.

psychological distress for both abusers and their families and with social problems such as divorce, child abuse, and unemployment (NIAAA, 1987). The economic costs—direct and indirect—of alcohol abuse may be as high as $120 billion a year (Moos, Finney, & Cronkite, 1990).

THE BIOPSYCHOSOCIAL PERSPECTIVE

The dominant model for the study of alcoholism in the United States today is described by the term *biopsychosocial*. It encompasses the study of genetic, physiologic, psychological, sociocultural, and behavioral factors associated with alcoholism. Decades of research have revealed an increasingly sophisticated picture of distinct clinical subtypes (Cloninger, 1987), with an implicit assumption that alcoholism is always multifactorial (Gilligan, Reich, & Cloninger, 1987). Currently, our best paradigm for exploring the factors that cause alcohol abuse—the biopsychosocial perspective—is less useful in explaining the *experience* of alcohol abuse (its meaning to the alcoholic) or in addressing such concepts as responsibility. Existential psychotherapy, on the other hand, focuses on just such areas of inquiry. It is based on belief in the abuser's responsibility (and privilege) to define, not just the meaning of his alcoholism, but of his life itself. When used in concert with an informed biopsychosocial understanding, it adds not just another, but a more profound, dimension to alcohol treatment.

ALCOHOLISM TREATMENT

In the United States, over a million people enter treatment for alcohol abuse each year (Saxe et al, 1983). Many different treatment modalities are currently in use. Holder et al (1991) discuss thirty-three of them, including only those that have been subjected to at least one controlled clinical trial. Some of these include self-control training, social skills training, stress management training, hypnosis, residential milieu therapy, confrontational interventions, marital therapy, cognitive therapy, individual psychotherapy, group psychotherapy, aversion therapy, and Alcoholics Anonymous.

The large number and variety of treatments reflect our incomplete understanding of the multiple factors influencing alcoholism, the lack of consensual outcome criteria for successful treatment, and sometimes the lack of documentation of results. Moos et al (1990), in their long-term study of alcoholism treatments, suggest that the roles played by life context and coping skills (the factors they consider most strongly influential in long-term outcome) are inadequately addressed in most alcoholism treatment programs, even those whose short-term outcomes are good.

Probably significant in such coping difficulties is the pervasive use of denial among alcoholics. A biopsychological explanation of this phenomenon is that alcoholics are compromised in their ability to perceive or interpret internal cues due to a predisposition to labile regulation of arousal (Tarter, Alterman, & Edwards, 1983). As a result, they learn to avoid attending to their own internal states. They seek distraction from their confusing emotions and can become estranged from their own subjective lives.

EXISTENTIAL PSYCHOTHERAPY AND ALCOHOLISM TREATMENT

The Concept of Being

In existential psychotherapy, the entire focus of attention is on subjective and inter-subjective experience. Put alternatively, it is concerned with the individual's *being* in the world, a condition shared by us all in that we must each experience it uniquely. The concept of being requires awareness, in the deepest possible sense, of one's unique *presence* in the present as it becomes the future. Therefore it can only be approached through one's own immediate experience. It requires a willingness to *encounter,* to engage with one's full attention, in the present moment, one's layers of pretense and diversion. We each construct a veil of distracting irritations and plea-sures, of mental busywork, designed to protect us from awareness of our deepest existential concerns: death, isolation, responsibility, and how we are to find meaning in our lives. Continuous awareness of such profound problems of existence would cause us terrible anxiety. Our diversions, if they are effective—that is, flexible and mature—allow us to go about our daily lives relatively unencumbered.

Alcoholism and Being

However to *remain* disengaged from such awareness, to refuse ever to "think deeply not about the way one came to be the way one is, but *that* one is" (Yalom, 1980, p. 11) is to live a constrained and fragile psychological life in which the deep self is cloistered from awareness. The alcoholic does live just such a tenuous life, chroni-cally estranged from the deep self; in the long run, addiction, rigid and suffused with denial as it is, is not an effective defense against existential anxiety.

In existential psychotherapy, we presume that if one wants to experience the full dimensions of what it means to exist, the depth of one's being in the world, one must access the deep self and allow it expression to the relatively outer self and thence to the interpersonal relationship if desired. Generally, such access can only be main-tained reliably through disciplined pursuit, just as diligence is required to sustain mastery of the violin or the stamina of the runner. Certainly therapists must be will-ing to forge these paths in their own mental lives if they are to have any hope of help-ing others who feel unable to do so. Alcoholics, with their avoidance of uncomfort-able emotion, are usually skeptical of the value of tolerating sustained discomfort.

ALCOHOLISM AND EXISTENTIAL AWARENESS; CHEMICAL ARMOR AND A FALSE FUTURE

The chronic warding off of existential awareness is often experienced as an illusion that one is "in control" of one's life. This is a common attitude among alcoholics. Since their drinking provides a particularly predictable subjective experience, they become particularly sensitized to the discomfort of unpredictable events. In addition, as suggested earlier, people who become alcoholics may have unusually labile arousal regulation and hence be especially uncomfortable in the face of change.

Alcoholics know that by drinking, they can give themselves the comfort and reassurance of a known future and superimpose it like camouflage over the unknown that actually lies ahead. The fact that this chemical future is false because it is contained within the illusory reality of their addiction may eventually become troublesome. But until it does, drinking serves as a rigid and powerful chemical armor against an unappealing option—living life as it is.

THE DECISION TO SEEK TREATMENT

Occasionally in life, we experience what Irvin Yalom (1980) calls *boundary situations,* situations in which our usual defenses fail in the face of some severe stressor and we become flooded with anxiety, more aware than usual of our existential vulnerability. Alcoholics who seek treatment are often motivated by such experiences, particularly ones that remind them of their mortality. Their physicians, for example, may have told them, for the first or the tenth time, that they were killing themselves. Or they may have had a brief glimpse of the denied deep self buried beneath their chemical armor. In any case, they decide to change.

THE CASE OF MR. P

Mr. P is a 30-year-old man who recently resumed outpatient treatment for a fifteen-year history of alcohol abuse and dependence. He first sought treatment two years ago after he was seriously injured in a car accident in which the intoxicated driver, his friend, was killed. Mr. P states that he can still clearly remember his shock and outrage at his friend's death and the stark realization that struck him "like an ice pick in my chest" that it could just as easily have been him who died. Death had "never seemed personal" before.

In direct response to this event, according to the patient, he entered and successfully completed a thirty-day inpatient alcohol treatment program. Though he had been in and out of various alcohol programs since he was a teenager, mostly under parental pressure, he describes this program as his first real commitment to stopping drinking.

He has been generally successful at not drinking for the two years since, except for an occasional "one or two beers." He has attended Alcoholics Anonymous meetings religiously and found them helpful. He has, however, continued to have a conflictual and dependent relationship with his parents; has been unable to define meaningful work for himself or sustain a satisfying relationship; and has been finding the temptation to drink increasingly irresistible over the last several months, to the point that he feels his sobriety "is beginning to crumble" for the first time since his inpatient treatment. These are the concerns being addressed in treatment.

Earlier we mentioned the tendency for the alcoholic to use denial diffusely as a defense. We associated this with a habitual tendency to avoid focusing on his own internal states or emotions. We also discussed the concept of encounter as crucial in existential psychotherapy. As it seems likely that the alcoholic patient (here male), with his pattern of immediate retreat in the face of emotional discomfort, will find it difficult to sustain an attitude of encounter, we reiterate how essential it is that the therapist (here female) remain stalwart in its pursuit. This is to in no way suggest that she should limit her empathy or sensitivity to the patient's limits but, rather, model for him tolerance of emotional discomfort as implicit to a process of self-discovery. Such tolerance is particularly important for the alcoholic because it is a capacity that is essential to his maintaining sobriety.

The therapist should also give the patient her full attention—intellectually, emotionally, and intuitively—so that he will experience her presence as fully as possible. Again, this is in part modeling to enhance his experience of the present moment.

An example of this process follows:*

Therapist: Mr. P, what do you want from your parents? *(Long pause. The patient moves around in his chair and then settles down with his elbow on the table and his head pressed against his hand. He looks down with a confused expression. His leg is shaking.)* I notice your leg is shaking.

Patient: (Laughs) Yes. *(He is still looking down.)*

T: I wonder where you are right now.

P: Well, last session I was really angry with my parents, and I felt constricted. *(He puts his hand up to his heart.)*

T: Where in your body do you feel your anger?

P: In my chest. *(He takes a deep breath.)*

T: How did that feel?

P: It felt like I was blowing out some steam.

T: Your voice cracked when you made that statement.

P: Yes, well . . . *(Pause.)* I guess the feelings of my anger go from my heart up to my throat.

T: Can you envision being in the same room with your parents?

P: Oh, yeah.

T: Can you do that now?

P: (He closes his eyes.) It's uncomfortable. I feel like I'm being watched closely and judged, like they don't trust me. *(He opens his eyes. He seems stiff.)*

T: Try, if you can, to stay with the feelings that come up.

P: OK. *(He closes his eyes again.)* My body feels rigid just visualizing them. I'm at their house attending my sister's birthday party. I really don't want to be there, and my parents are asking me to stay for dinner.

T: How do you feel?

P: Pulled, frustrated, I feel like exploding. *(He pauses.)*

T: Stay with that sensation.

P: I can feel my face turn red, and my arms feel like the blood is rapidly pumping through them. I want to yell at both my parents and tell them I'm sick of them pulling

---

Editor's note: The existential approach illustrated here may not be appropriate for certain alcoholic clients (for example, those in early stages of recovery). Yet, as the authors imply, it may be more appropriate than is generally assumed.

at me. *(Talking loud.)* I want acceptance from them for who I am and not for who they want me to be. *(Silence. He is breathing heavily, and his upper body and head are wavering from side to side. His hands are in fists and are on the arms of the chair. His eyes are still closed, and his jaw is clenched.)*

T: This issue is clearly very difficult for you.

P: (His eyes are still closed.) Yes, it is. *(He sounds angry.)*

T: What's happening for you right now?

P: I think I need to come down from this anger.

T: I wonder if I was pushing you too hard.

P: No, no. *(He smiles, seemingly embarrassed.)*

T: What are you thinking?

P: Well, now I feel lighter somehow, like I couldn't lift anything heavy right now. Kind of a feeling of being immobilized.

T: Are there any other images or thoughts that you can attribute to these feelings?

P: Probably experiencing the anger in here. I guess just thinking about what I want from my parents brings these feelings out.

T: How are you feeling now?

P: I feel uplifted.

T: Can you describe what that feels like?

P: Just that there's more lightness, really, I don't feel so burdened. It helps to get in touch with how my body reacts to what I'm thinking. I guess using alcohol kept me from feeling anything. I can't explain it.

T: Actually, you've explained it very clearly.

We might note here that the work the patient is doing is focused heavily on tolerating and communicating his internal states. He does not appear to be ready to encounter issues such as his own responsibility for his relationship with his parents, which, from an existential psychotherapy perspective, will eventually have to be addressed. Even though there is little reference to alcohol in this vignette, the experience of sustaining uncomfortable emotion and finding that he can get through it is directly relevant to the process of recovery, as was discussed earlier.

SUMMARY

Alcoholism is a pervasive problem in the United States today. The biopsychosocial perspective underlies our current approach to understanding and treating alcoholism. While effective in studying populations, this approach does not address the alcoholic's subjective experience or such qualitative issues as meaning and responsibility. Existential psychotherapy, with its focus on immediate, subjective experience, personal meaning, and other concerns related to the fact of existence, can augment other approaches to alcoholism treatment. The attitude of encounter, central to existential psychotherapy, is particularly relevant for helping the alcoholic break the typical cycle of denial and avoidance and therefore directly useful in the patient's recovery.

REFERENCES

Cahalan, D. (1987). *Understanding America's drinking problem: How to combat the hazards of alcohol.* San Francisco: Jossey-Bass.

Cloninger, C. (1987). Neurogenetic adaptive mechanisms in alcoholism. *Science, 336,* 410–416.

Gilligan, S., Reich, T., & Cloninger, C. (1987). Etiologic heterogeneity in alcoholism. *Genet. Epidemiol. 4,* 395–414.

Holder, H., Longabaugh, R., Miller, W., & Rubonis, A. (1991). The cost effectiveness of treatment for alcoholism: A first approximation. *Journal of Studies on Alcohol, 52,* 517–540.

Moos, R., Finney, J., & Cronkite, R. (1990). *Alcoholism treatment: Context, process, and outcome.* New York: Oxford.

National Institute on Alcohol Abuse and Alcoholism (1987). Sixth special report to the U.S. Congress on alcohol and health. Washington, DC: U. S. Department of Health and Human Services.

Saxe, L., Dougherty, D., Esty, K., & Fine, M. (1983). The effectiveness and costs of alcoholism treatment (Health Technology Case Study 22). Washington, DC: Office of Technology Assessment.

Tarter, R., Alterman, A., & Edwards, K. (1983). Alcoholic denial: A biopsychologic interpretation. *Journal of Studies on Alcohol, 45,* 214–218.

Witters, W., Venturelli, P., & Hanson, G. (1992). *Drugs and society,* 3d ed. Boston: Jones and Barlett.

Yalom, I. (1980). *Existential psychotherapy.* New York: Basic Books.

EI CASE FORMULATION—Mr. P

Traditionally, substance abuse has been treated nonexperientially—either medically, behaviorally, or cognitively. Experiential strategies, when they were used, were considered both questionable and gratuitous. Yet substance abusers notoriously fail in traditional treatment, and core issues remain festering.

This case shows that there is a key place for experiential liberation strategies in the treatment of substance abusers. Properly timed and offered, experiential strategies minister to the preverbal-kinesthetic bases for the abuse and catalyze alternatives for change.

The client in this study seems hyperconstricted. He's dependent on his parents, unable to find meaningful work, and discouraged about his relationships. His alcoholism appears to be a mask for this desolation, both elevating and—at requisite times—quelling his moods. By allowing herself to be fully present to Mr. P, the therapist helped him to become present in return, to deeply center himself.

Quite readily, therefore, the therapist is able to invoke the actual with Mr. P and invite him into uncomfortable terrain. She directs his attention to his shaking leg, for example, and to the constriction he feels in his chest. She underscores his "deep breath," which helps him to "blow off steam." She then notes how his voice cracks when he speaks and invites him to explore the sensation.

Each step of the way, the therapist keeps Mr. P focused on what is happening in his body, his gestures and his mannerisms. While this might evoke resistance in some clients, Mr. P seems to have worked through much of his resistance and ably rises to the challenge.

Mr. P begins to feel great anger well up in him and physically senses himself enlarging. The therapist then suggests a visualization designed to amplify that anger—being in a room with his parents. At first, Mr. P stiffens when picturing this scene; but soon he feels his blood pumping and his face reddening, and suddenly he wants to *explode.* He wants to "yell" at his parents, he says, and to declare his independence.

By mirroring this material back to Mr. P, the therapist helps him to realize how liberating and forceful it is and how capable he is of bearing it. The therapist is sensitive to Mr. P's limits, however, and does not push him to exceed those limits. In fact, by *asking* him about his limits, she tacitly encourages him to stretch them.

By the end of their session, Mr. P feels "lighter," "uplifted," and markedly less "burdened." He has gone into his hell, as Rollo May would say, and emerged with more authority. While he will eventually need to actualize this authority, as the authors indicate, we must not underestimate what he has already done. Specifically, he has already laid the groundwork for such actualization by widening the latitude of his consciousness. He has become more of an occupant, less of a prisoner of himself; and he has engaged his expansive and constrictive dreads *soberly,* increasing, thereby, his chances of transforming them soberly.

NOTES ON THE SINGLE WOMAN: THE ANNE SEXTON COMPLEX

Ilene Serlin

Ilene Serlin, Ph.D., A.D.T.R., is a professor of psychology at Saybrook Institute, a licensed psychologist, and a board member of the humanistic psychology division of the American Psychological Association. She has studied Gestalt, existential, and archetypal psychology with Laura Perls and James Hillman.

In this intimate commentary, Ilene Serlin explores the dynamic interplay between freedom and limitation (or Dionysian and Apollonian yearnings) in the lives of her single women clients. By comparing and contrasting the struggles of the poet Anne Sexton with those of Maria, Serlin richly animates a female existential view. Specifically, Serlin shows how debilitating oppositions between the sexual and spiritual and the wild and ladylike can be fruitfully encountered and transformed.

Maria walked in one day crying, "My mother died when she was forty-five years old, my stepmother did not live past forty-five, Anne Sexton committed suicide when she was forty-five, and I, being forty-five, am afraid that I will not make my forty-sixth birthday." That week, Maria took an overdose of sleeping pills.

What was the mystery of her identification with Anne Sexton? How was Maria part of a tradition of women, from Anne Sexton to Sylvia Plath to Marilyn Monroe, who identified with a tragic heroine whose creativity led to death? These women wrestled with the ultimate existential concerns of freedom and limitation, but in a way that was unique to their particular roles as women. The aim of this commentary is to discuss how existential psychotherapy can be relevant to this group of women, by outlining the course of treatment with one individual woman.

The high numbers of my women clients who struggled to express their creativity and who were alone was of deep concern to me. These talented women, most of whom had not had children, balanced the needs for autonomy with the needs for relationship, felt vulnerable, and faced aging alone. Their creativity was not in the service of work and consciousness, but in the service of the unconscious; they immersed themselves in journal writing, doomed love affairs, and dreams. Like many women, they knew how to swoon, and their form of surrender was sexual, mystical, and ecstatic. Darkness exerted a strong pull and death a romantic fascination. Death was often envisioned as a dark or ghostly lover. The current movie *Dracula* speaks of the archetypal combination of death, blood, and bliss. Instead of denying death, as is so common in our culture, these women experience death as a morbid fascination, an obsession, an addiction; in fact, as a denial of living. Finally, in defining themselves as women-selves in a repressive society, these women often experience being misunderstood, with conflicts between sexuality and spirituality, between images of whore and virgin, between being wild and being ladylike. Their difficulty in freeing themselves from creative blocks, from death, and from constricted sexuality seem to be related to their difficulty in separating from their mothers and standing alone.

The more I became concerned with these issues, the more I felt that women needed alternative role models to these romantic, tragic heroines. Can women be creative, alone, separate, loving, and still thrive? What would it take, therapeutically, to help them? And what can we learn about this complex in women, the conjunction of creativity, spirituality, sexuality, and darkness, so that other women can be helped?

In an obituary for Anne Sexton, the poet Denise Levertov wrote,

> We who are alive must make clear, as she could not, the distinction between creativity and self-destruction. The tendency to confuse the two has claimed too many victims. (quoted in Middlebrook, 1991, p. 397)

I call the pattern of romanticizing and identifying creativity with self-destruction and death the "Anne Sexton complex." How women might have this complex yet still live and balance their finite ordinary lives with their expansive selves is the subject of this commentary. This investigation will take the form of the case history of one woman, whom I will present, phenomenologically, using her own words. I will review the major themes of her life and connect them with the themes of Anne Sexton's life. Finally, I will draw some conclusions about how the Anne Sexton complex is a particular way of living out fundamental existential themes for some women, how it relates to existential theory, and how psychotherapy can rewrite the story to eliminate the tragic ending.

THE CASE OF MARIA

When Maria came for her first session, I was impressed with her grace and intelligence. She was petite, her blond hair was pulled back, and she was artfully dressed and groomed. She spoke about her life with clarity and insight and seemed serious about helping herself in therapy.

Born in the Southwest, she had three sisters, a stepbrother, and a stepsister. Maria described her mother as "like Anne Sexton. She never really wanted children and was restless," playing out the role of the 1950s conventional American housewife. Maria's mother and sisters, she said, "were all dependent women, not able to stand on their own feet, not able to make a stand for themselves." Her mother died when Maria was 19, and her father left at the same time. Sent to live with an uncle, Maria had recurring images of being an orphan. At age 30 or 31 she was raped, and she said that life never came back together for her after that. She went to live with her sister in an attempt "to find family" but found that it didn't work. Instead, she came to Boston, where she had been trying to create a new life for the past year and a half. She worked in a corporate office with mostly men, still had not made any friends, and was very lonely.

Freedom

While acknowledging that she had managed to break away from the role her mother had played out, Maria was still not enjoying her freedom. Ironically, she imagined that housewives envied her independence and fantasized that she was spending her time partying and being romanced. Instead, she worked hard and came home to an empty apartment, where lovely objects were tastefully arranged. Nothing messed up her life, no one interrupted, and she had everything just as she wanted. What was missing? Other people, mess, life, and a meaningful focus. When I asked her how she was using her creativity, she said she had no outlets. She called herself a "closet artist" and knew that she had to "dig down" and find out what her life's calling was supposed to be. She was becoming increasingly isolated. Sadly, she said she was "getting scared. I work all day and cry all night, and life is getting out of control." Drinking was an effort for her to find "spirits," or courage to connect and create. Her freedom was a "false freedom," she said, since she actually stayed in her apartment all weekend. The poignant picture I received was of a beautiful woman torn between a fearful independence and a need for connection.

Dreams

Ghostly Lover   The first dream Maria told me about was a powerful one for her, one in which her high school boyfriend Dennis appeared, saying "Call me." They were the "first" for each other, and seemed destined for marriage. They then both married others and lost touch (until recently, when they became available to each other again). He married someone "safe," said Maria. "I had too much passion." He stayed with Maria as a fantasy, but she felt that she lived more in fantasy than in reality. She said, "I've never really been on the earth. [I'm] ethereal . . . [and] never owned property." The theme of being attached to fantasy, to what has been called the Ghostly Lover, and of therefore not having lived life fully haunted Maria and was a continuing theme of our work.

The Sacrifice of the Witch   She then told me of a significant dream: "A man and a woman are traveling together. He is from a Latin American country. She carries with her a little creature—it might be a bird. It seems small and fits in between her hands. They enter a forest and come upon a community of people living in the forest. To honor the man, they take the woman and tie her to a cross. They set the cross on fire, and she is burned to death." Maria explained that upon awakening, she kept trying to make it come out better, to convince herself that she didn't die, but she reasoned that she had to have died. She could not have survived the burning cross.

Maria called this her first *sacrifice dream.* Her associations were that she gave an animal, her symbolic self, to the man before she herself was sacrificed. She did have a black cat and felt close to animals, but, she said, "Women were burned at the stake for living alone and talking to animals." This meant to Maria that they were close to their instincts. She said, "I always said I'd be burned as a witch. I am a threat, but to whom? To the established order because I've always been self-sufficient." Her early memories were of being called "the single type," taking care of herself and living alone. When I asked her what quality she might have that threatened others, she cried, saying, "I'm out of touch with my power. I have no idea what it might be." Despite this, Maria described herself as very competent at work, sometimes threatening to others, with a strong intuitive sense of their dynamics. She longed to use this capacity constructively, to be a healer, but she did not know how. Tearful, she described the sacrifice dream as about *transformation,* the ability to find the inherent power in a dangerous or pathological situation.

Virgin/Whore   In another dream, Maria was drinking and dressed like a gypsy. Images of the whore came up as Maria described how her mother wanted her to be wholesome and ladylike and disapproved of her being a dancer. Maria was fascinated with the image of the whore, danced topless once, and had a friendship with a woman who was a prostitute.

As she described this image to me, I was struck with Maria's blond beauty. She was always dressed in white. She said she was called Madonna at work, and she was afraid of the whore image. Maria had been raped, and she was afraid after the rape that people would accuse her of inviting it. She tried to not to "look as if she were inviting trouble," and she was afraid that her past would create problems in her relationships with men. As she talked, she normally sat in a composed and ladylike way. Yet when she laughed, and when she drank, a whole different, bawdy and life-affirming side emerged. She had a wonderful sense of humor, which she credits with having saved her in the past.

Sleeping Beauty

For the last thirteen years, Maria has been celibate. She felt that she had to purify herself, to let something die so that she would be ready for something new.

Just before her suicide attempt, Maria had a dream of crashing cars. She was surrounded by "paramedics and a woman in white [her therapist] standing over me," she said. "I asked the woman whether I would live or die. I know now that it was my unconscious breaking through, ready for a big change."

When Maria took the sleeping pills, she had been drinking. She later described the sensation while drinking as one of drifting off. Pills, for her, intensified the speed of the drifting, until the point where she blacked out. Later, Maria discovered a journal entry she had scrawled during that time. It included the telephone number of her Ghostly Lover. She remembers or reconstructs that she was dreaming about him. She describes the feeling as being "in another grip . . . like another force had given over. I was compelled . . . and fearless in it, too. I was willing to go." Going into a state of suspended animation while in perfect physical condition and awakening to the Ghostly Lover is like the story of Sleeping Beauty. Death, oblivion, dreams, and the Ghostly Lover are all intertwined.

Ironically, Maria awoke from her swoon to see real paramedics in white standing over her. They took her to the hospital. Among the few possessions she packed to take with her was the biography of Anne Sexton, which she continued to read while in the hospital. As in *The Portrait of Dorian Gray,* life paralleled art, and art paralleled life.

Transformation

The following is an account of Maria's treatment and what contributed to her recovery.

In the hospital, Maria asked me if it were possible to reverse the trend. I said, "Yes, if you're willing to give birth to yourself over and over again, to rediscover your innocence." I asked who I was to her, and she said, "the figure in the dream of whom I asked, Will I live or die?" Apparently I was a nurturing mother figure to Maria, one who would lend her strength as she weighed life and death or foster her strength to create her own life. Later she said that the figure in the dream that held her small animal, or her "self," made her feel safe. I also made her feel safe. "You validated me . . . carried me along until I could do it for myself . . . because it's a long journey back. (*Laughs.*) Something got set in motion . . . the idea of risk. I remember writing in my journal, 'Be willing to risk your own life—even death itself.' I've gained something, but only because I was willing to lose it, lose my life. It reminds me of the New Testament scripture: 'He who shall lose his life shall find it.'" Her dreams and her lover were two-edged, about freedom and limitation and how to integrate them in life. Being willing to risk her own life, like the image of sacrifice in her dream, allowed Maria to later really choose life.

Groups were an important part of the treatment structure, and Maria discovered that she liked living with people: "What turned it around was having people around. I've not been alone since." She enjoyed attention from the men and began to experience herself as a woman. She began to consider calling Dennis (the "Ghostly Lover" with whom she had actual contact recently) and ending her relationship with him, sensing that she needed to do this in order to be available for a real man and to live.

She understood that it had been only eight months since her contact with Dennis, but since then she had lost twenty pounds and gone into a deep depression. Thinking of his message in her previously mentioned dream as a "call," we talked of all the times in life when one might hear a call to the forbidden, to mystery and danger. For Maria, the call was to the underworld, and Dennis was an imaginary guide: "He played a part in my hitting bottom." Her task, however, was not to remain in the underworld but to disintegrate and reintegrate into real life in community and creativity.

When I asked her what changed for her, she said, "It took a near-death experience to give me life. It was like being reborn, starting from scratch." When I asked what it felt like to have life come back, she said, "It feels rather amazing . . . wonderful . . . just to feel. I didn't know I was cut off from my feelings. Now I know. The only access was through my dreams. I feel younger. I was getting ready to grow old and die. I'd been doing that for a long time. There was no sex in my life, I was like a little old lady." At this point, she expressed a willingness to "dare to connect. Instead of reading about it, I'd rather be out experiencing freedom. . . . I've not been able to watch TV since last April. Life is more interesting than watching TV."

Later that month, Maria came dressed in gold, with gold earrings and a suntan. Expressing a new interest in diet and health, she noticed the transition from lunar to solar imagery. She said: "You know my love affair with cats. This is a night world calling, related to moons and cats, to the unconscious and dreams." Her new solar energy related her to the day world, to sunshine and overtness.

Thinking back over her journey, Maria felt that it was all leading somewhere hopeful. "I marvel a lot these days at the turn my life has taken. Something got rolling, and I couldn't have planned it." Her tone of voice expressed a new innocence. "It feels like a rebirth. I feel like a child struggling to express myself, my brain wiped clean, having to relearn. I've given a lot of thought to the long period of celibacy—I think it was a really healthy thing. An opportunity to get to know myself, my own body and myself as a woman."

New Life

Soon after leaving the treatment center, Maria had a dream about "messy sex." She was ready to "mess up" her "pretty apartment" with another person and give up some of her carefully managed control. She thought of herself as "completing a cycle . . . coming back to myself. My hair is long and blond again. I feel alive."

The next month, she met a man and moved in with him and his 16-year-old son. He was of Mediterranean descent; he and his children were dark, but his former wife was blond. Themes of dark and light were coming together. She remembered how in her dream the dark man had kept her little animal safe, and she said she felt safe with this man.

The choice of being with him came out of her newfound courage. She said it was like her choice of whether to live or to die. It was a leap of faith. "You have to be able to go around the corner to see what is there. I knew it was risky. But I chose to live."

Maria described another change in terms of her need for freedom. She said, "I've always been independent and free. Now I don't want to be so free. I'm really happy, comfortable, letting him be the boss. I don't need my own car." Maria was trying to find a balance between the dependent-housewife stereotype, which she was fleeing, and a freedom that left her isolated. She was finding her way to a mutually determined interdependence, which meant negotiating long hours over household tasks and objects. Maria admitted enjoying this process: "I've never had an opportunity to care for people, to clean, someone else to shop for." I noticed that there was a certain pride in her use of the word *us*. As she put it: "I knew the meaning of life was in relationship, but I didn't know how to 'get' a relationship. I also wasn't able to go on alone." Here Maria was expressing a new balance between needs for work and needs for nurturance, a balance especially difficult for many women (Bateson, 1989, p. 240; Gilligan, 1982, pp. 62–63).

When I asked her about the similarities and differences between her story and Anne Sexton's, she said, "I am like Anne Sexton in that we both have a strong identification with our mothers. Anne Sexton also has similarities with my mother. My mother was a woman caught, or trapped, in the politics of the 1950s, not allowed to express herself in any domain other than in the context of home and family. Like many women in the 1950s, Anne Sexton sold cosmetics out of her home for awhile—the same brand of cosmetics my mother sold. I have come to understand that I have lived my mother's unlived life." In both Maria and Anne Sexton's families, the basic bond was between the "women. Men were observers. Coming to Boston was an attempt to break away. I was always attempting to have my own life. Even my sisters were controlling me." There was "too much enmeshment in the maternal womb. My own mother died when I was 19. I was literally thrown out into the world. I still needed a lot, was still a baby. I stayed in that little girl neediness. It's time to grow up and have a life. I'm still an adolescent. Staying virginal was a way of staying attached to my mother and pleasing her. But I'm older than her now. She died just twenty-eight days before her forty-sixth birthday." Like Anne, Maria had always experienced a strong pull downward. "Something drew me down, and I couldn't stop it. There really was a sense of going down." When Maria returned to her sister's house, she was aware of seeking a feminine environment, one closer to the earth and feminine values. However, there the death pull "began to get very strong, to pull me. Both of my sisters also have a struggle. My older sister didn't think I'd live past 46." There was the thought that "one of us will succeed in killing ourselves . . . almost like a curse." About their similarities in age, Maria observed, "It is perhaps a symbolic age, to cross the threshold that midlife presents to us and to meet the challenges that growing older represents." On the other hand, unlike Anne Sexton, Maria had a strong sense of being close to her father. Their drinking bonded them, and she once noted in a journal that she was "daddy's girl."

Maria's effort to break away from her home and individuate herself parallels the hero's journey. The hero must confront challenges, learn to be alone, overcome darkness, and bring his newfound wisdom back to his home and community. Missing are comparable stories for the heroine's journey, which could have provided a road map or sense of hope for Maria. She said, "While I was in the middle of it, I didn't understand all those dreams. I felt that everything that happened was absolutely necessary. You know how some people say, 'You got me on the rebound'? I say, 'You got me on the rebirth.'

"What is it that saved me? I don't know. Maybe their having died saved me, in that I was able to examine their lives and learn from their lives. I tried to understand why they died, perhaps so that I wouldn't have to follow them. But I had lost hope, and it has been asked how I got it back. It came back gradually. I think I entrusted my 'self' to others while I worked on the problem, while hope grew again. Others carried me while I was relearning who I am. Because today I am not who or what I was. What I was is lost to me—it has been sacrificed. I am in the process of reinventing my life. But I had to lose it in order to find it. I, of course, didn't know that this was what was happening. I know about it only in retrospect. The question has been asked, How does one decide whether to live or die? I decided to die. Maybe you have to decide to die before you can decide to live. I still decide daily. We take time before going to sleep at night to say what we are grateful for that day. I sometimes now say that I am grateful for my life. That is a big thing to say, and I feel it."

She then had a dream about a house burning down to ashes. However, in the dream was an image of a "phoenix rising from the ashes." What was burning? "All my preconceptions of security. I tried to move back to my home state—to my sister's house—so that her family would be my family, but that blew up. There is nothing left to hold onto. It is the 'Alchemical Negrito,* a blackening, getting to the essence.' The suicide attempt (and depression leading up to it) was the beginning of the return. All the parts, in ritual sacrifices, sacrificed over and over, until the sacrifice was complete." It is now time to "get to the essence of the spark of life, to find my own voice, my own spirituality." In a new dream, she "was choosing a bird for a pet." There were "lots of white birds. A yellow bird, peering down, asking to be picked. Expectant attitude. A spiritual dream. The bird is the soul. White birds are a purity of soul. A yellow bird is some sort of divine being. So many white birds, just one yellow one. Actually, I want to buy a yellow canary, a bird that sings. Brings beauty again."

Maria and her lover share a sense of spirituality. They say grace together before meals and "gratefuls" before bed. It is "good to share that," she says. She experiences "a sense of calm, serenity, grace." They have been talking about marriage. It's "very scary," she says, but they are "creating rituals together." Helping each other with the "soul losses" they experienced. She had tried "feminist, spiritual" paths alone and

---

*From the perspective of alchemy, the Alchemical Negrito is the dark phase, the phase of blackened metal, which precedes the metal's transformation into gold.

now needs to do her soul and spirit work with another person. She notices, "People romanticize being a little bit crazy. I think I used to. I'm much more concerned with daily life now, being real. I don't think the purpose of life is to be happy, just to live it." When she is scared, Maria recognizes that she thinks of Dennis and takes refuge in fantasy, but then she "can tell the difference between a fantasy and everyday life."

Recently, Maria came in reporting that the relationship was stable and a source of comfort for both of them. She had just survived her forty-sixth birthday. Maria had had a dream in which she remembered one line: "You will not live beyond the 9s." Upon reflection, she understood that 45 was 5×9 and that $4 + 5 = 9$. The number 9 was also symbolic of pregnancy, the period of gestation before something comes to fruition. She called her period of celibacy and hibernation her period of *dormancy:* "like I just went to sleep, turned it all off, Sleeping Beauty, a butterfly in a cocoon." There was now "so much willingness to comingle, to share our lives. I was attracted to men who were wrong. I just made the decision to stop. The change was imperceptible, unconscious. If I had intended to do it, I couldn't have." When I asked her what difference it made that she understood her journey in these terms, she said, "Some people have a need to study metapsychiatry, spirituality. I think I'm one. My sisters are not. I've been on this quest, the need to know, to understand." Commenting on the descent necessary for her rebirth, she said, "Other people don't really descend. Perhaps what was different was that the beginning of my journey was a conscious choice to make the quest. Without the descent and sacrifice, no change would have occurred. I had to kill part of myself." The image of an animal with its foot in a trap came up, an animal which had to gnaw off its foot in order to survive.

Maria commented on the difference between her descent and Anne Sexton's descent. "Anne Sexton worked with the unconscious: It was her 'art.' I think what makes my work with the unconscious different is that for the most part, my trusting the unconscious has its basis in awareness and spirituality. If you trust the unconscious and are one with it, you *are* unconscious and act from this unconsciousness. But if you trust the unconscious and are aware, *as a witness,* [of] its workings in your life and in your dreams and respectful of its power to both create and to destroy, you stand apart from it and are not identical with it. I think the difference is between a conscious descent and an unconscious one." By descending thoroughly, by being celibate and mostly containing the psychic process in journals rather than acting it out self-destructively (as did Anne Sexton), Maria was able to find the path to ascend.

Maria just finished reading Anne Sexton's biography by Diane Middlebrook. At the end of the reading, she felt "really sad" but also found "something sweet, something reclaiming" in it.

In summary, what were her similarities to Anne Sexton? Both were fascinated by death and darkness and both were very close to their mothers and the other women in the family, but this very attachment condemned them to live out the women's unfinished business. Both rebelled against the conventional role of housewife, experiencing a split between a heightened sexuality and ladylike behavior, images of the whore and the madonna, and needs for freedom and security. Both exhibited strong intuitive abilities, uncanny powers, healing abilities, and felt close to images of the witch. Both turned and returned to spirituality as salvation, looking for grace and redemption. Both were hungry for spirit, but spirit impregnated with the matter of the tribe, of culture, and the body. And both were heroines without adequate role models and with incomplete journeys of return.

Maria said she was different from Sexton in that she was less obsessed with suicide and closer to her father. She also wanted to be married, to care for another person and to be interdependent.

Let us now turn to Diane Middlebrook's biography of Anne Sexton to see how Anne Sexton's life exemplified the heroine's journey as a descent (Perera, 1981).

ANNE SEXTON

Anne Sexton, the first publicly described "confessional poet," died in 1974 at the age of 45. She came from a conventional middle-class background and worked as a fashion model but went on to win professorships, international recognition, and a Pulitzer Prize.

Sexton's mother was described as an inconsistent nurturer, a heavy drinker, and a poet. Sexton begged for her love and admiration, competed with her, and both wished for and dreaded her death. Both parents were conventional role models. Although Sexton tried to live a conventional life, she understood that "One can't build little white picket fences to keep nightmares out." The combination of a puritanical New England climate and a feverish sexuality ran through her family, causing eruptions and conflict. Maria, too, experienced a conflict between conventional values and heightened, almost hysterical sexuality, with a lack of a healthy sensual outlet.

Raised with strict ideas of propriety, Sexton expressed a guilty rage toward mothers in her poem "The Double Image." At least Sexton's mother, as a poet, provided a creative role model, whereas Maria's mother did not. Anne Sexton, with Adrienne Rich and Sylvia Plath, was preoccupied with and wrote about the conflicts between motherhood and writing.

Anne Sexton was extremely close to her great-aunt, Nana, whom she called a "twin," and who suffered a breakdown. Later, Anne came to understand one aspect of her illness as a form of loyalty to Nana, much as Maria understood her virginity as a form of loyalty to her mother.

The eruption of repressed and intense sexuality took the form, as it did in Maria's dreams, of witch imagery. Sexton wrote:

> I have gone out, a possessed witch,
> haunting the black air, braver at night;
> dreaming evil, I have done my hitch
> over the plain houses, light by light:
> lonely thing, twelve-fingered, out of mind.
> A woman like that is not a woman, quite.
> I have been her kind. (Middlebrook, 1991, p. 114)

In Sexton's poems, the housewife becomes an adulteress and witch while the poet is a magic maker. These are all a consequence of breaking out of the conventional woman's role. The witch image, however, is polarized into good witch and bad witch. Like Maria, Sexton had "good-witch" energy; she was empathic, intuitive, and had ways of "knowing." The bad witch was destructive, hysterical, and selfish. *The Radcliffe Quarterly* called Sexton "a contemporary witch" (Middlebrook, 1991, p. 356). Hysteria, whether in Freud's Victorian women or in these women, was a form of resistance to social repression. The forms their hysteria often took were the split personality of the vamp and the little girl.

Given the double bind of convention and impulse, breakdown could be seen as a logical response. Sexton's breakdowns allowed her to express herself authentically in a way that would not be accepted or understood in ordinary society. *Being* "crazy," in the R. D. Laing sense, was her meaning-making response to crazy binds.

> The mental hospital [is] a metaphorical space in which to articulate the crazy-making pressures of middle-class life, particularly for women. The home, the mental hospital, the body: these are woman's places in the social order that apportions different roles to the sexes; and woman herself is the very scene of mutilation. (Middlebrook, 1991, p. 274)

Sexton and Maria were both strongly connected, through their bodies, to the women in their families. Sexton reimagined God as a woman and associated female grace with the breast. Her own mother was named Mary. In "O Ye Tongues," Sexton's poetry is described: "Like a nursing mother's face, God's face bends over the world; and as the infant's tongue connects with the mother's breast, the poet's tongue connects with the uninterruptable attention of this Other, the milk of the skies" (Middlebrook, 1991, p. 355). Sexton imagined death as reconnecting with the mother as the source of all: "I wish to enter her like a dream, . . . sink into the great mother arms I never had" (Middlebrook, 1991, p. 395). To die meant to come home to mother.

Sexton had what she described as a "lust" for suicide and identified with Sylvia Plath, the poet who had already committed suicide. Sexton was somewhat envious of Plath's suicide, of its theatricality, of the attention it received, and of the end to suffering. She said: "I'm so fascinated with Sylvia's death: the idea of dying perfect, certainly not mutilated. . . . To lose your virginity is to be mutilated; virginity is unopen, not yet spoiled. . . . Sleeping Beauty remained perfect" (Middlebrook, 1991, p. 216). Taking pills preserved her perfection. Being Sleeping Beauty also expressed her desire to remain a child, an object of fantasy, dependent.

Sexton and Maria both came from conventional American families with strong ideas about what constituted "proper, ladylike behavior." Both rebelled and, in different ways, refused to be domestic. The rage they felt was partially expressed in a pull toward independence but primarily in killing off parts of themselves. Both experienced a strong split between their Little Girl, Madonna, and Virgin sides and their Whore and Vamp sexuality. The frustrated combination of sexuality, knowing, power, and anger came together in the image of the "Witch." They were both very attached to their mothers and searched for a form of feminine spirituality that would embody nurturance and grace. Both were beautiful and needed beauty in their lives but preferred to die as Sleeping Beauty rather than risk imperfection. Both sought to balance freedom and security, meaning and emptiness, loneliness and relationship. Both saw death as warm arms, as a release from the struggle of living.

At a memorial service for Sexton, her friend and fellow poet Adrienne Rich observed:

> We have had enough suicidal women poets, enough suicidal women, enough self-destructiveness as the sole form of violence permitted to women. (Middlebrook, 1991, p. 397)

MARIA'S ESCAPE

How did Maria escape death? What can we learn from her heroine's journey and descent into the underworld that might help other suicidal women? First, we will look at her case in terms of existential theory and follow this with a description, in her own words, of the major turning points of her psychotherapeutic journey.

Existential Theory

This case can be understood in terms of four major existential theorists. The first is Yalom (1980), who describes the confrontation with death as one of the primary existential challenges. Certainly Maria faced death, both symbolically and in reality. Her fundamental challenge was whether she would choose to live. Ironically, facing death can bring the courage to live and to create. Rollo May (1975) notes: "By the creative act . . . , we *are* able to reach beyond our own death. This is why creativity is so important, and why we need to confront the problem of the relationship between creativity and death" (p. 20). Although Maria has the aesthetic sensibilities of an artist, she has devoted her artistic vision to her inner world and fantasy and now needs to turn it outward to the task of creating a real life in relationship with others. May states that the role of the artist is to express the general conditions of the culture through symbol and the courage of the artist is the greatest kind of courage. Insofar as both Maria and Anne Sexton embody artistic sensibilities struggling to create life through symbol and the imagination, they demonstrate the existential task of creating in the face of death. If they create themselves and their own lives, however, it may be asked what "self" they are creating. Are they creating false selves and role expectations or authentic selves and authentic lives? Bugental (1987) stresses the importance of authenticity and subjectivity in the creation of a self in the world: "Our subjectivity is our true home, our natural state, and our necessary place of refuge and renewal. It is the font of creativity, the stage for imagination, the drafting table for planning, and the ultimate heart of our fears and hopes, our sorrows and satisfactions" (p. 4). To the extent that both Maria and Sexton were struggling to create, not just any selves, but experientially coherent authentic selves, subjectivity was a necessary aspect of their creativity. Finally, the confrontation between life and death, the courage to create in the face of death, and the authenticity of a subjective self can be organized into a paradoxical model. May comments that "Genuine joy and creativity come out of paradox" (Schneider, 1990, p. 7). In Schneider's (1990) paradoxical model, the human psyche is described as a continuum of constrictive and expansive possibilities. The dread of constriction and expansion promotes dysfunctional extremism or polarization, whereas confrontation with or integration of the poles promotes optimal living

(p. 27). Insofar as Maria and Sexton oscillated between the poles of expansion out into life and withdrawal into depression and a fantasy world (light and dark imagery, sexuality and spirituality), these extremes can be understood as resting on a continuum, with the therapeutic task being to name and integrate the poles.

However, the solitary journey toward independence emphasized by most existential theorists may be modeled after the heroic journey toward consciousness. The pull toward unconsciousness and the need for nurturance and interdependence as part of a woman's journey may not be adequately described in existential theory. This case raises the question of the role of relationship and caring within the context of existential theory.

The Psychotherapeutic Journey

What helped Maria face her darkness, integrate opposites, descend, and find renewal? What about this journey is unique to women?

First, I invited Maria to stay present to her pain, her distortions, and the denied and projected parts of herself. As the therapist, I stayed present to my own familiarity with Maria's issues and felt my way into her pain. Although I did not disclose any of the facts of my own life, I nevertheless let the emotional resonance of my empathy speak for itself nonverbally. When her pain became too great, we contained it with humor and with her writing. *Presence* was a critical part of the sessions, as I listened to her silence, to her presence (*dasein*), and gave her my immediate, kinesthetic, and profound attention. I trusted my own bodily response to the way she made me feel, including my tears, and the desire to hold her hand when she was in the deepest part of her suicidal depression. I had a sense of *invoking the actual* when I attempted to help Maria feel the experiential component of her symbolic material. Only later in the sessions did Maria let me know that as she had felt that something very dark lay ahead, she was looking for a therapist who could contain and accompany her. We both sensed this desire and allowed it to emerge in the sessions. All I might need to do in the sessions would be to comment simply, Why the tears? thus opening the way for her disclosures. Once she was able to express her emotions, Maria could let me see not only her expansive, independent, and capable side, but also the small side— the little girl who needed to be held and contained. We named the parts of herself that emerged and helped her to accept and integrate them. To contain her, I used the reality of the therapist-client encounter to help her express difficult material, to experience trust in a relationship, and to connect our work to the future potential of our relationship. Finally, I used an aesthetic perspective that enabled her to see her life as a composition, to bring her extremes into a more integrated whole, and to apply her creativity to her actual life.

An essential part of Maria's healing was to see her individual story in a larger cultural perspective. The balance between nurturance and work, and the themes of sacrifice, homelessness, and the closeness between death and rebirth, are especially close to the psyche and psychotherapy of women. Sacrifice was the basis of the early primordial fertility rites and was a necessary part of the spring rebirth. Feeling sacrificed to the dominant patriarchal culture and experiencing the plight of homelessness through the dispossession of an archetypal place in the world brings women together in a bond of empathy and shared humanity. This bond can also unite a female client and female therapist in an empathy of an intense, preverbal sisterhood. When asked what made the therapeutic difference, Maria chose to describe her experience of my empathy in terms of how Enki created two servant-mourner figures who "groaned with" the goddess Erishkigal in sympathy (Perera, 1981, pp. 69–71). To "groan with" implies a way of being with a client that does not distance but noncognitively "feels with" her experience and allows her to descend into the underworld, transform the pain into image and symbol, and re-emerge stronger.

As we worked, I followed and stayed with Maria in her progress and changing imagery. The first series of images had to do with "clearing the underbrush," or clearing the space for change to happen. This meant letting go of her sexuality, her car, activities and vestiges of her old life, and of illusions that her sisters could provide a home for her and that her Ghostly Lover could provide a relationship. The second set of images had to do with her descent. These had to do with her experiencing her aloneness, her nakedness and vulnerability, tracking the images in her dreams and journals, and experiencing her images of fire, darkness, crosses, and sacrifice. During this period, Maria focused on her readiness to create her own life and to meet another person without any "baggage" or encumbrances from her past. When she did meet a man, she was free and ready to move into a relationship with clear intentions of creating a stable home and a place for herself. Her third set of images had to do with rebirth, light, and interdependence. Staying with Maria's process meant trusting the logic of her psyche and helping her to put her images and experiences into the context of a meaningful story.

Concretely, how did Maria experience our work and the therapeutic relationship, and what was its effect on her? Here is a description in her own words:

> I am only beginning to understand the relationship between Ilene and myself. If it had just been the benefit with just anyone, it wouldn't have made a difference who I was talking to. But I had tried to talk to several people, and basically I was faced with total lack of understanding, either not wanting to understand what I was talking about because it was too personal and painful or unable to understand because it was too foreign to their experience or because they were totally unable to listen to another person and hear what she is saying. In any event, the world offered me nothing of care or concern for my experience or my feelings. It was unable and unprepared to give me anything to help me in my suffering. I just suffered, and by asking them to listen, and getting no response, my suffering was increased.
>
> So not anyone will do. With Ilene, she did listen, but I think also she did more. She was a witness to my suffering; she felt what I was feeling and felt for me. She didn't intervene or try to change my feelings or thoughts. She allowed me to process my dreams and my experiences as they arose.
>
> There are moments when I have nothing to say, and we just sit in the quiet. These moments can be so comfortable—time almost seems to stop. It is difficult to put the experience into words. Once I referred to it as a "holy moment"—such peace and quiet and closeness. Just letting the moment be.
>
> Sometimes I have just sat quietly weeping, and Ilene is just there.
>
> I have always known, somehow, that she sincerely cares—perhaps seeing tears in her eyes while I was telling a dream or my feelings. I was even concerned when I was in the

middle of a suicide attempt to mention in my "note" that her bill should be paid. This work requires, I believe, a degree of selflessness. I am very grateful to Ilene.

Her witnessing of my suffering has made a difference. Just being seen and heard by another. And her listening and sharing in my deep mourning. I remember sitting and telling her of some experience or dream and watching her eyes fill with tears. It had an impact on me. I still remember the sense of that moment. My suffering moved another. She had no agenda of her own. Not trying to change me, or teach me, or show me. She just listened and quietly mourned with me.

The ability to listen is a rare quality, born of love. The ability to sit in silence is even more rare—a holy moment when two sit as one. The feeling has no need for explanation—indeed cannot be explained. It is a wordless experience that occurs in the silence.

Once a week, for an hour, I was listened to.

REFERENCES

Bateson, M. (1989). *Composing a life.* New York: Atlantic Monthly.

Bugental, J. (1987). *The art of the psychotherapist.* New York: Norton.

Gilligan, C. (1982). *In a different voice.* Cambridge: Harvard University Press.

Harding, M. (1975). *The way of all women.* New York: Harper & Row.

Heilbrun, C. (1988). *Writing a woman's life.* New York: Ballantine Books.

May, R. (1975). *The courage to create.* New York: Bantam.

Middlebrook, D. (1991). *Anne Sexton.* Boston: Houghton Mifflin.

Perera, S. (1981). *Descent to the goddess: A way of initiation for women.* Toronto: Inner City Books.

Schneider, K. (1990). *The paradoxical self: Toward an understanding of our contradictory nature.* New York: Plenum Press.

Serlin, I. (1977). Portrait of Karen: A gestalt-phenomenological approach to movement therapy. *Journal of Contemporary Psychotherapy, 8,* 145–152.

Serlin, I. (1992). Tribute to Laura Perls. *Journal of Humanistic Psychology, 32*(3), Summer.

Yalom, I. (1980). *Existential psychotherapy.* New York: Basic Books.

EI CASE FORMULATION—Maria

Many women in our society feel split. On the one hand, they are told to restrain themselves—to be good little girls, dutiful mothers, and competent but subordinate businesspeople. On the other hand, they are encouraged to indulge—to be wildly attractive, ecstatically sensual, and ethereally magical or intuitive—in short, to be goddesses.

This split is even more intensified when, from young ages, girls are taught to repress either polarity and to conform to polarizing ideals.

Maria is a casualty of restrictive (or, in our terms, *hyperconstrictive*) social and familial influences. She is proper, dutiful, and Apollonian, as Nietszshe might say, and she has domesticated tastes. Yet she has a fire burning within her—just as her mother had; and the fire is threatening to consume her.

Her inability to get centered, then, to become deliberate and integrated, sets up a fierce oscillation in Maria. Her fear of venturing out into the world, of enlarging herself, pulverizes her into embedding and domesticating herself. Her fear of obliterating herself, on the other hand, of irrevocably choking herself off, propels her to inflate and romanticize herself. And so the cycle goes.

By the time Maria starts therapy, she sees only two alternatives, either a life of depression, or *death* (a total, unencumbering release). The latter, of course, was Maria's mother's solution, and Sexton's. Yet Dr. Serlin holds out another alternative for Maria.

By being intimately *present* to her, Dr. Serlin conveys to Maria three important sentiments: (1) she is safe, (2) she is heard, and (3) she is understood. This, in turn, helps Maria to feel safer and more accessible to herself and to risk fuller contact with Dr. Serlin.

Although Maria has difficulty invoking the actual in her waking life, the opposite is true in her dream life. Dr. Serlin capitalizes on this ability by listening to and reflecting back the salient themes she hears in Maria's dreams and by inviting Maria to immerse herself fully in these themes. Maria, in turn, is able to *experience* her dream symbolism (e.g., sterility/bawdiness, impotency/divinity) and not simply report on it.

When the experiences become too intense for Maria, Dr. Serlin invites humor, writing, or just simply *being* to enable her to regroup.

In the final stages of their work together, Maria begins to see a third, more integrative option to her plight. She begins to see that she can *survive* her orgiastic impulses—as well as her counterreactions to those impulses. She can be bold, she realizes, but she does not have to be deific; and she can be demure without fear of disintegrating.

The relationship with Dr. Serlin, accordingly, provides a laboratory for Maria. It enables her to try out new roles and to test those roles in her outside life. Eventually, she is able to become "messier" in her life—to abandon her sterile apartment, forgo her compromising celibacy, and mate with a charismatic man. Simultaneously, however, she is able to embrace this man's household, nurture his son, and stabilize her life with rituals. She is able to become *interdependent,* in other words, and to redeem the travails of her heroines.

A WIDOW'S EXPERIENCE: THE CASE OF ELVA

Irvin Yalom

Irvin Yalom, M. D., is one of the leading existential therapists in America. He is a psychiatrist and professor emeritus at Stanford University, and he is the author of such books as Group Psychotherapy, Existential Psychotherapy, Love's Executioner, *and* When Nietzsche Wept. *His most recent books have stressed literary forms to convey existential therapy.*

While the route to liberation for many clients is expansion, *as we have defined that term, for some it is the "full-throttle" reverse. Such is the case with Irv Yalom's study, Elva. Yalom sug-*

Source: Irvin Yalom, *Love's Executioner* (New York: Basic Books, 1989).

gests that because of her sense of entitlement, Elva was primed for disillusionment. Neither her arrogance, status, nor indulgent nature could inure her to the bruises we all must sooner or later face and for which we must all pay a price. Yet Yalom shows how Elva—sometimes painfully, sometimes humorously—begins to accept this sobering plight and, hence, the plight of mortality.

I greeted Elva in my waiting room, and together we walked the short distance to my office. Something had happened. She was different today, her gait labored, discouraged, dispirited. For the last few weeks there had been a bounce in her steps, but today she once again resembled the forlorn, plodding woman I had first met eight months ago. I remember her first words then: "I think I need help. Life doesn't seem worth living. My husband's been dead for a year now, but things aren't getting any better. Maybe I'm a slow learner."

But she hadn't proved to be a slow learner. In fact, therapy had progressed remarkably well—maybe it had been going too easily. What could have set her back like this?

Sitting down, Elva sighed and said, "I never thought it would happen to me."

She had been robbed. From her description it seemed an ordinary purse snatching. The thief, no doubt, spotted her in a Monterey seaside restaurant and saw her pay the check in cash for three friends—elderly widows all. He must have followed her into the parking lot and, his footsteps muffled by the roaring of the waves, sprinted up and, without breaking stride, ripped her purse away and leaped into his nearby car.

Elva, despite her swollen legs, hustled back into the restaurant to call for help, but of course it was too late. A few hours later, the police found her empty purse dangling on a roadside bush.

Three hundred dollars meant a lot to her, and for a few days Elva was preoccupied by the money she had lost. That concern gradually evaporated and in its place was left a bitter residue—a residue expressed by the phrase "I never thought it would happen to me." Along with her purse and her three hundred dollars, an illusion was snatched away from Elva—the illusion of personal specialness. She had always lived in the privileged circle, outside the unpleasantness, the nasty inconveniences visited on ordinary people—those swarming masses of the tabloids and newscasts who are forever being robbed or maimed.

The robbery changed everything. Gone was the coziness, the softness in her life; gone was the safety. Her home had always beckoned her with its cushions, gardens, comforters, and deep carpets. Now she saw locks, doors, burglar alarms, and telephones. She had always walked her dog every morning at six. The morning stillness now seemed menacing. She and her dog stopped and listened for danger.

None of this is remarkable. Elva had been traumatized and now suffered from commonplace post-traumatic stress. After an accident or an assault, most people tend to feel unsafe, to have a reduced startle threshold, and to be hypervigilant. Eventually time erodes the memory of the event, and victims gradually return to their prior, trusting state.

But for Elva it was more than a simple assault. Her world view was fractured. She had often claimed, "As long as a person has eyes, ears, and a mouth, I can cultivate their friendship." But no longer. She had lost her belief in benevolence, in her personal invulnerability. She felt stripped, ordinary, unprotected. The true impact of that robbery was to shatter illusion and to confirm, in brutal fashion, her husband's death.

Of course, she knew that Albert was dead. Dead and in his grave for over a year and a half. She had taken the ritualized widow walk—through the cancer diagnosis; the awful, retching, temporizing chemotherapy; their last visit together to Carmel; their last drive down El Camino Real; the hospital bed at home; the funeral; the paperwork; the ever-dwindling dinner invitations; the widow and widower's clubs; the long, lonely nights. The whole necrotic catastrophe.

Yet, despite all this, Elva had retained her feeling of Albert's continued existence and thereby of her persisting safety and specialness. She had continued to live "as if," as if the world were safe, as if Albert were there, back in the workshop next to the garage.

Mind you, I do not speak of delusion. Rationally, Elva knew Albert was gone, but still she lived her routine, everyday life behind a veil of illusion which numbed the pain and softened the glare of the knowing. Over forty years ago, she had made a contract with life whose explicit genesis and terms had been eroded by time but whose basic nature was clear: Albert would take care of Elva forever. Upon this unconscious premise, Elva had built her entire assumptive world—a world featuring safety and benevolent paternalism.

Albert was a fixer. He had been a roofer, an auto mechanic, a general handyman, a contractor; he could fix anything. Attracted by a newspaper or magazine photograph of a piece of furniture or some gadget, he would proceed to replicate it in his workshop. I, who have always been hopelessly inept in a workshop, listened in fascination. Forty-one years of living with a fixer is powerfully comforting. It was not hard to understand why Elva clung to the feeling that Albert was still there, out back in the workshop looking out for her, fixing things. How could she give it up? Why should she? That memory, reinforced by forty-one years of experience, had spun a cocoon around Elva that shielded her from reality—that is, until her purse was snatched.

Upon first meeting Elva eight months before, I could find little to love in her. She was a stubby, unattractive woman, part gnome, part sprite, part toad, and each of those parts ill tempered. I was transfixed by her facial plasticity: she winked, grimaced, and popped her eyes either singly or in duet. Her brow seemed alive with great washboard furrows. Her tongue, always visible, changed radically in size as it darted in and out or circled her moist, rubbery, pulsating lips. I remember amusing myself, almost laughing aloud, by imagining introducing her to patients on long-term tranquilizer medication who had developed tardive dyskinesia (a drug-induced abnormality of facial musculature). The patients would, within seconds, become deeply offended because they would believe Elva to be mocking them.

But what I really disliked about Elva was her anger. She dripped with rage and, in our first few hours together, had something vicious to say about everyone she knew—save, of course, Albert. She hated the friends who no longer invited her. She hated those who did not put her at ease. Inclusion or exclusion, it was all the same to her: she found something to hate in everyone. She hated the doctors who had told her that Albert was doomed. She hated even more those who offered false hope.

Those hours were hard for me. I had spent too many hours in my youth silently hating my mother's vicious tongue. I remember the games of imagination I played as a child trying to invent the existence of someone she did not hate: A kindly aunt? A grandfather who told her stories? An older playmate who defended her? But I never found anyone. Save, of course, my father, and he was really part of her, her mouthpiece, her animus, her creation who (according to Asimov's first law of robotics) could not turn against his maker—despite my prayers that he would once—just once, please, Dad—pop her.

All I could do with Elva was to hold on, hear her out, somehow endure the hour, and use all my ingenuity to find something supportive to say—usually some vapid comment about how hard it must be for her to carry around that much anger. At times I, almost mischievously, inquired about others of her family circle. Surely there must be someone who warranted respect. But no one was spared. Her son? She said his elevator "didn't go to the top floor." He was "absent": even when he was there, he was "absent." And her daughter-in-law? In Elva's words, "a GAP"—gentile American princess. When driving home, her son would call his wife on his automobile telephone to say he wanted dinner right away. No problem. She could do it. Nine minutes, Elva reminded me, was all the time required for the GAP to cook dinner—to "nuke" a slim gourmet TV dinner in the microwave.

Everyone had a nickname. Her granddaughter, "Sleeping Beauty" (she whispered with an enormous wink and a nod), had two bathrooms—two, mind you. Her housekeeper, whom she had hired to attenuate her loneliness, was "Looney Tunes," and so dumb that she tried to hide her smoking by exhaling the smoke down the flushing toilet. Her pretentious bridge partner was "Dame May Whitey" (and Dame May Whitey was spry-minded compared with the rest, with all the Alzheimer zombies and burned-out drunks who, according to Elva, constituted the bridge-playing population of San Francisco).

But somehow, despite her rancor and my dislike of her and the evocation of my mother, we got through these sessions. I endured my irritation, got a little closer, resolved my countertransference by disentangling my mother from Elva, and slowly, very slowly, began to warm to her.

I think the turning point came one day when she plopped herself in my chair with a "Whew! I'm tired." In response to my raised eyebrows, she explained she had just played eighteen holes of golf with her twenty-year-old nephew. (Elva was sixty, four foot eleven, and at least one hundred sixty pounds.)

"How'd you do?" I inquired cheerily, keeping up my side of the conversation.

Elva bent forward, holding her hand to her mouth as though to exclude someone in the room, showed me a remarkable number of enormous teeth, and said, "I whomped the shit out of him!"

It struck me as wonderfully funny and I started to laugh, and laughed until my eyes filled with tears. Elva liked my laughing. She told me later it was the first spontaneous act from Herr Doctor Professor (so that was *my* nickname!), and she laughed with me. After that we got along famously. I began to appreciate Elva—her marvelous sense of humor, her intelligence, her drollness. She had led a rich, eventful life. We were similar in many ways. Like me, she had made the big generational jump. My parents arrived in the United States in their twenties, penniless immigrants from Russia. Her parents had been poor Irish immigrants, and she had straddled the gap between the Irish tenements of South Boston and the duplicate bridge tournaments of Nob Hill in San Francisco.

At the beginning of therapy, an hour with Elva meant hard work. I trudged when I went to fetch her from the waiting room. But after a couple of months, all that changed. I looked forward to our time together. None of our hours passed without a good laugh. My secretary said she always could tell by my smile that I had seen Elva that day.

We met weekly for several months, and therapy proceeded well, as it usually does when therapist and patient enjoy each other. We talked about her widowhood, her changed social role, her fear of being alone, her sadness at never being physically touched. But, above all, we talked about her anger—about how it had driven away her family and her friends. Gradually she let it go; she grew softer and more gentle. Her tales of Looney Tunes, Sleeping Beauty, Dame May Whitey, and the Alzheimer bridge brigade grew less bitter. Rapprochements occurred; as her anger receded, family and friends reappeared in her life. She had been doing so well that, just before the time of the purse snatching, I had been considering raising the question of termination.

But when she was robbed, she felt as though she were starting all over again. Most of all, the robbery illuminated her ordinariness, her "I never thought it would happen to me" reflecting the loss of belief in her personal specialness. Of course, she was still special in that she had special qualities and gifts, that she had a unique life history, that no one who had ever lived was just like her. That's the rational side of specialness. But we (some more than others) also have an irrational sense of specialness. It is one of our chief methods of denying death, and the part of our mind whose task it is to mollify death terror generates the irrational belief that we are invulnerable—that unpleasant things like aging and death may be the lot of others but not our lot, that we exist beyond law, beyond human and biological destiny.

Although Elva responded to the purse snatching in ways that *seemed* irrational (for example, proclaiming that she wasn't fit to live on earth, being afraid to leave her house), it was clear that she was *really* suffering from the stripping away of irrationality. That sense of specialness, of being charmed, of being the exception, of being eternally protected—all those self-deceptions that had served her so well suddenly lost their persuasiveness. She saw through her own illusions, and what illusion had shielded now lay before her, bare and terrible.

Her grief wound was now fully exposed. This was the time, I thought, to open it wide, to debride it, and to allow it to heal straight and true.

"When you say you never thought it would happen to you, I know just what you mean," I said. "It's so hard for me, too, to accept that all these afflictions—aging, loss, death—are going to happen to me, too."

Elva nodded, her tightened brow showing that she was surprised at my saying anything personal about myself.

"You must feel that if Albert were alive, this would never have happened to you."

I ignored her flip response that if Albert were alive she wouldn't have been taking those three old hens to lunch. "So the robbery brings home the fact that he's really gone."

Her eyes filled with tears, but I felt I had the right, the mandate, to continue. "You knew that before, I know. But part of you didn't. Now you really know that he's dead. He's not in the yard. He's not out back in the workshop. He's not anywhere. Except in your memories."

Elva was really crying now, and her stubby frame heaved with sobs for several minutes. She had never done that before with me. I sat there and wondered, *"Now what do I do?"* But my instincts luckily led me to what proved to be an inspired gambit. My eyes lit upon her purse—that same ripped-off, much-abused purse; and I said, "Bad luck is one thing, but aren't you asking for it carrying around something that large?" Elva, plucky as ever, did not fail to call attention to my overstuffed pockets and the clutter on the table next to my chair. She pronounced the purse "medium-sized."

"Any larger," I responded, "and you'd need a luggage carrier to move it around."

"Besides," she said, ignoring my jibe, "I need everything in it."

"You've got to be joking! Let's see!"

Getting into the spirit of it, Elva hoisted her purse onto my table, opened its jaws wide, and began to empty it. The first items fetched forth were three empty doggie bags.

"Need two extra ones in case of an emergency?" I asked.

Elva chuckled and continued to disembowel the purse. Together we inspected and discussed each item. Elva conceded that three packets of Kleenex and twelve pens (plus three pencil stubs) were indeed superfluous, but held firm about two bottles of cologne and three hairbrushes, and dismissed, with an imperious flick of her hand, my challenge to her large flashlight, bulky notepads, and huge sheaf of photographs.

We quarreled over everything. The roll of fifty dimes. Three bags of candies (low-calorie, of course). She giggled at my question: "Do you believe, Elva, that the more of these you eat, the thinner you will become?" A plastic sack of old orange peels ("You never know, Elva, when these will come in handy"). A bunch of knitting needles ("Six needles in search of a sweater," I thought). A bag of sourdough starter. Half of a paperback Stephen King novel (Elva threw away sections of pages as she read them: "They weren't worth keeping," she explained). A small stapler ("Elva, this is crazy!"). Three pairs of sunglasses. And, tucked away into the innermost corners, assorted coins, paper clips, nail clippers, pieces of emery board, and some substance that looked suspiciously like lint.

When the great bag had finally yielded all, Elva and I stared in wonderment at the contents set out in rows on my table. We were sorry the bag was empty and that the emptying was over. She turned and smiled, and we looked tenderly at each other. It was an extraordinarily intimate moment. In a way no patient had ever done before, she showed me everything. And I had accepted everything and asked for even more. I followed her into her every nook and crevice, awed that one old woman's purse could serve as a vehicle for both isolation and intimacy: the absolute isolation that is integral to existence and the intimacy that dispels the dread, if not the fact, of isolation.

That was a transforming hour. Our time of intimacy—call it love, call it love making—was redemptive. In that one hour, Elva moved from a position of forsakenness to one of trust. She came alive and was persuaded, once more, of her capacity for intimacy.

I think it was the best hour of therapy I ever gave.

EI CASE FORMULATION—Elva

Like many of us, Elva is invested in being "special," in being immune and invulnerable. Beyond many of us, however, Elva has created a kind of religion around this stature, and the trappings are readily apparent. She is bloated with self-importance, ridiculing toward others, and numb to calamity. She is isolated but magically protected by her husband.

It's not that Elva revels in these aggrandizements—far from it. She is both appalled and tormented by them. Yet she is compelled to engage them, to deflect her obliterating wounds.

Dr. Yalom's task is to offer Elva an alternative to this debilitating plight. He invites her to be more real with him, for example, and more vulnerable. He enables her to grieve for her husband and laugh at her condescending quips. Finally, he helps her to become more comfortable with herself and to relinquish her inflationary props.

Then Elva is robbed, and her world comes crashing down. She is stripped of worth, hope, and even her therapeutic trust. Whereas before she could rely on her illusions to elevate her, now she can see only realities—cold, hard, and annihilating. Dr. Yalom allows Elva to "sit with" these realities and refrains, wisely, from pacifying her.

But then a fundamental shift occurs. Dr. Yalom opens up to her and lets her see his own insecurities about living. He tells her, in effect, that he, too, feels small in many ways and that he, too, is anxiously mortal. This disclosure seems to bolster Elva a bit. It helps her to feel accompanied, contained, and inspired to continue forward.

If Dr. Yalom can make it, she seems to feel, then perhaps she can, too; and if he can risk intimacy with her, then perhaps she is worthy of being intimate with.

The degree to which Elva can feel significant on her own, bereft of her immunities, is eloquently illustrated by the final scene. By challenging her to share the contents of her purse with him, Dr. Yalom helps her to see the absurdity of those contents and the importance, by contrast, of the one who possesses them. What is cash, he asks, in comparison with her value as a person? What are notions, photographs, and bits of memorabilia in comparison with the living relationship they share?

In short, Elva is introduced to her mortality by Dr. Yalom. She is deflated some by this introduction, and hurt, but she is, at the same time, revitalized by it. At long last she can simply be herself, she realizes, without fear that she will lose herself. She can be constrained, flawed, and inept; but she can also find room to soar, to genuinely laugh and love.

AN EXISTENTIAL-SPIRITUAL PERSPECTIVE: THE CASE OF SARA

Paul Bowman

Paul Bowman, Ph.D., is a licensed psychologist in private practice in San Francisco, who has taught at, among other places, John F. Kennedy University, Orinda, California. He was educated at the California Institute of Integral Studies. His clinical and research interests focus upon existential, psychoanalytic, self-psychological, and meditative approaches to growth and change.

While traditional therapies frequently pathologize reports of spiritual transcendence, transpersonal orientations sometimes inflate their significance. By drawing upon the assumptions of existential-phenomenology, Paul Bowman illustrates a productive middle way. This "way" challenges clients to approach their spirituality dialectically—in the ongoing context of their maturation.

One of the defining frontiers of any psychological theory is the dialogue it establishes with religious traditions in general and spiritual experience in particular. *Spiritual experience* is the encounter with one's "ground of being" (Tillich, 1963). It is the moment of self-transcendence where one grapples with and discerns the essential meanings of one's life, one's "place" in the universe, and the values that characterize how one lives. Because these issues are central to the self-reflective life and because they are realized in moments of extraordinary clarity with an urgency and authority all their own, they demand attention in the articulation of any definitive psychological system. The different traditions of psychology are distinguishable in part by the way in which they characterize this ineffable relationship between the psyche and its "ground."

Freudian psychology's emergence out of nineteenth-century science cast it essentially at odds with the religious traditions of its day. Whereas the writings of the American psychologist William James addressed what were basically philosophical questions (James, 1901–02/1987), Freud was a scientist who approached the psyche from a positivist, biomechanical point of view. Within a "scientific" psychology, the nonrational spiritual experience was subordinated to defensive or pathological categories. When viewed as a social institution, religion was a transference en masse of the Oedipal father (Freud, 1930/1973), a defense on a grand scale against the societally repressed. The individual religious experience was similarly reduced to, at best, a regression in service of the ego and, at worst, a psychotic return to the womb.

Self-psychology differs from Freudian drive theory in its emphasis on relationship as the basis for psychological motivation and development (Stolorow, Brandchaft, & Atwood, 1987). The self is established and maintained through its self-object ties, not the control of its instinctual gratifications. Whether archaic and pathological or age appropriate and mature, the need for self-object bonds are unremitting throughout one's life (Kohut, 1984). The spiritual experience is seen as a manifestation of the need for an idealized self-object bond, a self-soothing relationship with one's "ground of being." Though Kohut acknowledged that this need for idealized union can have pathological or defensive manifestations, his theory recognized the legitimacy of a mature relationship to one's spiritual ideal which strengthens and upholds the psychological self.

Jung recognized this same potential for a mature, self-enhancing relationship to the transcendent (Jung, 1938), and with the humanistic and transpersonal movements which followed him, invested it with central importance in his psychological schema. These theories abandoned the traditional psychodynamic view, placing the emphasis, instead, on an expanded developmental model. Psychological growth and change begins at birth and extends to include not only psychological maturity but transcendental experience as well (Maslow, 1971; Wilber, 1977). When the instinctual and relational needs of the person are met and mastered, they give way, under the driving force of an inherent urge for growth, to an encounter with self as spiritual being. Thus spiritual, self-transcendent experience is the end point and natural culmination of a singular process of psychological development.

Each of these models approaches spiritual experience in a unique way and, within its limitations, articulates a particular aspect of this human experience. The psychodynamic theories are adept at identifying the pathological or ego-defensive qualities of the experience. They tend, however, to devalue spirituality as a whole, failing to differentiate the self-transcendent from the regressive—the pre-egoic from the transpersonal, if you will (Wilber, 1980). The growth models, on the other hand, often inflate the importance of ego transcendence, placing it hierarchically above psychological maturity in the developmental sequence. This bias tends to obscure the differences between the defensive, or pathological, aspects of non-ego-based experience and the psychologically sound, and invites the substitution of "spiritual growth" for psychological development. And though self-psychology recognizes the distinction between mature and regressive spirituality, its emphasis on the self-enhancing quality of the self-object relationship minimizes the inherently nonpsychological, self-transcendent aspects of the experience.

Thinkers in the existential tradition have approached this dimension of human experience in a unique, though characteristically varied, fashion. While Kierkegaard was staunchly theistic, elaborating the givens of his "existential" world as a means of clarifying and strengthening his Christian faith (May, Angel, & Ellenberger, 1958), the post-World War II European existentialists approached these same concerns from a decidedly atheistic stance. Common to both, however, and elaborated in the American tradition of existential psychotherapy (May, Angel, & Ellenberger, 1958; Bugental, 1978; Yalom, 1980) is an emphasis on examining the reality of experience as it is lived, a phenomenological approach that attempts to suspend the prejudice of one's beliefs "about" existence and return "to the things themselves." This methodology proves ideal for the encounter with spiritual experience because it strips away both the spirit-inflating bias of the humanistic/transpersonal models and the psychodynamic theories' tendency to reduce and pathologize. Existential therapy is an encounter with the client's experience as it is lived. With its emphasis on process over theory, it is uniquely suited to the exploration of a phenomenon that for any given client, may have self-enhancing, self-transcending, and self-avoiding characteristics.

THE CASE OF SARA

Sara was referred to me by a therapist who knew of my involvement with Buddhist meditation. A student of yoga for many years, Sara had taken up a (meditative) sitting practice with her recent move to the Bay Area. She came to our first session complaining of generalized anxiety and depression. The anxiety was chronic and escalating; the depression was occasional and acute. There was a family history that suggested a predisposition to affective disorders. She was 40 years old and, despite holding a master's degree and having a work history that included professional positions, she was currently underemployed as a department-store clerk. She had impulsively surrendered her previous career to follow her live-in boyfriend to San Francisco and had been unable to find an appropriate job here. In a pattern that was uncomfortably familiar to her, she was angry at again having fallen prey to the demands of a narcissistic man.

Sara was the older of two daughters born to an academic Catholic father and a European Jewish mother. She originally described her mother as having little impact on the family; except during her occasional bouts of depression, she kept up the house and home with little emotional presence. Sara's younger sister was similarly sullen and withdrawn. Her father, on the other hand, was a force to be reckoned with. He was narcissistic and oblivious to the emotional needs of his wife and children, at times actively suppressing their affective display. He was an avid outdoorsman, politically progressive, and involved in many community causes. He set the tone for all the family activities and vacations; conversations around the dinner table always centered upon him; and, with his provocative and daring questions, he was idealized as "cool" and "liberated" by Sara's boyfriends and girlfriends alike. All three women in the family loved and resented him and were unquestioningly drawn into his spell— especially Sara, her father's favorite. The original goals of the therapy, the second in her adult life, were to uncover and work through the bonds that tied her to these types of men and to discern and act upon her own emotional responses to their narcissism.

In the fourth session, just as our work together was getting under way, Sara's life took a dramatically unexpected turn. Her mother was diagnosed with terminal cancer, and she immediately left treatment to travel back to the family home. Two months later, she returned to San Francisco. Her mother was dead, she had no job, and her boyfriend had announced in her absence that he was leaving her. Understandably devastated, this quick succession of losses completely overwhelmed the original issues that brought her into treatment. She was now in crisis, requiring support in the working through both of her grief at her mother's death and the loss of the narcissistic relationship around which her life had formerly revolved. She felt crushed, empty, and, though not suicidal, hopelessly alone. Her only reason for remaining in San Francisco was her therapeutic relationship with me. And in a risk that revealed more about her complete isolation than the strength of our relationship, she chose to stay on, hoping that she would find in therapy the help she needed to rebuild her life.

I became increasingly concerned with Sara's atypical responses to her own grief, if one can aptly use this term in the face of such a confluence of losses. Though she tearfully recounted the last weeks of her mother's suffering, railed against her father's inability to empathize, and was furious at her boyfriend's extraordinarily bad timing, there was something frozen and immobile at the heart of her grief reaction. At times her body would stiffen, her fists would clench, and her eyes would shut tightly. A sob would be choked off in her throat, and, when she opened her eyes moments later, she would be unable or unwilling to recount the thoughts that had prompted the episode. It was clear to us both that her grief was being held in check in the face of some great loss, one that lay deeper than the events of recent weeks. In spite of her knowledge of the therapeutic process and her willingness, in theory, to let her grief reaction run its course, there was a core of affect that she simply could not allow herself to feel: a "dark void" that she had long sensed but fearfully suppressed.

At this point, now several months after Sara's return to therapy, I was uncertain as to how to proceed. Session after session, she would begin to engage the feelings of grief and loss only to draw up short in the same moment of frozen tears. In many ways, her life was moving forward. She had new boyfriends, a challenging new job, and a renewed social life. In therapy, she recognized familiar patterns in these relationships: her disappointment at the needs the man in her life would not address, her rage at him, and a paralyzing fear of abandonment that would force her back into compliant submission. Her transference onto me as someone whose needs she must narcissistically appease was also mobilized. She brought gifts of food and flowers to several sessions, trying to secure the support that she was increasingly dependent upon. But at the emotional core of our work, something remained fixed and unyielding. No amount of empathy, focus on defenses, or exploration of her internal experience would nudge her into the center of her grief. In that "dark void" was an experience of a loss of connection—a loss of self that no amount of trust in me or in the process of therapy could restore.

Sara's Spiritual Experience

Sara had been practicing meditation since moving to San Francisco and was becoming increasingly involved in the activities of several local centers. One had scheduled a retreat with a visiting teacher she had previously worked with and trusted implicitly. Over a two-day retreat with him, something in her capacity to contain her experience of grief profoundly shifted; and, in our next session, she was able to articulate a significantly deeper level of affect and memory. What had transpired that weekend and the material that flowed out from it became the turning point in her therapy.

The schedule of the retreat followed a fairly typical protocol: no conversation, little sleep, simple food, and long hours of focused attention guided by the teacher. Her meditation practice was similarly standard; following the in-and-out flow of her breathing for hours on end and watching with ever-deepening sensitivity as the sensations and thoughts passed into and out of her awareness. She was quickly brought face-to-face with the material that had frequented our weekly sessions, the same emotional "doorway" into her grief that had heretofore remained shut. But in the midst of this meditative environment, and with the gentle encouragement of a warm, compassionate teacher she had long admired, inexplicably, the doorway opened.

Instead of being overwhelmed with grief and loss, Sara's attention was subsumed in a profound state of meditative absorption. Termed *samadhi* in Sanskrit, in Buddhism it is the hallmark of a deepening meditative state, an experience of riveted focus that leaves one relaxed, unresistant to the ongoing flow of internal perception, and attentively poised. She felt deeply at peace, emotionally safe, and yet intimately engaged with the stream of memory and insights that were later to be therapeutically "unpacked." But during those two days, the emotional significance of her memories was not important to her. Instead, she was experiencing an emotional safety and anxiety-free openness that was her greatest achievement in self-acceptance to date. Within this "spiritual" context, she had realized a capacity to bear witness to her psychological process as never before, and with this new perspective she returned to psychotherapy.

In the weeks and months that followed, she returned regularly to this store of material, each time with a greater exposure to its emotional impact. What she recovered was a host of disavowed memories of her mother. From her earliest days, she recalled her mother's episodic withdrawals, not only into depression but into mania, as well. A survivor of the Holocaust that claimed nearly every other member of her family, Sara's mother entered into her marriage in a fragile emotional state. Sara's father truly loved his wife and would try to please her, but he was helpless to affect her wild mood swings. Following both of her pregnancies, she was engulfed in postpartum depressions and was hospitalized and given electroshock therapy. She would periodically cycle in and out of mania. Her husband would look on helplessly as she acted out self-destructive fantasies. During one manic episode, Sara's mother rented storefront space and filled it with odds and ends purchased at garage sales. Sara remembers the look of despondency on her mother's face as the impact of what she had done began to sink in.

It was in the face of this emotional volatility that Sara turned from her mother to her father for emotional support. Sara's initial attempts to bond with her mother—the earliest postpartum links—were thwarted by her mother's emotional preoccupations. Sara's "dark void" was probably connected to these early experiences of dependency and disconnection—an utterly overwhelming emptiness that threatened to snuff out her psychological life. After countless failures to bond with her mother, she turned to her father, a stable presence who, though exacting a narcissistic price, was a consistent alternative to her mother's abandonments.

Over the next two years, Sara gradually came to terms with and worked through the emotional dilemmas of these early relationships. She put in context the helplessness and rage she felt at her dependency on narcissistic men and the paralyzing fear that arose at the thought of leaving them. She came to see that her father's control of her mother's ebullience was his own fear of her manias; how, indeed, every member of the family had conspired to maintain her mother's stability, often at the expense of their own emotional lives. She further recognized that her initial hopes for a consistent and supportive emotional relationship were correct and trustworthy, and she established a marriage with a man who was capable of attending to her needs as well as his own.

Though an elaborated account would be too extensive for this summary, it is fair to say that Sara's therapy ended after this period with her work largely completed. Her grieving was resolved, her potential for intimacy well-established, her abandonment traumas well-remembered, and the frustrations with the dependent relationship style developed with her father largely worked through.

Formulations and Theoretical Considerations

What, then, are we to conclude about the meditative experience that had such an impact on Sara's therapeutic progress? This experience could be viewed in many different ways depending on the theoretical perspectives. From a drive/conflict perspective, for example, Sara's *samadhi* experience might be interpreted as largely defensive. At the very least, it would be seen as an isolation of affect, a regression in service of the ego which split off her emotional responses in order to minimize the ego-threatening impact of a flood of childhood memory. The features of her psychological state in the months following the experience corroborate this interpretation, for as she gradually returned in therapy to the memories and insights she had so comfortably observed during the retreat, she was frequently stunned by their emotional impact.

While the drive/conflict model has its clinical relevance, it nevertheless fails to address key features of her experience. Most important, the ego-sustaining effects of Sara's "defensive" maneuver were enduring. The "regression in service of the ego" is a state-specific event, with the defenses effectively eliminating the conscious threat only so long as the material is relegated to the unconscious. When the isolation of affect breaks down, the ego is once again subject to being overwhelmed. Sara, however, experienced a fundamental change in her orientation toward her childhood material that helped her to integrate the emotional experiences she had previously split off. For the months of working through that followed, she remained unafraid of her formerly ego-threatening memories. Her anxiety was largely gone, and she was able to experience emotions that she previously could not have tolerated. Something fundamental had been re-organized in her psyche, something that carried forward beyond the state-specific moments of the meditation.

The self-psychological view offers a similarly plausible, yet limited, interpretation. A case can be made that Sara's spiritual experience was a successful internalization of the idealized self-object relationship. In the presence of an idealized teacher, she found the strength to retrieve her previously disavowed memories, soothed by the presence of a man who encouraged her, and who was later internalized as her own unique meditative self-object. Though it could be noted that Sara turned to this idealized figure at a time of therapeutic impasse—a split between the "good" soothing teacher and the "bad" frustrating therapist—the impact of the experience on her therapy was nevertheless productive. Over the months of our ongoing work, she drew upon this newly internalized self-soothing capacity, making it possible to go forward with the uncovering aspects of therapy as internal self-structure was rebuilt.

Sara's experience does not perfectly fit this model either, however. For Kohut, the self-restorative, "structure-building" experiences take place gradually and incrementally. Whether through the course of years of childhood development or the incremental accretions of the psychotherapeutic process, the "transmuting internalizations" that build self-structure are only gradually internalized. For Sara, on the other hand, something profoundly life-changing had occurred over a single weekend. Though it could be said that this moment was the outcome of the months of therapeutic and meditative labor that had come before, this was not, in any conventional sense, a "therapeutic" event. It was, rather, a "spiritual" moment, one that made use of capacities to contain her experience that were beyond the resources of her ego.

From the vantage point of the humanistic and transpersonal perspectives, Sara's experience was nothing short of a definitive developmental achievement. It was a "peak experience," which marked Sara's recognition of her identity at a transpersonal level (Maslow, 1971). Though Sara was comfortable with this perspective, and while her meditation teacher willingly characterized her experience in such terms, the model does little to address the uniquely psychological ramifications of the experience. Far from being the culmination of her developmental process, this event occurred very early in our therapeutic work. It was the necessary establishment of a psychological capacity to tolerate a greater range and magnitude of emotions. Her meditative experience was clearly a *trans-egoic* event, therefore, which, in its own right, is not adequately reducible to a *pre-egoic* pathological interpretation. But it is equally important to stress the personal elements within such transpersonal events. For Sara, in spite of the "spiritual" achievement of being able to bear meditative witness to her own internal process, there was much psychological work still to be done.

From the outset, my work with Sara was existential in style; i.e., it emphasized process and downplayed theoretical considerations in order to let her experience reveal its own particular meaning. Returning after her mother's death in a state of crisis, she was initially stabilized by an empathic articulation of her grief. Then, when her progress was halted by material she could not face, she turned to her meditation practice for support, finding a new perspective on herself there, one that enhanced her ability to tolerate the disavowed emotions. The therapy that followed was a simple elaboration and working through of childhood material. Yet, as she herself had intuited when she sought out a therapist who would be sensitive to her meditative practice, this elaboration initially required a reorienting of her sense of self in relation to the traumata.

From the latter formulation, then, I believe one can discern the existential approach to working with spiritual experience. Central is the emphasis on elucidating the client's personal meaning over a reifying adherence to a theory or a psychological belief. In lieu of jumping to theoretical conclusions about the defensive or developmental significance of her spiritual experience, the focus of our work stayed on how *Sara* experienced it. We concentrated on how her capacity to tolerate painful emotions was enhanced by the meditation rather than on the legitimacy of meditative experience itself. Sara's meditative experience was profound and life-changing in its own right. And though the religious literature has long insisted that spiritual experiences of this kind are ultimately ineffable, I believe it is nevertheless a compelling and necessary task to "unpack" their meaning psychologically. What made this articulation *existential* was the attempt to remain open to the impact of her experience on all levels—from the pathological to the transcendent, the mundane to the sublime.

For Sara, meditatively engaging her "ground of being" enabled her to return to her psychological world strengthened and encouraged. It facilitated a process of self-recovery and healing that was otherwise unavailable. Within the existential view, spiritual experience may serve a variety of functions, from the developmental to the avoidant and defensive. What marks the essential character of this orientation is its emphasis on attending to the various meanings of each individual's encounter with his or her own "ground of being."

REFERENCES

Bugental, J. (1978). *Psychotherapy and process: The fundamentals of an existential-humanistic approach.* Menlo Park, CA: Addison-Wesley.

Freud, S. (1930/1973). Civilization and its discontents. In *The standard edition of the complete psychological works of Sigmund Freud, Vol. 21.* New York: International Universities Press.

James, W. (1901–02/1987). *William James: Writings 1902–1910.* New York: Viking.

Jung, C. G. (1938). *Psychology and religion.* New Haven: Yale University Press.

Kohut, H. (1984). *How does analysis cure.* Chicago: University of Chicago Press.

Maslow, A. (1971). *The farther reaches of human nature.* New York: Viking.

May, R., Angel, E., & Ellenberger, H. (Eds.). (1958). *Existence: A new dimension in psychiatry and psychology.* New York: Basic Books.

Stolorow, R., Brandchaft, B., & Atwood, G. (1987). *Psychoanalytic treatment: An intersubjective approach.* Hillsdale, NJ: The Analytic Press.

Tillich, P. (1963). *Morality and beyond.* New York: Harper & Row.

Wilber, K. (1977). *The spectrum of consciousness.* Wheaton IL.: Quest.

Wilber, K. (1980). The pre/trans fallacy, *Revision, 3* (2).

Yalom, I. (1980). *Existential psychotherapy.* New York: Basic Books.

EI CASE FORMULATION—Sara

This case is integrative on at least two fronts—its approach to spirituality and its approach to therapy.

With regard to spirituality, three modalities are considered—the analytic, the transpersonal, and the existential.

While the analytic tends to minimize and the transpersonal to magnify spiritual experience, according to Dr. Bowman, the existential steers midway in between. In other words, it holds spirituality in *suspense,* both appreciating and bracketing its role.

Sara is hyperconstricted when she enters therapy with Dr. Bowman. She is depressed, anxious, and dependent on dysfunctional men. Ostensibly, this constriction stems from her father, who controlled and dominated her. At a deeper level, however, it originated with her mother's volatile, psychotic state.

The facts of this case, however, are not as important as Sara's *experience* of the facts, and this is Dr. Bowman's focus. He encourages her meditation practice, for example, and empathically facilitates her disclosures. He attunes to the *process* of her communications and restricts discussion of their content. On the other hand, he also senses when content discussions are appropriate to contain her overpowering fears.

Gradually, Dr. Bowman invites Sara to expand experientially, to conceive of herself beyond her lover's (and father's) control. He encourages her to express thoughts and feelings about disconnecting, asserting, and making it on her own.

But then her mother dies, and the deepest layers of her anxieties are laid bare. She feels lost, adrift, and bathed in a "dark void." Whereas before she feared social independence, she now fears *cosmic* independence—from structures, boundaries, every kind of constraint!

By invoking the actual with Sara, Dr. Bowman is able to bring her to the brink of these anxieties, but not into their core. Even vivifying her resistance does not budge her, although it eventually may have, after a protracted period. It is only through her meditative sitting practice that she is able to confront her chaotic dreads and to deepen, as a result, her capacity to bear those dreads.

The sitting practice, therefore, initiates a process for Sarah—it clears a space; but it does not complete her work. This is left to the long hours in therapy, tirelessly reexperiencing and deepening her meditative discoveries and applying them to her life.

In sum, Dr. Bowman addresses Sara's sitting practice as she lives and experiences it—and neither minimizes nor glorifies it. He supplements his own approach with it because he realizes its usefulness to Sara; but it does not replace his own experiential work with her. To the contrary, he views it as complementary to that work. It provides more time for her to be present to herself, to deepen her observations, and to increase her tolerance for pain. There are at least three general differences, however, between the sitting practice and therapy: (1) it involves less interpersonal intimacy; (2) it places less emphasis on acting experiences out; and (3) it places less value on the meaning-contexts or implications of one's observations.

THE INNER SENSE OF THE CHILD: THE CASE OF JOEY

Steve Curtin

Steve Curtin, Ph.D., is a psychologist and former elementary school teacher. Dr. Curtin is a graduate of Saybrook Institute, where he trained with James Bugental, and is a member of the American and California Psychological associations. Dr. Curtin is currently writing a book on existential therapy with children.

One way to help children make informed and adaptive choices, according to Steve Curtin, is to heighten their subjective sense of self. This helps them to shift from detached and impersonal styles of behavior to engaged and "uniquely personal" dispositions. The challenging case of Joey, Dr. Curtin proposes, is a cogent demonstration of his view.

What is an "existential child case"? If I search for such a case in my notes, I cannot find one. Nowhere is there a note that starts with "he/she is struggling to discover his/her subjective self." Yet, as I think about individual child clients that I have seen, most of them were struggling with that very issue. Many child victims of abuse have learned to numb themselves. This helps them forget physical and emotional trauma. Other children have lived in families where they were actually punished for exposing internal feelings and experiences. Thus children can be taught not to attend to internal experience.

Every child struggles with the dialectic involved in sorting out internal cues from external ones. "Did you really want that toy, or did you want it because your brother had it first?" This is a common parental question, to which most children reply, "I don't know." Sometimes parents are relieved that the child has no pressing need or wish. Others require the child to search further within, to try harder to know the meaning of their actions.

The focus of the existential therapeutic process with children is to heighten their subjective experiences of themselves. This process leads to the discovery of *meaning* in children's behavior, meaning of which they may have limited awareness.

To the extent that subjective experiences are brought to awareness in the relationship with the therapist, the child becomes cognizant of his/her "inward sense" (Bugental, 1978). With this awareness, the child has some experience of *choosing* his/her behavior, what Bugental (1978) calls "subjective sovereignty." For the child, the awareness of choice often results in a sense of empowerment. For example, a child who flees conflict has a different felt experience if he/she experiences him/herself as *choosing* to run away instead of seeing the environment as causing him/her to run away.

There is no "perfect" case. Every therapeutic encounter brings with it a multitude of interdependent factors that muddy the waters of therapeutic progress. Any one session or fragment of a session can be viewed in many ways. In the case that follows, the therapist's attention is directed toward facilitating the child's awareness of internal feeling, and sensations. None of the techniques used in existential therapy are exclusive to one school of therapy. As Rollo May (1983) states, "Existential analysis is a way of understanding human existence rather than a system of 'how to's'" (p. 151). Thus the therapist uses strategies that help the child shift from "detached, impersonal statements [or behavior]" to "more emotional and uniquely personal elements" (Bugental, 1987, p. 13).

THE CASE OF JOEY

This case involves a 3-year-old child who was brought in by his mother because of her concern that he was not adjusting well to his parents' separation.[1] Joey was expressive, intelligent, and artistic. His presenting complaints included soiling his pants at preschool, wetting his bed nightly, masturbating when playing alone, acting aggressive with other children, and being inappropriately affectionate with adults other than his parents.

In cases like Joey's, there is a natural tendency to focus on getting answers to the factual questions commonly posed by the judicial system. The need to obtain information for purposes of determining custody was the primary reason for the referral. There was much consternation on the part of the parents and the court that the child's developmental age made most factual content questionable. The hope of the court was that a therapist might be able to sort out fact from fiction in this case.

When I met this child, he was clinging to his mother and would not separate from her. He sat in a corner of my office and watched me from a distance. As I directed his attention to the surrounding games, puppets, toys, and art material, he showed little response. He huddled close to his mother's side and watched me. His mother prompted him to play with the toys, but to no avail.

In his art of therapy courses, James Bugental cautions therapists to take small steps. In the context of child therapy, "small steps" involves engaging the child in the familiar. In the office, many objects (games, puppets, toys, books) are familiar to children. Children are drawn to these objects and use them without prompting. Their natural curiosity begins the engagement process. With Joey, these objects provided a means of establishing his presence in the room. Therapy began when he was able to separate his attention from avoiding being there to something in the room. Often the very presence of the therapist, a stranger to the child, prevents the child from being in the room. Familiar objects can begin to focus the child on the therapeutic space.

To meet Joey, I began to place puppets on the couch next to him. At first he ignored them. As I moved the puppets, nodding heads and wiggling arms, he looked at them from the corner of his eye. Often the initial action of such children is to push the puppets away, and that was Joey's response. This action can evoke several responses in the therapist. In this case, I chose to deepen my presence by making a noise of surprise and pushing the puppets back. After several pushes, Joey picked up two of the puppets and had them fight with one another. The struggle between the puppets was half-hearted and brief. Following this action, he sank further into his mother's side and hid from me.

Quietly, I asked if he was hiding from the fighting or from something else. His response was to kick the puppets onto the floor. My response was, "Oh, it has to do with the puppets. Is it what they did, or is it something else about them?" Joey turned further away from me. I got some plain paper and colored pens. He looked at the pens with obvious interest. As he reached for them, I asked him to draw something about the puppets. He made a number of marks on the paper with the black and the red pens. When asked to talk about the drawing, he described it as "the mommy bunny [nursing] the baby bunny." He then presented the drawing to his mother. I asked him, "How's the baby bunny feeling?" "Good." "What does the baby bunny feel about the puppets?" "Bad!" "What kind of bad?" His response was to curl up on the couch in the fetal position.

By the next session, Joey was able to walk to my office from the waiting room unattended by his mother. He asked to check on her frequently, but he always returned from the waiting room without prompting. Much of his play in this session was exploratory. He opened all the cabinets and touched everything. He picked things up and played mostly with the objects that were familiar to him. When he found something unfamiliar, he attempted to discover its properties on his own. He made no attempt to engage me directly and clearly avoided asking me for help in identifying the unfamiliar objects.

In our third session, he spontaneously placed all the puppets other than the wolf in a corner and hid there with them. As he cowered there, I asked him to tell me what was happening. He pointed to the wolf puppet and said, "That's the big bad wolf!" I asked him what he felt about the wolf. He visibly shivered. Speaking about the other puppets and him, I said, "You all look scared. Is anyone *not* afraid of the wolf?" He got a female adult doll from the toy basket and placed it on the floor between the wolf and the hiding spot. He continued to shiver. "You still look scared," I said. He nodded and left the room again to check on his mother. Upon returning this time, he turned his attention to the dollhouse.

All of my focus with thematic material is to follow the client's lead. It is like placing the rails down as quickly as the child lays the railroad ties. As a stronger alliance develops, it is possible to stimulate further exploration of thematic elements. With Joey in this early stage of therapy, some limited interventions toward diverging or expanding were possible.

Later in the third session, Joey played with the dollhouse. He used only the adult female doll and a boy doll. The play was not remarkable other than that the two dolls were inseparable. His play was quiet, and the drawing he made afterward consisted of lines with no description. Joey's movement in this session indicated his need to find a way to confront his fear. Rather than focusing on why he is afraid and attempting to allay those fears, the existential approach is to focus on his internal attempts to come to grips with these fears. Living involves fear. It is what we do with our fear, not necessarily what it is, that sets up lifelong patterns and habits. Existential therapy focuses on the *experience* of the fear rather than on its content. Avoiding the content trap allows the therapist to focus on the larger dilemma of how this or any child will cope with the fears present in any lived experience.

During the sessions that followed, the "big bad wolf" was always present. Dolls, puppets, and Joey were all afraid of the wolf. The child felt vulnerable all the time. Therapeutic efforts were made to focus Joey on the *experience* of fear rather than on *what* was fearful. "Interpersonal press" (Bugental, 1987) was used to influence the child to try on a variety of "personal" resolutions to his crisis rather than restrict his search to the first resolution that offered relief. Emphasis was placed on reflecting back to Joey his human predicament, with increased attention on the strategies he used in attempting to contain his fear.

The evolving theme for Joey was how he would attempt to control his fear of extinction. Over time, Joey moved from relying on external forces to finding internal forces. Thus in the initial play, Joey struggled to have various puppets, dolls, and the therapist control the wolf.

At times, Joey was content with each of these external strategies. In one session, a puppet was made into a judge, and the wolf retreated. In another session, a doll became a police officer and killed the wolf. In the next session, the wolf returned, and Joey was forced to confront the wolf on his own. When he failed, he sought protection from a maternal doll and left the session sucking his thumb.

In this kind of play the child identifies individuals in his real world whom he expects to protect him. These may include his mother, his grandparents, officers of the court, uncles, or other adults from the child's daily life (perhaps father's new companion, the mail carrier, a neighbor, or friends of his parents). Reliance on these external forces provides temporary relief.

After four months of weekly therapy and a series of sessions focused on flight (using the dolls to act out moving out of state), a new strategy emerged. Joey split his self into three figures. One of the dolls became the "real Joey." This doll was a twin of another doll except that the other one had a few more scratches. This second doll he named the "other Joey." This doll was always given to the father doll when visitation was reenacted. The third doll was a girl doll whom Joey named after a real-life friend, Amy. Amy was not afraid of the wolf and was able to yell and confront it. Amy and the "real Joey" were constant companions.

The therapeutic effort was aimed at heightening Joey's experience of this splitting up of the self. Each time this strategy was acted out in the play, I explored with Joey how each of the facets of the triad felt inside as events moved forward. In order to clarify with Joey the advantages and disadvantages of splitting, I attempted to elicit from him what it was like to feel separate from the others in the triad.

The Amy doll, meanwhile, yelled at the wolf each time he came to take the "other Joey." Amy tried to protect the "other Joey" as the "real Joey" watched. In each session, I pressed Joey to describe what it was like for the Amy doll to confront the wolf. He would describe feelings of anger and hostility toward the wolf. The power of these feelings would often be described with clenched fists and angry facial expressions. Joey could sense the energy in his hands and face. It made these body parts solid—"like rocks that can hurt but can't break," as Joey put it.

The "other Joey" was frequently described as "holding" the fear. He was described as a fugitive from danger (external and internal). He did not want to feel anything except safe. This "safe feeling" was felt when the wolf was vanquished. At the same time however, Joey described the "other Joey" as feeling nervous about his safety, not quite assured.

The "real Joey" doll was described as a *watcher* who often exhorted the Amy doll to express anger at the wolf. From a distant and detached place, the "real Joey" was feeling anger while being protected from the threat the wolf symbolized.

Over the next three months, Joey continued to alternate between the triad and adult figures. Slowly the "real Joey" doll joined the Amy doll in confronting the wolf. It was always Amy, however, who initiated the confrontation. Over time, the difference between the experience of the "real Joey" and "Amy" diminished. The attempts to use adult figures (the "judge" and "mother" dolls) to contain the wolf diminished in frequency as "real Joey" and "Amy" merged.

I pressed Joey to experience the "judge" and "mother." Role-playing these figures increased his sense of what it feels like to *be* them. In the role-play, he felt "taller" and had more resources (such as calling the policeman!) to cope with his feelings of fear. Joey talked about what he would do when he got "bigger" (*bigness* represented a state of fearlessness).

In the next series of sessions, Joey used the experience of *bigness* to make his own attempt to control the wolf. In one session, he placed the wolf in a jail he had made of fences and placed army men outside the enclosure. The wolf broke free. In another session, Joey took a rock, stoned the wolf, placed the wolf in the garbage can, and announced that it was dead "for good." When he left the session, the wolf was still in the trash. This effort to control the wolf directly was repeated over several sessions.

With each session, Joey displayed less energy in the process of killing and throwing away the wolf and took less time doing it. More of his energy was directed toward playing with the dollhouse and with other figures. His focus turned toward the "family" of dolls, who acted out daily tasks and events. He made drawings that reflected an interest in the emerging self. The drawings were primitive, consisting primarily of lines and spirals, but Joey identified himself, and occasionally his mother or a friend, in these drawings, sometimes paired with hearts or flowers. He also made drawings that he labeled the "mean dad." These drawings had only one figure in them.

Up to this point, Joey's fear was projected onto the toys and drawings. In the next series of sessions, he began to act out containing the fears in several skits. The first of these skits involved "hearing a noise outside the door of the office." First he hid, then we slowly opened the door and searched the office building for the "big bad wolf" or the "mean dad." This search was extensive, and Joey was relieved when the wolf was not found. The emphasis was placed on the strategy of finding "safe" places.

With this change in strategy, Joey became actively involved in containing his fear. His whole being—body and mind—was engaged in this struggle. The focus was on *real time*. The threat was in the here and how. The sessions seemed longer as the child tried out his strategies in the moment. Now the therapeutic effort was toward Joey's experience with these individuals. Paraphrasing and gentle challenges were used to get Joey into what it felt like to display his real feelings and needs with three powerful people: the dad, the mom, and the judge.

This process was seen when Joey devised a skit that involved using the phone to call the judge. One significant theme was consistently present in these conversations: He was telling the truth. He said, for example, "My dad really is mean." The effort was directed toward establishing that his word or perceptions had validity. Joey's inherent need to be validated slowly outweighed the other strategies. Joey told the judge secrets that he thought would make the judge jail the father. The child was using the strategy of "telling the truth" to gain protection from the authority figure.

During this same series of sessions, a "ghost dad" emerged in the boy's drawings and in his play with the dollhouse. This imaginary dad made the "family" acceptable. In the mind of the child, there had to be a "dad" in order to have a "real family." In the process, the three dolls ("real Joey," "other Joey," and Amy) became modified. "Real Joey" and Amy became siblings who lived with the mother and father.

"Other Joey" was present only when contact with "mean dad" occurred. "Other Joey" was becoming an artifact. Joey described him as "just there." It appeared, from Joey's description, that both "mean dad" and "other Joey" were not felt in the body but were in the head, as memories.

With his emerging inner strength, Joey shifted his attention from the intrapersonal to the interpersonal world. We saw this child start with hoping that forces in the material world would protect him. Over time, he turned to his own personal resources. Initially, these resources were fragmented and detached from the self, but as he gained confidence, he developed strategies that reflected greater personal power. Finally, he voiced his intentions to the others in his world. He finally saw himself as an agent for change in his world rather than a helpless figure.

While Joey was able to change in many positive ways, the factual needs of the court were not met. When I met Joey, he was difficult to engage. Using familiar objects with attention to mirroring his actions, I was able to forge an alliance. As Joey demonstrated his strategies for coping with his fear, I pressed him to continue the search process. His willingness to share the search process with me allowed for a deeper appreciation of Joey's experience. Included in that experience were Joey's feelings, strategies, and worldview. Being with Joey or with any child in that deeply felt experience allows the therapist to model a commitment to action (i.e., trying out strategies). Joey's journey from external to internal resources and his newly developed courage represented an effective use of the model provided by the therapist. In his willingness to voice *his* needs, it was clear that Joey was acting intentionally (Bugental, 1987). Put simply, Joey's therapeutic efforts led to expanded awareness of his hopes, dreams, and wishes coupled with the courage to voice them to the court and to his parents.

NOTE

1. Some changes were made to protect the identity of the child. Also, the therapeutic contact with this child extended over several years and involved more material than presented here.

REFERENCES

Bugental, J. F. T. (1978). *Psychotherapy and process.* Reading, MA: Addison-Wesley.
Bugental, J. F. T. (1987). *The art of the psychotherapist.* New York: Norton.
May, R. (1983). *The discovery of being.* New York: Norton.

EI CASE FORMULATION—Joey

Child therapy too often caters to adult needs and forgets the needs of the child. The child's subjectivity is considered peripheral in such instances, measurable behaviors indispensable.

In this case, Dr. Curtin describes a subject-centered, step-by-step approach to child therapy. Through play, metaphor, and encounter, Dr. Curtin helps Joey to experience himself, to immerse himself in his wounds, and to find the capacity for overcoming these wounds.

Joey feels hyperconstricted, we find—abused, minimized, and exposed. His father appears to be the catalyst for these perceptions, but they are suffused throughout Joey's world. His expansive acting out—bedwetting, soiling, acting aggressively, and so on—may be ways to counter these helpless feelings and attract the support he requires.

Dr. Curtin cultivates an atmosphere of gentle challenge for Joey. The approach he takes, the games he offers, and the creativity he encourages all bespeak opportunities for Joey's self-renewal.

By allowing Joey to take the lead in play acting and by reflecting his experiences back to him, Dr. Curtin helps Joey to look at his fears—such as the "big bad wolf"—and find ways to redress those fears. As his alliance with Joey strengthens, Dr. Curtin facilitates ever deeper explorations with him, drawing him supportively into his terror. Each step of the way, Dr. Curtin stays with Joey's experience and keeps him focused on that experience. He avoids digressive interpretations that could divert Joey from his engagement.

Slowly, by mobilizing an assortment of characters within himself, Joey is able to confront the wolf. The "real Joey," for example, gradually asserts himself as the Amy doll inspires him to risk. Through the Amy doll, Joey is able to confront what he had formerly found unmanageable—yelling at the wolf—and to empower himself in other areas of his life. The "judge" and "mother" dolls also help him to experience this bigness and the real-life strength that they offer to him.

In the final stages of his therapy, Joey is able to talk about his fears directly ("My dad really is mean") and directly explore his role in restraining his father.

In short, Dr. Curtin has been able to methodically invoke the actual with Joey. By cultivating an atmosphere of trust, encouraging creative play, and raising Joey's consciousness of his experience, Dr. Curtin facilitated the resources for Joey to expand. The meaning created out of this expansion proved pivotal, ultimately elevating Joey from his victimization.

DIALOGICAL (BUBERIAN) THERAPY: THE CASE OF DAWN

Maurice Friedman

Maurice Friedman, Ph.D., is codirector of the Institute for Dialogical Therapy and professor emeritus of religion, philosophy, and comparative literature at San Diego State University. He is one of the leading existential scholars in America and author of The Worlds of Existentialism, The Healing Dialogue in Psychotherapy, Dialogue and the Human Image, Religion and Psychology, *and numerous studies of the philosopher Martin Buber.*

Maurice Friedman's case study of Dawn demonstrates the healing quality of Martin Buber's I-thou relationship. For Buber, the I-thou relationship is the ability to be open and present to another while remaining open and present to oneself. This "healing through meeting," as Friedman views it, fosters genuineness, spontaneity, and trust. Dawn is able to confirm these outcomes following her therapy with Dr. Friedman.

> *All real living is meeting.*
> —MARTIN BUBER, *I and Thou*

In my book *The Worlds of Existentialism* (Friedman, 1991), I point to a crucial and still not sufficiently recognized issue that divides existentialists: whether the *self* is seen as central, with the relation between selves a dimension of the self, or whether the *relation itself* is seen as central, with the self coming into being precisely through that relation.*

This same issue carries over into existential psychotherapy. Whereas many existential psychotherapists see the self as the touchstone of reality, even while recognizing the world of intersubjectivity, as does Sartre (M. S. Friedman, 1991, pp. 186–200) or that *Dasein ist Mitsein,*[†] as does Heidegger (M. S. Friedman, 1991, pp. 180–186), the dialogical psychotherapist starts with the "between" as the touchstone of reality.

By dialogical psychotherapy, we[‡] mean a therapy that centers on the *meeting* between the therapist and his or her client or family as the central healing mode, whatever analysis, role playing, or other therapeutic techniques or activities may also enter in. If the psychoanalyst is seen as an indispensable midwife in bringing up material from the unconscious to the conscious, this is not yet "healing through meeting." Only when it is recognized that everything that takes place within therapy—free association, dreams, silence, pain, anguish—takes place as a reflection of the vital relationship between therapist and patient do we have what may properly be called *dialogical psychotherapy.*

What is crucial is not the skill of the therapist but, rather, what takes place between the therapist and the client and between the client and other people—what my wife, Aleene Friedman, calls *the healing partnership* (A. M. Friedman, 1992). Only as a partner can a person be perceived as an existing wholeness. To become aware of a person, Buber (1988, p. 70) points out, means to perceive his or her wholeness as a person defined by spirit; to perceive the dynamic center that stamps on all utterances, actions, and attitudes the recognizable sign of uniqueness. Such an awareness is impossible if, and as long as, the other is for me the detached object of my observation, for that person will not thus yield his or her wholeness and its center. It is possible only when he or she becomes present for me in genuine dialogue.

The psychological is only the accompaniment of the dialogue between person and person. What is essential is not what goes on within the minds of the partners in a relationship but what happens *between* them. For this reason, Buber is unalterably opposed to that psychologism that wishes to remove the reality of relationship into the separate psyches of the participants. "The inmost growth of the self does not take place, as people like to suppose today," writes Buber, "through our relationship to ourselves, but through being made present by the other and knowing that we are

---

*This is a point I expanded upon in my recent essay, "Intersubjectivity in Husserl, Sartre, Heidegger, and Buber" (Friedman, 1993).

[†]Literally translated: "To exist is to be with others."

[‡]By *we,* I mean all those who associate themselves with dialogical psychotherapy and, in particular, the members of the Institute for Dialogical Psychotherapy in San Diego, founded and codirected by James DeLeo, Richard Hycner, and myself. The institute, now in its tenth year, has a two-year training program that is now in its fifth year. I am grateful to Drs. DeLeo and Hycner for helpful suggestions in revising this case study.

made present by him" (Buber, 1988, p. 61). Being made present as a person is the heart of what Buber calls *confirmation.*

Confirmation is interhuman, but it is not simply social or interpersonal, for unless one is confirmed in one's uniqueness as the person one can become, one is only seemingly confirmed. The confirmation of the other must include an actual experiencing of the other side of the relationship—a bold imaginative swinging "with the intensest stirring of one's being" into the life of the other so that one can, to some extent, imagine quite concretely what another is feeling, thinking, and knowing and add something of one's own will to what is thus apprehended (Buber, 1988, p. 60). This *inclusion,* or "imagining the real," does not abolish the basic distance between oneself and the other. It does not mean, at any point, that one gives up the ground of one's own concreteness, ceases to see through one's own eyes, or loses one's own "touchstone of reality." Yet at the same time one swings over into the life of the person one confronts, through whom alone one can make her present in her wholeness, unity, and uniqueness.

Inclusion, or imagining the real, must be distinguished from that empathy that goes to the other side of the relationship and that identification that remains on one's own side and cannot go over to the other. True confirmation means precisely that *I* confirm *you* in your uniqueness and that I do so from the ground of my uniqueness as a really "other" person. Only inclusion can confirm another because only inclusion really grasps the other in his or her otherness and brings that other into relationship to oneself. Only inclusion can produce that confirmation by the therapist that begins to replace the disconfirmation that the patient has experienced in family and community. This confirmation comes from understanding the patient from within and from going beyond this, as Hans Trüb suggests, to that second stage when the demand of the community is placed on the patient (Friedman, 1991, pp. 497–505). This demand enables the patient to go back into dialogue with those from whom he or she has been cut off.

THE CASE OF DAWN

After taking part in a therapy group that I co-facilitated, Dawn, a 40-year old Caucasian woman, came to see me for four years in individual and couples therapy. Dawn complained that Bob, her husband of ten years, never talked to her but spent his hours at home watching television and that he did not do his share of taking care of the children when she was home or baby sitting when she went to graduate school. She told me of a time when she broke the television set in a fit of anger and Bob simply replaced it. Dawn's response to this troubled, tense family atmosphere was to show signs of depression: She lost interest in and enjoyment of sex, her concentration and sleep were disturbed, she displayed low energy, and she had periods of sadness. The flat affect with which she told me how her children were having night terrors clearly indicated the depth of her depression and its impact upon her family.

In order that Dawn might attain some degree of symptom relief, I referred her to a psychiatrist who gave her antidepressants. With the support of our therapy and the help of the antidepressants, the intensity of her symptoms subsided. In time, it became clear that her current tense family atmosphere was only the immediate pre-cipitating factor in her depression. Its deeper roots were found to lie in her family of origin, particularly her troubled, ambivalent relationship to her father. Her father's rages frequently resulted in the physical abuse of Dawn and her mother, abuse that he seemed unable to stop. As our therapeutic dialogue unfolded, Dawn came to under-stand that she felt the need to be asexual in order to protect herself from her father's implicit sexual interest in her. At the same time, Dawn's father had valued boys over girls as a sign of his own manliness, with the result that Dawn did not value being a girl.

Dawn experienced a good deal of rivalry with her younger sister, who played the feminine, seductive role in opposition to Dawn's "tomboy," though by no means masculine, stance. Dawn's mother had a positive relationship with Dawn's sister pre-cisely because she was very feminine and flirtatious. During the girls' high school years, Dawn's mother had pulled one of Dawn's old papers out of her drawer and told her sister to submit it in her own name. Dawn's sister not only received an A for this paper but won a statewide prize for it. When Dawn protested, her whole family came down on her, telling her that she was being selfish.

What struck me most forcefully about Dawn was the enormous contrast between her evident intellectual superiority and her inner sense of her self. Dawn's need to compare herself with others seemed to stem from a basic distrust in her relationships with others. Only this can account for the veritable split between Dawn as an active, well-functioning person on the outside and Dawn as the inferior person that she saw herself as being.

My therapeutic goals grew out of my dialogical approach to the therapy that was taking place between Dawn and myself. At first I tried to help Dawn and Bob com-municate by first seeing Dawn alone and then seeing Dawn and Bob together. At the same time, I was helping Dawn to stand up for her own *entitlement,* a term I take from Ivan Boszormenyi-Nagy's contextual therapy (Boszormenyi-Nagy & Krasner, 1986). After Bob moved out, at Dawn's request, I saw my task as helping Dawn adjust and understand her circumstances. This included working on overcoming her depression and helping her to get into a more active relation to her own life, includ-ing creative expression. This was done through individual, couples, and family ther-apy, including, at times, Dawn's sister.

I saw as the *basic* goal of our therapy helping Dawn enter into dialogue and a rela-tionship of trust. My therapeutic interventions included (1) exploring her family of origin and pointing out patterns such as Dawn and her siblings as *delegated children,* a term of Helm Stierlin's (1974); (2) encouraging her to express her feelings, espe-cially her feelings of anger; (3) getting her to write down her dreams; (4) bringing a divorce mediator to group therapy; (5) sending her to a psychiatrist for medication; (6) discussing her school plans with her; (7) suggesting support groups; (8) sending her for psychological testing; and (9) discussing how her daughter's adolescent act-ing out had brought back Dawn's problems with her sister, mother, and husband.

Analyzing the past, however, was never the main focus of our therapeutic dia-logue. It was done only for the sake of re-presenting the past and inviting ever deeper layers of her walled-off self to enter into a relationship of trust.

There is clearly room in dialogical therapy for techniques and interventions such as those I mentioned above. But the techniques should always be only *accompaniments* to the real matter, which Buber (1958, pp. 132f.) aptly describes as the "regeneration of the atrophied personal center." In reflecting upon our relationship, it became clear to me that the healing of Dawn's personal center happened through the meeting between us.

The goal of Dawn's therapy was neither to preserve her relationship with Bob nor to establish her in a new long-term relationship after Bob departed. Nor was it any specific matter, such as overcoming her anxiety and depression, getting her to be able to write papers, or healing her inner split. What was essential, rather, was the relationship of trust that developed between us over the four years in which we entered and re-entered dialogical therapy. My support, facilitation, confrontation, silence, questioning, reinforcement, interpretation, and modeling were always grounded in a relational stance.

My approach to Dawn's therapy was at times insight-oriented, at times process-oriented, and at times support-oriented. But it always evolved from the relationship and returned back to my relationship with her. This was true even when I tried traditional Gestalt therapy techniques, such as asking Dawn to play different roles in her family or to move from chair to chair, addressing herself from the standpoint of some member of her family that she had just spoken to.

I did not simply impose these actions on Dawn but explored with her when it was helpful. The same is true of my interpretations. I did not offer them as authoritative pronouncements but, rather, asked her whether they rang a bell and modified them in dialogue with her. Thus choosing therapeutic goals and objectives became a responsibility that Dawn and I shared. This is unlike the technique of many psychodynamic or behavior therapists, who see it as their task to set goals, and unlike the technique of process-oriented therapists, who see it as the task of the client to set goals.

At the same time, it is important to recognize that this dialogical psychotherapy differs in kind and not just in amount from the trust that Dawn might have established in a relationship of friendship or love. There was, as Buber insisted, a "normative limitation of mutuality" (1958, pp. 132–134). Dialogical therapy, too, rests upon the I-Thou relationship of openness, mutuality, presence, and directness. Yet it can never be fully mutual. There is mutual contact, mutual trust, and mutual concern with a common problem, but there is not mutual inclusion. The therapist can and must be on the patient's side, too, in a bipolar relationship, but the therapist cannot expect or demand that the patient practice such inclusion with him (M. S. Friedman, 1985, pp. 169–194).

Dawn and I shared a mutual contract and trust without which there could be no healing through meeting. We also shared the mutuality of common concern. We were talking about Dawn's problems, yet we were concerned in common with the sickness and distortion of community and family life of which her "problems" were only an aspect. But there could not be an expectation of mutual inclusion: namely, that Dawn should experience my side of the relationship or concern herself with my problems and with healing me.

It is equally important to recognize that inclusion, or "imagining the real," was necessary *from my side* if the habitual mistrust on which Dawn's life and actions were established was to be healed to the point where she could enter a relationship of trust with me and, later, with others.

What is most impressive about this therapy was the remarkable change I witnessed in Dawn during the years of therapy and during the more than six years since it was concluded. (We have stayed in touch sufficiently so that I am in a position to judge this.) This was precisely her movement from virtual isolation to being a person-in-relationship, a person ready and open for give-and-take with others. Over the years, I witnessed in Dawn a gradual but unmistakable warming, opening, flowering, and maturing.

Because I approached Dawn's therapy from the standpoint of the healing dialogue, it seems both fitting and meaningful to conclude this account of Dawn's case with Dawn's own evaluation of our relationship.

> When I think about our therapeutic relationship, it is the *process* that stands out in my memory, not the content.
>
> Up until the time I met Maurice, I had always "picked out" a male authority figure (usually a teacher or psychologist), put him on a pedestal, and obsessed about him a lot—not usually in a romantic or sexual way, although there was an erotic element. I just wanted him to like me and approve of me and to think I was smart and interesting. A real relationship, though, was terrifying to me—I kept my distance and rarely ever talked to them. The greater the attraction, the greater the fear.
>
> When I first met Maurice, I could feel myself wanting to fall into this same pattern with him. However, I could never quite feel intimidated by him—although I think I really wanted to. He was too human for that. I never felt that I had to be interesting or smart, good, bad, happy, or sad—it just wasn't something I had to be concerned with. If the therapist can be human and fallible, that gives me permission to be human and fallible, too.
>
> This was an entirely new experience for me. I soon found that I was involving myself in relationships with other "male authority figures" with much less fear and anxiety than I had felt in the past. I also became aware that I no longer wanted the kind of superior/inferior, vertical type of relationship that I used to seek out. I think this change is, by far, the most valuable result of my therapy relationship with Maurice. I am, in general, much better able to relate to others in an adult-to-adult way. I am much less intimidated or awed by position, titles, or accomplishments. I believe that if I ever again become involved in an intimate relationship with a man, it will be on a healthier basis—there will be fewer neurotic needs to deal with.
>
> I think there were a number of reasons why my relationship with Maurice was different. I believe I sometimes intimidated people with my intense neurotic needs, and Maurice was never intimidated. I was never able to seduce him into my little games, thank God. He always responded to me as simply "me" and did not classify me or categorize me or try to fix me because there was something wrong. In our relationship he never objectified me, and he didn't allow me to objectify him. Sometimes when I read books or articles written by Maurice I am very impressed, but I'm never impressed with him when I'm with him.
>
> In my relationship with my husband, Maurice helped me to understand that it wasn't Bob or me that was necessarily inadequate—it was our relationship. In my relationship

with Maurice, I began to realize that I wanted a "relationship," that relationship was important and life-sustaining and that Bob and I both deserved to be involved with those with whom we could have a "relationship."

Seeking to get my neurotic needs met leads to death. Relationship, with all its imperfections, is life—I know that very well now, and my first teacher in this area was Maurice. But because he doesn't need to be my teacher, I am now able to be my own teacher. And because he doesn't need me to follow in his path, I am now free to find my own.

REFERENCES AND RECOMMENDED READING

Boszormenyi-Nagy, I., & Krasner, B. R. (1986). *Between give and take: A clinical guide to contextual therapy.* New York: Brunner/Mazel.

Buber, M. (1958). *I and Thou,* 2d ed., (R. Smith, trans.). New York: Scribner.

Buber, M. (1988). *The knowledge of man: A philosophy of the interhuman,* with an introductory essay (chap. 1) by M. Friedman (Ed.) (M. Friedman & R. Smith, trans.). Atlantic Highlands, NJ: Humanities Press International.

Friedman, A. M. (1992). *Treating chronic pain: The healing partnership.* New York: Insight Books, Plenum.

Friedman, M. S. (1985). *The healing dialogue in psychotherapy.* New York: Jason Aronson.

Friedman, M. S. (1991). *The worlds of existentialism: A critical reader,* 3d ed. Atlantic Highlands, NJ: Humanities Press International.

Friedman, M. S. (1992). *Dialogue and the human image: Beyond humanistic psychology.* Newbury Park, CA: Sage Books.

Friedman, M. S. (1992). *Religion and psychology: A dialogical approach* (chaps 1–3, 12–15). New York: Paragon House.

Friedman, M. S. (1993). Intersubjectivity in Husserl, Sartre, Heidegger, and Buber. *Review of existential psychology and psychiatry.*

Heard, W. G. (1993). *The mystery of the healing between.* With a foreword by M. Friedman. San Francisco: Jossey/Bass.

Hycner, R. C. (1991). *Between person and person: Toward a dialogical psychotherapy.* Highland, NY: Center for Gestalt Development.

Stierlin, H. (1974). *Separating parents and adolescents: A perspective on running away, schizophrenia, and waywardness.* New York: Quadrangle/The New York Times Book Co.

EI CASE FORMULATION—Dawn

The emphasis in this case is on the relationship, the naturally unfolding encounter. Although technical strategies are referred to, they are consistently viewed as secondary. By contrast, the relationship—with all its experiential fervor—is viewed as primary.

From the EI standpoint, Dawn is hyperconstricted. She is depressed, lethargic, and sexually unresponsive. She becomes explosive at times (e.g., smashing her television set to get her husband's attention), but these extravagances are temporary; basically, she is inert.

Her profile suggests a life of relentless depersonalization. Her father sexually abused her; her mother discounted her accomplishments; and her sister took credit for her labors. Moreover, despite her demonstrable gifts, she was never able to transcend these circumstances productively.

Dr. Friedman offers Dawn three primary alternatives to her plight: (1) a real relationship, (2) a chance to experiment with that relationship, and (3) a chance to *experience* herself experimenting with that relationship. Before Dr. Friedman can emphasize experiential elements in their relationship, however, he must first attune to the symptoms that are most relevant to Dawn—clarifying her family dynamics, for example, helping her to assert herself with her husband and elevating her with medication. These engagements are worked out in dialogue with Dr. Friedman and ever within the context of their bond.

As she is ready to expand experientially, Dr. Friedman allows more of himself into the relationship and challenges her with a variety of exercises. These exercises, however, which include role-playing and attention to her affect, are still subordinate to the relationship with Dr. Friedman, which is the primary context for change. It is as if Dr. Friedman poses tacit relationship questions to Dawn, even in the midst of her exercises: "What is going on between *us* right now, Dawn? Are these exercises making sense to you? Do you feel I'm pushing too hard, or not hard enough? Are you expecting more from me than I can deliver? Do you need support from me right now? Silence?"

Such inquiries, tacit as they may be, deeply invoke the actual with Dawn and extend the possibilities for her recovery. In time, Dawn learns to use her relationship with Dr. Friedman to optimal effect. She is able to question his authority, for example, and to risk affirming her own opinions. He, in turn, is able to show his foibles to her and to lessen her anxieties about power.

By the end of her therapy, she is able to be *present* to herself, to be more expansive. She finds new meaning in relationships, moreover, and new ways to express herself in these relationships, especially with those in authority.

By stressing the encounter then—over and above other vehicles by which to invoke the actual—Dr. Friedman reminds us of an oft-neglected power in professional circles—love.

REFLECTIONS ON THE DEPRESSED AND DYING: THE CASE OF CAROL

Tom Greening

Tom Greening, Ph.D., has been a therapist for thirty-six years and the editor of the Journal of Humanistic Psychology *for twenty-three years. He is also a professor of psychology at Saybrook Institute in San Francisco, the author of* Existential-Humanistic Psychology, *and a poet.*

In this somewhat ironic portrayal of his work, Tom Greening shows how a traditionally trained practitioner can touch his clients experientially. By "being there," and "not panicking in the face of the pathology," he poignantly sets his clients free.

Carol's childhood, adult life, psychotherapy with me, and dying were all full of pain. Was there any value to all that pain, and to her and my attempts to heal it, numb it, ignore it, share it, confront it, transcend it?

She came to me for help in 1959, when I was just out of graduate school. I had been hired by Jim Bugental and Al Lasko as a staff psychologist in their Los Angeles group practice. I was not prepared for a client like Carol. At first, she appeared to be a fairly well-functioning, if neurotic, young woman. She was my age (28), an attractive, intelligent grade school teacher who loved folk music. In spite of my help, or perhaps because of it, she deteriorated into an overweight, depressed, suicidal, accident-prone victim.

She often phoned me for emergency support. One time she called because the skeleton of her dead mother was coming out of the closet of her apartment to grab her and take her to hell. Carol had already swallowed a lethal dose of pills and was surrendering to her mother. She had called me in a final attempt to clutch at life. I was indignant, outraged. I told her that was a terrible thing for her mother to do and ordered Carol to tell her mother that I said so and that I demanded she go back in the closet and stay there. Carol did this, her mother retreated, and Carol threw up the pills.

This was not the turning point I hoped it would be, however. We went on like this for eight more years. Finally, Carol felt somewhat better and concluded we'd done all we could together. I was relieved to be free of the burden of trying to help her. I did not see her for twelve years.

Then, in 1979, she called to congratulate me on a book I'd published, and we agreed to meet to review and reflect on what we had done together. She was still overweight and sad, but she was also strong and wise. She felt our psychotherapy work together had been "successful" and was grateful for it. I told her I supervised psychologists in training and asked her what had "worked" in our struggles together that I could pass on to others. She immediately answered, with clarity and conviction:

"Tell them to do three things: (1) be there; (2) don't panic in the face of the pathology; and (3) hold out a positive vision of what can come from the pain."

I confessed to Carol that based on my experiences growing up and in graduate school, when I first saw her I hadn't the faintest idea of what it meant to "be there." I'd read Rogers on congruence and heard Buber and Rogers discuss I-Thou encounter in their famous 1957 dialogue at the University of Michigan, but I'd never had an actual experience of myself or anyone else "being there." Instead, I had tried to "do" things, including psychotherapy with Carol. In the process of failing with her, I learned, unwillingly and inadvertently, to be there with her.

I admitted to Carol that I had certainly panicked in the face of her pathology (graduate school had not prepared me to combat skeletons), but I had doggedly refused to let my panic or her dead mother dominate my relationship with her.

I don't know what positive vision I had held out for Carol during her therapy. In 1959, I was still imbued with reductionistic, pathology-oriented models from psychoanalytic training and academic psychopathology courses. Rollo May's book *Existence* was published in 1958, but I didn't read it until a few years later. In confronting nothingness with Carol I could only draw on the knowledge of existentialism I had acquired from reading novels by Sartre and Camus. The positive visions of Abe Maslow, Jim Bugental, and others that led to the development of existential-humanistic psychology also did not come to my attention until I had been working with Carol for several years.

When we talked in 1979, Carol's emphatic prescription of the three things therapists should do impressed itself upon me as a reminder of what I have taken so long to learn and what I have often learned more with help from clients than from teachers. I currently have a client who is giving me an advanced (or remedial?) course in Carol's principles of psychotherapy, and we are both indebted to her more than she will ever know.

That is because she died in 1989. Here is how she did that: She got cancer, had surgery, had severe and mismanaged postoperative pain, took control of her pain management and recovery, elicited support from caretakers, went home to recover with her playful dog, found the continuing pain and daily struggle too hard, and gave up.

And in the process, she and I went one final round with the lessons she had taught me. I spent time being there with her, and we connected in a deep and peaceful way, sitting, talking, reminiscing, sharing jokes, playing with her dog, listening to music, and doing some more psychotherapy. She had never heard music on a compact disc player, so I played blues and folk music for her, some of which she knew and some of which she learned to love for the first time. There are times in life when Bessie Smith is the best doctor. And even if you don't hear Gabby Pahanui until you are on your deathbed, he is worth waiting for.

Carol's niece and nephew lovingly cared for her to the end. Her nephew is the son of her brother, whom she hated for abusing her as a child. Her love for her nephew, and his love for her, helped heal those old wounds. She died peacefully, "being there," not panicking in the face of the final pathology, guided by a positive vision of living . . . and dying.

I wrote four poems about Carol. The following is one of them.

POSTPONED REMEMBRANCE

Driving to a deathwatch by the beach
a memory I don't want tries to reach
into my mind; I twist away—
I cannot deal with it today.
One death at a time, that's enough.
More than enough, actually—
As the bumper-sticker says,
"I'd rather be sailing."

I've brought a rare guitarist's record
to entertain my friend.
Our tastes get very specialized
when we get near the end.

And so the beat goes on;
there's still a song for her to sing,
and rhythms in the dusk
to help us both defer
the silence that will come.

Today's visit over, I drive inland
along the hamburgered boulevard,
away from the coastal fog and
the part of my barnacled brain
that sank there.
I'll be back again
until her song ends
and the ebbing evening tide
reveals what I would hide.

EI CASE FORMULATION—Carol

The case of Carol highlights *clients'* perspectives on therapeutic effectiveness. So often we (as therapists) become smug. We believe that only *we* know what is good for our clients, and that clients (*because* they are clients) are hopelessly inaccurate. Yet clients' views of what is therapeutically significant correlate better with therapeutic outcomes than do therapists' views (Lambert, Shapiro, & Bergin, 1986), and it is their views, of course, that ultimately count.

When clients do elaborate on what is helpful to them (as we have seen in this section), they almost invariably focus on experiential and relationship factors. They cite qualities such as the therapist's warmth, for example, or his listening ability. They highlight his empathy, or the way he helps them emotionally.

Dr. Greening is successful with Carol precisely because his *process* of relating to her supersedes his technique of approaching her, precisely because—in spite of himself—he offers her a preverbal-kinesthetic *experience* rather than a prescription.

The factors Carol cites as salient—"being there," "not panicking in the face of the pathology," and "holding out a positive vision" are remarkably compatible with EI liberation strategies. Being there and not panicking in the face of pathology, for example, are directly analogous to "presence." Similarly, holding out a positive vision is parallel to "invoking the actual."

Like many gifted young practitioners, Dr. Greening offered these qualities almost in spite of himself, in spite of his sophisticated training. Yet his "doggedness," as he puts it, and his staunch determination to help palpably shine through to Carol. He exhibits this with his willingness to stand by her in her most fretful, suicidal periods; with his spontaneous indignation toward her mother which, in turn, inspires Carol's spontaneous indignation; and with his personable sharing with her which, in turn, encourages her to share.

Carol begins to die by the end of her work with Dr. Greening, but inside she appears to thrive. She has come to terms with her expansiveness, in other words, and the constraints so cruelly imposed. She has found hope with Dr. Greening, strength; and he, in turn, has found an exemplar of the highest and most courageous kind.

References

Lambert, M., Shapiro, D., & Bergin, A. (1986). The effectiveness of psychotherapy. In A. Bergin & S. Garfield (Eds.), *Handbook of psychotherapy and research* (pp. 157–212). New York: Wiley.

SUMMARY
AND CONCLUSION

In this book, we have proposed that psychology needs a new scale —*beyond* physiology, environment, cognition, psychosexuality, and even interpersonal relations; and *toward* existence (in all its brute forms).

Existential-integrative psychology is one step toward such a conception.

Existential-integrative psychology is the "ground" or context out of which traditional psychological standpoints arise. The basis for existential-integrative psychology is phenomenology—a richly descriptive, qualitative method for investigating human experience. Although phenomenology was formalized by Edmund Husserl at the beginning of the twentieth century, it has a profound literary and artistic heritage.

The core existential-integrative position is that human experience (or *consciousness,* in the full sense of that term) is both *free*—willful, creative, expressive—and *limited*—environmentally and socially constrained, mortal. To the extent that we deny or ignore this dialectic, we become polarized and dysfunctional; to the extent that we confront (or integrate) it, we become invigorated and enriched.

The freedom-limitation dialectic is characterized clinically by the capacities to constrict ("draw back," make oneself "small"), expand ("burst forth," make oneself "great"), and "center" oneself. (The freedom-limitation dialectic, in other words, is the *range* within which we can constrict, expand, and center ourselves.) *Dread* of either constriction or expansion (across many psychophysiological dimensions) fosters equally debilitating counterreactions to those polarities; *confrontation* with (or integration of) the modalities, on the other hand, promotes dynamism and vitality.

What are the implications of our existential-integrative formulation? The key implication, we believe, is that existential psychology is wider (theoretically and clinically) than is generally assumed. For example, while it is true that we stress experiential domains of functioning (i.e., *affectivity*), we also acknowledge the import of biological and mechanical levels of our being—the engagement of the world through chemistry, nutrition, reinforcement contingencies, and Aristotelian logic. Correspondingly, while we, indeed, emphasize immediate and kinesthetic dimensions of experience, we concurrently appreciate the interpersonal antecedents to those dimensions—childhood separation/attachment issues, for example, or the traumas of sexual/aggressive imbalance.

Finally, while we acknowledge the compatibility of our paradigm with tradition-ally privileged clientele (or subjects), we also see its value for a broader and more diverse population. This is a population with which students and practitioners increasingly interact; and it is one that is significantly more amenable to our approach than is generally appreciated—as we have seen. For example, who among this population *would not* benefit from attunement to the preverbal, openness to the spiritual, and acknowledgment of life's tragedies? Who among them would fail to profit from attention to their constricted or expanded worlds; or cultivations of "aliveness," obviousness, and actuality at appropriate junctures?

Indeed, who among them would be unable to benefit from encounters that reach them personally, not merely objectively; and from fundamental opportunities to cre-ate meaning in their lives?

Few, we believe—on all counts.

This book is but a beginning. Yet it is an essential one, we believe, for the many students intrigued by psychology's depths. To the extent that we have aroused these students and enabled them to consider existential psychology anew, we have amply realized our task.

ACKNOWLEDGMENTS

Page 45 "Hitchcock's Vertigo: An Existential View of Spirituality" reprinted from *Horror and the Holy* by Kirk J. Schneider by permission of Open Court Publishing Company, Chicago and La Salle, Illinois.

Page 67 Kierkegaard, Søren, translated by Walter Lowrie, from *The Concept of Dread.* Copyright © 1957 and renewed by Princeton University Press. Reprinted by permission of Princeton University Press.

Page 70 From *The Portable Nietzsche* by Walter Kaufmann, editor, translated by Walter Kaufmann. Translation copyright 1954 by The Viking Press, renewed © 1982 by Viking Penguin Inc. Used by permission of Viking Penguin, a division of Penguin Books USA Inc.

Page 72 From *The Myth of Sisyphus and Other Essays* by Albert Camus, translated by J. O'Brien. Copyright © 1955 by Alfred A. Knopf, Inc. Reprinted by permission of the publisher and Hamish Hamilton, Ltd.

Page 92 "What Psychology Can Learn from the Existentialists" from *Toward a Psychology of Being* by Abraham Maslow, 1968. All rights reserved. Reprinted by permission of the publisher, Van Nostrand Reinhold.

Page 102 "Rollo May: Personal Reflections and Appreciation" by James F. T. Bugental in *Perspectives, 2*(1), Summer 1981, pp. 30–31. Reprinted by permission.

Page 105 "R. D. Laing Remembered" by Kirk J. Schneider in *Journal of Humanistic Psychology,* vol. 30, no. 2, Spring 1990, p. 39. Copyright © 1990 Sage Publications, Inc. Reprinted by permission.

Page 108 "For Ronnie Laing" by Thomas Greening in *Journal of Humanistic Psychology,* vol. 30, no. 2, Spring 1990, p. 43. Copyright © 1990 Sage Publications, Inc. Reprinted by permission.

Page 108 "Master of Duality: Some Personal Reflections about Jim Bugental" by Kirk J. Schneider. This article was originally published in *The Script,* newsletter of the International Transactional Analysis Association, volume 8, number 4, June 1983. Reprinted by permission.

Page 111 Reprinted with the permission of The Free Press from *The Denial of Death* by Ernest Becker. Copyright © 1973 by The Free Press.

Page 144 From *The Paradoxical Self: Toward an Understanding of Our Contradictory Nature* by Kirk J. Schneider. New York: Plenum Publishing Corporation, 1990, p. 85. Reprinted by permission.

Page 286 "I Never Thought It Would Happen to Me" from *Love's Executioner and Other Tales of Psychotherapy* by Irvin D. Yalom. Copyright © 1989 by Irvin D. Yalom. Reprinted by permission of BasicBooks, a division of HarperCollins Publishers, Inc., and Penguin Books Ltd.

INDEX